ecpr PRESS

Croce, Gramsci, Bobbio and the Italian Political Tradition

Richard Bellamy

ecprPRESS

First published by the ECPR Press in 2014

The ECPR Press is the publishing imprint of the European Consortium for Political Research (ECPR), a scholarly association, which supports and encourages the training, research and cross-national co-operation of political scientists in institutions throughout Europe and beyond.

ECPR Press
University of Essex
Wivenhoe Park
Colchester
CO4 3SQ
UK

Typeset by ECPR Press

Printed and bound by Lightning Source

British Library Cataloguing in Publication Data

A catalogue record for this book is available from the British Library

ISBN: 978-1-907-301-99-5

www.ecpr.eu/ecprpress

Contents

About the Author

Richard Bellamy is Director of the Max Weber Programme at the European University Institute in Florence, on extended leave from his position as Professor of Political Science at University College London (UCL). In 2012 he was awarded the British Academy's Serena Medal 'for eminent services towards the furtherance of the study of Italian history, literature, art or economics'. His Italian publications include *Modern Italian Social Theory* (Polity and Stanford, 1987) and (with Darrow Schecter) *Gramsci and the Italian State* (Manchester University Press, 1993) and critical editions of Beccaria, Gramsci and Bobbio. He has also written extensively on liberalism and pluralism, democracy, constitutionalism, rights and citizenship, and political legitimacy in the EU.

Acknowledgements and Preface

This collection could be said to offer either a promissory note that the various projects to which these essays can be regarded as exploratory contributions will finally see the light of day, or a settling of accounts and admission that they will never be completed. Optimism of the will leads me to hope the former, while pessimism of the intellect forces me to acknowledge that I have now moved on to other topics and my energies are devoted for the foreseeable future to rather different matters. These pieces were published between 1984 and 2005, with the majority dating to the 1980s and early 1990s, when I was writing my PhD on Benedetto Croce, producing my two books devoted to Italian issues – *Modern Italian Social Theory: Ideology and Politics from Pareto to the Present* (Polity and Stanford University Press, 1987) and (with Darrow Schecter) *Gramsci and the Italian State* (Manchester University Press, 1993), and editing translations of works by Norberto Bobbio, Antonio Gramsci and Cesare Beccaria. At the time I went so far as to sign contracts to write monographs on Croce and Bobbio and I also had an ambition to write a history of Italian political thought in the eighteenth and nineteenth centuries – a sort of prequel to my *Modern Italian Social Theory* (the title of this volume was the publisher's, the subtitle – *Ideology and Politics from Pareto to the Present* – being a more accurate guide to its contents). In the event, none of these books materialised but the essays collected here can be seen as fragments of these various projects.

Apart from a host of encyclopaedia articles and reviews written for the TLS among other publications, this book collects pretty much all my substantive contributions on these topics. I have excluded four articles. Two have already been republished elsewhere: 'From ethical to economic liberalism - the sociology of Pareto's politics', *Economy and Society* 19, 1990, pp. 431–55 and 'Between economic and ethical liberalism: Benedetto Croce and the dilemmas of liberal politics', *History of the Human Sciences* 4, 1991 pp. 175–95, provided sections 2 and 3 respectively of Chapter Four of my *Liberalism and Modern Society: An Historical Argument* (Polity and Penn University Press, 1992). Two were published in fairly obscure places but I decided that obscurity was well deserved. They reproduce more or less unchanged two chapters of my PhD and really ought to have been more thoroughly revised before publication. For the record, they are 'Croce, Hegel and Gentile and the doctrine of the ethical state', *Rivista di Studi Crociani* XX, 1983, pp. 263–81, XXI, 1984, pp. 263–81, and 'Liberalism and historicism – Benedetto Croce and the political role of idealism in Italy c.1890–1952', in A. Moulakis (ed.), *The Promise of History*, (Walter de Gruyter, 1985), pp. 69–119. With the exception of Chapter Four, which also derives from my doctoral thesis, I have not revised the pieces included here beyond a few minor stylistic changes. 'An Italian "New Liberal" theorist – Guido De Ruggiero's *History of European Liberalism*', *Historical Journal* 30, 1987, pp. 191–200, appeared in an extended version as Chapter Three of my *Rethinking Liberalism* (Continuum

Press, 2000). I have decided to include it here as well because it complements in various ways the Croce–Gramsci–Bobbio dialogue that runs through much of the volume, given that, in many respects, De Ruggiero can be thought of as being in dialogue himself with all three, as well as with his teacher Giovanni Gentile.

I also decided to include one non-Italian piece: an article on 'Hegel's conception of the State and political philosophy in a post-Hegelian world', published in 1986. My reason for doing so is that this article offers what might be called the non-Italian, contemporary political theory context of these early pieces. This was the period of the liberal-communitarian debate and the engagement with Hegel and Marx by serious analytical political philosophers – notably, for me at any rate, Charles Taylor, G. A Cohen, Steven Lukes, Raymond Plant and David Miller. An education begun in Cambridge and continued in Florence at the EUI was completed, formally speaking, as a Post-doctoral Research Fellow at Nuffield College, Oxford. Many of the Hegel-Marx, Liberal-Communitarian-Marxism debates were played out before my eyes during my time at Oxford by the figures mentioned above – along with parallel historical debates hosted by Tony Judt, who took on the role of looking after Oxford-based historians of modern Italy on Christopher Seton-Watson's retirement. It was in this period that I first began to write up my doctoral research for publication. So these pieces reflect that eclectic, not to say eccentric, mix of influences, involving – as I put it in the Preface to *Modern Italian Social Theory* – an attempt to reach Oxford destinations by the Cambridge road.

Unsurprisingly, it will be noted that my views are not always consistent over the course of the book – on a number of topics they evolved over time. Yet that does not mean the later positions are necessarily more accurate than the earlier ones. These pieces were written for different occasions and reflect different preoccupations on my part. Just as in each case I have tried to place the particular ideas of the thinker concerned in a given intellectual and political context, so these essays also belong to different contexts and are best read in that light. In particular, most of these essays belong to a world where the Soviet Union still existed and Italy had the largest Communist Party outside the Soviet bloc, while at the same time Britain was experiencing 11 years of Mrs Thatcher, the collapse of the Labour Party and the rise of the Social Democrat Party (SDP). All but the most abstract and unworldly political philosopher is likely to view the topics addressed in these essays somewhat differently pre-, during and post this period.

My first permanent academic position – as a lecturer at the University of Edinburgh – coincided with the United Kingdom's very first research assessment exercise. In those halcyon days this exercise was so light-touch that I was blissfully unaware of its existence until the head of department happened to mention that he had included my Italian book in a list he had been obliged to compile of works produced by the department 'of singular originality'. As he remarked, my publications seemed to qualify on both counts since they were on matters so obscure as to be 'singular' and by that token alone 'original'. That was not entirely fair even with regard to British and American scholars, a select and pioneering few of whom had begun to explore many of the Italian figures discussed here, but was certainly not true of the great wealth of Italian scholarship on which I was able to draw. So it is a pleasure to be able to record here my gratitude for the help I have received from both sets of academics. Duncan Forbes, Jonathan Steinberg, Paul Ginsborg and Quentin Skinner acted successively as my PhD supervisors while at Cambridge, with Dennis Hay, Maurice Cranston, Athanasios Moulakis, and Anthony Pagden performing a similar role while I was based at the EUI in Florence. While a Post-doctoral Research Fellow at Nuffield College Oxford, Tony Judt, Christopher Seton Watson, Dennis Mack Smith (who kindly gave me his Croce library – many presents from the philosopher), W. H. Walsh, and John Robertson also offered various kinds of moral and intellectual support, not least by reassuring me that work on Italian political thought was a promising area of research, as did from further afield Jo Femia, Adrian Lyttleton, Percy Allum, John Davis, Harold Acton, Bruce Haddock, H. S. Harris, David Forgacs, Martin Clark and Walter Adamson. I am also very grateful for the help of all kinds offered by my contemporaries in the field, especially Stephen Gundle, Martin Brown, Edward Chaney, Bob Lumley, Christopher Duggan, James Martin, Carl Levy, Virginia Cox and Darrow Schecter. Among Italian scholars, I am indebted to the early encouragement I received from Raffaele Ajello and Guiseppe Ricuperati for my forays into the Italian eighteenth century and especially from Eluggero Pii, whose early death deprived me of a good friend and the academy of a great scholar. Vittorio Sainati and Enrico de Mas provided invaluable advice on my PhD, while Franco Sbarberi, Virgilio Mura, Giuliano Marini, Michelangelo Bovero, Furio Cerutti, Pietro Costa and above all Danilo Zolo fostered my studies of twentieth-century Italian political thought. Andrea Campana, Vittorio Bufacchi, Nadia Urbinati, Luca Bacelli, Antonino Palumbo, Roberta Sassatelli, Barbara Henry, Debora Spini, Anna Loretoni, Mario Piccinini, Mario Diani, Roberto Franzosi and particularly Emilio Santoro also offered succour, friendship and support of various sorts along the way. A special mention is owed to Dario Castiglione, without whom this collection would never have appeared. I apologise in advance for any people I have forgotten. Recalling what seems a whole other life is a difficult task but I am grateful to you all. This volume is dedicated to all the above-mentioned Italian friends and scholars of Italy, including any one I have inadvertently passed over, in gratitude for your intellectual and emotional companionship over the years.

I am indebted to the following publishers for allowing me to reproduce, with some minor stylistic revisions, the articles and book chapters republished here. They first appeared as follows:

1. 'Social and Political Thought 1890–1945', in A. Lyttleton (ed.), *Liberal and Fascist Italy*, Short Oxford *History of Italy* vol. 6, (Oxford: Oxford University Press, 2002), ch. 10, pp. 233–48. Published here by kind permission of Oxford University Press.

2. '"From metaphysics to economics" – Antonio Genovesi and the development of the language of commerce in 18th century Naples', in Anthony Pagden (ed.), *The Languages of Political Theory in Early Modern Europe*, (Cambridge University Press, 1987), pp. 277–99. Published here by kind permission of Cambridge University Press.

3. 'Introduction' to C. Beccaria, *On Crimes and Punishment*, ed. R. Bellamy, (Cambridge University Press, Cambridge Texts in the History of Political Thought, 1995), pp. viii–xlvi. Published here by kind permission of Cambridge University Press.

4. 'Hegel's conception of the State and political philosophy in a post-Hegelian world', *Political Science*, XXXVIII, 1986, pp. 99–112. Published here by kind permission of Sage.

5. 'What is living and what is dead in Croce's interpretation of Hegel', *Bulletin of the Hegel Society of Great Britain* IX, 1984, pp. 5–14. Published here by kind permission of the Hegel Society of Great Britain.

6. 'A modern interpreter: Benedetto Croce and the politics of Italian culture', *The European Legacy: Towards New Paradigms* 5, 2000, pp. 845–61. Published here by kind permission of Taylor and Francis.

7. 'An Italian "New Liberal" theorist - Guido De Ruggiero's *History of European Liberalism'*, *Historical Journal* 30, 1987, pp. 191–200. Published here by kind permission of Cambridge University Press.

8. 'Gramsci, Croce and the Italian political tradition', *History of Political Thought* XI, 1990, pp. 313–37. Published here by kind permission of Imprint Academic.

9. 'Introduction' to A. Gramsci, *Pre-Prison Writings*, ed. R. Bellamy, Cambridge Texts in the History of Political Thought (Cambridge, 1994), pp. ix-xxviii. Published here by kind permission of Cambridge University Press.

10. 'A Crocean critique of Gramsci on historicism, hegemony and intellectuals', in *Journal of Modern Italian Studies* 6 (2), 2001, pp. 209–229. Published here by kind permission of Taylor and Francis.

11. 'Gramsci, Walzer and the intellectual as social critic', *The Philosophical Forum* 29, 1998, pp. 138–59. Published here by kind permission of Wiley.

12. 'The advent of the masses and the making of the modern theory of democracy' in T. Ball and R. Bellamy (eds), *The Cambridge History of Twentieth Century Political Thought* (Cambridge: CUP, 2003), pp 70–103. Published here by kind permission of Cambridge University Press.

13. 'Introduction' (pp. 1–30), Norberto Bobbio, *Which Socialism?: Marxism, Socialism and Democracy*, ed. R. Bellamy, (Polity Press, 1987). Published here by kind permission of Polity Press.

14. 'Introduction' (pp. 1–15), Norberto Bobbio, *The Future of Democracy*, ed. R. Bellamy (Polity Press, 1987). Published here by kind permission of Polity Press.

15. 'Norberto Bobbio: the rule of law and the rule of democracy', *Iris: European Journal of Philosophy and Public Debate* III, 5 April 2011, pp. 53–60. Published here by kind permission of Florence University Press.

References in the text follow the style of the original publication.

Richard Bellamy
December 2013

To Dario, Emilio and my many other Italian friends
and fellow scholars of Italy.

Introduction

Studying the Italian Political Tradition

The Italians can stake a reasonable claim to have invented modern politics. From ancient Rome onwards, they conceived politics as the product of the competition for power between different social groups pursuing diverse and often incompatible goals, with the political arts concerned with the management of that competition and the disagreements and conflicts it produces. Italian politicians and theorists of politics alike, the two often being one and the same, were all too aware of the gap that often exists between the ideals we hold and the realties that stand in the way of their implementation. They also saw how the need to engage in real politics can alter the character of those political ideals – often for the worse but also, in so far as it can motivate a willingness to compromise with others to accommodate their ideals as well as one's own, for the better. In various ways, this contrast between political ideals and the reality of politics runs through these essays and the ideas of the thinkers they examine.

The pieces collected here do not come close to constituting a history of the Italian political tradition. Among many omissions, the most notable are the absence of any treatment of the political thought of either the Renaissance or, more glaringly for this volume, the *Risorgimento*.[1] Along with two chapters dealing respectively with the two major figures of the Neapolitan and Milanese Enlightenments, this volume offers at best a discussion of certain core ideas of the main political thinkers of the post-unification period. As a way of contextualising these latter pieces, Chapter One provides an overview of social and political theory in Italy circa 1890–1945. However, all the thinkers explored here engaged with and developed certain motifs that were characteristic of a longer, distinctively Italian, political tradition. The first part of this introduction, therefore, briefly sketches these themes and indicates how they shaped the thought of the writers examined in this book.

---

1. The one *Risorgimento* figure I have tentatively attempted to explore is Giuseppe Mazzini, and at one time had thought of producing a new edition of his *Duties of Man* but failed to interest a publisher in the project. Fortunately, Nadia Urbinati managed to do so – *see* S. Recchia and N. Urbinati (eds) *A Cosmopolitanism of Nations: Giuseppe Mazzini's Writings on Democracy, Nation Building, and International Relations*, Princeton, Princeton University Press, 2010. For my own attempts at some sketchy reflections on his thought, see the following review essays: 'Writing for the cause', [review of D. M. Smith, *Mazzini*, Yale University Press], *TLS*, Aug 5 1994, p. 3; 'Contemporary reflections on Mazzini's *Thoughts Upon Democracy in Europe*', *Il Pensiero Politico*, 36, 2003, pp. 122–4; and 'Mazzini' in E. Craig (ed.), *The Routledge Encyclopedia of Philosophy On Line*, London, Routledge, 2003, http://www.rep.routledge.com/article/DC112

The second part of this introduction addresses more methodological and personal issues. It describes the motivations that led to the composition of the individual articles and chapters collected in this volume. Re-reading these essays, I became aware that they themselves reflected a certain historical context – that of the academic and political discussions of the 1980s and early 1990s involving the liberal-communitarian debate, on the one hand, and the reaction of the British left to both eleven years of Mrs Thatcher and the collapse of the Soviet bloc and with it, if slightly later, the waning of the allure of Western Marxism, on the other. They also arose out of a belief that history could both be politically engaged and make a contribution to contemporary philosophical debates. As the subtitle of my later study of *Liberalism and Modern Society* was to put it, these essays formed 'an historical argument' in both a methodological and substantive sense that I attempt to sketch here.

Political thought in Italy[2]

A self-consciously Italian political tradition only developed in the nineteenth century, when the *Risorgimento* inspired a number of contrasting visions of a united Italy. Prior to that, political theorists tended to identify with the regimes and traditions of a given region and were often employed by local rulers to support their claims to power. Nonetheless, one can detect three general themes that recur from the post-Roman period up to the present. The first theme concerns the competing attractions of the two Romes, not only in the straightforward form of Emperor versus Pope and later the Church versus the anticlerical supporters of the secular state, but also in the guise of the opposition between the active and the contemplative life, social emancipation and heavenly salvation. The second theme relates to the respective strengths and weaknesses of *signorie* and communes, monarchies and republics – an opposition that likewise broadened into a more general contrast between authoritarian and democratic rule, force and consent. The first theme reflects the fact, peculiar to the Italian situation, that the papacy operated as a territorial as well as a spiritual power. The second is equally specific to Italy in that it is a classical theme which acquired new life with the rise of the city-states and principalities in the later Middle Ages. The third theme arises from the struggles in which these polarized conceptions of politics partook and that they partly generated: namely, a recurrent linking of the idea of Italian unity with order and an end to sectarian and inter-state strife, on the one hand, and to the foreign domination that often accompanied them, on the other. All three themes were also at various times linked to the contrast between a more secular, democratic and industrial north and a more religious, feudal and agrarian south; the unification of Italy required the leadership of the one and its absorption of the other, with most of Italy's problems stemming from the north's difficulties in fully doing so.

2. This section draws on my entry 'Political theory', in P. Hainsworth and D. Robey (eds), *The Oxford Companion to Italian Literature*, Oxford, OUP, 2003.

These themes are intertwined, mixing in all available combinations as circumstances changed, and some of them at least can be found in all the significant Italian political thinkers – be they of a broadly empiricist or rationalist persuasion. Thus, the autocratic ambitions of the papacy between the thirteenth and fifteenth century engendered an intermittent conciliarist reaction within the Church, which urged the need for consultation with the Council of Bishops, an argument that drew on and fed into debates about the benefits of oligarchical and republican governance in the communes. Likewise, the theocratic aspirations of popes to establish a right to the temporal power of the Roman Empire, and to assert their spiritual ascendancy over all civil rulers, came to be matched by similar claims to a universal secular authority on the part of emperors. From the beginning, communes and principalities aligned themselves with both camps – most notably in the clash between Guelfs and Ghibellines. These ideological battles continued in new configurations up until the *Risorgimento*, when the neo-Guelfism of Antonio Rosmini-Serbati and, most particularly, of Vincenzo Gioberti, who advocated that the papacy should take the lead in Italian unification, was counterposed by the largely anticlerical views of liberal monarchists and radical democrats, notably Giuseppe Mazzini, and then endured as the post-war rivalry between communists and Christian democrats.

The clash between Church and Empire, commune and principality, informs the writings of the three major political thinkers of the Middle Ages and Renaissance: Dante Alighieri, Marsilio da Padova, and Niccolò Machiavelli. All worked within the largely secular and neo-Aristotelian paradigm of politics that had been established by Thomas Aquinas. Writing in the wake of Henry VII's abortive Italian expedition, Dante envisaged him taking on the mantle of the Roman Empire and establishing the universal peace and political unity between the different peoples of the world necessary for the collective enterprise of human knowledge and culture to achieve its full potential. Marsilio, by contrast, in the *Defensor pacis* (1324), framed his case against the disruptiveness of clerical pretensions to rule in the context of communal assertions that popular government was the bastion of freedom against tyranny. Yet the 'Defender of the Peace' proved to be his work's dedicatee, Ludwig of Bavaria, in his successful Italian invasion of 1327–30. However, the full separation of Church from state in the form of a neat distinction between politics and morals, Christian or otherwise, only came with Machiavelli a century afterwards. For him, politics was essentially instrumental to the establishment of order and civic liberty, depending on qualities that were specific to the political arts. Although an advocate of the commune in his *Discorsi* (c. 1517, published posthumously in 1531), the conclusion of the *Principe* (1513, published posthumously in 1532) repeats the call for a princely figure capable of liberating Italy from the flood of foreign invasions.

The elaboration of Machiavellian '*ragioni di stato*' (reason of state) by thinkers such as Gaspare Scioppio, Giovanni Bolero and Ludovico Zucolo continued into the seventeenth century. It was counter-posed by the religious, if heretical, Platonic utopianism of Giovanni Bruno and Tommaso Campanella. The Counter-Reformation gave new impetus to the battle between Church and state, culminating in the defences of toleration and civil authority by Paolo Sarpi and Pietro Giannone. As Franco Venturi has noted, the development of a secular science of politics during the eighteenth century continued likewise to oscillate between the radical, republican utopianism of figures such as Francesco Mario Pagano and the drive of reformists like Pietro Verri, Cesare Beccaria and Antonio Genovesi to enlighten despotic rulers. Yet, as Venturi conceded, this distinction is a little too neat – each group had elements of the other, and both identified the Church and feudal system as the chief barriers to social and political change.

The French Revolution reopened the question of Italian unification. Whilst radical democrats such as Carlo Cattaneo, Giuseppe Ferrari and Carlo Pisacane adopted a positivist position and looked to the empiricist and realist tradition of Machiavelli and the Enlightenment reformers, liberal supporters of Pius IX (such as Gioberti) or of Cavour (such as Bertrando Spaventa and his brother Silvio) tended to be philosophical idealists, who constructed an Italian heritage going back to Marsilio Ficino and Giambattista Vico. Not surprisingly, the most important figure of the period, Giuseppe Mazzini, straddled the various traditions, identifying God with the people and supporting both republicanism and monarchy.

With Italy finally united, the aim became to 'make Italians'. Liberalism, fascism, and communism drew prominent support from both idealists (such as Benedetto Croce, Giovanni Gentile and Antonio Gramsci) and positivists (such as Gaetano Mosca, Alfredo Rocco and Achille Loria) but – as Chapter One details – regardless of ideology or methodology, they shared a desire to unite 'legal' Italy to the 'real' Italy, north and south. Once again, the theme of Italian unity was viewed through the lens of the other two themes, with different thinkers linking or counter-posing moral and social reform, on the one hand, and the importance of force and consent, on the other. The respective roles of north and south in this enterprise was a central issue among the positivist meridionalisti, Marxists such as Gramsci and idealists like Croce; though here, too, all the different ideological positions drew support from thinkers across the spectrum of the various methodological approaches. However, whatever their stance, defenders of democracy were relatively thin on the ground, though Carlo Rosselli and Piero Gobetti, both killed by fascists, are honourable exceptions. Post-war Italian politics continued to be dominated by the opposition between the two Romes represented by communism and Christian democracy, with those – such as Norberto Bobbio – who attempted to offer a social and liberal democratic alternative to both remaining an important but minority intellectual and political force. While the centre-left had hoped to make this strand of thought the basis of a second republic with the collapse of the two traditional ideological groupings post-1989, that expectation has thus far proved forlorn.

The Italian tradition in the Anglo-Saxon mirror:
Cambridge roads and Oxford destinations

My interest in the topics covered by these essays largely grew out of my undergraduate study of the history of political thought at Cambridge in the late 1970s, while much of the research for them was carried out while a PhD student – first at Cambridge and then at the European Institute in Florence in the early

1980s. This research was then extended, elaborated and written up while I was a post-doctoral research fellow at Nuffield College in Oxford and then a fellow in history at Jesus College in Cambridge in the mid to late 1980s. Though some of the essays date from the 1990s, they have their origins in the work I carried out in this period. During this time, I gradually moved from intellectual history to contemporary political theory, though in a number of respects I sought to combine the two. This combination was the fruit of my experience of the rather different intellectual environments of Cambridge and Oxford and, as I put in the Preface of my study of *Modern Italian Social Theory*,[3] represented an attempt to reach Oxford destinations by the Cambridge road.[4]

A key figure for my undergraduate education was Duncan Forbes and it was the inspiration of his lectures and supervisions on the thinkers of the Scottish Enlightenment and of Hegel that inspired me to study first the Italian Enlightenment and then Benedetto Croce. The essays on Genovesi and Beccaria that form Chapters Two and Three had their origins in my initial and abortive PhD under Duncan that had as its focus the influence of the Scottish Enlightenment's account of the passage from feudalism to commercial society on the Italian, and especially the Neapolitan, Enlightenment.[5] The basic thought behind this project had been that Scotland and southern Italy, in particular, shared certain characteristics as poor countries with continuing elements of feudalism linked to richer, more commercial neighbours, prompting an Italian version of the 'rich country–poor country' debate in Scottish political economy, in which the Neapolitans drew divergent conclusions from similar premises to the Scots, not least with regard to the benefits of free trade.[6] However, these essays tackle a different, if related, topic: namely, how far an associationist psychology based on the pursuit of happiness and self-interest, of a kind suited to a commercial ethic, could overcome the traditional concern that such attitudes and the love of luxury that accompanied them led to the corruption of public morality.

The different responses of Genovesi and Beccaria to this issue reflect in part the contrast between southern and northern Italy. Both were on the reformist more than the utopian side of the Enlightenment, providing ideological support

---

3. Richard Bellamy, *Modern Italian Social Theory: Ideology and politics from Pareto to the present*, Cambridge, Polity and Stanford, Calif., Stanford University Press, 1987.

4. As I noted above, much the same aspiration still characterised my second book, with that approach signalled by its subtitle: *see* Richard Bellamy, *Liberalism and Modern Society: An historical argument*, Cambridge, Polity and University Park, PA, Penn State University Press, 1992.

5. I published a preliminary study of the Scottish side of this debate as Richard Bellamy 'From feudalism to capitalism – history and politics in the Scottish Enlightenment', in A. Moulakis (ed.), *The Promise of History*, Berlin/New York, Walter de Gruyter, 1985, pp. 69–119.

6. *See* the pioneering essay by Istvan Hont, 'The "rich country–poor country" debate in Scottish classical political economy' in I. Hont and M. Ignatieff (eds), *Wealth and Virtue: The shaping of political economy in the Scottish Enlightenment*, Cambridge, Cambridge University Press, 1983. On the Naples–Scotland parallels and contrasts, *see* the splendid study of John Robertson, *The Case for the Enlightenment: Scotland and Naples 1680–1760*, Cambridge, Cambridge University Press, 2005.

for the policies of enlightened monarchs. Yet, the one had to engage far more with prevailing Catholic thinking than the other. Consequently, Genovesi's solution to the dilemma noted above was to present the new commercial ethos as a reinterpretation of traditional Catholic natural law, using the language of the Catholic metaphysician to express and in certain respects transform the arguments of the merchant found in the new political economy. By comparison, Beccaria's reasoning was thoroughly secular and in some ways came at the problem from the opposite end. If Genovesi wished to show how the correct exercise of natural rights served public utility, Beccaria argued that rights could be upheld through the pursuit of public utility: directly in the case of punishment, where the abuse of rights involved in torture failed to serve – and possibly subverted – its ostensible public purpose; indirectly in the case of commerce, where upholding the right to trade and freedom of contract promoted the public utility of increasing wealth.

The concern with philosophers who found themselves somehow between utility and rights,[7] most especially in their attempt to balance self-interest and virtue in their accounts of commercial society, was one that was undoubtedly fostered – even if subconsciously at first – by the contemporary debates in political philosophy and politics in the late 1970s and early 1980s.[8] This was the period when John Rawls and Ronald Dworkin were displacing utilitarianism as the main discourse of Anglo-American analytical political theory and replacing it with contractarianism and rights.[9] Yet, as the libertarianism of Robert Nozick made evident, there was a potential difficulty in deploying the liberal language of rights-based justice for the solidaristic social purposes favoured by many on the liberal left. This was the challenge posed by the communitarian critique of contemporary liberal individualism, which drew on Aristotle, Hegel and Marx.[10] Within the UK, interest grew in the liberal idealists and the new liberalism of the late nineteenth and early twentieth centuries. They seemed to many to offer an alternative, communitarian form of liberalism that might bring together these two schools of thoughts in a way that favoured a form of liberal socialism. This project had been encouraged in Britain by the impact of Mrs Thatcher on British public life and the implosion of the Labour Party in fraternal civil war between social democrats and Marxian socialists. Finding a way to avoid the respective

---

7.   The phrase is, of course, a reference to H. L. A., Hart 'Between utility and rights', *Columbia Law Review*, 1979, vol. 79, pp. 828–46.

8.   It had also informed my undergraduate dissertation, which I also revised for publication while in Oxford and published as 'William Godwin and the development of the "New Man of Feeling" ', *History of Political Thought*, 1985, vol. VI, pp. 411–32.

9.   I published an overview of this shift from utility to rights in contemporary Anglo-American political philosophy in Italian as '*Rinascita della filosofia politica anglo-americana?*', *Teoria politica*, 1989, V., pp. 93–10.

10. I wrote a review of this debate at the time, published as 'Defining liberalism: neutralist, ethical or political?', in R. Bellamy (ed.), *Liberalism and Modern Social and Legal Philosophy, Archiv für Rechtsund Sozialphilosophie*, Beiheft nr. 36, 1989 pp. 23–43, which I later revised considerably as Chapter Five of my *Liberalism and Modern Society*.

pitfalls of all three of these dominant ideologies – neoliberalism, revisionist social democracy and old-style labourism – whilst offering a view of socialism that could respond to both the liberal and the communitarian impulses appeared at the time an important intellectual project.

The initial decision to study Croce for my PhD had been motivated by rather more innocent academic concerns, basically an interest in the philosophy of history stemming from my Cambridge training in the history of political thought and the opportunity to work with Quentin Skinner when he returned from Princeton to take up the Chair of Political Science. However, the rewriting and development of this research in the essays published in Parts 2, 3 and 4 of this collection was very much framed by these Oxford debates. What I came to think, though, was that a genuinely historical investigation of the origins of the theories that were being deployed in these discussions might reveal whether their underlying assumptions really were tenable today. Therefore, I sought to put my Cambridge training in the service of contributing to Oxford arguments.

To give a flavour of the nature of the mindset in which these pieces were written, I have republished as Chapter Four a non-Italian article on 'Hegel's conception of the state and political philosophy in a post-Hegelian world'.[11] Chapter Five on Croce's critique of Hegel was written more or less at the same time, and involves a parallel refection on whether an Hegelian version of liberalism is really tenable without adopting Hegel's metaphysics. I did toy for a time with the thought that one could possibly take on the German's metaphysical baggage and so remain true to the Hegelian ontology. However, once I gave up on that idea, the crux became whether the communitarian-liberal thesis involved, at best, an elegy for a world we have lost. In the end, I came to believe this might well be the case. Investigating this thesis in the context of the rather more conflictual historical terrain of early twentieth-century Italy – rather than the comparatively cosy academic world of Victorian Oxford inhabited by T. H. Green and his followers – was, in this regard, a sobering experience. Chapter Six is, in some respects, the last of three attempts to explore the interactions between Croce's liberal historicism and his engagement with the politics of his time.[12] In many ways, it is also the most sympathetic treatment of his endeavour that tries to give

---

11. Other pieces written at this time that belong to this project are 'Hegel and liberalism', *History of European Ideas*, 1987, vol. 8., pp. 693–708 and 'Isaiah Berlin, T. H. Green and J. S. Mill on the nature of liberty and liberalism', in R. Harrison and H. Gross (eds), *Jurisprudence: Cambridge Essays*, Oxford, Clarendon Press, 1992, pp. 257–85 and republished as Chapters One and Two of my *Rethinking Liberalism*, London, Continuum, 2000 (Chapter Seven of this collection, on De Ruggiero, is also Chapter Three of that one). A similar impetus lay behind my edited book on *Victorian Liberalism: Nineteenth century political thought and practice*, London, 1990 (prompted in part by Mrs Thatcher's evocation of Victorian values) and *Liberalism and Modern Society*.

12. The other two attempts, not republished here, are: 'Liberalism and historicism – Benedetto Croce and the political role of idealism in Italy c.1890–1952', in A. Moulakis (ed.), *The Promise of History*, Berlin/New York Walter de Gruyter, 1985, pp. 69–119 and 'Between economic and ethical liberalism: Benedetto Croce and the dilemmas of liberal politics', *History of the Human Sciences*, vol. 4, 1991, pp. 175–95.

the strongest reading possible of his delicate balancing act between swallowing Hegelian metaphysics and descending into historical relativism. However, Croce himself was undoubtedly a rather conservative liberal. Chapter Seven turns to a more radical figure, Guido De Ruggiero. He was a great admirer of the post-Green British new liberalism that many contemporary communitarian liberals were seeking to revive. At that time – and perhaps even today – his *History of European Liberalism*, which R. G. Collingwood had translated, was treated as a textbook rather than a philosophical and political intervention. So, studying the origins of this text seemed to offer a perfect opportunity to engage in a historical investigation of these Oxford arguments through the prism of the Italian mirror. The result of that exercise was largely responsible for my seeking to write my own counter-De Ruggiero, in *Liberalism and Modern Society*.

Part 3 develops similar themes but in the context of an examination of the political thought of Antonio Gramsci. The Sardinian is by some way the best-known political theorist of this period outside Italy. During the 1980s he was held up as offering an alternative strategy for the left – one that avoided the pitfalls of orthodox Marxism and its Soviet embodiment, on the one hand, and social democracy, which was deemed fatally flawed due to its compromise with liberalism, on the other. Within the UK, both aspects were then linked to an analysis of Mrs Thatcher's hold on British politics and the development of a socialist counter-hegemonic strategy. Thirty years on, it may be hard to imagine how seriously such views were taken but, at the time, the group of Gramscians around *Marxism Today*, who included Stuart Hall, Martin Jacques and Eric Hobsbawm, were viewed as among the leading strategists of the left.

Chapters Eight and Nine dispute two aspects of this use of Gramsci. The first aspect was the claim that Gramsci's thought could be adapted to the politics of contemporary Britain. This claim had a certain credibility due to the fact that the Italian Communist Party (PCI) was at that time the main opposition party in Italy and claimed to be adopting a strategy for promoting revolution within the context of a liberal-democratic parliamentary regime that had been first developed by its former leader. The second aspect was the view that Gramsci's strategy involved a departure from Marxism, in so far as it accorded a certain independence to the political superstructure from the economic base. That independence was deemed to be not simply pragmatic and tactical but also carried over to his view of the future communist society, when a 'true', participatory form of democracy would finally be possible. These chapters indicate how Gramsci's thought was both grounded in the very different political problems of pre-second-world-war Italy, which was anything but an established liberal-democratic regime, and also largely orthodox in its Marxist assumptions and limited to the production methods of the late nineteenth and early twentieth century. The unconventional aspects of his Marxism may have derived from his being the product of an Italian tradition of political thought but that renders his thought even less suitable for tackling the problems of contemporary, post-industrial democracies.

The use and abuse of Gramsci raises a number of more general issues over and above the correct interpretation of the Sardinian's thought. First, there is the issue of the coherence of immanent critique. Gramsci followed Croce in developing a historicist epistemology and ontology. On this account, political ideals had to be formulated in ways that related to the social, economic and political reality they addressed. As with Croce, the risk with this strategy is that it either falls into historical relativism and a possible justification of the *status quo* or involves an implied immanent teleology of a progressive kind which, at best, amounts to little more than wishful thinking. Second, this issue raises in its turn the question of whether it is either necessary or possible to develop political ideals autonomously from considerations as to how far they can be realised. Finally, both issues relate to the problems of whether socialist goals should or could be pursued via liberal means – and, if so, if this entailed radically altering the nature of socialism – and the extent to which these means themselves are ideals or reflect the realities imposed by the human condition.

The first issue of the nature of immanent critique is discussed in relation to Croce in Chapter Six and is raised again with regard to Gramsci and Croce in Chapter Ten and Gramsci and Walzer in Chapter Eleven. Gramsci accused Croce of being caught on the first horn of this dilemma and idealising the prevailing hegemony of the liberal regime in Italy. Yet, not only is that critique unjustified but Gramsci himself can be regarded as being caught on the second horn and adopting a progressive teleology. To some extent that makes his theory less prone to the conservatism that potentially afflicts Walzer's account of social criticism. However, it does so by assuming to know the underlying meaning of history. By contrast, Croce's view offers the sort of agonistic and radical theory that some recent interpreters, such as Ernesto Laclau and Chantal Mouffe,[13] have wanted to attribute to Gramsci. Croce's theory was an attempt to see the ideal and the real as in constant, dialectical tension. On his account, willed and conscious action always followed from the conceptual understanding of current historical circumstances. Yet in understanding the past so as to act in the present, both ideas and reality were changed. Moreover, in contrast to the natural world, the human world is capable of being interpreted in a variety of different ways, with those self-interpretations largely constituting that world. As a result, there was no imminent teleology to human history, given that different individuals and societies could come up with different reasonable understandings of themselves and the nature of the good life.

The second issue enters here. Both Croce and Gramsci, insisted that ideal theory also needs to some degree to be attuned to the nature of the reality it seeks to grasp and change. However, whereas in Gramsci's case that ultimately meant that the 'true' ideas where those that developed the forces of production in maximal ways, Croce attempted to relate the ideal to the real in a less functionalist and more open ended manner. On his account, while ideals have a degree of autonomy from reality, individuals should see themselves as subject to the judgment of history. By regarding their actions as contributing to posterity, he believed individuals would

---

13. E. Laclau and C. Mouffe, *Hegemony and Socialist Strategy: Towards a radical democratic politics*, London, Verso, 1985.

be motivated to act responsibly towards those present and future others whose lives they affect and in whom they consequently continue to live. In this way, Croce's historicism sought to promote an immanent form of moral judgement that was neither teleological nor relativist. As a result, he also disputed the view that moral judgement was by its nature transcendental and *a priori*. On the contrary, the justification and legitimacy of ideals did not derive from their meeting abstract theoretical criteria such as coherence, consistency or universalisability but through their practicality, acceptability and durability – features that could only emerge through an engagement with the reality of the social world, including the diverse ideas of those who inhabit it.

With regard to the third issue, Gramsci certainly believed that socialism involved a non-liberal form of democracy that he adapted from both Marx and the Italian tradition of the ethical state. However, this argument involves highly contentious assumptions as to the ultimate compatibility of human conceptions of the good and the possibility for their harmonious co-ordination. If one accepts that conflicts between these conceptions may be not only contingent but also inherent to the plurality of human values, the partiality and fallibility of human reasoning and the limited resources available to us, then forms of politics that are both liberal and democratic remain inevitable as mechanisms to mediate and resolve our ongoing disagreements.[14] A major flaw of the Marxist tradition has been a failure to acknowledge that the circumstances of justice and politics are not entirely economically derived – the products of a class-divided society, destined to wither away with the passing of these divisions.[15]

To a degree, Croce's 'metapolitical' liberalism was also underdeveloped in this regard. He says comparatively little about the nature of the political institutions that are likely to sustain the sort of agonistic and dialogical politics he came to embrace. He criticised both neo-liberal defenders of the free market, such as Luigi Einaudi, and liberal socialists, such as Carlo Rosselli, for confusing contingent liberal practices with the liberal ideal. However, he was adamant that even a metapolitical form of liberalism was incompatible with either the fascist or communist ethical state. Moreover, when he did discuss the relationship between the state and civil society within his 'ethico-political' view of history it was in relatively conventional liberal-democratic terms. Moreover, notwithstanding his own idealist leanings, he was in this respect largely indebted to the Italian realist and positivist tradition, especially Gaetano Mosca.

Part 4 turns to this tradition. As Chapter Twelve shows, the neo-Machiavellian, empirical theory of democracy was not an Italian invention but Italian thinkers – particularly Vilfredo Pareto and Gaetano Mosca – played a key role in its development. Originating as a critique of Marxist and socialist aspirations for 'true democracy', it became transformed into an alternative account of the way

---

14. I have explored this theme in my *Liberalism and Pluralism: Towards a politics of compromise*, London, Routledge, 1997.

15. S. Lukes, *Marxism and Morality*, Oxford, Oxford University Press, 1985.

democracy works. Norberto Bobbio was the pre-eminent political theorist of post-war Italy. Throughout his long career a key feature of his intellectual activity was to open a dialogue with the Italian Communist Party centred on convincing them that socialist goals are not just compatible with liberal democratic means but also are only plausible and justified in so far as they pursued and realised in this way. These debates go back to the late 1940s and 50s but became particularly crucial in the 1970s, when the PCI became the largest single party, and again in the late 1980s and early 1990s, after the collapse of the former Soviet bloc, when a majority in the PCI decided to change its name and character to become a social-democratic party.[16]

Chapter Thirteen focuses on the debates of the mid 1970s and the essays later collected in Bobbio's book *Which Socialism?*[17] The point of departure of Bobbio's discussion returns us to the debate on the Hegelian conception of the state outlined in Chapter Four. He criticised both the Marxist and the neo-liberal arguments for a withering away of the state and the absorption of its functions by civil society, be it in the form of a direct democracy among workers or a self-regulating market. However, Bobbio also disputed the neo-Hegelian thesis that the ethical state could absorb civil society. Like Croce, he views state and civil society as being in constant tension. The crucial task, therefore, is to develop viable forms of democracy capable of mediating between the two spheres. On the one hand, the state needs to be responsive to civil society but, on the other hand, state regulation is required to control the power of certain social actors, such as large corporations. Bobbio was also a pioneering advocate of the need for certain forms of international democracy to govern the relations between states,[18] although this dimension of his thought is not discussed here. As ever, Bobbio remained a realist concerning the practicalities of this double process of democraticisation – triple if one adds the international dimension. As he famously argued in the essays collected in *The Future of Democracy*,[19] examined in Chapter Fourteen, democracy promises more than it can deliver. Since individuals do not form a collective entity, democracy will always compromise individual autonomy, while societies are too complex to allow for their complete democratic governance. For this reason, Bobbio advocated a minimal view of democracy that raises appropriately limited expectations. Democracy may have little intrinsic merit – it may not encourage greater solidarity among citizens or produce good decisions. However, forcing governments to follow the rules of the game and stay within the law curbs the worst excesses of arbitrary power.

---

16. For an account of these debates, *see* Bellamy, *Modern Italian Social Theory*, ch. 7.

17. N. Bobbio, *Quale Socialismo?: Discussione di un 'alternativa*, Turin, Einaudi, 1976.

18. *See*, for example, Norberto Bobbio, 'Democracy and the international system', in D. Archibugi and D. Held (eds) *Cosmopolitan Democracy: an agenda for a new world order*, Cambridge, Polity Press, 1995, pp. 17–41.

19. Norberto Bobbio, *Il futuro dell democrazia*, Turin, Einaudi, 1984.

Nevertheless, Bobbio was far from rejecting the socialist ideal – indeed, his short book of the 1990s on *Left and Right*,[20] which became a bestseller in Italy, insisted on the continuing relevance of notions of social equality. Alongside his sober and restrained view of real democracy, Bobbio retained a certain faith in ideal democracy as yielding a less minimalist view of the foundations of the social order. This tension is explored in Chapter Fifteen. Bobbio returned to the social contract tradition for the derivation of the basic rights that lie at the heart of the legal constitution underpinning a democratic society. The term 'socialism' entered the Italian language as a term of criticism of Beccaria's appeal to the social-contract tradition in his *On Crimes and Punishments*, examined in Chapter Three. Bobbio reaches similar conclusions but sees the egalitarian character of contractarianism in a positive light. Drawing on Rawls, he sees the idea of a social contract as encapsulating the linking of liberalism and socialism, liberty with equality and justice, which he advocates. However, this maximal view of constitutionalism and the rule of law is potentially at odds with his minimal view of democracy. In this regard, Bobbio's thought seems thoroughly Italian in character, shaped by the antinomy between the two Romes, theory and practice, the legal ideal and the social and political reality, that, as we have seen, has framed the Italian political tradition from the very beginning.

This judgment should not be understood as a criticism or as yielding a pessimistic conclusion. Given the current parlous state of Italian politics, the desire to escape the weight of the past would be understandable. Yet that is never wholly possible. Political theory is necessarily bound by the historical circumstances in which it is located and the dominant modes of thought of the political culture with which it engages form a part of those circumstances. In this respect, political theorists cannot but reach Oxford destinations by the Cambridge road – some merely do so in a more self-conscious fashion than others. It is one of the merits of the Italian thinkers explored here that, for the most part, they do so in a highly reflexive manner. However, that does not mean one is doomed to repeat past mistakes – merely, that recognising those mistakes and correcting them is to some degree always a matter of confronting and working through the events and ideas that shape one's thinking and of passing historical judgment upon them. As I have noted, my own reading of Italian political thought certainly reflects certain Anglo-Saxon preconceptions and prejudices. Nevertheless, the exploration of a different political culture to one's own also forces one into critical reflection on the assumptions of one's own tradition. While hopefully not an '*inglese italianato, diavolo incarnato*', my subsequent studies of liberalism and democracy have certainly been more sceptical and realist as a result of considering them through the Italian mirror than they might otherwise have been. In that respect, though I have more or less abandoned the direct study of the Italian political tradition in my most recent work, it retains a marked Italian character that reflects the influence of my earlier engagement with it in the essays collected in this book.

---

20. Norberto Bobbio, *Destra e sinistra: ragioni e significati di una distinzione politica,* Roma, Donzelli, 1994.

Chapter One

Italian Social and Political Thought: 1890–1945

'We don't like Italy as it is today.' As the intellectual entrepreneur Giuseppe Prezzolini observed, this pithy observation made by Giovanni Amendola in 1910 summed up the sentiments of a whole generation of social and political thinkers. Despite their very different methodological and ideological perspectives, they agreed to a remarkable extent that the unified Italy had not realised the hopes and aspirations of the *Risorgimento* period. At best, the resulting disillusionment produced an incisive if invariably polemical critique of Italian political institutions that not only unmasked the divide separating the 'legal' from the 'real' Italy but also served to deepen the analysis of liberal-democratic systems more generally. At worst, this dissatisfaction produced a nihilistic and cynical antagonism towards most features of modern societies, combined with a dismissive contempt for the concerns of ordinary people.

The main preoccupation of Italian social and political theorists was with the Machiavellian issues of 'force' and 'consent'. The Italian state's lack of 'force' was manifested in its inability either to defend and promote itself externally or to uphold law and order internally. The absence of 'consent' allegedly arose from a failure to 'make Italians', with the result that few people identified strongly with the new state. Relatively little attention was paid to the key questions of liberal democracy, namely the protection of individual liberties and the accountability of governments. These were dismissed as pseudo-problems that were meaningless; impossible to conceptualise adequately or solve in themselves; making sense only as aspects of the state's primary role as the focus of the collective strength and will of a people. Indeed, the view that Giolittian Italy had failed to either act sufficiently forcefully or promote a suitably strong consensus had a tendency to shade into a critique of liberalism and democracy *tout court*. Ironically, a more favourable appraisal of both the Giolittian era and liberal democracy only occurred when the fascist regime in its turn transformed such positive opinions into an oppositional perspective.

This chapter will first survey the various critiques of Italian liberal democracy made up to and immediately following the First World War and then examine attempts to produce alternatives of both a fascist and a communist character; finally, it will explore the revaluation of both liberalism and democracy produced by the Resistance.

The critique of liberal democracy

In Italy, as elsewhere, late-nineteenth-century philosophical culture was dominated by two schools of thought – idealism and positivism. The former not only drew on Kant and Hegel but also had native roots, particularly in Vico, and encompassed thinkers as diverse as the liberal Catholics Vincenzo Gioberti and Antonio Rosmini and the anticlerical Neapolitan Hegelians Francesco de Sanctis, Angelo Camillo de Meis and Bertrando and Silvio Spaventa. The positivist school of thought was similarly eclectic, looking to the thinkers of the French and British Enlightenments, their nineteenth-century heirs, notably Auguste Comte, J. S. Mill and, towards the end of the century, Herbert Spencer and certain of his Italian followers, such as Antonio Genovesi, Cesare Beccaria and Carlo Cattaneo. It also encompassed a broad spectrum of positions, from largely 'methodological' positivists such as Pasquale Villari, whose main concern was to promote the 'scientific' and empirical study of socio-economic processes, to 'systematic' positivists such as Roberto Ardigò, who espoused a materialist epistemology and saw positivism as a complete philosophy.

The idealists were the most influential school in the first decade of the newly united Italy, most particularly through their links with the ruling Historic Right, in whose administrations de Sanctis and Silvio Spaventa served. Predominantly from the south and inspired by the Hegelian doctrine of the ethical state, they were largely concerned with constructing a 'legal' Italy capable of exercising moral authority over its citizens. By contrast, the 1870s to the 1890s were the decades of the positivists, whose attention was focused on the social conditions of the 'real' Italy. Although the positivists were mainly from northern Italy, thanks to the studies of Pasquale Villari, Sidney Sonnino and Leopoldo Franchetti this issue came to be epitomised above all by the 'Southern Question'. In general, the positivists of this generation had greater faith in the progress of society than the idealists. Whereas de Sanctis, de Meis, and Silvio Spaventa, for example, believed the state, guided by the intellectual class, had the crucial if daunting task of educating the lower classes and creating a national political culture, the positivists hoped this transformation could be brought about by the processes of modernisation – albeit with the state facilitating the development of southern industry by de-regulating agrarian contracts, removing protectionist customs duties and tempering some of the operations of the free market with discreet social measures.

However, in other respects the positivists shared many of the views of the idealist camp. They were similarly contemptuous of the transformist politics that followed the fall of the Right, seeing it as a crucial block to any constructive reform, and often became critical of parliamentary democracy in general as a result. Their emphasis on the south as somehow encapsulating Italy's problems also caused them to share certain conservative prejudices of the neo-Hegelians, encouraging them to ignore the new and rather different issues raised by the growth of an urban working class in the north and to favour somewhat anachronistic policies that idealised the potential position of a new class of independent peasant proprietors, which they somewhat naively expected to emerge from the introduction of more capitalist farming methods. Finally, despite differences in method and approach, they were likewise preoccupied with 'making Italians', seeing social and economic improvements in largely moralistic terms. This latter aspect was particularly evident in Ardigò's concern with human psychology, which fed into the Italian school of positivist criminology, represented above all by Cesare Lombroso. Though he adopted occasionally contradictory opinions on specific topics, Lombroso's basic thesis was that penalties had to match the psychological type of the criminal rather than the crime. Though he employed racist theories as well, he saw social conditions and political institutions as the prime influences on human behaviour. For example, in his 1895 book *Anarchists* he argued against the use of the death penalty or other severe punishments for anarchists on the grounds that their activities were in large part caused by Italian society's backwardness and injustice.

The writings of the positivists of the 1870s and 1880s bequeathed an ambiguous legacy to their successors in the 1890s. The attention paid to social reforms combined with the progressive and modernising sympathies of this generation of positivist writers was to pass into socialism, mixing in various ways with Marxism to become the ideology of the Italian labour movement. The major socialist writers of the 1890s – Filippo Turati, Achille Loria, Napoleone Colajanni, Enrico Ferri and Saverio Merlino – all espoused a complex (and at times contradictory) mix of Darwin, Spencer and Marx (whose names formed the subtitle of Ferri's *Socialism and Positive Science* of 1894). Their espousal of reformism stemmed from the resulting belief in the need for an evolutionary approach, which involved passing through the capitalist stage, and the empiricist desire to find practical solutions to specific problems; whilst their emphasis on moral leadership reflected the traditional concern of the intellectual elite with educating the masses. Yet the result was to lay them open to attacks from both the left, for collaborating with a flawed political system and promoting bourgeois capitalism rather than the interests of the proletariat, and from the right, for typifying the materialistic, populist, moderate politics they associated with *Italietta* or 'little Italy'.

The intellectual reaction against reformism from around 1900 is standardly associated with the attack on positivism by a new generation of idealist thinkers. It is portrayed as a reactionary assault on the materialism of the modern world linked to a vague yearning for spiritual values. As we shall see, this characterisation is certainly partly true, even if, ironically, there was a partial reconciliation of the Catholic Church with Italian democracy in this period, with the publication of *Rerum Novarum* in 1891. Catholic modernisers, such as Romolo Murri and Ernesto Buonaiuti, however, found little sympathy from either the Church or the fiercely anticlerical idealist school. The acutest critiques of Italian democracy, though, came from the positivist camp and from the left.

The most incisive and theoretically important of these critical analyses stemmed from the elite theories elaborated by the positivist thinkers Vilfredo Pareto and Gaetano Mosca. Despite superficial similarities in their views, their criticisms were very differently motivated. Born in Paris in 1848 and initially based in Florence prior to taking up the Chair of Political Economy at Lausanne University in 1893, Pareto was a classic liberal deeply influenced by Spencer and, more particularly, J. S. Mill. For much of the 1890s, he expressed support for the cause of organised labour. He saw 'popular socialism' as a legitimate reaction to the 'bourgeois socialism' practised by the Italian political class gathered around Crispi and his successors, which employed state monopolies and economically disastrous protectionist tariffs to buy votes and adopted increasingly coercive measures to suppress unrest. He also sympathised with individual socialists, such as Colajanni, sharing many of their progressive hopes. However, a convinced economic liberal, he had never accepted either the efficiency or legitimacy of state intervention in the economy, regarding it as merely increasing political power and patronage. His coruscating deconstruction of *Socialist Systems* in 1902 and his later fascist sympathies arose largely because he felt that, from 1900, the balance had swung the other way. Instead of counterbalancing 'bourgeois socialism' in ways that might have established a liberal economic system, 'popular socialism' simply threatened to take its place. Its apparent democratic credentials notwithstanding, socialist ideology, particularly its reformist variant, was simply a mechanism for promoting the interests of a particular group of politicians.

By contrast, Gaetano Mosca, who was born in Palermo in 1858, belonged to the conservative southern intelligentsia. Unlike Pareto, he doubted the capacity of the lower classes to participate in politics and had little insight into the plight of northern workers. Whilst attacking the governments of the so-called left, he idealised those of the right as the work of public-spirited citizens.

These differences were reflected in their respective versions of elite theory. Both argued that, irrespective of the form of government, be it monarchy, aristocracy or democracy, a relatively compact minority always ruled. Moreover, they also agreed that mass democracy in many ways extended rather than constrained the possibilities for elites to govern. Though Mosca, in particular, bickered with Pareto continually over who took precedence in having formulated this thesis, in fact they developed it in quite different ways.

Pareto's argument, given most fully in the massive *Treatise of General Sociology* of 1916, may have dispensed with the earlier Italian positivists' faith in the progressive evolution of modern society but shared their emphasis on social psychology rather than social structures. A rigorous mathematical economist, who pioneered modern welfare economics, Pareto believed the primary question confronting the social scientist was why individuals were invariably moved by 'non-logical' motivations rather than self-interested 'logico-experimental' instrumental reasoning. He believed the answer lay in humans being motivated by a number of basic emotional 'residues' which could then be manipulated by certain sorts of argumentation, which he called 'derivations'. Though he enumerated some 52 residues, the most important were 'the instinct of combinations' and the 'persistence of aggregates'. Pareto believed the rise and fall of governing classes reflected altering balances of these two residues within the elite, with the first favouring the cunning needed to rule through consent and the latter a more conservative desire for strength. He argued that societies tended to alternate between periods of prosperity, when the skills of persuasion were at a premium, and of austerity, when policies of law and order were demanded. He linked the

Giolittian period with the former, suitably situated between the periods of coercive rule of Crispi and Mussolini. Reformist socialism, on this account, was simply an ideology or 'derivation' employed by the prevailing ruling class to maintain their power. Like democracy, with which it had an affinity, it was well suited to elites employing the consensual methods of the 'instinct of combinations', giving their rule a veneer of popular legitimacy. In common with other anti-democrats discussed below, Pareto was more sympathetic to revolutionary syndicalism, which in his view reflected the forceful 'persistence of aggregates'. However, he believed its claims were just as illusory, amounting to little more than rhetorical gestures to legitimise a counter-elite's bid for power. Though he initially welcomed fascism, it was as a confirmation of his social theory rather than because of agreement with its ideals. He remained an economic liberal and had no sympathy with the syndicalist strand in fascist ideology. However, his disillusionment with democracy led him to the paradoxical belief that a free market involving minimal state intervention could only be maintained by an authoritarian state that did not have to bargain with democratically entrenched vested interests. Had he lived, Mussolini would soon have disabused him in this regard and he would undoubtedly have been as critical of the fascist regime as he had been of Giolitti.

Though Mosca shared Pareto's doubts about both popular sovereignty and socialism, his account of the ascendancy of a political class was more truly sociological. Minorities always rule because they form a more coherent group, able to act with greater consistency and coherence and to organise themselves better than the necessarily more diffuse and inchoate majority. He agreed with Pareto that universal suffrage promoted the corrupt and devious political skills of the flatterer, the wheeler-dealer and the populist demagogue. He also believed that terms such as 'popular sovereignty' and the 'common good' were simply ideological 'political formulae', whereby a ruling class legitimised its position. However, he departed from Pareto in believing that the elite ideally should be, and in fact often was, the most capable of ruling. However, the qualities making the group best-fitted to rule altered as societies evolved. Thus, the rulers of the industrial age required rather different talents to those of the feudal era, where military prowess was at a premium. A deputy from 1909 to 1919, he opposed the introduction of universal suffrage in 1912 but ultimately accepted the need to come to terms with mass democracy and to concentrate not on its debunking so much as its reworking, so that it would produce a democratic meritocracy committed to liberal values and possessing the administrative skills essential for the efficient and just government of contemporary societies. Crucial to this scheme was his doctrine of 'juridical defence'. Mosca argued that a political system had to be so designed as to mix the 'aristocratic' and the 'democratic' tendencies within any society, producing in the process a balance between the 'autocratic' and 'liberal' principles of government. Unlike Pareto, he saw electoral competition between elites and openness to demands and recruitment from the lower strata as mechanisms for reducing rather than exacerbating corruption. For they ensured that rulers could further their own interests in governing only by taking account of the interests of the ruled in good government.

The idealist revolt against positivism echoed many of these criticisms of mass democracy but linked them to an attack on the materialism of the positivist method. By far the most prominent figure in this movement was the philosopher Benedetto Croce. The nephew of Silvio Spaventa, with whom he lived following the tragic death of his parents in an earthquake, he first came to prominence through his critique of the evolutionist Marxist theories of Loria, Ferri and others in the 1890s. Croce had been encouraged to study Marxism by Antonio Labriola, a philosophy professor at Rome University and a former student of Bertrando Spaventa. In a series of influential essays published first in French by Georges Sorel between 1895 and 1898 and then in Italian by Croce in 1902 as *Essays on the Materialist Conception of History*, Labriola had argued that Marxism was, above all, a theory of revolutionary praxis, which involved raising the consciousness of workers concerning their exploited condition within capitalist societies. He inveighed against the reformist conceit that revolution was a process inherent within the very development of industrial societies. Croce agreed with Labriola that Marxism was above all a practical philosophy geared to political action. He even dubbed Marx 'the Machiavelli of the proletariat'. However, he questioned the coherence of certain Marxist propositions, notably the law of the falling rate of profit, and disputed both the materialist ontology and the utilitarian morality that he believed underlay Marxism. Instead of helping Labriola promote a more critical, sophisticated and revolutionary Marxism, Croce briefly became Italy's foremost critic of Marx.

The most intellectually lively and revolutionary branch of Italian socialism was at this time the syndicalist movement. Inspired by Sorel, it also spawned an important Italian literature, including contributions by Enrico Leone, Arturo Labriola, Paolo Orano and Sergio Panunzio. Belief in the inevitably corrupt and transformist character of parliamentary democracy was once again fuelled by the southern origins of most of the main syndicalist intellectuals. Fiercely workerist in orientation, syndicalism focused on unions and spontaneous activism centred on the myth of the general strike. Once again, moral transformation was emphasised over social and political reform. Deeply antagonistic to reformist compromises with bourgeois democracy, syndicalists also disputed the Leninist strategy of organising revolution via a vanguard party.

Though Croce admired Sorel's austere morality, he had little time for the movement's other adherents. Indeed, its essentially negative and anarchic tendency led to it attracting the very extreme and, as he eventually thought, irrationalist forces of the right that he was soon to regard as his prime opponents. Rising to prominence with the general strike of 1904, syndicalism was declared 'heretical' at the Florence Socialist Party conference of 1908. Nevertheless, their breakaway organisation, the Italian Syndical Union (USI) did pretty well, claiming 800,000 members in 1920. Many, such as Panunzio, Orano and Angelo Olivero Olivetti, later espoused fascism.

From 1900 Croce devoted himself to elaborating his own distinctive 'Philosophy of Spirit'. Along with his collaborator, Giovanni Gentile, who had also written an influential idealist interpretation and critique of Marx in 1899, he employed his review *La Critica* to promote a revival of the idealism of de Sanctis and Spaventa. Croce's idealism had its roots in the contention that human creativity, thought and morality not only were not instrumental in character, even if practical action was, but were also distinct from each other. Thus, his first major work, the *Aesthetic* of 1902, was devoted to defending art as the 'pure expression' of artistic 'intuition' rather than the desire to communicate a given idea – the role of philosophy – or a practical programme – the realm of politics.

Influenced by Gentile, Croce historicised this doctrine as a dialectic of the distinct moments of the Beautiful, the True, the Useful and the Good. The first two represented the theoretical aspects of spirit, the last two its practical aspects. Whereas the second and fourth included the first and third respectively, the latter pair were totally independent from the former. Thus, it was possible to write a philosophy of art but art was not itself philosophy. Likewise action that was practically useful was not of itself moral but could only be assessed as such after further and entirely separate reflection. However, Croce did not believe there were absolute standards of Beauty, Truth, Utility and Goodness either. Rather, these were all matters of historical judgement in the light of prevailing circumstances and their suitability as responses to the particular issues they were addressing.

Croce's historicist belief that present action always entailed an engagement with conditions inherited from the past seemed to make his doctrine more positivist and conservative and less radically idealist than many, including his friend Gentile, had initially supposed. Indeed, he was partly moved in this direction by what he came to see as the irrational and voluntaristic tendencies of certain thinkers whom he had initially greeted as fellow-travellers. Chief amongst these were the Florentine intellectuals Giovanni Papini and Giuseppe Prezzolini, whose journal *Leonardo* Croce cautiously welcomed as a suitable expression of youthful iconoclasm, and the various nationalist writers gathered around Enrico Corradini's journal *Il Regno* and the poet Gabriele d'Annunzio, whose work Croce initially praised. The first group had seen Croce's aesthetic as an anti-naturalist paean to the human capacity for self-invention, the 'Man-God' as Prezzolini's review was entitled. However, Papini's 'magical pragmatism' and his relentless debunking of all attempts at a systematic philosophy, including Croce's own, soon created strong divisions between them. When Papini broke with Prezzolini and founded the proto-futurist *Lacerbo*, along with D'Annunzio he became a byword for a certain Nietzschean 'decadence' and irresponsibility that Croce saw as amongst the chief ills of the modern age. Likewise, Croce's conservative desire to revive a sense of '*Patria*' and a strong state capable of maintaining law and order, combined with his criticisms of socialist reformism and an aristocratic liberal concern over mass democracy, all aligned him with the second group. But, as he put it in an important essay of 1911, a patriotic faith was one thing, ill-considered nationalist programmes for imperial expansion quite another. To his dismay, he found Gentile apparently endorsing both the extreme tendencies he was attempting to reject. He used Prezzolini's new philo-Crocean journal *La Voce* to launch an attack on his collaborator's 'actualist' philosophy. The crunch came with the First World War. Whereas Papini, d'Annunzio, and Gentile saw it as a purifying bloodbath that would foster a spiritual regeneration of the Italian people and allow the convention-breaking qualities of the superior sort of individual to flourish, Croce advocated neutrality and doubted Italy's capacity to fight. He saw intervention as an unholy alliance of the decadent irrationalists, with their empty quest for national and individual glory, and the democratic populists, moved by a Utopian commitment to the abstract and illusory ideals of international solidarity and a war to end all wars.

Revolution and reaction

Croce was right, the war did place Italy's fragile economy and democracy under tremendous strain, with the Red Years of 1918–20 being swiftly followed by the Black reaction and the Fascist seizure of power in 1922. From the perspective of social and political theory, the most significant event in the former period was the factory occupations in Turin and the theorisation of them by the Marxist thinker Antonio Gramsci. Of Sardinian origin, Gramsci had come to Turin to study linguistics at the university but quickly became involved in socialist circles and embarked on a career as a political journalist. Gramsci had already achieved a certain notoriety through having appeared to side with Mussolini's faction by advocating entry into the war and in greeting the Russian Revolution as going against Marx's *Das Kapital*. Gramsci argued that revolution arose not as a direct result of changes in the mode of production but through workers becoming conscious of the available opportunities for revolt and having the desire and capacity to exploit them. He saw intervention as a way of creating the appropriate revolutionary spirit and conditions. Though influenced by revolutionary syndicalism, the chief inspiration for his thinking came from Labriola and Croce. However, his revisionism notwithstanding, he remained firmly within the Marxist camp, both theoretically and politically. The material base might not determine the superstructure but it certainly conditioned it, whilst the party played a central organisational role as against the unions.

This underlying orthodoxy is apparent in Gramsci's view of the factory councils. These originated from the internal factory commissions that were set up after the war. Gramsci saw them as potential soviets, offering a new form of workers' democracy suited to a modern industrial economy. He believed participation in the management of the factory gave workers a sense of their place within the system of production and exchange. He envisaged an international network of factory councils, which would replace the market as the means whereby supply and demand could be tailored to each other. Along with Palmiro Togliatti and Umberto Terracini, he used their journal *L'Ordine Nuovo* to militate for the development of a whole system of factory councils and, crucially, provide them with the intellectual leadership of the party. When northern factories were occupied in September 1920, he made the councils the key organ of the movement.

The occupations ultimately collapsed, in part due to lack of support from the unions and the Italian Socialist Party (PSI), and in 1921 Gramsci and his colleagues joined the secessionists from the PSI in forming the Communist Party of Italy

(PCd'I). Gramsci was in Moscow at the time of the March on Rome, as the PCd'I delegate to the Comintern, but soon began to analyse the fascist phenomenon. He now developed his earlier insights into the role consciousness played in the creation of a revolutionary praxis. Gramsci believed that contemporary production-line methods and the big monopolistic corporations with which they were associated had created the objective conditions for communist forms of social and political organisation to emerge. However, he also argued that the mature liberal democracies of advanced capitalist societies had much more sophisticated ways of winning the consent of the populace to a system that actually worked against their interests than were available in less developed countries. Ironically, therefore, the weakness of Russia's political institutions had allowed Lenin to mount a political revolution even though the propitious economic circumstances had yet to obtain. The fascist seizure of power and the direct use of the state to defend capital similarly testified to the relative backwardness and fragility of Italy's economy and democracy. In Britain and the United States, industrialists had been able both to create a new kind of factory worker without recourse to state coercion and to evolve forms of mass democracy that obtained the passive allegiance of workers to the political system. He believed a revolutionary strategy suited to Italy's *sui generis* situation now had to be elaborated – one which built links between the northern workers and the southern peasants and established tactical alliances with other parties opposed to fascism.

Gramsci regarded the goal of such linkages as the forging of a collective revolutionary consciousness rather than reformism. However, many of the existing PCd'I leaders feared tactical alliances with non-workers would dilute the revolutionary commitment of the Party. His argument, though, was more in tune with Comintern thinking than theirs and in 1924 he was elected a deputy, returned to Italy and formed a new Party leadership. Following Mussolini's withdrawal of parliamentary immunity, he was arrested and sentenced to twenty years, four months and five days of imprisonment in 1928. From 1929 he worked on the *Prison Notebooks*. These elaborated many of his earlier ideas. Of particular importance was his notion of 'hegemony' or ideological power. As I noted above, he saw the capacity of liberal regimes to win the consent of the populace as requiring a modification of revolutionary tactics. A 'war of position' had to be fought within the institutions of civil society so as to win people over before a successful 'war of movement' or frontal assault could be mounted on the state. He defended the Marxist credentials of this thesis via a critique of positivist historical materialism, inspired by a critical reading of Crocean historicism. Seriously ill, he suffered a series of strokes and died in 1937, shortly after receiving an unconditional discharge.

Many of Gramsci's views were devised as self-conscious reversals of fascist positions. Whereas he saw fascism as a totalitarian ideology imposed from above via the forced organisation of people within its corporate structures, he sought to make Marxism an equally all-encompassing and 'total' conception of the world but one that would emerge from below, through the democratic organisation of workers within civil society.

Many commentators doubt whether fascism can in fact be dignified with having anything as coherent as a philosophy. Indeed, Mussolini's success was in part to make the fascist movement an anti-party that harnessed the support of groups as disparate as the irrationalist iconoclasts around Papini and d'Annunzio, certain revolutionary syndicalists, the disaffected petty bourgeoisie and conservatives desirous of a return to law and order – though the latter group, who initially included both Mosca and Croce, gradually deserted him from 1925 onwards. However, at least two thinkers tried to give him a theory: Giovanni Gentile and Alfredo Rocco.

Giovanni Gentile, who joined the party in 1923, sought to align fascism with the neo-Hegelian's doctrine of the ethical state. He hoped thereby to provide it with a lineage going back to the *Risorgimento* period, which allowed him to designate fascism as the true heir of the Italian liberal tradition. But he also gave this doctrine a personal twist that derived from his own 'actualist' philosophy. The subjectivist extreme of idealism, in politics this theory led him to identify the force of the state with the consent of the people – a position that conveniently justified the fascist seizure of power. He saw the state as the expression of the collective will of the people, with corporatism the most suitable means for organising this will. The state's role was not that of a mediator between individuals, as most liberal doctrines suggested; the state existed within each individual as the expression of his or her true interests. Fascism had an almost mystical and spiritual quality for Gentile – a position his followers Ugo Spirito and Arnaldo Volpicelli attempted to radicalise in the direction of a Sorelian revolutionary syndicalism.

By contrast, the other main fascist theorist, Alfredo Rocco, operated from positivist and explicitly reactionary premises. A prominent Nationalist thinker and jurist, he had worked out most of his ideas before the war. He viewed the nation as a quasi-biological organism with which the individual could be almost totally identified. A fierce critic of liberalism, which he associated with an egoistic economic individualism, his ideal was a form of industrial *ancien régime*, comprising a strong state governed by the new feudal class of industrialists. He advocated replacing 'disorganised' capitalism with a corporatist state of hierarchically organised socio-economic groupings that allowed industrial leaders to discipline the individual to boost national production and engage in imperialist expansion. When the Nationalist Association merged with the Fascist Party in 1923, he quickly rose to prominence. As Minister of Justice from 1925–32 he was, with Giuseppe Bottai, instrumental in turning this corporatist doctrine into law in the 'Charter of Labour' of 1926. Indeed, positivism was generally more influential than idealism on fascism. For example, the ideas of Ferri and Lombroso largely shaped the design of the Fascist penal code. However, on the whole, fascist theory limply followed rather than directed fascist practice, with the legal Italy separated as never before from the real Italy.

Opposition and resistance

Given Gentile's prominence as the ideologist of fascism, it was entirely fitting that his erstwhile friend and fellow idealist Benedetto Croce should lead the opposition, drafting a famous reply to Gentile's *Manifesto of Fascist Intellectuals* of 1925. Like many Italian liberals, Croce had initially supported Mussolini in the regrettably common belief that fascism was better than socialism. Once it became clear that fascism aspired to create a new type of regime rather than merely strengthening the hand of the liberal state, he quickly changed tack. He found Gentile's conception of the ethical state particularly repugnant. Invoking his important distinction between ethics and politics, Croce argued that civil society was the realm of ethical life whilst the state was simply a utilitarian institution concerned with efficient governance. Consent might be forced but only in the sense that, to be durable, it had to reflect the force of circumstances – including the demands and needs of citizens. In his histories of Italy from 1871 to 1915 and of nineteenth-century Europe, he sought to defend the practice of liberal institutions, attributing their collapse to irrationalism and materialism. He also presented his historicist philosophy as a 'metapolitical' 'religion of liberty'. Human history, he claimed, resulted from individuals reconceptualising the world in new ways and so preparing the ground for innovative action to alter the world in the future. Put another way, in Croce's view, we change the world via the different ways we come to understand it.

Although Croce defended traditional liberal political and economic institutions, such as representative democracy, the rule of law and the market, he regarded their relationship to liberalism as historically contingent. Thus, he took issue with the free-market economist Luigi Einaudi, arguing that even socialist economic measures could serve liberal purposes in certain circumstances. However, he also disputed the view of the socialist liberal Carlo Rosselli, who argued that liberty was necessarily linked to social justice as the means for realising it. For Croce, individual liberty was the crucial concept and included the freedom to interpret justice in differing ways according to changing historical circumstances.

Nonetheless, Rosselli's position was extremely important within the non-communist anti-fascist movement. In the 1920s, a similar argument had been developed by Guido De Ruggiero, and Piero Gobetti. Gentile's star pupil, De Ruggiero sided with Croce, producing his *History of European Liberalism* in 1924, whilst the precocious 23-year-old Gobetti first published Rosselli's thesis in his Turin journal *La Rivoluzione liberale*. Both thinkers had been tremendously impressed by the socialist movement and, unlike Croce, had sided with it against the fascists from the first. Historicist liberals like Croce, they were arguably more aware than he was of the importance of industrial labour within modern economies and hence of the legitimacy of labour's claims. Though Gobetti was sympathetic to the Russian Revolution, learning Russian in order to follow it more closely, he – like De Ruggiero – was nevertheless antipathetic to forms of collectivism that crushed rather than fostered individuality. Whereas Rosselli sought to liberalise socialism, they wished to socialise liberalism – most importantly by linking it to a mass movement. This last aspiration was ultimately a failure. Again, like Croce, they became interested in Protestantism, attributing (albeit to differing degrees) the absence of a liberal spirit amongst Italians to the pervasiveness of Catholicism. Though Croce argued that fascism was but a 'parenthesis' in Italian history, for Gobetti it was Italy's 'autobiography' – testimony to the absence of a moral revolution amongst the Italian people.

During the Resistance, the Party of Action revived the theme of 'Justice and Liberty'. Rosselli and his brother had been killed on fascist orders in 1937 and Gobetti died in exile aged only 25 in 1926. Their arguments, however, were picked up and developed by Guido Calogero, the major figure in the movement, as well as Augusto Monti and Norberto Bobbio. However, it remained influential only amongst fellow intellectuals. Instead, the two dominant ideologies of post-war Italy were to be the two religions of communism and Christian democracy. Both parties became partially reconciled to liberal democracy: the one (under the leadership of Togliatti) in the Gramscian spirit of a strategic manoeuvre whilst building a counter-hegemony; the other, though tainted with acceptance of fascism via the Lateran Treaty, was led by Alcide de Gasperi to a similarly pragmatic acceptance that no realistic alternative existed. Regrettably, ideologists of each side were to continue to concentrate more on the ideal than the real Italy, placing moral uplift above institutional, social, and economic reform.

Part One:

Enlightenment and Reform

Chapter Two

'*Da metafisico a mercatante*': Antonio Genovesi and the Development of a New Language of Commerce in Eighteenth-Century Naples[1]

Genovesi's appointment in 1754 to the specially created chair *di commercio e di meccanica* at Naples University marked, as Franco Venturi has noted, the full flowering of the complex of political and cultural developments which made up the Neapolitan enlightenment.[2] Yet this event is perhaps too easily seized upon as representing the birth of a secular science of politics, a transition, as Genovesi jokingly said of his new position, from *metafisico* to *mercatante*.[3] In this essay, I wish to show how these two elements were fused, as Genovesi sought to give them coherent expression in a new language of politics adapted to the needs of modern commercial society.

Born in 1713 at Castiglione near Salerno, Genovesi was the first son of a family of small landowners fallen on hard times. He was educated for the priesthood, being ordained in 1737, when the death of his uncle gave him enough money to continue his studies in Naples.[4] Neapolitan intellectual life was at this time undergoing a profound change. The Cartesian and Platonist philosophies that had dominated

1. Professors Raffaele Ajello and Giuseppe Ricuperati very kindly encouraged my early Neapolitan studies, whilst Dott. Eluggero Pii has generously shared his intimate knowledge of Genovesi with me. I am grateful for his comments on an earlier version, and for those of Anthony Pagden, the participants at the Florence conference and John Robertson and Judith Shklar. Research for this paper was made possible by a Leverhulme study-abroad studentship and a grant in aid of research from the British School at Rome.

2. Franco Venturi, *Illuministi italiani*, T.V., Riformatori napoletani, Milan-Naples,1958, pp. ix–xiii, 3–43; 'Il movimento riformatore degli illuministi meridionale', *Rivista Storica Italiana* LXXIV, 1966, pp. 5–26; *Settecento riformatore* I, Turin, 1969, ch. 8, pp. 523–644; and 'Antonio Genovesi', *Terzo Programma*, n.s., II, 1970, pp. 15–24.

3. Letter of 23 February 1754 to Romualdo Sterlich in 'Lettere familiari', in G. Savarese (ed.) *Autobiografia e lettere*, Milan, 1962, p. 78. This view, held by Venturi (*see*, e.g. *Settecento riformatore* I, pp. 552–3, 'Antonio Genovesi', pp. 18–20) and, with a different emphasis, by R. Villari, (*see* 'Antonio Genovesi e la ricerca delle forze motrici dello sviluppo sociale', *Studi Storica* XI, 1970, pp. 26–52), has been criticised by Paola Zambelli in *La formazione filosofica di Antonio Genovesi*, Naples Morano, 1972, pp. 421–37, who has demonstrated the continuity of Genovesi's theological interests, though without reference to his economic doctrine (*see* esp. pp. 709–94). The most recent analysis of the reason for Genovesi's change of chair, based on the various versions of his autobiography, is provided by Eluggero Pii, *Antonio Genovesi – dalla politica economica alla 'politica civile'*, Florence, 1984, pp. 9–21.

4. *Vita di Antonio Genovesi* in *Autobiografia*, pp. 7–14.

the previous fifty years still prevailed but their three main representatives, Pietro Giannone, Giambattista Vico and Paolo Mattia Doria, were all to die in the 1740s and an important new current of thought, fervently anti-metaphysical in character and stressing the experimental method of Newton, was growing up in opposition to them.[5] As Vincenzo Ferrone's recent study has shown, these two intellectual traditions were grouped into two opposing camps centred on the Accademia degli Oziosi, founded in 1733 and supported by Vico and especially Doria, and the Accademia delle Scienze, formed by Celestino Galiani and Bartolomeo Intieri the year before.[6] Whilst the *veteres* attacked the 'material and carnal science' of the *Principia* and the *Opticks*,[7] the *novatores* regarded them as models for the study not just of the natural world but of humanity and society as well, reading Mandeville, Bayle and, above all, Locke to this purpose.[8] As a result, Vico and Doria's dispute with the *novatores* was more than a simple defence of humanist learning. Their complaint was that the rigorous application of the empirical method of the natural sciences to the study of society was incompatible with Catholic morality and, indeed, was likely to have a deleterious effect on social mores *tout court*.

This was a central issue in contemporary Naples. The formation under Carlo Borbone in 1734, of an independent Neapolitan state, free from Austrian or Spanish domination, had produced hopes for a comprehensive reform of the administration and legal system, to revive a society hitherto crippled by feudal privileges and systematically plundered by foreign rulers.[9] The Accademia delle Scienze had been formed with the express aim of providing suitable.intellectual tools for this purpose. Its chosen models were Holland and, especially, England, whose commercial success was attributed less to the intervention of the sovereign than to the existence of a culture and laws favourable to economic achievement, a conclusion drawn from Jean-François Melon's influential *Essai politique sur le commerce* (1734).[10] The debate between *veteres* and *novatores* was therefore motivated by two divergent views of the nature and merits of economic development. The former stressed the social character of commerce. This aimed

5.   In addition to the Books and articles by Franco Venturi cited in n. 1, *see* Raffaelo Ajello, 'Cartesianismo e cultura oltramontana al tempo dell' "*Istoria Civile*" ', in R. Ajello (ed.), *Pietro Giannone e il suo tempo*, 2 vols, Naples, 1980, pp. 3–181, esp. 88–105 and Vincenzo Ferrone, *Scienza, natura, religion – mondo Newtoniano e cultura italiana nel primo '70*, Naples, 1982, esp. chs 5 and 6.

6.   Ferrone, *Scienza, natura, religione*, pp. 501–15, 525–45. On Intieri and Galiani *see*, in addition to Ferrone, Franco Venturi, 'Alle origini dell' illuminismo napoletano: dal carteggio di Bartolomeo Intieri', *Rivista storica italiana* (RSI) LXXI, 1959, pp. 416–56 and Fausto Nicolini, *Un grande educatore italiano, Celestino Galiani*, Naples, 1951.

7.   P. M. Doria, quoted in Ferrone, *Scienza, natura, religione*, p. 539.

8.   Their manifesto declared that 'We expressly ban the discussion of metaphysics or general systems', quoted in *ibid.*, p. 502.

9.   Franco Venturi, *Settecento riformatore*, I, pp. 29ff.; R. Ajello, 'La vita politica napoletana sotto Carlo di Barbone: "La fondazione ed il tempo eroico" della dinastia', in *Storia di Napoli* VII, Naples, 1972, pp. 461–984.

10. Ferrone, *Scienza, natura, religione*, pp. 554–67.

not at individual enrichment but at 'mutual aid', a practice which required 'a most virtuous education and good training'.[11] The latter sought to legitimise commercial practice by elaborating a lay, utilitarian model of society, based on immutable economic laws reflecting those of the Newtonian cosmos, the principle of which was human self-interest. The contrast between the two was thus that whereas Doria's concern with Christian morality led him to place economic development within a general scheme of social justice, Intieri and Galiani's view of morality and justice was entirely economic in orientation.[12] This led to a revised theory of human nature, involving the reduction of human psychology to certain basic passional drives which could be, in A. O. Hirschman's suggestive term, 'harnessed' to the needs of society.[13] The essential elements of this vision are clearly deployed in Ferdinando Galiani's *Della moneta* (1750), a work which, as Ferrone has shown, completed the programme for a new social ethic begun by his uncle Celestino in the 1730s. Ferdinando argues against 'the disdain and loathing of those few, who arrogate the venerable name of "savants" ' for human acquisitiveness. Rather, 'the desire for gain; or to live happily' is the equivalent in the moral sciences to gravity in the physical. Since 'man is a complex of passions, which move him with unequal force' these can be studied and used to procure for humanity the maximum utility or happiness.[14]

According to his autobiography, Genovesi began by maintaining his independence from these two camps, filling the gaps in his provincial education with elements gleaned from both. In many respects his distinctive contribution resides in the manner in which this continued to be the case, so that his work reflects the conflicts felt by contemporaries in adopting the new theory of society as elaborated by Galiani. His greater affinity with the *novatores* is nevertheless clear in his admiration for Newton.[15] Newton did not, however, move him in the direction of scepticism or atheism but rather provided him with a key for resolving traditional religious concerns about the new commercial ethic. An attempt at such a solution can be found in his early works on metaphysics but this route was eventually closed to him, when ecclesiastical opposition prevented his gaining the chair of theology in 1748. His subsequent involvement with Intieri and Galiani is explained in the *Vita* entirely in terms of these external circumstances and lead almost immediately to the setting up of the new chair *di commercia e di meccanica*

---

11. P. M. Doria, *Del commercio del regno di Napoli*, 1740, in E. Vidal, *Il pensiero civile di P. M. Doria negli scritti inediti: con il testo del manoscritto 'del commercio del regno di Napoli'*, Milan, 1953, p. 162, quoted in Ferrone, *Scienza, natura, religione*, p. 597.

12. *See* R. Ajello, 'La critica del regime in Doria, Intieri e Broggia', in *Arcana iuris: diritto e politica nel settecento italiano*, Naples, 1976, pp. 389–427.

13. A. O. Hirschman, *The Passions and the Interests: Political arguments for capitalism before its triumph*, Princeton, 1977, pp. 16–20.

14. Ferdinando Galiani, *Della moneta*, 1750, Alberto Merola (ed.), Milan, 1963, pp. 36, 39, 55–6.

15. E. Pii, *Antonio Genovesi*, pp. 11–12.

by Intieri, with him in mind.[16] This suggests that the shift from *metafisico* to *mercatante* was less a change of purpose than of the path by which he chose to pursue it. The first part of this essay will therefore show how he fused the new and the old in a theory of human nature inspired by Newtonian cosmology. The second part will then illustrate how he used this 'moral anthropology' to reconcile the claims of morality and commerce.

I

The group gathered around Celestino Galiani had already gone some way towards developing a Newtonian science of society. The following example of his thinking will serve as a useful point of comparison with Genovesi's rather different use of these ideas:

> Just as in Newtonian physics one traces the forces and the laws with which these function, and having found out what they are we use these as principles to reason about other phenomena, so in the study of man, one who knows how to reason and observe well, can deduce from certain of his constant traits the forces, which are usually one or more passions combined together and having traced what these are, understand his [man's] character [...] to the extent of being able to act as a fortune teller or prophet by predicting without danger of erring what he will do in the various positions, or combination of circumstances in which he might find himself. [17]

Although Genovesi's willingness to read and comment on authors such as Hobbes and Mandeville got him into difficulties with the religious authorities, there can be little doubt about the orthodoxy of his views.[18] He could not therefore accept Galiani's theory without considerable modification. He certainly appreciated the potential of both Newtonian method and cosmology to provide an unassailable basis for the new political and moral sciences:

---

16. *See* Franco Venturi, 'Alle origini dell'illuminismo napoletano: dal carteggio di Bartolomeo Intieri'. Intieri quickly realised the potential of Genovesi as an educator (e.g. letters to A. Cocchi in *ibid.*, no. viii, 12 December 1752, pp. 440–1: no. x, 16 January 1953, p. 443; no. xi, 20 February 1753, p. 444; no. xiv 12 February 1754, p. 448) and regarded Genovesi's appointment to the new chair as 'the culmination of his life's work', no. xv, 18 June 1754, p. 449. Genovesi records his debt to Intieri in his autobiography (*Autobiografia*, pp. 29–34) and the 'Discorso sopra il vero fine delle lettere e delle scienze', dedicated to Intieri (reproduced in *ibid.*, pp. 275–6).

17. Letter to Bottari, 12 August 1730, quoted in V. Ferrone, *Scienza, natura, religione*, p. 569. Particularly useful for an understanding of Galiani's ideas is the unpublished manuscript 'Della scienza morale', discussed by Ferrone in *ibid.*, pp. 420–42.

18. *See* G. Galasso, 'Il pensiero religioso di Antonio Genovesi', *RSI*, LXXXII, 1979, pp. 800–23 and, more generally, P. Zambelli, *La formazione filosofica di Antonio Genovesi* Naples, Morano, 1972.

The *Mathematical Principles* of cavalier Newton, the *Physico-Theology* of Derham, the work of Niewentit, and others of a similar kind, are worth a hundred thousand volumes of the idle tales and equivocations of these Avincennists, Averroists etc [...] Here is the real metaphysics.[19]

His use of Newtonianism was not, however, free from a continuing concern with certain axioms of traditional Christian theology. He was particularly worried that certain Newtonian ideas, such as the concept of the ether and of empty space as God's sensorium, could lead to the Spinozist heresy of identifying God and Nature.[20]

Genovesi objected to such ideas on the grounds that they denied the doctrine of creation. For Genovesi, the universe was to be considered as the product of God's will, its laws being in conformity with its nature and hence not binding on God, Who existed outside and separated from His creation.[21] He therefore accepted the argument from design but firmly attacked concessions to any kind of hylarchic principle because, in his view, this led to atheism[22] and to the rejection of the freedom of God's will and of humanity's. He preserved both by seeing each component of the universe as endowed with its own principle of action proper to its nature and governed by the mechanical laws whose working was directly dependent on the will of God.[23]

Genovesi had essentially discovered a *via media* between a passive conception of matter, acted upon by an omnipresent and omnipotent God, and a view of matter as active and dynamic and self-ordering. There are, therefore, two tiers in Genovesi's view of the world system – a rational order created by God and

---

19. *La logica per gli giovanetti*, 1766, 7th edn, Naples, 1836, Book V, ch. 5, para. xiv *II* V, p. 268. Where possible, I shall quote from Venturi's selection of Genovesi's writings in *Illuministi italiani*, T.V., pp. 47–330, hereafter *II* V. Genovesi followed Newton in making this transition from natural to moral philosophy, particularly the 31st question of the *Optics*.

20. *Delle scienze metafisiche per gli giovanetti*, 1763, Venice, 3rd edn 1803, 1, ch. 6, para. xv and 2, ch. 3, para. ii. Ferrone, following N. Badaloni in *Antonio Conti: un abate libero pensatore tra Newton e Voltaire*, Milan, 1968, pp. 203–8 and E. Garin, 'Antonio Genovesi storico della scienza', in *Dal rinascimento all'illuminismo*, Pisa, 1970, pp. 223–40, argues that in the earlier *Disputatio physic-historica de rerum corporearum origine et constitutione*, 1745, Genovesi had read Newton in a neo-Stoic key, seeing the universe as a self-sufficient system, a theatre of active processes ordered by an immanent *anima mundi* (*Scienza, natura, religion*, p. 612). Yet here, too, Genovesi seems to be saying that although Newton *could* be read in this manner, citing Clarke and Whiston as examples, it would be against both Newtonian method ('*non fingo...*') and religion to do so – regardless of the motives of those, like Clarke, who aimed to defend religion in this way (*see* the 'Disputatio' in *Disciplinorum metaphysicarum elementa*, T.V., new edn, Venice, 1779, pp. 99–100). Thus, whilst Genovesi fully appreciated the cultural significance of Newton, he was very careful, right from the start, to disassociate himself from both 'conservative' and 'radical' wings of Newtonianism. *See also* the 'Proemio' to the *Elementa physicae experimentalis*, 2 vols, Naples, 1791 (published posthumously), I, p. vii and II, Book IV, ch. 13, paras. ix, x.

21. *Metafisica*, Part 1, ch. 1, and ch. 6, para. xiii.

22. *See ibid.*, Part 1, ch. 2, para. v and the passage of the *Elementa physicae* cited in note 19, where he praises the natural theology of Ray, Derham and Nieventit.

23. *Ibid.*, Part 1, ch. 6, para. xii.

a secondary system of self-regulating natural processes. The first is constituted by an underlying created order, in which humanity, in common with everything else, has its place; the second by the mechanisms which preserve this order and develop it. The two taken together constitute the basis of Genovesi's moral science: 'Therefore the first foundation of the moral sciences is human nature: the second the relations between things, which surround us: the third the laws of these relations'.[24]

In an analogous manner, Genovesi also divided human nature into two parts – animal and rational. By virtue of our animal nature, we are subjected to all the 'animal laws' (*leggi della animalita*) and all those of the spirit and of reason with respect to the mind.[25] Humans qua animals are sensate beings with an infinite number of appetites and natural desires which they seek to satisfy.[26] Genovesi examines the consequences for humanity of this state, both internally and externally, each time invoking the laws of mechanics to do so. There are two forces which govern the world system – 'the *centripetal and the centrifugal*' [*la centripeta e la centrifuga*'].[27] Humankind, as a finite, limited being, is subject to the same laws which regulate all other bodies in the universe: the laws of attraction and collision.[28] The dialectic of these two forces preserves the natural order. It is therefore the source of all good but also, because of the imperfect nature of finite beings, of all evil. On the one hand, political evil derives from humans living in society and the inevitable clash of individuals seeking to satisfy their private interests associated with the force of collision. On the other hand, the force of attraction is a source of gain for humankind, society providing them with the security and company necessary to their existence. Happiness and the good for humankind are to be found in the equilibrium of these two forces.[29] Genovesi therefore rejects the idea that the public good can develop out of the pursuit of selfish ends. He takes this argument further with reference to the internal structure of humans. The conflict of desires, the pressures of the external world, cause pain and arouse passions within them. To describe this phenomenon, Genovesi again has recourse to the two universal forces of attraction and repulsion derived from Newtonian cosmology. These two forces, called at different times *concentriva* and *diffusiva* or *espansiva* and *coattiva* and *direttiva*, are also defined in the more usual terminology as 'self-love' ('*l'amor proprio*') and 'love of the species' ('*l'amor della spezia*').[30] Genovesi uses this schema in order to criticise those theorists who sought a metamorphosis of destructive passions stemming from self-love

24. *Logica*, Book V, ch. 5, para. xxxi, *II* V, p. 270. *See also* F. Aratathe (ed.), 'Proemio' to the *Della Diceosino o sia della filosofia del giusto e dell'onesto*, 1766, Milan, 1973, pp. 25–7.
25. *Diceosino*, Book I, ch. 1, para. i, p. 32.
26. *Ibid.*, Book I, ch. 1, para. ii, p. 32.
27. *Metafisica*, Part 1, ch. 2, para. i.
28. *Ibid.*, Part 1, ch. 8, para. 1; *Diceosina*, Book I, ch. 1, para. x, p. 37.
29. *Metafisica*, Part 1, ch. 8, 'Dei mali'.
30. *Logica*, Book V, ch. 5, para. xxxiv, *II* V, p. 271; *see also Diceosina*, Book 1, ch. 1, para. xvii, p. 42, where they are also called '*due interni principi motori, simpatici ed energetici, che sono essenziali alla nostra natura*'.

into virtuous social action. His principle targets were Hobbes and Mandeville. The verisimilitude granted to Mandeville's theory derives, he argues, from its superficiality – he is *un filosofo di corteccia*. Self-love is basic to human survival but, here following Shaftesbury, so is sympathy with the rest of humankind and the latter can in no sense be seen as derivative from the former.[31] Both, claimed Genovesi, explicitly breaking with the associationist psychology of Locke which had been adopted by Galiani and others, are innate, fixed principles within humans.[32] On the same grounds, he attacks what he calls the Hobbesian view that society can be seen as the product of enlightened self-interest:

> the error of both of them is to have made the *concentriva* alone the primary force, and the other the effect and result of that. Shaftesbury has shown the error of this: and if there is something in nature which the philosophers have demonstrated, it is this truth in the learned work of this Englishman.[33]

Human happiness is thus to be found in the harmony of these two forces, which regulate both the world and human nature. Genovesi consequently rejects as artificial any suggestion that different political systems could affect human behaviour. For example, he criticises Montesquieu's tripartite division of the forms of government, each with its own principle, as a 'Fable [*Romanzo*]: neither well founded in nature, nor in the principles of nature'.[34] Different forms of government simply reflect the balance of the two forces within humankind. As Enrico De Mas has observed, such a view is strange, given that he had earlier accused Montesquieu of subverting religion and morals by attempting to see them as the outcome of natural processes.[35]

---

31. *See Metofisica*, Part 3, ch. 7, paras x–xv. P. Zambelli has demonstrated the influence of Vico's criticism of Hobbes on Genovesi, *La formazione filosofica di A. G.*, pp. 557–61. This has suggestive consequences for his later economic theory (*see Elementorum metaphyisicae*, T. IV, Naples, 1754, Book I, ch. 4, paras xxxii–ill; *see also*, A. O. Hirschmann, *The Passions and the Interests*, pp. 17–19, for a revealing discussion of Vico's *Scienza nuova*, paras cxxx–xxxv).

32. Genovesi's rejection of this aspect of Locke is clearly shown in his epistolary exchange with Antonio Conti on the origin of ideas (*Lettere familiari*, 2nd edn, Venice, 1787, pp. 2–30, esp. letter 2, pp. 3–28). Genovesi defines innate ideas as '*naturali inclinazioni dell'animo, [...] naturali leggi, per cui siam portati al nostro ultimo fine, simili in ciò alle leggi naturali della materia; ovvero quei giudizi, che naturalmente vengono in capo a tutti, e che son dette prime e naturali verità*' (pp. 23–4). This debate forms the core of G. Gentile's chapter on Genovesi in *Storia della filosofia italiana: dal Genovesi al Galluppi*, 2nd edn, 2 vols, Florence, 1937, I, ch.1, which is, to my mind, more accurate in its conclusions than N. Badaloni, *Antonio Conti*, pp. 204–10 and 'La cultura', pp. 823–8.

33. *Logica*, Book V, ch. 5 para. xxxvi, *II* V, pp. 272–3.

34. *Spirito delle leggi del Signare di Montesquieu con le note dell'Abate Antonio Genovesi*, 4 vols, Naples, 1777, I, Book III, ch. 4, n. 2, p. 56. Genovesi's annotations to Montesquieu's *Esprit des lois* (written 1766–9) were published posthumously. They have been discussed in detail in Enrico De Mas, *Montesquieu, Genovesi e la edizione italiane dello 'Spirito delle Leggi'*, Florence, 1971, esp. pp. 59–169. De Mas's study provides, in many respects, the best philosophical treatment of Genovesi's social thought. He omits to mention, however, Genovesi's concept of '*collisione*' and this, to my mind, flaws his discussion of the linking of passion, reason and interest.

35. E. De Mas, *Montesquieu, Genovesi*, pp. 108–9.

Genovesi resolves this possible contradiction by appealing to the laws of the created natural order. Genovesi raises the problem that his theory might appear to lead to some form of determinism itself. Taking on the role of devil's advocate, he argues that, if humanity is to be seen as being moved solely by 'physical causes' rather than moral imperatives, then there would be no point in engaging in moral philosophy at all.[36] To counter this, he takes a qualitative, if not strictly logical, leap in his argument. Human nature is unchangeable but not unmodifiable– humanity is 'elastic' ('la forza della natura umana è elastica').[37] Humans are led by nature, but an understanding of this is communicated to them by the passions. Passions derive from the law of collision. But since Genovesi maintains the mind-body distinction,[38] an aspect of how the external world affects us is our rational perception of it:

> A false and harmful point of view will arouse a harmful passion and man will be led by that passion (that is by nature whipped up by the passion) to his misery. A truer view of the same thing, and more connected to our interests will arouse a useful passion; and we will be led by it to our happiness. Our happiness or our misery therefore depends upon what aspect things present to us, and make us love or hate them. So do, or should do, the true and good theories of morality. The theory of relations is therefore essential to good morals.[39]

This passage (and there are many like it) demonstrates the crucial bridge Genovesi created between the naturalistic and rationalistic models of human action which he had adopted. Hirschman has shown how the concept of 'interest' became a new paradigm in eighteenth-century moral theory, mediating between selfish and socially orientated passions.[40] Genovesi puts it to much the same use, though in his own way. He identifies utility, happiness and interest as the rational perception of the natural order which enables humans to avoid the pain consequent on the force of collision. Reason is simply defined as 'the calculating faculty' ('la facolta calcolatrice').[41] Reason cannot of itself, therefore, provide moral guidelines. These derive from the law of nature, which humans know by a religious and moral sense or instinct and which reason seeks to interpret.[42] Thus, although humans are susceptible to an infinite variety of habits and customs, their essential nature remains the same, ruled by the law of nature 'which links all the parts of this world, fixing in each its nature, its relations and the particular laws'.[43]

---

36. *Logica*, Book V, ch. 5, para. xxxviii, *II* V, p. 273.
37. *Diceosina*, Book I, ch. 1, para. xvi, p. 41, 'Discorso sopra il vero fine delle lettere e delle scienza', *II* V, p. 119.
38. *Metafisica*, Part 3, ch. 2, para. xv.
39. *Logica*, Book V, ch. 5, para. xl, *II* V, pp. 273–4.
40. A. O. Hirschmann, *The Passions and the Interests*, pp. 42–8.
41. *Diceosina*, Book I, ch. 2, para. i, p. 44.
42. *Ibid.*, para. iii, p. 45, 41.
43. *Ibid., Logica*, Book V, ch. 5, paras XLV–VII.

This law necessarily forms the basis by which humans must order themselves if they want to achieve the 'minimum of ills' ('*minimo de' mali*') – *viz.* the best possible happiness that limited and imperfect beings can enjoy.[44] To adopt other criteria is to court disaster:

> If the nature of things; if man; if the relations which man has; if the civil body, and its relations, if the interest of man and of the Republic, etc [...] are not the foundation of the laws, the laws clash with physical nature, and do not endure, or are undermined in an infinite number of ways. The true rule therefore, the first, the immutable, is to turn to nature herself.[45]

This is achieved by rationally using the springs of human action, the passions, to encourage humankind to pursue their interest – what Genovesi calls the maxim of *etica fisica* – namely that:

> IT IS NOT REASON WHICH RESTRAINS THE PASSIONS, BUT ALWAYS THE GREATER [passion] RESTRAINS THE LESSER: and if reason acts as a restraint, it does so by exciting a greater [passion].[46]

The art of government thus consists in leading humans from false and harmful passions and seeking to imprint in their hearts 'a stronger passion, but truer, that is more in accord with personal and common interests'.[47] Genovesi had therefore discovered a use for theory in the moral world, since knowledge of the law of nature is necessary to promote human happiness. Moreover, such action is not to be regarded as morally indifferent, or a mysterious manipulation of vice to good ends, but is the outcome of virtue. Virtue is precisely this perception of the moral order without which humanity would be led not just to evil but equally to pain and unhappiness.[48] If humanity's reason were not involved, as, for example, Genovesi thinks Mandeville argues, humans could be no more capable of virtue than an animal or a plant.[49] Instead, Genovesi follows Shaftesbury in believing that humanity has a natural propensity for virtuous action that develops with their intellect, that is, their rational perception of the moral order.[50] Virtue and interest necessarily coincide; to separate them is only hypothetically possible, as in the false theories of Hobbes and Mandeville. Occasional ambiguities in Genovesi's opinion here merely reflect the uncertainties in the political language of the time.[51] Genovesi firmly rejects the notion that a society could be built on interest alone, or indeed that a people exists without virtue, since morals and religion are innate

---

44. *Diceosina*, Book I, ch. 2, para. ii, p. 45.
45. *Logica*, Bk. V, ch. 5, para. xliv.
46. *Ibid.*, para. 1 x, *II* V, p. 279.
47. *Metafisica*, Part 3, ch. 6, para. xxi.
48. *Diceosina*, Book I, ch. 1, para. viii. p. 35; ch. 2, para. v, p. 46.
49. *Ibid.*, ch. 1, paras iv and v, pp. 33–4.
50. *Metafisica*, Part 3, ch. 7, para. xiv.
51. A. O. Hirschman, *The Passions and the Interests*, pp. 46–7.

sentiments within humankind.[52] Like Shaftesbury, he argues that human's self-interest can only be truly found in reference to their end as implanted in their nature. Each creature, plant and so on is part of a universal system of things, in which the end of each is resolved with that of the whole. Virtue and interest are identified, since to do evil to oneself and to subvert the order of things are one and the same thing.[53] Genovesi has simply combined this theory of morals with his physical description of the workings of human passion inspired by Newtonian cosmology. Reason cannot change humanity's end, which is fixed by their natural constitution, but is merely the means by which they fulfil it.[54]

It would be wrong to see Genovesi's moral order as immutably fixed, his concept of virtue based on the traditional Christian qualities of restraint and abnegation – ideas developed by Muratori and Doria earlier on in the century.[55] It was noted above how Genovesi's conception of Newtonianism achieved a middle way between the set laws which govern the component parts of the world and active properties inherent in these parts themselves. Genovesi transfers this to the moral sphere when he argues that the ethical code governing human actions can be reduced to the axiom 'preserve the equilibrium by preserving rights'. (*serba l'equilibrio con serbare i diritti*').[56] Genovesi in this respect provides an early prototype for the minimalist liberalism of today. A baseline of rights is there to provide a safety net against the abuse of freedom but not a set of goals for human action. This is simply, again in liberal fashion, the pursuit of happiness. Human rights are simply those properties of mind and body with which they are endowed as created beings. These in turn are preserved by the law of nature which orders the whole chain of being.[57] The dynamic element is provided by human reason, which develops with experience and eases humanity's passage through this vale of tears.

It is here, in his adoption of a programme for progress through the practical use of reason, that Genovesi's second debt to contemporary scientific culture becomes evident. Reason, he argued in his inaugural *Discourse on the True End of the Arts*

52. *Metafisica*, Part 2, ch. 4, para. iv. *See* Enrico De Mas, *Montesquieu, Genovesi*, pp. 112–21 for an important discussion of Genovesi's notes to *Esprit des lois*, Book III, ch. 7. *Diceosina*, Book I, ch 10, para. viii, p. 164.

53. Shaftesbury, *Inquiry Concerning Virtue and Merit*, 1699: 'We have found, that to deserve the name of *good* or *virtuous*, a creature must have all his inclinations and affections, his dispositions of mind and temper, suitable, and agreeing with the good of his *kind*, or of that *system* in which he is included, and of which he constitutes a PART. To stand thus well affected and to have one's affections *right* and *entire*, not only in respect of oneself, but of society and the public: this is *rectitude, integrity*, or VIRTUE. And to be wanting in any of these, or to have their contraries, is *depravity, corruption* and VICE'. Book II, Part 1, sect. I, in D. D. Raphael (ed.), *British Moralists 1650–1800*, 2 vols, Oxford, 1969, I, para. ccv, p. 175. Compare *Diceosina*, Book I, ch. 3, para. xviii, p. 60.

54. *Metafisica*, Part 3, ch. 6, para. xxxii.

55. On Doria, *see* R. Ajello, 'La critica del regime in Doria, Intieri e Broggia', and compare Muratori's chapter on luxury in *Della pubblica felicita*, 1748, ch. 19, with its attack on Melon, to the view of Genovesi in *Lezione di commercio*, Part 1, ch. x, *II* V, pp. 177–208, discussed below.

56. *Diceosina*, Book I, ch. 1, para. xx, p. 44, chs 3 and 4.

57. *Diceosina*, Book I, ch. 3, para. xiv, p. 58, *Lezione di commercio*, Part 1, ch. 1, paras x–xv.

and Sciences (1753), is what separates humanity from the brutes, bringing them closer to God. It is what directs their other faculties. Through its use they are able to satisfy their wants in increasingly better ways. Tracing the hypothetical development of a nation from barbarity to civilisation he notes how:

> Reason, on the basis of the relations of the things which surround us in our life, makes the arts and perfects them with regard to their relations to our end [...] Experience, which is the point arrived at by reason in different times and subjects, discovers in brief new relations and new uses, and therefore improvements and perfections, and will do so to the extent that such a nation, which in its origin was closer to dumb beasts than reasoning beings, finds itself as superior to the former as it had been similar to them at its birth.[58]

There can thus be a science of politics which can be put to practical use to educate the populace and promote good habits in them.[59] The progress of society is not inevitable but goes hand in hand with the development of reason and the consequent regulation of the passions in humankind.[60] Hirschman has suggested that the attractiveness of interest as a new paradigm for explaining human motivation was its predictability – the constancy with which it was held to operate within human beings. For Genovesi, interest still had unpleasant notions of egoism, which he diffused by linking it with reason and virtue. Only then would humankind's interest emerge, for only by the practical application of reason to discover and observe nature's laws could humans lessen the burden of their earthly existence, cease to be animals and become truly human again.[61] That the arts and sciences should be put to the useful task of furthering human (as opposed to individual) happiness was thus a moral obligation which it was the duty of the intellectual class to spread amongst the people.[62]

The *Discorso* clearly aligns Genovesi with the *novatores* and against the *veteres*. The culture of contemplation, of *ozio*, runs the risk of corrupting the community and precipitating a return to the bestial state.[63] It is, in the modern sense of the word, otiose; and he significantly justifies this view via a criticism of Greek philosophy, which, he claims, produced the dark ages of scholastic thought.[64] The decisive break came with the Renaissance and the works of Galileo and Bacon, which liberated Europe from the 'barbarism' into which it had fallen.[65]

---

58. 'Discorso sopra il vero fine delle lettere e delle scienze', *II* V, p. 89.

59. *Ibid.*, p. 100.

60. 'Ragionamento sul commercio in universale', *II* V, pp. 136–7.

61. Hirschman, *The Passions and the Interests*, pp. 48–56. Genovesi's 'Lettere accademiche su la questione se siano piu' felice gli' ignoranti che gli schienziati', (1764), in *Autobiografia*, pp. 359–66, deals with this theme, e.g. Letter 2, p. 375.

62. 'Discorso sopra il vero fine delle lettere e delle scienze', *II* V, pp. 118–25. My interpretation of the *Discorso* follows E. Pii, *Antonio Genovesi*, pp. 23–44.

63. *Discorso*, p. 89.

64. *Ibid.*, pp. 92–6.

65. *Ibid.*, pp. 96–7.

Progress requires the enlightenment of the populace. Reason must therefore cease to be the preserve of an intellectual elite:

> One cannot say that reason has reached maturity in a nation, when it still resides more in the abstract intellect than in men's hearts and hands [...] It is like the jewels which sparkle but do not nourish us. Reason is not useful until it has become a practical reality, nor does it become such until it is so diffused in the customs and arts, that we adopt it as our sovereign rule, almost without realising it.[66]

The *Discorso*, dedicated to Intieri, ends with a survey of the state of the kingdom of Naples and looks to the spreading of enlightenment (*lume*) amongst the country's artisans and peasants[67] and the consequent 'multiplication, improvement and, the perfectioning of foodstuffs, commerce and the arts'.[68]

The *Discorso* has been called 'the manifesto of the Neapolitan Enlightenment',[69] assigning a definite role to intellectuals in promoting economic progress via a programme of cultural reform and education of the populace. The emphasis on education is important for a correct understanding of the precise nature of Genovesi's endorsement of commercial practice. He specifically avoids the essentially naturalistic theory of the development of human morality of Hobbes and Mandeville, which Celestino Galiani adopted. The framework of Genovesi's thinking remains essentially theocentric and hence anti-sociological.[70] It is not the development of society as such which produces the improvement of human customs and manners; rather, the influence of the latter leads to the former. This view was no doubt reinforced by the bitter experience of Neapolitan history, in which intellectual repression went hand in hand with a backward and archaic social system. The duty and rationale for human improvement, therefore, required a foundation outside the contingencies of social progress in the God-given laws of attributes of human nature and reason.[71] Our obligations to others and to ourselves are fixed in a manner that avoids the moral parody of *The Fable of the Bees*. The elements of a commercial ethic are nevertheless clearly present. Our goals are no longer prescribed by our place in the hierarchy of being. The cosmic order is not fixed for all time but is a complex of interrelated and dynamic atoms. The result of the application of the atomistic model to the microcosm of society is that the individual, ruled by his or her own thoughts and desires, becomes the basic unit for explaining and legitimating social relations. Our purposes are closely related to our moral duty to use our God-given cognitive and physical capacities. In practice, this entails us finding our goals within our own nature and devising the means to satisfy and fulfil our desires, a duty enshrined in certain

---

66. *Ibid.*, p. 100.
67. *Ibid.*, p. 110.
68. *Ibid.*, p. 123.
69. E. Pii, *Antonio Genovesi*, p. 26.
70. *Discorso*, p. 88.
71. *Ibid.*, pp. 89–90, 124–31.

basic and inalienable rights. Genovesi was able to provide thereby a theological motive for the capitalist way of life. The life of endless accumulation, which, in Doria's neo-Platonist perspective was one of vice and slavery to the passions – a turning away from what is intrinsically good – is endorsed by Genovesi as the exercise and fulfilment of our spiritual capacity. Reason ceases to be concerned with contemplation of the eternal forms but is instrumental to the pursuit of our worldly goals. Genovesi thereby provided a model of the capitalist individual, who works to satisfy his or her desires as a God-given vocation, which would be almost archetypically Weberian were it not for the fact that it arose in a Catholic rather than a Protestant milieu. Finally, it is to be noted that, although Genovesi's theory is in many respects paradigmatically liberal and individualist in character, he is careful to avoid the dangers of egoism. The individual's pursuit of his or her own good is related at a basic level with the rights of others to act similarly. In this manner, he reconciled the new language of commerce with the concern with morality and social justice of Doria and Broggia.

II

Having outlined the main features of Genovesi's *antropologia morale,* I wish briefly to sketch how he adapted it to the needs of commercial society. The impetus to translate his social theory directly into a study and defence of commerce came less from his new teaching duties than from the terrible famine of 1764.[72] It was generally agreed that this had arisen from the series of bad harvests that had occurred since 1758. It thereby brought to an end a period of general European prosperity that had encouraged an optimism in the inherently progressive nature of social processes amongst Neapolitan reformers.[73] The spectacle of this national disaster had a profound effect on Genovesi, convincing him of the need to put forward a programme for the reform of the practices – most particularly those stemming from numerous local and feudal privileges – which had so weakened agricultural production. Genovesi's observations were informed by an attempt to provide empirical documentation of the kingdom's ills. However, what was strikingly new and original was the organisation of these ideas within a general theory of economic development, derived from his revised account of human nature. The principal aspect of Genovesi's proposals was the need to erode feudal landlords' hold on the land and to free the peasants from their virtual serfdom so that they were in a position to profit from their own labour.[74] The rationale for the theory was provided by his justification of the acquisitive ethic examined in the previous section.

---

72. E. Pii, *Antonio Genovesi*, pp. 165–70.

73. P. Villiani, *Mezzogiorno tra riforme e rivoluzione*, 2nd edn, Bari, 1973, p. 26.

74. A. Genovesi, 'Preface to Cosimo Trina, *L'agricoltore sperimentato*, 1764', in *Autobiografia*, pp. 342–55.

The two volumes of his *Lezioni di commercio o sia di economia civile* appeared in 1765 and 1767 respectively. He begins by making the step from *metafisico* to *mercatante* outlined above.[75] Humans are born, he argues, with certain innate properties:

> But although these things are inseparable from us; they can nevertheless be modified in an infinite number of ways. Our happiness depends on a wise modification of them, and from the reasoned use, that we make of them: misery from their abuse.[76]

This is increasingly the case as societies grow and become more complex. Needs increase and their satisfaction becomes more complicated, so that friction and hence pain is potentially greater. Yet in reality the opposite occurs, since the larger number of ties binds society together more tightly and enables more people to be sustained above subsistence level than in primitive society.[77] These are the two objects of trade and industry (both products of human reason): to increase the wealth of the nation and hence the size of the population.[78] What holds society together is the law of nature, duty to which is encouraged by education and religion.[79] Human beings are educated via their passions; above all, the desire to eschew pain, which Genovesi calls their interest. But it is not simply a selfish desire. Two forces, the self-regarding and the social, operate in human beings. The latter, 'the sympathetic principle' ('*il principio simpatico*'), which he distinguishes from 'rational self-love' ('*un amor proprio riflesso*'), being 'the source of three-quarters of human actions'.[80] Again, he rebuts the suggestion that any sort of felicific calculus could be applied by a benevolent legislator to encourage good customs in people without appealing to reason and virtue.[81] In debate with Rousseau, he argues that the arts and science, in so far as they are used to promote social and economic progress, can only spread virtue rather than vice.[82] The traumatic effect of the plague and famine of 1763–4 made his attack on the supposed happy condition of primitive man all the more poignant.[83] Humans

---

75. On the genesis of Genovesi's economic theory *see*, in addition to the articles and Books already cited in note 1, Franco Venturi, 'Le *Lezione di commercio* di Antonio Genovesi – Manoscritti, edizioni e traduzioni', in *RSI* LXXII, 1960, pp. 511–38 and E. Pii, 'Le origini dell'economia "civile" in Antonio Genovesi', *Il Pensiero Politico* XII, 1979, pp. 334–43 and *Antonio Genovesi*, ch. 5.

76. *Delle lezioni di commercio o sia d'economica civile*, 2 vols, 2nd edn, Naples, 1768–70, Part 1, ch. 1, para. xxi, p. 36.

77. *Ibid.*, Proemio, p. 12.

78. *Ibid.*, introduction to Part 1, pp. 17–18, ch. 16, para. I, p. 342.

79. *Ibid.*, ch. 1, para. xxxii.

80. *Ibid.*, ch. 2, para. vi.

81. *Ibid.*, ch. 1 para, xxxii, and note a.

82. *Ibid.*, ch. 10. para. ii.

83. This is essentially the message of the 'Lettere accademiche', e.g. letter 1, p. 373. *See* F. Venturi, *Settecento riformatore*, I, pp. 605–10.

in the primitive state are little better off than animals, moved by physical springs alone and incapable of virtue. It is only when they can consciously take control of their own destiny that humans can be capable of moral action. Commerce is thus rehabilitated by Genovesi as the free application of the arts and science to the pursuit of the *summum bonum*, human happiness.[84]

Nothing better illustrates the transformation of morals achieved by Genovesi than his treatment of luxury.[85] Vico and Doria had both regarded luxury as pernicious to society. Vico's 'ideal eternal history' is often regarded as an early prototype of the stadial theory of social progress but it clearly emerged from an intellectual framework which the proponents of stadial theory (notably the Scots) consciously sought to supersede. For Vico, the founding of society is an act of God for humanity's preservation and greater ease. Humankind's attempts to better their condition determine the phases of history but this process has a limit in the final stage of luxury. Thus

> Men must feel necessity, then look for utility, next attend to comfort, still later amuse themselves with pleasure, then grow dissolute in luxury, and finally go mad and waste their substance.[86]

Significantly applying his theory to the history of Rome, Vico argued that the objective of statecraft should be the direct furtherance of the public good. Only when this became the chief priority of all members of the community was a state likely to escape entering the cycle of decadence and decline. The decline of Rome and the *ricorso* to a second barbarism is attributed to the importing of 'Asiatic' luxury. Vico's condemnation of luxury was thus very much that of the civic moralist and was endorsed by Doria, who regarded it as something 'which by its very nature is a vice and poison in the republic'.[87] It was crucial to Genovesi's defence of commerce that he amend this view, for it set an unacceptable limit to human progress and was at odds with the individualist premises of his theory of economic growth. The originality of this step is underlined by the fact that even Ferdinando Galiani, in *Della Moneta*, had argued that despite its good effect '[i]t is nevertheless always true that luxury is the infallible sign and warning of the imminent decadence of a state'.[88]

Hume played a crucial role in providing Genovesi with arguments to counter these objections. Hume's *Essays* and his *History of England* provided a model of economic development that Genovesi in many respects made his own. There are various reasons for the affinities between their thought, mainly deriving from a common concern with the relative economic development of rich and poor countries and the key role played by agriculture in providing a surplus to be spent

---

84. *Lezioni di commercio*, Part 1, ch. 22, paras. ix, xxxiii, *II* V, pp. 224–5 , 243–4.

85. *Ibid.*, Part 1, ch. 10, in *II* V, pp. 177–208.

86. G. B. Vico, *La scienza nuova*, 1744, Fausto Nicolini (ed.), 2 vols, Bari, 1974, 'degnita' LXVI, para. ccxli, *see also* LXVII, para. ccxlii.

87. P. M. Doria, *Del commercio*, p. 209, quoted in Ferrone, *Scienza, natura, religione*, p. 599.

88. *Della moneta*, p. 242.

on manufacture. For both, their commitment to the undoubted benefits accruing from commercial wealth necessitated a reappraisal of the moral consequences of luxury.[89] Hume, in the essay 'Of refinement in the arts', had defended luxury from the views of both moralists and libertines:

> by proving, *first*, that the ages of refinement are both the happiest and most virtuous; *secondly*, that wherever luxury ceases to be innocent, it also ceases to be beneficial; and when carried a degree too far, is a quality pernicious, though perhaps not the most pernicious, to political society.[90]

Genovesi essentially repeats Hume's arguments, using them to steer a careful path between Mandeville and Rousseau. Both Mandeville, who regards luxury as the product of vice, and Rousseau, who sees it as productive of vice, are wrong. Rather, Genovesi believes, there is a level of luxury that is essential to both the civilisation and virtue of a nation, without which a people is subject simply to the gifts of fortune. Genovesi agrees that amongst the springs of human action is greed. But although one cannot change vice into virtue, it is possible to take advantage of it for the public good: 'Human art cannot make nature, but it can regulate it' (*reggerle*).[91]

Genovesi followed Hume in maintaining that, whilst excessive luxury was destructive of society in arousing the desire for gain and hedonistic pleasure above all else, a certain degree of it was required if a nation was to leave the savage state:

> this moderate luxury should rather be called propriety, decency, and gentility of a civilised people, than luxury: and far from being a vice is a virtue, being a mean between tough and sordid parsimony, and foolish and vain prodigality.[92]

Genovesi's reappraisal of luxury went hand in hand with a revised view of how wealth was created in a community. Vico and Doria had argued that wealth must be sought as a public rather than a personal good if its corrupting effects were to be forestalled. Genovesi, however, drew upon Hume to argue that economic growth was the end product of the individual pursuit of personal and family interest; since 'the nature and main force and activity of political bodies derives from the nature

---

89. 'Of commerce', *Essays Moral, Political and Literary*, Oxford, 1963, pp. 259–74. Hume's *Essays* and *History* were appreciated early on in Italy. As the Florentine *Novelle letterarie* noted: '*il signor Hume si e proposto in questi suoi Discorsi Politici il grande oggetto d'essere utile anche agli homini che nasceranno; e di piu' non li ha scritti per la sola nazione. Il commercio è una delle parti piu' esseziale della sua opéra.*' (vol. XVI, no. 3, 17 January 1755, p. 42). The *History of England* was regarded as '*un modello per tutti quei che vogliono accingersi a scrivere una qualche storia*', (vol. XIX, no. 48, 1 December 1758, p. 67). On the Italian reception of the Scottish Enlightenment, *see* F. Venturi, 'Scottish echoes in eighteenth-century Italy', in I. Hont and M. Ignatieff (eds), *Wealth and Virtue*, Cambridge, 1983, pp. 345–62. I am indebted to John Robertson's chapter, 'The Scottish Enlightenment at the limits of the civic tradition', in *ibid.*, pp. 137–78, for my understanding of Hume's economic theory.

90. *Essays*, p. 267.

91. *Lezione*, Part 1, ch. 10, para. ii, pp. 178–9 and *ibid.*, para. vii, p. 181.

92. *Ibid.*, para. xli, p. 206.

and force of families and the nature and force of persons'.[93] Luxury and wealth are a product of the human desire to 'distinguish ourselves' (*di distinguersi*).[94] This desire exists in even the most primitive peoples, who adorn themselves with bangles or brightly coloured clothes – a point illustrated by a quote from the description of 'the character of the Anglo-Saxons marvellously painted by Sig. Davide Hum'.[95] It becomes much more complicated in commercial society, where the marks of distinction are 'no longer natural, but representative' (*rappresentatrici*).[96] Once money and manufactured goods have been introduced, the incentives to work are potentially unlimited. For these provide an infinite source of different forms of wealth by which individuals can distinguish themselves from each other.[97] Genovesi had no wish, as previous moralists had done, to attack this natural human propensity, merely to regulate it.[98] This is again done with reference to both the laws of nature and the laws of mechanics.[99] The former merely confer the obligation to respect the rights of others in their individual pursuit of happiness; the latter provide the means of educating the passions in conformity with the social interest.[100]

Genovesi shared the view of the Scottish economists that luxury distributes wealth and destroys privilege, in particular that stemming from feudalism.[101] Again following Hume, he gave a classically Scottish account of the decline of feudalism that was to become a standard feature of the works of Neapolitan reformers.[102] 'In a polite nation [*una nazione politica*]', he says, 'one cannot do without a thousand things which luxury begins to make necessary'.[103] 'As a result,

93. *Lezione*, Part 1, ch. 1, para. ii, p. 19.

94. *Ibid.*, ch. 10, paras xv–vi, in *II* V, pp. 187–8.

95. *Ibid.*, n. 1, pp. 188–9.

96. *Ibid.*, para. xvii, pp. 189–90.

97. *Ibid.*, paras. xviii–xxv. pp. 190–4.

98. *Ibid.*, para vii, p. 181.

99. *Ibid.*, para. viii, p. 181.

100. *Diceosina*, Book 1, ch. 3, para. v, pp. 52–3.

101. *Lezioni de commercio*, Part 1, ch. 22, para. xxiv, in *II* V, pp. 193–4. I have discussed the interpretation by the Scottish economists of the Idea of Progress in 'From feudalism to capitalism: history and politics in the Scottish Enlightenment', in A. Moulakis (ed.), *The Promise of History*, Berlin-New York, 1985, pp. 35–50.

102. *Lezione*, Part 1, ch. 22. *II* V, pp. 218 ff., discussed in G. Giarizzo, 'La storiografia meridionale del settecento', *Vico-la politica e la storia*, Naples, 1981, pp. 175–239, esp. 198–201. Genovesi's own version of the stadial theory is in *Lezione*, Part 1. ch. 17, paras i–vii, pp. 140–9 and is analysed by E. Pii, *Antonio Genovesi*, pp. 230–3. Genovesi's follower, G. M. Galanti, had the relevant passages of Hume's *History* (Appendix III) and William Robertson's *A View of the Progress of Society in Europe* translated, and applied their insights in his own study *Della descrizione geografica e politica della Sicilia*, Naples, 1782. This use of the stadial theory for the analysis of the transition from feudalism to capitalism in Naples culminated in David Winspeare's *Storia degli abusi feudali*, Naples, 1811. See G. Giarrizzo, 'La storiografia meridionale', for the fullest account of this movement.

103. *Lezione*, Part 2. ch. 9, para. xi, *II* V, pp. 215–16.

the landowners begin to dissipate their wealth and hence their economic power in conspicuous consumption. The consequent substitution of cash for service relationships frees the peasants from oppressive feudal dues and, ultimately, enables them to become a class of independent small proprietors. Genovesi believed that this would inevitably be a slow process. Significantly, he regarded the role of the state as consisting not in the outright abolition of feudalism but in the protection of the individual's right to his labour, 'the capital of the poor'. This would eventually have the desired effect of increasing the wealth of the nation and, more importantly, would result in its being distributed in an equitable fashion.[104] It does not lead to a classless society, since individuals will still be distinguished by natural talents, skills, occupations and so on, but to a meritocracy suited to the desert-ethic of a market society.[105] Finally, he did not believe that the bonds between states created by commerce would replace war, as Melon and Montesquieu had argued.[106] The Seven Years War had provided ample evidence that this was not necessarily the case, and he maintained a strong neo-mercantilist attitude with regard to the dealings between states. This largely derives from the realistic strain in Genovesi and does not contradict the principle of a fundamental equilibrium that is at the heart of his social theory. It is merely a recognition that relations between states are likely to be harder to regulate than those within them, so that the desire for gain is likely to get the upper hand. Nations must simply be prepared for this eventuality.[107]

The commercial growth of England, in particular, represented for Genovesi a model of economic development for the new kingdom of Naples. This had nothing to do with English constitutional arrangements but with the principles which had been applied to arouse the commercial instinct in human beings.[108] Genovesi, unlike many later Neapolitan thinkers such as Filangieri, was not particularly interested in the institutional arrangements of individual governments but grounded his theory, as we have seen, on eternal laws of nature that were identifiable by reason. What was important was the constancy of human nature at all times and places and of the natural order that regulated it.[109] This was realised not by constitutional reform but via a system of legally recognised rights.

---

104. *Ibid.*, ch. 22, paras xxii, xxxv–vii, pp. 461, 483–7.

105. *Ibid.*, Part 1, chs 3 and 4.

106. Hirschman, *The Passions and the Interests*, p. 80; E. De Mas, *Montesquieu, Genovesi*, pp. 157–61.

107. *Spirito delle leggi*, Book XXI, ch. 14, n. 2, I, p. 346. *Spirito delle leggi*, Book XX, ch. 2, n. 1, I, p. 266, *Lezione di commercio*, Part 1, ch. 19, para. vii, *II* V, p. 406.

108. As De Mas notes, Genovesi barely comments on Montesquieu's famous chapter on the English constitution, except to mention that it is about England (*Montesquieu, Genovesi*, p. 157, n. 46; *Spirito delle leggi*, Book XIX, ch. 27, II, n. 1, p. 250). He makes the reasons clear in his introduction to J. Carey's *An Essay on the State of England*, in which he emphasises not the political structure of England but the principles that have been used to arouse the commercial drive within man, *II* V, pp. 144–56.

109. *Diceosina*, Book I, ch. 3, para. xvi, p. 59.

Although Hume's defence of English commercial practice is at the heart of Genovesi's view of the modern economy, he takes issue with him on two key points that reflect both the special circumstance of Naples and salient differences in their social theory and which reveal the nature and limits of Genovesi's endorsement of commerce. First, he notes a certain inconsistency between Hume's analysis of money and luxury and his criticisms of banks and paper credit. In a chapter of the *Lezioni* devoted to the topic, he argues that an influx of money stimulates labour and industry by increasing demand and that Hume ignored these benefits, outlined in the essay 'Of money', when he came to attack Law's schemes in 'Of public credit'. After all:

Signor Hum himself calls money 'the oil of the commercial wagon'.[110] Therefore when he claims not to have ever understood the force of this word 'circulation', wishing to declaim against the abuses of paper money, he pretends to be ignorant of its true utility, in order to be able to become more severely heated [in his criticisms].[111]

Genovesi was free from his British contemporaries' concern with the undermining of values in an economy based on money and credit.[112] In part, this reflects the perspective of a poor country, which did not run the dangers of pricing itself out of the market,[113] but his faith in the continued industriousness of the workforce also derived from a different view of the springs of human action. Hume regarded morality and justice as a product of the progress of society. His reservations sprang from the fact that he had never completely overcome his scepticism about the long-term prospects for virtue under capitalism. Genovesi, in contrast, grounded moral identity in humankind's God-given rational capacities to follow and develop their nature according to certain eternal and immutable laws. For Genovesi, reason was not the mere slave of the passions, constrained by the conventions and requirements of society. Religious qualms apart, he was all too aware that social arrangements, such as those of his own country, often arise in a quite arbitrary fashion and can be thoroughly bad; he was therefore unwilling to accept such a theory. Rather, human reason mirrors divine reason in making society as well ordered as the natural world. For it to be otherwise could be to put in question the meaning and value of human existence.

Commercial activity is thus an extension of Genovesi's view of human activity in general. Seen in terms of Genovesi's social theory it becomes the expression of human virtue rather than in conflict with it. It derives from the free, rational

---

110. Hume's actual words are: 'it is the oil which renders the motion of the wheels more smooth and easy', *Essays*, p. 289.

111. *Lezione*, Part 2, ch. 7, para. xv, *II* V, pp. 96–7.

112. On this debate, *see* J. G. A. Pocock, *The Machiavellian Moment*, Princeton, 1975, chs 13 and 14.

113. *See* Istvan Hont, 'The "rich country–poor country" debate in Scottish classical political economy', in Hont and Ignatieff (eds), *Wealth and Virtue*, pp. 271–315.

exercise of humanity's innate faculties towards their end – the least possible pain.[114] This does not lead to a rapacious war of conflicting individual appetites but to a higher development of the equilibrium of passion, which exists at all times, reflecting the forces that regulate the motions of celestial bodies. The preservation of the laws of nature hence constitutes humanity's true duty and interest.[115] Although commercial civilised societies are not free from evil and pain, and luxury has a tendency to increase human greed, on balance, humans are immeasurably better off. They are freed from the bare struggle for existence and tied to their fellows by stronger mutual bonds.[116] Utility and interest are in this way redefined to coincide with virtue and justice:

> From all of the above, one easily understands that in nature these words, just, honest, virtue, useful, interest, can only be foolishly separated. If keeping intact our God given rights, our own and those of others, is justice, it is also honesty and true moral virtue. And if this is the law of equilibrium between the *concentriva* and *espansiva* forces; and this equilibrium alone can provide our present happiness; it alone is truly useful and our real interest. If injustice is but to offend the rights either of the ruler of the world or others; this same would be vice. And if this tends to divide our basic forces, to put them in conflict with each other and bring us pain and misery; vice cannot be the true utility [...] Who is wise or stupid enough that he would know or dare to arrest the course of the universe? We are subject to it, fools or wise men, whether we like it or not, in spite of our scorn.[117]

Genovesi was too religiously orthodox to accept the secular theory of utility based on a hedonistic individualism propounded by Celestino Galiani. Indeed, Galiani's *Della Scienza morale* was too out of tune with the dominant mores of the age for it even to be published. Genovesi sought to devise a theory of utility that was both more social in orientation and in tune with traditional religious ethics. The *metafisico* was thus never absent in his writings on commerce. His moral philosophy presupposed a total philosophy of the created order of nature, hinging on a metaphysics and natural theology of design, the Chain of Being, teleology, order, hierarchy and mind–body dualism. His achievement was to exploit the language of the theologian to express the new values of the merchant.

---

114. *Lezione di commercio*, Part 1, ch. 1, para. xv, *II* V, pp. 30–1. Genovesi's moral reservations and maintenance of a theocentric framework in his justification of modernity invites comparison with the similar project of Locke: *see* John Dunn, 'From applied theology to social analysis: the break between John Locke and the Scottish Enlightenment', in Hont and Ignatieff (eds), *Wealth and Virtue*, pp. 119–36.

115. *Ibid.*, para. xxxix, p. 51.

116. *Ibid.*, ch. 16, *passim*, esp. para. ii, n.a., pp. 343–4, ch. 19, para. v, n.h., pp. 404–5.

117. *Diceosina*, Book I, ch. 3, para. xviii, p. 60.

Chapter Three

Between Utility and Rights: Cesare Beccaria's *On Crimes and Punishments*

Beccaria's classic study *On Crimes and Punishments* belongs to the category of works that are much cited and little read. In Beccaria's case the reasons for this relative neglect are twofold. First, until recently even those who have attempted to read him, either in the original or in translation, have had to rely on a corrupt text.[1] Second, the context provided by Beccaria's other writings and those of his circle is rarely known, so that the background assumptions on which his argument rested have either appeared obscure or simply been misconstrued. As a result, Beccaria has come to be pigeon-holed as one of the founding fathers of a putative tradition of classic penal reformers and the distinctiveness of his contribution has been recognised only rarely. However, his argument was more complex than most previous commentators have appreciated, anticipating in an original way some of the solutions and difficulties of contemporary philosophers of punishment.

Punishment forms part of a wider system of social organisation and is sustained by a broad range of social practices, attitudes and institutions. Beccaria's argument for penal reform reflected a whole new discourse about the nature of society and the need for social change more generally; it has to be read as part of this larger movement. Therefore, some knowledge of the intellectual, social and political circumstances that prompted and shaped Beccaria's famous work forms a necessary preliminary to any analysis of the text.

Beccaria wrote his treatise whilst a member of a short-lived group of intellectuals known as the 'Accademia dei pugni', or the Academy of Fisticuffs. This society, which lasted from 1762 to 1766, consisted of a small number of young men who regularly met to discuss and study together. Self-consciously modelled on the circle of French *philosophes* gathered around the *Encyclopedie*, they were a far less formal association than the numerous other literary societies and academies that abounded in Italy at this time. The name was adopted by Pietro Verri, their prime mover, when he learned that their discussions had the reputation of becoming so heated that they ended up in a fight. Between 1764 and 1766, members of the 'academy' also published the periodical *Il Caffe* as a means of disseminating their ideas.

Although their interests were wide-ranging, their activity was essentially centred on winning over the Austrian rulers of Lombardy to a broad programme of reform and to bringing attention to themselves as potential agents of these changes within the imperial administration. The Habsburgs had held Lombardy since 1707

---

1. I give an account of the fascinating history of Beccaria's text and its subsequent French and English translations in 'A note on the texts', in Richard Bellamy (ed.), C. Beccaria, *On Crimes and Punishments and Other Writings*, Cambridge, 1995, pp. xli–xliv.

but did not begin the process of reform until the end of the War of the Austrian Succession in 1748. The initial impetus in Lombardy, as elsewhere, was the need to improve the administration of finances and the economy in order to reduce the massive deficit created by the war. As Beccaria indicated in his inaugural lecture as Professor of Cameral Sciences, the most significant element of the reform programme was the completion of a new land register, the *catasto*. Begun in the 1740s, it was completed by the Florentine official Pompeo Neri in 1757. Outlining his aims in an important report in 1750, which set the agenda for all later reforms, Neri had proposed the abolition of all taxes, except for those on land, and the removal of all the exemptions allowed to nobles and the Church. The new register also offered an opportunity for redrawing the provincial and district boundaries, a review of the methods employed for the collection of taxes and a reappraisal of customs tariffs.

These measures brought the Habsburg regime into conflict with the Lombard establishment, for they threatened the independence and privileges of Church, patriciate and aristocracy. These groups resisted the reforms through numerous legal battles and appeals to precedent. Initially these countermeasures had some success. However, the further deterioration of state finances due to the Seven Years War of 1756–63 gave a fresh stimulus to the reorganisation of the province and its integration into the political structure of the Empire. In 1759 a new impetus was given to the reform movement by the appointment of Count Carlo di Firmian as Minister Plenipotentiary, whom Beccaria came to regard as his protector. Supported by the Austrian Minister of Foreign Affairs, Count Kaunitz, the next decade witnessed a concerted attack on ecclesiastical powers and immunities and the undermining of the position of local notables.

Beccaria's and his colleagues' writings belong to this second phase. Members of the ruling aristocracy, they nevertheless rejected the juridical mentality of their parents. Pietro Verri's clash with his father was particularly emblematic of this generational conflict. Gabrielle Verri had played an important part in the counter-attack of the Milanese establishment against the incursions of the Austrian government, defending in a series of works the local legal and administrative traditions of the Lombard region. Pietro, however, bitterly criticised the antiquarian and jurisprudential culture that then dominated in Milan and placed all state affairs in the hands of lawyers and scholars. Unlike his brother Alessandro, and Beccaria, he never took a legal degree. Instead, he escaped to fight in the Seven Years War. When he returned to Milan in 1761, after an unsuccessful attempt to seek employment in Vienna, it was as a champion of the very reforms his father was attempting to block.

When Verri renewed his acquaintance with Beccaria in 1761 he found a willing disciple. Born in 1738, the eldest son of a reasonably wealthy noble family, Beccaria had become similarly estranged from his parents, due to their attempts to prevent his marriage to Teresa Blasco, whom they considered socially inferior. As he confessed in his letter to André Morellet, his 'philosophical conversion' to the writings of the French Enlightenment dated from this period.[2] Rousseau's recently

---

2.   Letter to André Morellet, in Beccaria *On Crimes*, p. 122.

published *La Nouvelle Héloise*, in particular, offered a new discourse of moral sensibility that echoed his own romantic temperament and concerns. His first child, born in 1762, was symbolically named Giulia, after Julie – the heroine of the novel. Encouraged by Verri, in whose house he and his wife found temporary refuge, Beccaria's conflict with his family developed into a thoroughgoing critique of the values and social system that underlay their opposition to his marriage. The passages in *On Crimes* dealing with parental tyranny are only the most obvious indicators of the links Beccaria made between the organisation of the family and that of society as a whole. Like Verri, his aim became the substitution for the existing irregular, particularist and custom-bound legal system, based on hereditary rights and the personal rule of the monarch and nobility, of a regular, centralised and rational system of justice that was equal for all and grounded in the rule of law.

Against the traditionalist thinking of the lawyers and the Church, Verri, Beccaria and their circle placed the developing languages of political economy and of a secular morality that sought to harness and cultivate, rather than to repress, the passions. Verri's writings on these subjects provide the necessary starting point for any consideration of Beccaria's thought. For Beccaria's ideas largely developed through daily discussion of his friend's views. Indeed, Verri played a major role in initiating and eventually editing Beccaria's most important work.

Whilst in Vienna, Verri had drafted his *Elements of Commerce* (1769), which he later published in *Il Caffè*. This treatise reflected the neo-mercantilism of writers such as Jean-François Melon and François Véron Duverger de Forbonnais, who tempered their advocacy of *laissez-faire* with a continuing role for the state, particularly in fostering domestic manufacturing industry, and a general concern to discourage foreign imports in order to secure a favourable national trade balance. Although he later modified the protectionist aspects of his views, ultimately favouring the abandonment of all restrictive practices such as guilds or the granting of monopolies, for example, Verri remained largely indifferent to physiocratic ideas. He argued that stimulating the manufacturing and the export market would bring about an increase in agricultural production and a rise in population of their own accord. More in tune with the advanced economic theories of the time were his ideas on luxury and equality. Here Verri followed David Hume in believing that luxury provided a necessary incentive for work and industrial innovation, both creating wealth and destroying privilege in the process, by forcing landowners to dissipate their wealth in conspicuous consumption, and with it their economic power. To foster further the breakdown of feudal ties, he advocated the abolition of *fidecommessi*, entails and other special rights of nobility that restricted the exchange of property and the free movement of labour. He contended that the commercial system not only required a more formally egalitarian society, in which there were no social barriers to freedom of contract and to trade, but also led to the resulting prosperity being more equally distributed. In addition, Verri shared Hume's conception of money as a universal commodity that oiled the wheels of commerce by providing a uniform medium of exchange, and had corresponding worries about the dangers of paper credit and inflation. Beccaria's lectures of 1769–70, posthumously published as *Elements of Public Economy*, developed substantially similar arguments.

Verri's programme fitted with the interventionist tendencies of the Habsburg regime and their central concern with increasing state revenue. Even the egalitarian aspect of Verri's thought found an echo in the Austrians' desire to dismantle those privileges of the *ancien régime* that stood in the way of the process of centralisation and reform. The earliest publications of the group gathered around Verri were concerned with championing particular economic and fiscal policies associated with his theories. Verri began his campaign with an essay on the salt tax (1761) and from 1762–3 was engaged in composing his extensive *Considerations on the Commerce of the State of Milan*, in which he provided a comprehensive analysis of the decline of Lombard trade and the need to revive it through legal reform, internal free trade and the abolition of the tax farm. Beccaria's first publication was a pamphlet *On the Monetary Disorders and their Remedies in the State of Milan in 1762*, in which he employed his skills as a mathematician to advocate a stable rate of exchange, in preference to Milan adopting its own currency, as the best means of facilitating trade. Running through all these proposals was a desire to reduce the laws regulating trade to a more systematic order that reflected the rational economic calculations of individuals rather than a complex pattern of entrenched traditions, privileges and special interests. Both Verri and Beccaria were able to fashion powerful criticisms of the existing system with these new analytical tools. For instance, Beccaria's brief essay on smuggling of 1764 offered a classic early application of the mathematical formulation of rational choice theory in order to quantify how high tariffs could be before contraband proved worthwhile. Although many of their specific suggestions were ignored, the activity of these reformers brought them to sufficient prominence for the Austrian government ultimately to place many of them in important positions within the Lombard administration. Both Verri (in 1765) and Beccaria (from 1771) ended up on the Supreme Council of the Economy, a body that had been created partly in response to their ideas.

Underlying these economic proposals, with their attack on feudal attitudes and practices, was a new account of human motivation and morals. The link between economics, ethics and psychology was provided by the concept of happiness – the subject of Verri's *Meditations on Happiness* of 1763; this was published shortly before Beccaria's treatise on punishment and, at the time, was occasionally attributed to him. Giuseppe Ricuperati has called this book, rather than Beccaria's more famous work, the true 'manifesto of the Accademia dei pugni'. Enunciating a conception of legitimacy that was to be fundamental to Beccaria's argument, Verri declared that

> The end of the social pact is the well-being of each of the individuals who join together to form society, who do so in order that this well-being becomes absorbed into the public happiness or rather the greatest possible happiness distributed with the greatest equality possible.

In accordance with the lessons of the new political economy, the maximisation of public wealth and happiness required the equal protection of individuals. Behind his qualified utilitarian goal lay a hedonistic psychology and associationist epistemology principally derived, albeit with important modifications, from Locke, Helvétius and Condillac. Verri shared the contemporary view that the passions were the springs of human action. However, he continued to accord reason a decisive role in the refinement and direction of our passional urges. Moreover, he treated the flight from pain rather than the pursuit of pleasure *per se* as the decisive factor. Happiness, therefore, consisted of more than the passing enjoyment of mere pleasurable sensations. Rather, it was achieved via the rational pursuit of our interests through the removal of obstacles to well-being, such as poverty. In this way, the spread of ideas or enlightenment and the programme of economic and social reform came together, with the one producing the other and promoting in the process the progressive civilisation of society, by providing for the greater satisfaction and refinement of human needs.

Similar assumptions underlay Beccaria's writings. His study of crimes and punishments has often been treated as narrowly focused on the issue of penal reform. Even Verri, who grew jealous at the fame the work brought his 25-year-old protégé, was apt to dismiss it as a limited exercise that he had set his young companion in applying the reformer's ideas to a specific problem. The book was much more ambitious, however. Beccaria sought to establish a legal framework that reflected the general programme of the reformers to replace the existing system of semi-feudal privileges, customs and honours with a new conception of social organisation, based on a regular system of justice involving equal laws for all. This project was intimately connected to the Academy's understanding of human nature and their views on political economy, which furnished him with the principles that guided his work. His purpose was to make punishment the chief instrument of reform by leading human beings, via their reason and passions, to the progressive promotion of the public happiness. As we shall see, however, Beccaria conceived this proposal in essentially liberal terms, as requiring the state to allow individuals to pursue their own happiness in their own way so long as they did not harm others in the process.

As Beccaria made clear in his prefatory note 'To the reader', appended to the fifth edition in reply to his critics, his aim was to provide an entirely secular account of the origins and function of law. He studiously avoided appeals to either revelation or natural law, making a clear distinction between God's justice, which was best left to Him, and terrestrial justice. The foundation of Beccaria's theory was human nature and, in particular, 'ineradicable human sentiments'.[3] Beccaria shared Verri's positive evaluation of the function of pain. Whilst he believed 'pleasure and pain are the motive forces of all sentient beings', he thought 'every act of our will is always proportional to the strength of the sensory impression that

---

3.   Beccaria, *On Crimes*, p. 10.

gives rise to it'.[4] As he later specified, this meant that 'the proximate and efficient cause of actions is the flight from pain, their final cause is the love of pleasure', since 'man rests in good times and acts when in pain'.[5] Indeed, in his *Elements of Public Economy* (1769) he maintained that even the prospect of pleasure or of greater utility acted upon us only indirectly, via the pain resulting from the anxiety associated with the possibility of its not being achieved.[6] In this way, Beccaria was able to avoid one of the classic dilemmas confronting a social ethic based on a hedonistic psychology – namely, the worry that people will prefer either a very low level of contentment or base pleasures to the struggle to achieve quantitatively and qualitatively higher levels of fulfilment. On his view, we can never be fully satisfied. We are continuously driven on by the fear of being deprived of our present pleasures, combined with a constant dissatisfaction with those pleasures created by the possibility of there being even greater pleasures to be attained. The resulting continual expansion of human needs was at the heart of his account of the progress of society, explaining the development of commerce through the multiplication of luxury goods as well as the role of law.

Beccaria followed the empiricist argument of Locke and Helvétius in attributing all human knowledge, including morality, to the operation of impressions upon our senses. However, he did not interpret this process in a totally mechanistic or deterministic manner. In common with Verri, he retained an element of the rationalist view in attributing a distinct function to human reason in the ordering and synthesising of our sense impressions. Moreover, far from reason being the slave of the passions, as in Hume, both the Italians believed that the distinctiveness of human beings lay in their capacity to control and channel them rationally. Civilisation resulted from the cultivation of this capacity. The spread of ideas or enlightenment became in this way directly related to the promotion of reform.[7]

This modified empiricist epistemology provided the basis for Beccaria's attempt to place the law on what he regarded as a more rational footing. In general terms, law had to be clear and punishment speedy, certain and an economical deterrent, so as to ensure an indisputable association of ideas between pain and crime. A rational legal system required that laws be as precise as possible, with judicial discretion reduced to a minimum, so that all citizens knew where they stood and could reason accordingly.

This approach, though present to some degree in Helvétius, was to become very influential, especially through the work of Jeremy Bentham, who found Beccaria's work extremely suggestive. Bentham credited him with being 'the father of *Censorial jurisprudence*' – the first thinker to attempt a critical or 'censorial', as opposed to a merely expository, account of the law, which sought to demystify and correct the prejudices and confused reasoning that guided most contemporary

---

4.   *Ibid.*, pp. 21, 41.

5.   *Ibid.*, p. 157.

6.   *Ibid.*, p. 163.

7.   *Ibid.*, ch. 42.

legal decision-making. Indeed, Beccaria provided Bentham with one of his most important tools of criticism. For Beccaria not only followed Locke in seeking to analyse complex ideas into their simple, experience-related parts. As H. L. A. Hart has observed,[8] he also anticipated Bentham's elaboration of this technique in order to deconstruct the supposed logical fictions that in their eyes constituted the bulk of our traditional legal and moral concepts. Both thinkers appreciated that terms such as 'right', 'duty' and 'obligation' could not be defined readily in terms of concrete material objects and their effects upon us. As Beccaria put it, such words were 'abbreviated symbols of a rational argument and not of an idea'.[9] It was necessary, therefore, to look not for definitions of these words alone but of the complete sentence or argument within which they were employed. Only then would it be possible to translate such statements into others in which the words to be explained did not appear and were replaced instead by things which could be directly experienced and analysed in terms of pleasure and pain – a procedure Bentham called *paraphrasis*. For both thinkers, notions of obligation and of duties, which lay behind doctrines of rights, were all abbreviations for the argument that we will suffer a sanction unless we behave in a particular way. As a result, our basic legal and political vocabulary boiled down to the possibility of punishment, or the infliction of pain, if we do not act in a stipulated manner. The establishment of the right to punish, therefore, provided the key to our understanding of the whole legal and political system and, consequently, was the starting point for Beccaria's theory.

Beccaria agreed with Hobbes that the asocial state was one of war, and that fear and the desire for security provided the motivation for uniting to form society. Characteristically, it was the prospect of pain rather than of pleasure that moved us to act. However, he was far from believing that we sacrificed all our liberty to the Leviathan in return for the protection it offered us. On the contrary, he contended that we give up only the smallest portion of our liberty, that is, that portion necessary for us to enjoy the remaining part in peace and tranquillity.[10] As a result, law was justified only to the extent that it was limited to what was required to preserve the maximal amount of individual liberty possible.

Beccaria employed the idea of a social contract more as a theoretical device for setting limits to the legitimacy of law than as an actual historical act to explain its origins. However, in the same chapter he made reference to a classic utilitarian justification for law. If there were a sufficiently large secondary literature on Beccaria to contain interpretative disputes, this combination of contractarian and utilitarian arguments would no doubt have given rise to 'the Beccaria problem'. For it is generally argued that the utilitarian argument either negates the contractarian or renders it unnecessary and *vice versa*. On the one hand, utilitarians have tended

---

8. H. L. A. Hart, 'Bentham and Beccaria', in *Essays on Bentham*, Oxford, Oxford University Press, 1982, ch. 2.

9. Beccaria, *On Crimes*, p. 12.

10. *Ibid.*, p. 11.

to regard the notion of a social contract as either redundant or a pernicious fiction. If the purpose of government is to secure optimal welfare then our obligation to obey any law lasts so long as it performs this function better than any alternative and no longer. Contractarian notions of consent and related considerations of natural rights seem beside the point and merely serve to help individuals withdraw from supporting the general good. On the other hand, social-contract theorists have suggested that utilitarianism fails to show a sufficient degree of equality of concern and respect for the differences between individuals. They accuse utilitarians of potentially sacrificing the individual to the greater good of society as a whole. From their perspective, the contract argument appears as a way of ensuring that individuals are not used as a means for some collective purpose.

The seeming confusion arising from Beccaria's mixture of these apparently conflicting arguments draws additional plausibility from the fact that the first English translation of Beccaria's book wrongly credited its author with making 'the greatest happiness of the greatest number' the benchmark of all laws and other human arrangements. In the hands of Bentham, this principle became the sole foundation of morals and legislation and was employed by him in a merciless attack on all contractarian and rights-based arguments. However, although Bentham owed the wording of his formula – if not the ideas behind it – to this source, and in spite of the fact that all subsequent English translators have continued to attribute it to Beccaria, the Italian never employed the phrase. His exact words were 'the greatest [*massima*] happiness shared among the greater [*maggior*] number'.[11]

Unfortunately, even this formulation offers a poor guide to Beccaria's meaning. The notion of division might suggest that he had in mind average as opposed to aggregate utility, whilst the use of the comparative (*maggior*) instead of the superlative (*massima*) potentially indicates that he might have meant 'the greatest happiness of the majority' rather than of the 'largest number'. However, Beccaria's discussion of the utilitarian injunction elsewhere reveals that such inferences would be wrong and that his own wording here is also misleading and imprecise. In these other passages, it becomes clear that his meaning is much closer to that expressed by Verri in his *Meditazioni*, cited above, who, together with Hutcheson, Helvétius and (less directly) Bacon and Rousseau, inspired his thesis. From these sources, it emerges that Beccaria was concerned to maximise equally the happiness of each person – a goal he shared not just with Verri but with other members of the *Caffe* group. Thus, in the *Fragment on Smells* (1764) he defines the public good as 'the greatest sum of pleasures, divided equally amongst the greatest number of people', whilst in his *Reflections on the Barbarousness and Civilisation of Nations and on the Savage State of Man* he went so far as to describe 'barbarity' as a disequilibrium between knowledge and opinion, on the one hand, and 'each individual's needs and greatest expectations of happiness', on the other. More importantly, in his *Elements of Public Economy* he defined the sovereign as the 'just and equitable distributor of public happiness' and this latter

---

11. *Ibid.*, p. 7.

as 'the happiness of all those individuals that are subject to him'. Consequently, he included amongst his list of 'false ideas of utility', enumerated in ch. 40 of *On Crimes*, any attempt 'to give a multitude of sensible beings the symmetry and order of brute inanimate matter' or doctrines that 'separate the public good from the good of each individual'.[12]

There can be no doubt, then, that Beccaria took both the contractarian and the utilitarian aspects of his doctrine seriously and sought to combine them. Was this synthesis confused, as Bentham's remarks about Beccaria's 'false sources' and 'obscure notions' lead one to believe he thought? Or can a coherent thread be found that links the two into a form of contractarian utilitarianism, in which the good of the individual cannot be sacrificed to the common good? The general drift of Beccaria's theory suggests that he attempted the latter, anticipating in the process a number of arguments more usually associated with Bentham's most famous disciple and critic, J. S. Mill.

Like Mill, Beccaria contended that human welfare was tied up with the protection of certain basic interests, most particularly security of the person and possessions. The moral justification for protecting these interests, however, did not depend upon notions of natural right. Their basis lay in considerations of utility, as being essential to human life and the pursuit of happiness. Moreover, when individual interests came into conflict, utility again became the benchmark for resolving these clashes. Indeed, such reasoning underpinned Beccaria's understanding of the moral foundations of the state. Beccaria contended that our interests could not be guaranteed without the legal sanctions and regulatory mechanisms provided by government. However, as we saw, he believed that the agreement to obey the law involved a trade-off, whereby individuals sacrificed a part of their liberty to preserve the greatest possible liberty over all. Both the purpose and limits of government, therefore, were set by what Beccaria regarded as the utilitarian goal of securing the greatest possible happiness of each and every citizen. For to achieve this utilitarian goal we had to submit to a number of general rules which applied equally to all and which were upheld by some authoritative power. In this way, the idea of the social contract became both a means for expressing the central utilitarian concern that in minimising pain and maximising pleasure we show equal respect for the interests of each individual and a device for justifying our obligation to uphold this maxim. On this view, the only laws we could and should agree to were those concerned with the furtherance of human well-being, the most vital of which prohibited harm to our vital interests. As a consequence, the only rights that either states or citizens might validly claim flowed from their mutual obligation to preserve those human interests necessary to the reduction of pain and the promotion of happiness.

Beccaria's mixture of contractarianism and utilitarianism served to modify the latter in two main respects. First, the contract established that the purpose of government was to govern according to rules that promoted the public happiness

---

12. *Ibid.*, pp. 101–2.

by giving the greatest possible protection to the vital interests of each and every citizen, rather than by pursuing the greatest possible aggregate utility. Although it is not clear that Beccaria appreciated that his attempt to equalise happiness might conflict with his desire to maximise happiness, forced to choose between the two he invariably opted for the former rather than the latter. Second, by making the rules subject to a contract, Beccaria effectively blocked the collapse of rule-into act-utilitarianism, which would have allowed the government to weigh each case on its particular merits. Both these moves served to prevent the utilitarian reasoning which he employed as an effective tool of social criticism and reform being used to sacrifice the individual to the common good. These considerations were of the utmost importance for Beccaria's theory of punishment. They enabled him to escape some of the problems associated with purely utilitarian theories of economical deterrence and to adopt a compromise theory, not dissimilar to that proposed by contemporary philosophers such as John Rawls and H. L. A. Hart,[13] which found room for the concerns of retributivists as well.

Very briefly, the respective merits and demerits of the retributive and utilitarian views of punishment have been traditionally described as follows. For the utilitarian, punishment is forward-looking. Its basic purpose is the reduction of crimes, and hence pain, in the future. From this perspective, past wrongs cannot be undone, merely prevented from reoccurring by making illegal actions less attractive than legal ones. For the retributivist, in contrast, punishment is backward-looking. It follows from guilt and aims to ensure that wrongdoers suffer in proportion to their wrongdoing. Retributivists have made two general and related criticisms of the utilitarian view, both of which strike at the heart of Beccaria's theory. First, they claim that utilitarianism might lead to the imposition of excessive punishments for relatively minor offences. For the gain to society resulting from deterring multiple minor infractions of the law by administering a severe exemplary punishment, such as hanging someone for double-parking, might outweigh the pain caused to the unfortunate individuals selected to be made an example of. Second, they have argued that utilitarianism could even justify punishing an innocent person for a crime they did not commit: for example, if the real criminal could not be apprehended and a conviction was necessary to prevent people losing faith in the effectiveness of the forces of law and order and a consequent lessening of the deterrent effect of punishment. Indeed, they contend that utilitarianism creates no necessary connection between guilt and punishment at all, other than the rather tenuous link established by the likely undermining of the whole deterrent argument if people come to believe that individuals are simply punished arbitrarily. Utilitarians, in their turn, argue that the retributivist view is circular and vague, amounting to little more than the assertion that someone deserves to be punished because they deserve it. Such theories may be good at specifying who should be

---

13. J. Rawls, 'Two concepts of rules', *Philosophical Review* 54, 1955, pp. 4–13 and H. L. A. Hart, *Punishment and Responsibility: Essays in the philosophy of law*, Oxford, Oxford University Press 1968, ch. 1.

punished, namely the transgressor, but are less compelling at explaining why or how. The classic retributivist argument of the *lex talionis* ('an eye for an eye, a tooth for a tooth'), for example, proves rather imprecise when it comes to concrete cases. It is unclear, for instance, what form of punishment it decrees for a toothless person who has knocked out someone else's teeth.

Beccaria was well aware of the pros and cons of each of these theories of punishment and, in framing his own theory, aimed to draw on the former whilst avoiding the latter. His basic justification for why we should punish was utilitarian. One of the central points of his essay was that the existing system of criminal justice, which was essentially retributive in character, was far too arbitrary and often pointless. Essentially orientated around the *lex talionis*, its basic rationale was that crimes against the body politic should be punished by heaping suffering upon the body of the criminal. Beccaria ridiculed such notions as both useless and unjust. 'Can the wailings of a wretch', he asked, 'undo what has been done and turn back the clock?' Against such views, he asserted that there could be no other purpose for punishment than

> to prevent the offender from doing fresh harm to his fellows and to deter others from doing likewise. Therefore, punishments and the means adopted for inflicting them should, consistent with proportionality, be so selected as to make the most efficacious and lasting impression on the minds of men with the least possible torment to the body of the condemned.[14]

As we have seen, however, it is precisely at this point, when considerations of whom and how one should punish enter the discussion, that the utilitarian begins to get into difficulties. Beccaria clearly wanted to avoid these problems, since his two other main concerns in the book were that the present system frequently convicted the wrong person and that it exacted unduly harsh penalties. His solution was to introduce some of the retributivist arguments into his theory in ways that paralleled his contractarian view of utilitarianism. His argument was essentially that whilst the basic purpose and rationale of punishment was utilitarian, its application had to be limited by retributivist considerations of guilt. For the contractarian justification that Beccaria gave for the adoption of the utilitarian rules provided by the state made them subject to the limitation that they afforded each of us equal mutual protection of our basic interests, except in those circumstances where we intentionally broke the agreement.

As a result of this dual perspective on punishment, Beccaria made a similar distinction to that proposed by Rawls and Hart between the functions of the legislator and those of the judiciary.[15] The first should adopt utilitarian criteria for the framing of laws and punishments, the second employ retributive criteria when applying these rules to particular cases. Moreover, as Foucault has noted, the contractarian argument also enabled Beccaria to distinguish between the

---

14. Beccaria, *On Crimes*, p. 31.

15. *Ibid.*, pp. 12, 14–15.

public and the private spheres, restricting state action to the former. The legal rules merely operated as an external framework to regulate our social interaction, leaving us as much as possible to pursue our own affairs as we pleased. Punishment referred solely to the restitution of the legal order and to the legal personality of the criminal. Unlike later penal reformers, he did not aim at the rehabilitation of the criminal's moral personality as such.[16]

The power of the sovereign to punish offenders, therefore, only became a right to the extent that it was exercised in a manner 'most useful to the greatest number', whilst punishments were only just in so far as they did not go beyond what was necessary 'to unite together particular interests' and prevent society degenerating into a harmful state of warlike anarchy.[17] However, what utility entailed was not left to the sovereign's discretion but was determined by those laws that could have been agreed to, under a social contract between free and equal individuals, as providing for the greatest possible reduction of harm divided amongst the greatest possible number. Two important consequences followed from these criteria. First, punishment only became justified to the extent that the crime harmed society, that the punishment was proportionate to that harm and that the individual to be punished had violated the terms of the contract from which everyone benefited. Second, and far more radically, he contended that if the benefits of the legal system failed to be equitably distributed, so that the law promoted the happiness of some rather more than others, then it would not only justify but positively promote crime. In so arguing, Beccaria not only had the privileges and immunities of the Church and nobility in mind but also the maldistribution of property which gave rise to them. In such circumstances, he argued, it was entirely understandable that the poor should seek to 'break those bonds which are so deadly for the majority and useful only to a handful of indolent tyrants' by returning to a 'natural state of independence' in which, as members of a robber band, they could, for a time at least, 'live free and happy by the fruits of courage and industry'.[18] As Franco Venturi has observed, Beccaria moved at this point beyond reform and towards the discourse of utopia. It is little wonder that the term socialism was first coined in Italian by Ferdinando Facchinei, who intended it as a term of abuse, in his critique of Beccaria of 1765.

The best way to illustrate Beccaria's compromise theory is by examining two of his most famous arguments – his case against torture[19] and, for contemporaries the most original of all, his rejection of the death penalty.[20] Beccaria considered two different uses of torture. First, he examined the practice of judicial torture to get the criminal to confess to his or her crime. Beccaria objected that this procedure was both unjust and inefficient. It was unjust for largely contractarian

---

16. *Ibid.*, pp. 22–3, 74.

17. *Ibid.*, p. 11.

18. *Ibid.*, p. 69.

19. *Ibid.*, ch. 16.

20. *Ibid.*, ch. 28.

reasons. Torture involved punishing someone before they had been proven guilty. However, Beccaria argued, society had a duty to protect the individual until it had been 'decided that he had violated the pacts according to which this protection was provided'.[21] In other words, we had only submitted to abiding by the laws of the state to the extent that they offered us protection and any attempt to go beyond this remit was illegitimate. He condemned torture as inefficient, though, on largely utilitarian grounds. For a start, he saw no purpose in forcing someone to confess to crimes that could not be proven in some other way, since such offences would presumably be otherwise unknown and hence offered no bad example to others from which they had to be deterred. Even more importantly, though, torture undermined the deterrent effect of punishment. The weak, he claimed, would reason that they could be made to confess to any crime under torture and, on the principle that one might as well be hanged for a sheep as for a lamb, would have no incentive not to commit crimes. The strong, in contrast, would reason that they could withstand the pain and hence could break the law with impunity.

Both the internal evolution of judicial procedure and the impact of the empirical methods of the natural sciences on rules of evidence, a theme Beccaria developed elsewhere in his treatise, had made these latter arguments against torture relatively commonplace. More novel was his case against the second use of torture, as a means of punishment for exonerating guilt. Here, he employed the utilitarian reasoning that provided his basic justification for punishment to condemn the retributive use of torture as a means of removing the taint of infamy as pointless and so illegitimate. However, this argument had its dangers since utilitarian theorists of deterrence could be accused, as we saw, of a potential willingness to employ overly severe punishments to achieve their goal, in which case cruel and unusual punishments might be thought occasionally appropriate. Once again, therefore, Beccaria had to adopt a mixture of contractarian and utilitarian reasoning.

In fact, utilitarians can avoid the most simplistic versions of this charge by stressing that their goal is economic deterrence. In other words, they seek to use the least pain possible so as to maximise happiness over all. In general, this criterion entails that punishment is proportionate to the gravity, or harmfulness, of the offence. Beccaria certainly took this view, arguing that crimes ought to be categorised by the harm they inflicted on society and punished accordingly. He insisted that punishments should never be more painful than was necessary to prevent a given crime or outweigh in suffering the harm done to society by the misdemeanour they aimed to prevent. He also believed it important to ensure that criminals had an incentive to commit a lesser rather than a greater crime. Torture, he maintained, was too inflexible and rarely, if ever, possessed these necessary features. In spite of all the ingenuity that had gone into the devising of tortures, their adaptability was limited by the human frame, which could only stand so much. His condemnation of torture for being simply too crude drew additional support from his belief that the duration of a punishment had a greater effect on other people

---

21. *Ibid.*, p. 39.

than its intensity. Hard labour lasted over many years, for example, whilst it was difficult to prolong torture for more than a few hours or days without losing your victim. As a result, he doubted that tortures could ever be sufficiently refined so as to provide the carefully graded scale of punishments his deterrence argument required if a punishment was to be legitimate. Moreover, he also maintained that torture was essentially brutal and brutalising and as such was likely to increase violent crimes by desensitising people to cruelty.

Nevertheless, such thinking does not rule out torture on principle. Some of his arguments are empirically debatable. Torture, for example, might be prolonged and refined by administering it at weekly intervals rather than at one go. Nor does his case exclude the possibility that the cumulative effect of some minor but common crime could justify on utilitarian grounds a harsher penalty in order to stamp it out than a rare but grave offence. It does not even ensure that some barbarous penalty inflicted on an innocent person might not be allowable in certain rare instances, although we have already noted Beccaria's separate argument against this possibility. To prevent such exemplary punishments ever being justified, however unlikely they might be, Beccaria had to turn once again to the contractarian argument underlying his utilitarianism, whereby the utilitarian strategy was adopted as a means for giving equal weight and protection to the interests of every individual. According to this line of argument, although it might in some highly hypothetical case make sense to convict and torture a relatively innocuous person, it could never make good utilitarian sense to institute such a practice by giving the state the right to do so. In the language of modern utilitarianism, the contract bound the state to follow certain utilitarian rules rather than to weigh up all actions on the basis of utilitarian criteria. To allow any institution to do the latter involves handing over a wide degree of arbitrary power, the utility of which is highly doubtful.

This move becomes clearer in Beccaria's discussion of the death penalty. Beccaria believed that the most novel feature of his argument was the utilitarian claim that the death penalty could never have been established because to give the state the right to kill its members on a regular basis, even subject to numerous limiting conditions, could never be deemed useful or necessary for the protection of their interests. As with his argument against torture, the main part of this reasoning related to his belief that the death penalty was essentially wasteful and a doubtful deterrent. He argued that killing the criminal took a potentially useful member of society, who could have repaid his or her debt to society, out of circulation. Moreover, he believed that public executions rarely had a lasting impact on the population. With the exception of murder, the association between the sentence and the crime committed was hard to establish in people's minds and was soon over and as soon forgotten. Paradoxically, therefore, one needed a constant succession of capital crimes if the death penalty was to retain its effectiveness. Finally, capital punishment did not allow of any degree of proportionality, so that a criminal risking death had no incentive to moderate his or her behaviour in any way in the hope of a lesser sentence. In these cases, the death penalty offered an incitement to crime. Indeed, he believed that executions in general inured people to violence and in some cases even had the effect of glorifying the criminal by turning him or her into a martyr, thereby encouraging rather than deterring crime.

Although this reasoning clearly inspired later utilitarian arguments against the death penalty, such as Bentham's, it rests once again on speculative and possibly mistaken empirical assertions. A convict, for example, would have to break a lot of rocks and sew a good many mail-bags before he began to earn his keep, let alone render a return. As Beccaria's earliest critic – Ferdinando Facchinei – pointed out, it also would be difficult to make much of a deterrent out of hard labour, given the harshness of the average peasant's everyday existence. Of course, Beccaria's argument that the death penalty was an uneconomical deterrent had far greater plausibility in the case of the numerous petty offences for which it was still administered at the time, although we have already noted that, even here, difficulties might arise. However, whilst many of his contemporaries granted this much, even admirers, such as Denis Diderot, felt that capital punishment remained justifiable for murder. Beccaria's clinching argument, therefore, had to lie elsewhere. Namely, that it was the right to punish with death, rather than this or that particular use of it, which failed the test of utility, by giving the state a power which appeared contrary to the very purpose of the state and seemed to set it at war with its members, bringing it into disrepute in the process. He contended that to have granted such a power would have been contrary to the utilitarian calculation that provided the basis for the legitimacy of the state. 'For how', he wrote, 'could it come about that the minimum sacrifice of liberty made by everyone included the greatest good of all, life?'[22] Indeed, if, as Christians then claimed, suicide was wrong, the gift of life being a matter of God's will rather than our own, no one could be said to have a right to kill him or herself which could be surrendered to others in the first place. The only exception Beccaria entertained was that of an individual such as a revolutionary leader, whose exile or imprisonment might still constitute a threat to the very existence of the state. However, with the exception of this limiting case, he contended that the state's duty to protect our vital interests could never entail that it put itself at war with us.

Hegel regarded Beccaria's argument as revealing the ultimate absurdity of the contractarian conception of political obligation. In his view, the state was characterised by precisely this right to call on its citizens to lay down their lives. Other commentators, however, have been less convinced that a prohibition on capital punishment follows so inexorably from the contractarian position. For example, although Beccaria is often interpreted as having radicalised the Hobbesian account of the social contract, Hobbes himself did not deny the state the right to apply the death penalty in appropriate cases. On the contrary, he believed it was entirely rational that contractors would grant such a right in order to protect themselves from law-breaking by others. He merely contended that the condemned had no duty to obey in such circumstances. Similarly, Kant pointed out, in an important criticism of Beccaria's argument, that when the contractors cede to the

---

22. *Ibid.*, p. 66.

state a right to punish certain crimes by death, they cannot be regarded as literally willing their own capital punishment. Rather, they are seeking to create a system of law appropriate to a society which they know will probably contain murderers and other heinous criminals within it. The criminal does not will his or her own punishment, he or she merely opts to commit a punishable deed. From both the Hobbesian and the Kantian perspective, therefore, it is perfectly possible for the contractors to decide that the death penalty might be justified, either because of utilitarian considerations as to its general deterrent effect, as in the case of Hobbes, or for retributive reasons concerning its basic justice, such as Kant put forward. At most, Beccaria has simply provided grounds for believing that the utilitarian reasoning of Hobbes's contractors might be flawed. He could only have argued for the absolute injustice of the death penalty had he been prepared to employ some form of natural rights theory which treated all killing as intrinsically wrong.

Beccaria's later writings, most of which arose from his teaching and administrative duties and were not published during his lifetime, developed the essentially liberal reasoning underlying his theory of punishment. Refining his argument, he contended that utility required that the laws operate negatively, to prevent harm, rather than positively, to promote happiness – this latter being best left to individual initiative. As he put it in a fragment consisting of 'Reflections on manners and customs':

> Everything that is publicly useful does not need to be directly commanded, although one should prohibit everything that is harmful. Therefore, all laws that restrict the personal liberty of men have their limit and rule in necessity; and the laws that aim solely at positive utility must not restrict personal liberty.[23]

This thesis anticipates in a striking manner the indirect utilitarianism that was to inform Adam Smith's writings. It suggests that, had Beccaria lived longer, he might have followed Verri in abandoning enlightened despotism as the means of reform and embraced a form of constitutional liberalism.

Beccaria's book made a tremendous impact when it was first published. A comparatively short work, its literary quality and ability to synthesise some of the quintessential themes of the Enlightenment and bring them to bear on a particular issue quickly won it a wide audience. It attracted the praise of the French philosophes, who invited him to Paris and encouraged the preparation of a French translation by Morellet. Voltaire recruited Beccaria's work to his own campaign against various abuses perpetrated by the French legal system and prepared a *Commentary* on the text, which was regularly published along with subsequent editions of the Italian's book in French and other languages. The English edition of 1767 brought him to the attention of Bentham and was subsequently reprinted many times. Catherine the Great even invited him to Russia to help in the preparation of her *ukase* reforming the Russian penal code. Unfortunately, this immediate success proved a mixed blessing in both the short and the long term. Beccaria was

---

23. 'Reflections on manners and customs' in Beccaria, *On Crimes*, p. 157.

unnerved by his sudden fame and curtailed his visit to Paris. Pietro Verri, piqued by the fact that Beccaria rather than he was being credited as the leading light of the Milanese intelligentsia, broke with him. Deprived of Verri's support and that of his circle, Beccaria failed to complete any other major work. Instead, he confined himself to the role of practical reformer in his career as a prominent official in the Austrian administration of Lombardy. These reports reveal a continuity with his early theories. A memorandum of 1792, for example, proposed the abolition of the death penalty and further elaborated the views of his famous book. However, the dissemination of his ideas amongst other intellectuals now largely fell to others and the various distortions that came about in the process went uncorrected. The recovery of his views only began in the 1960s as a result of the scholarly efforts of Franco Venturi and Luigi Firpo. Sadly, both torture and the death penalty remain in use even in supposedly liberal-democratic regimes, committed to the principles Beccaria upheld. His book retains its value in suggesting why such policies are repugnant to the very purposes of political society.

Part Two

Hegel, Croce and Idealist Liberalism

Chapter Four

Hegel's Conception of the State and Political Philosophy in a Post-Hegelian World[1]

The relationship between the state, the realm of authority and justice (*Recht*), and civil society, the sphere of transactions between individuals, in Hegel's *Philosophy of Right* has been criticised by liberals and Marxists alike.[2] Both take issue with his claim that a political community is defined by a number of common moral goals that are logically prior to those of its members and that the legitimacy of the state flows from upholding these, rather than the particular interests of individuals in society. Liberals argue that the state is simply a means to the fulfilment of our private projects. It is subordinate to society, therefore, merely providing a legal and institutional framework for the adjustment and reconciliation of the divergent pursuits of its different members. Marxists go further, denying the necessity of the state at all. They regard social conflict as the product of the class divisions of capitalism, to be eliminated in a communist society in which the state will wither away. Whilst liberals accuse Hegel of substituting the plurality and freedom of society for the imposed uniformity of a preconceived metaphysical entity, the 'supra-individual' state, Marxists believe he has simply 'reified' the present system of coercion and class exploitation.

Recent communitarian critics of both liberalism and Marxism have come to Hegel's defence. They maintain that neither the individualism of the former nor the class analysis of the latter are capable of explaining the myriad relationships that make up society and define the preferences and ideals of its members. However, they are equally uneasy with Hegel's metaphysical explanation of politics. They regard

1. This article is based on research funded by the ESRC under its Postdoctoral Research Fellowship Scheme. Its contents are the responsibility of the author and do not necessarily reflect the views of the ESRC. Earlier versions of this paper were presented at seminars at Oxford and Lancaster Universities and at the seventh conference of the Hegel Society of Great Britain on Hegel's Philosophy of Right. I'm grateful to W. H. Walsh, Z. Pelczynski, Caroline Forder, Jon Brooks, Michael Rosen, David Miller and especially Raymond Plant for their valuable comments on these occasions and in private conversation.

2. This distinction is regarded as the 'antithesis of modern political thought' by R. N. Berki in his introduction to a collection of essays on *State and Society in Contemporary Europe*, Jack Hayward and R. Berki (eds), (Oxford, 1979). A similar claim is made by Z. A. Pelczynski in his very useful editorial introduction to *The State and Civil Society: Studies in Hegel's political philosophy* (Cambridge, 1984). My own interpretation is particularly indebted, even as a stimulus for disagreement, to the contributions of Pelczynski, Ilting, Plant and Walton to this volume.

the community as a product of its history and tradition and refrain from following Hegel and interpreting these processes as stages in the development of Spirit or the Idea, which gives to human affairs an inner meaning and rationality.[3]

Hegel's political philosophy, then, focuses on an important difference in three traditions of modern political thought – namely, three divergent ways of conceiving the relationship between the state and civil society, and hence of the role and nature of law, justice and morality (*Recht*) in regulating human affairs, which I propose to explore in this chapter. In the first section, I seek to defend Hegel from his liberal and Marxist critics. I maintain that this requires accepting not just his historical and sociological claims for the state but also the logical metaphysical status he accords to it. This, as I show in the second section, undermines the communitarians' interpretation of Hegel. Finally, in the third section I attempt to reinstate the Hegelian conception of rationality as a way of looking at contemporary political dilemmas in a post-Hegelian world, that is at a time when the historical community that gave rise to his theory no longer exists.

I

The traditional criticisms of Hegel turn on a double misunderstanding: either that the state is the reification of an empirical entity or that Hegel fits the facts into a preconceived logical scheme. These errors follow from the mistaken belief that Hegel's claim concerning the identity of the rational and real is historical rather than meta-historical. Hegel's concept of rationality derives from his *Logic* and is encapsulated in the reasoning behind the syllogism, whereby:

> Everything rational shows itself to be a threefold union or syllogism [of Universal, Particular and Individual], in that each of the members takes the place both of one of the extremes and the mediating middle.[4]

Even the most casual acquaintance with the *Philosophy of Right* (a glance at the table of contents of Knox's translation, for example) reveals this 'threefold mediation or syllogism' to be the organising principle of the work. Thus, the first syllogism – of Individual, Particular and Universal – is that to be found in Abstract Right. Here the individual will find the universal through seeking the fulfilment of the particular inclinations, needs and passions with which he or she was born, via the possession of property. Yet, even within this section, there is a threefold mediation of the Idea. The second mediation (adopting Hegel's abbreviation)

---

3.   Charles Taylor, *Hegel* (Cambridge, 1975) and Raymond Plant, *Hegel* (2nd edn, Oxford, 1983) both adopt this view. Their influential studies are discussed in section two. Other examples, which suggest that this is the new orthodoxy, are S. Avinieri, *Hegel's Theory of the Modern State* (Cambridge, 1972) and Bernard Cullen, *Hegel's Social and Political Thought* (Dublin, 1979).

4.   Hegel: *Hegel's Logic: Being Part One of the Encyclopaedia of The Philosophical Sciences* (1830) trans. William Wallace, 3rd edn (Oxford, 1975) para. 187 zus, (amended translation R. B.). *See,* too, paras 6 and 181. My concentration on the 'Hegelian middle' derives from the analysis of this passage by Emil Fackenheim, *The Religious Dimension in Hegel's Thought* (Chicago, 1967), ch. 4.

U-I-P, deals with contract – that is, the regulation of individual wills once they come into contact with each other for the purposes of commerce and exchange. The final meditation P-U-I, having the Universal as its mid-point, deals with the morality of commerce and exchange and the notions of fraud and crime. Similarly, the third part of the *Philosophy of Right*, ethical life, is both the final mediation of the syllogism, P-U-I, whilst containing within it all three mediations. Thus the family is a unity founded on the immediacy of feeling, civil society a 'system of needs' based on the satisfaction of particular desires through the forces of production, whilst the State is the unity mediated by the Universal, the common good. Finally, within the State itself there are the three moments of the concept. As Hegel expressed it in the *Encyclopaedia*:

> the State is a system of three syllogisms: (i) The individual or person, through his particularity or physical or mental needs [...] is coupled with the Universal, i.e. with society, law, right, government. (ii) The will or action of Individuals is the intermediating force which procures for these needs satisfaction in society, law, etc [...] and which gives society, law etc [...], their fulfilment and actualization. (iii) But the Universal, i.e. the State, government, and law, is the permanent underlying mean in which the individuals and their satisfaction have and receive their fulfilled reality, intermediation and persistence. Each of the moments of the concept, as it is bought by intermediation to coalesce with the other extreme, is brought into union with itself and produces itself [...] It is only by this triad of syllogisms with the same terms that the whole is thoroughly understood in its organisation.[5]

The rationality of the State, therefore, resides in the constitution that embodies this threefold mediation in a *conscious* manner; in the moments of the legislature, which establishes the Universal from the perspective of particularity, the crown, which enacts the Universal as individuality, and the mediating middle, the executive, which subsumes particularity and individuality under the Universal. This rather formal working out of the logic of the State may seem at first glance to have fully justified the chief qualms of Hegel's detractors. But if Hegel is to be true to the logic of his theory of the State then the immanentist interpretation of his thought must be as untenable as its transcendent–metaphysical opposite. To favour either one of these would rule out the possibility of the two other elements necessary for the threefold mediation, which is the lynch-pin of Hegelian philosophy.[6] Two examples, of the transcendent or liberal and the immanentist or Marxist critiques respectively, will serve to show how the logic of Hegel's argument works against both these interpretations.

---

5. Hegel, *Logic: Encyclopedia*, para. 198.
6. My interpretation here follows that suggested by Fackenheim, *Religious Dimension*, pp. 220–2 and in, 'On the actuality of the rational and the rationality of the actual', *Review of Metaphysics* XXIII, 1969–70, pp. 690–8.

According to the liberal view, Hegel's 'metaphysical theory of the State' rests on three, largely erroneous, propositions. In Hobhouse's succinct summary, they are 'first [...] that true individuality or freedom lies in conformity to our real will [...] second that our real will is identical with the general will, and [...] third that the general will is embodied more or less perfectly in the State'.[7] For the liberal, the unity of the Hegelian State is only achieved at the indefensible cost of imposing a putative rational will upon the empirical and often self-contradictory desires and inclinations of the individual. The agreements of the social world can then be interpreted as the product of will rather than convenience, their justification being that they express humankind's 'true' rather than their actual nature. However, since ordinary mortals are unlikely to perceive the underlying rationality of their social existence for themselves, the state is fully justified in stepping in to uphold the rational within the real, and if necessary impose it on its members.

For Hegel, however, the unity of the State is not and could not be based upon the simple identity of these three elements. Hegel does indeed regard action as a product of will, of choosing between the impulses and desires we have. However, these choices in turn presuppose certain evaluative decisions which are more than simple instrumental calculations of how best to satisfy the desires we have. For human beings are more than 'bare forked animals' with only natural biological needs to satisfy. The social activity of production provides new objects of desire, whose pursuit and satisfaction are matters of moral deliberation and choice. But this choosing retains its tripartite nature as relative both to the individual, to the particular society he or she happens to live in, and a non-relative morality presupposed by all collective and individual choosing. Thus, one cannot know the third aspect of the Universal without continual experience of the other two – namely, the Individual and the Particular – and as we have seen all three are constantly developed and re-enacted at all stages of Hegel's exposition of the *Philosophy of Right*. It is only in bringing together all three elements that the State can be said to embody 'concrete freedom'.

This thesis provides the rationale behind Hegel's view that people enter politics via the estates rather than directly. This argument is usually read in a totalitarian light as exhibiting the dangers of the 'organic' conception of the State, in which individuals are simply cells subordinated to the greater purpose of the whole. However, Hegel is not in any way denying individuality but merely pointing out that as such it provides no basis for coming to collective decisions. Hegel's reasons have a lot in common with more recent critics of participatory models of democracy. In Schumpeterian fashion, he argues that various external constraints influence individual choices to such an extent that the people are likely to be highly ill-informed as to what their interests really are and, as a result, will generally act either for irrational reasons or in pursuit of what they falsely conceive to be self-interest.[8] Moreover, Hegel adds that, even if they are right about their self-

---

7. L. T. Hobhouse, *The Metaphysical Theory of the State* (London, 1918), p. 71.

8. Joseph Schumpeter, *Capitalism, Socialism and Democracy*, 3rd edn (London, 1950), pp. 250–83; G. W. F. Hegel, *Philosophy of Right*, trans. T. M. Knox (Oxford, 1952), para. 301. Hereafter all paragraph numbers in the text refer to this work.

interests, then this could hardly be the basis of agreement on the general interest, even in the sense of achieving maximum want-satisfaction. Majoritarian voting is almost certainly going to produce consistent minorities whose interests are ignored or worse. As a result of these weaknesses, the electorate is open to just the sort of demagogic manipulation liberals fear. For without any sense of a common interest, public agreement is likely to be achieved through manipulation and force. Yet:

> this atomistic and abstract point of view vanishes at the stage of the family, as well as that of civil society where the individual is in evidence only as a member a general group.

It is through participation at the lower levels of associated life, in the family and workplace, that a group identity has meaning. At the lower level, people can share in the common good and adapt to each other's wants and feelings. It would be absurd to ignore these ties when considering national issues:

> To picture these communities as once more breaking up into a mere conglomeration of individuals as soon as they enter the field of politics, i.e. the field of the highest concrete universality, is *eo ipso* to hold civil and political life apart from one another and as it were to hang the latter in the air, because the basis could then only be the abstract individuality of caprice and opinions, and hence it would be grounded on chance and not on what is absolutely stable and justified (para. 303E).

Hegel's position is not the upshot of conservatism, bent on, in Henry Jones' phrase, 'moralising our social relations as they stand'.[9] There is no suggestion that one should be obliged to perform a given role; rather, his argument is that we become moral via our social roles. The estates perform a mediating function since the deputies, by representing the interests of civil society, are able to watch over and inform the executive in its care for the common good. Moreover, this common good is no mere aggregate of individual interests but an articulated conception of what the welfare of society as a whole requires. For, the authority of the state rests on providing the conditions for human self-realisation generally, not of this or that particular person or group. It is thus participatory at the base and representative at the top, only this combination is consistent with the 'threefold mediation or syllogism', which is the rationality of the State (para. 304).

A more powerful objection, though, is that Hegel's actual working out of the nature of the State belies the very possibility of such a mediation and that the logic of his conception of the State is itself fundamentally misconceived. This is the substance of Marx's famous blow by blow 'Critique of Hegel's doctrine of the State', which aims to demonstrate that if the empirical content is at variance with the logical premises, then the logic itself must be confused.[10] Marx methodically applies Feuerbach's 'transformative method' to the whole of the section of the

---

9.   H. Jones, *The Working Faith of the Social Reformer and Other Essays*, (London, 1910), p. 114.

10. K. Marx, 'Critique of Hegel's Doctrine of the State' (1843), in *Early Writings*, trans. R. Livingstone and G. Benton (Harmondsworth, 1975), pp. 4.

Philosophy of Right devoted to the State but, again, one famous example will suffice to show its limitations – namely, the attack on primogeniture. Taking up three paragraphs (paras. 305–7) in Hegel, Marx devotes several pages to it.[11] Hegel argues that it is necessary to have some class in the State besides the 'Universal class' or bureaucracy, which has the common good as its end. The estates incorporate the particularity of civil society within the State but are still bound by the class interests of day-to-day economic and social life. As a result, 'set hostility' between these interests was just as likely as 'the possibility, though no more, of [their] harmonisation'. Liberal theory tends to regard the legislature as a forum for airing grievances against the State and preventing undue incursion on the rights of individuals. Radicals, by contrast, whilst agreeing that the people are the best judges of their own interest, believe that the legislature should directly enact the common will of the people. As we saw, Hegel contends that neither is likely to occur whilst a concern with purely private interests dominates. The 'set hostility' which is the basis of the liberal position is as 'abstract' as the 'harmonisation' aimed at by the radical and can be changed 'into a rational relation (into a syllogism [...]) only if the middle term between the opposites comes into existence'. In the constitution as a whole, this task is performed by the executive. Similarly, within the estates 'one moment in them must be adapted to the task of existing as in essence the moment of mediation' (para. 304). This is the logical demand made by his theory and Hegel argued it was most likely to be met in his time by the landed aristocracy. Primogeniture and entailed estates made this class independent of both the State and business world. They sit in the upper house by right of birth rather than election and as such mediate between the lower house and crown since they share elements of both. Marx attacks this thesis, pointing out that the defence of entailed estates is at odds with Hegel's earlier definition of property as a projection of individual will. Primogeniture also breaks with the unity of the family, for the estate passes to one child alone. Marx seeks to show via these criticisms that the class Hegel picks out as most representative of the Universal interest, the landed aristocracy, is that which is inevitably subservient to particular ones, through its attachment to private property. At most, however, it must be conceded that Hegel does not always live up to his own principle that philosophy is limited by positive right and that philosophic thought must recognise the contingent as contingent, even when 'over-reaching' it. Life peers, for example, might fit just as well as aristocrats. Marx denies that the tensions of civil society can ever be overcome, that there can be mediating agencies that are not essentially representative of private interests, without the complete overcoming of private interest itself in communist society. In a sense, Hegel is making exactly the same point, since the State aims at the reconciliation of private interests with the needs of communal life. But he disputes that this can be done directly. To take any moment apart from the whole is to render it an abstraction. The landed class do not make a nonsense of elected assemblies, both have a role to play which is only justified

---

11. *Ibid.*, pp. 164–80.

by the common goal of the State. This is the point of the apparent contradiction in Hegel's account of the landed class, which, as Marx notes, Hegel himself comments on – namely, that their position involves 'hard sacrifices made for political ends'. Marx is correct to insist that Hegel's whole analysis is ontologically grounded but his critique fails because he does not penetrate to this ontological level.

Both the liberal and Marxist critiques have as their hidden premise the denial of the possibility of a mediation of the conflicts in civil society via the Hegelian middle. Liberal theory rejects the notion of a common good to which all individual life plans are subject.[12] Rather, they claim that the workings of civil society will generate some kind of compromise essential to the functioning of any society. Hegel retorts that there is nothing in this 'atomistic and abstract point of view' to form the basis for agreement beyond the mere requirement for survival – a contention possibly borne out by the current popularity of Hobbesian contract and rights theories amongst liberals. Marxism, by contrast, seeks to arrogate the power of *Geist* to humankind and thus abolish the need for the Hegelian mediation. 'True democracy' will be possible when nature has been completely transformed to reflect humanity's 'communist essence' and the divisions of civil society overcome. The antithesis of private interest and public good will be transcended when nature has been so mastered as to make the division of labour in the system of needs unnecessary.[13] But human solidarity is no more guaranteed by the satisfaction of our needs and interests in the Marxist than in the liberal version of society. For the abolition of class divisions via differential access to property does not, as the actually existing socialist countries of the former Soviet bloc amply demonstrated, mean the abolition of inequalities based on differential access to the organs of power.

Both the liberal and Marxist critiques assume an autonomous self – be it individual or collective – that does not have to seek common purposes through interacting with other autonomous selves. Like the liberal, the Hegelian State attempts to do justice to the conflicting autonomous plans of individuals. Like the Marxist, the Hegelian State seeks to 'overcome' these conflicts, yet without denying their reality. The political mediation offered by politics is the attempt to satisfy both these aspects. Yet, an objection remains that the rationality of the Hegelian State cannot be achieved in actuality – it is an ideal, theoretical construct that could not be made real other than through some form of totalitarian perversion of reality. How far the rational is real and the real rational becomes a crucial question, therefore.

12. This aversion was classically expressed by Isaiah Berlin in 'Two concepts of liberty', *Four Essays on Liberty*, (Oxford, 1969).

13. Marx 'On the Jewish question', *Early Writings*, pp. 230, 234.

II

Hegel's dictum concerning the rationality of the actual is frequently read in reverse, as meaning that what exists is *a priori* rational.[14] That 'What is rational is actual; and what is actual is rational'[15] has, however, by no means always been valid, but only came about at a particular stage of history, when the human desire for self-realisation put on flesh in the social institutions of the modern world. As Hegel makes plain in a gloss on this passage in the *Encyclopaedia* (para. 6), the central historical event was the advent of Christianity. The image of the incarnation of God in human form, with which the *Phenomenology* ends and Hegelian philosophy begins, makes possible a modern conception of freedom. The world is no longer construed as being created apart from humanity, the product of God's will, but is intimately connected with our own purposes and desires, through which *Geist* realises itself. 'Reason rules the world' because the Universal is implicit in human affairs:

> The *world spirit* is the spirit of the world as it reveals itself through the human consciousness. The relationship of humanity to it is that of the single parts to the whole which is their substance. And this world spirit corresponds to the divine spirit which is the absolute spirit.[16]

It is because reason has become actual, the principle of action, that the existing world can be examined for its rationality. Ethical life is thus the culmination of an historical process, set forth most succinctly in the Introduction to the *Lectures on the Philosophy of World History*, in which, via Christianity, the human will and the Idea of Freedom come to form 'the warp and weft in the fabric of world history', giving rise to the 'entire ethical life of nations'.[17] The dual nature of this process has seemed to justify the view that the Hegelian Idea is some sort of supernatural puppet master, manipulating human passions via the 'cunning of reason' to achieve its dark purpose – the construction of the State.[18] However, the progress of the Idea in history cannot be seen as something apart from the history of the people who make it up. Rather, it is the development of reason and hence of freedom within humankind. Just as the rationality of the State implies the Hegelian syllogism, so does history. It is perhaps best seen as an analogy of the moral development of the individual, each stage being a historical community embodying a particular mediation. Thus, primitive society is built on a natural

---

14. E.g. Sidney Hook's comment that 'One interpretation of the distinction between the actual and the existent gives us a sheer tautology, the other a scandalous absurdity.' 'Hegel and the perspective of liberalism', in C . D. Travis (ed.) *A Hegel Symposium* (Austin, TX, n.d.), p. 51.

15. Hegel, *Philosophy of Right*, p. 10.

16. Hegel, *Lectures on the Philosophy of World History: Introduction: Reason in history*, trans. H. B. Nisbet, with an introduction by Duncan Forbes (Cambridge, 1975), pp. 28, 36, 52–3.

17. *Ibid.*, p. 71.

18. As we shall see in Chapter Five, this was Croce's view, in B. Croce, *Ció che é vivo e ció che é morto nella filosofia di Hegel, in Saggio sullo Hegel*, 4th edn., Bari, 1948, e.g. pp. 90–95.

unity, that of the given order of things, and is paralleled by the unity of the family. The State, however, represents the highest unity because it is based on humankind's self-conscious shaping of the world in conformity with reason. Neither moment denies the other but, whereas in the earlier stage our natural impulses and desires shape our conception of ethical life, in the last stage they are in turn mediated via a conception of the common good itself. As a result

> The principle of modern States has prodigious strength and depth because it allows the principle of subjectivity to progress to its culmination in the extreme of self-subsistent personal particularity and yet at the same time brings it back to the substantive unity and so maintains this unity in the principle of subjectivity itself. (para. 260)

The Hegelian State was not conceived as crushing individuality but as realising it. However, Hegel's community is not a society as liberal individualism conceives it – the minimum degree of co-operation necessary for us to follow our private ends. For Hegel, our sense of self and framing of life plans is not done in isolation. What we value and think worthwhile is itself a social product, emerging from interaction with other people. The ties of love and friendship, our antagonisms and dislikes, our standards of excellence and all the other attitudes whereby we express our individuality cannot be conceived as purely private affairs, since they get their meaning in large part from a public language and set of norms. Therefore, the modern State in Hegelian terms is legitimate to the extent that its political and social institutions embody those related sets of practices which confer on the individual his or her identity and define his or her obligations to others, as *Sittlichkeit*. As we saw, this thesis is underwritten by a metaphysical argument. Hegelian philosophy is an enterprise in reconciliation of humankind to society by bringing humanity to consciousness of the working of *Geist*, of Spirit or Reason, in humankind and the world. Human history is perceived not simply a product of human will but as will seen as the emanation of the Universal as it is progressively realised in history.

Hegel can thereby claim, in the Preface to the *Philosophy of Right*, that the philosopher's task is not 'to construct a State as it ought to be' but to 'show how the State, the ethical universe, is to be understood'. Hegel believes that the nature of modern society is such that alienation can be overcome by a proper understanding of the social relations which govern us. For the actual is not the merely existing, but that which has been suffused with the rational. This argument poses a crucial question for contemporary neo-Hegelian communitarian theorists. For is it still possible to be an Hegelian without accepting the active trans-historical argument implied by the *Logic*, if the existential conditions for Hegelian belief have passed away?

This dilemma bedevils recent attempts to apply Hegel's political philosophy to the study of contemporary society. Charles Taylor's work, which has perhaps contributed the most to the current Hegel revival in political theory, illustrates these difficulties in a profound manner. A noted critic of the failings of a purportedly 'neutral' political science to describe the functioning of western institutions,[19] and of the 'atomism' of recent contractarian theories of the State,[20] he believes 'that Hegel has contributed to the formation of concepts and modes of thought which are indispensable if we are to see our way clear through certain modern problems'.[21] He claims that the democracies of advanced capitalist societies are currently undergoing, or are prone to, a legitimation crisis deriving from a lack of fit between the individual's position as a producer in civil society and his or her expectations from politics.[22] These two aspects of modern life are governed by two divergent views of individual freedom stemming from the Enlightenment. These are the romantic view of freedom as self-expression, prominent in radical forms of revolutionary Marxism, and the instrumental view of freedom as the rational satisfaction of certain innate desires, found in classical liberalism.[23] Taylor argues that Hegel was extraordinarily prescient in foreseeing this clash. Drawing on Hegel's account of French revolutionaries in the *Phenomenology*, Taylor contends that Hegel reveals the inadequacy of either view to provide a coherent picture of how the divergent life plans of different individuals might be reconciled in society without resorting to coercion or otherwise drastically reducing their freedom to act.[24]

As was shown in the first section, Hegel's solution is to reconcile these two strands of modern thought and aspiration. Taylor is equally adamant that Hegel's argument for harmonisation is only coherent in the context of his system as a whole. However, he regards its success as contingent on the validity of Hegel's interpretation of the course of human history; and herein lies its weakness. For whatever its merits for the analysis of the past, Taylor maintains that 'the development of modern civilisation in an increasingly industrial, technological, rationalised direction' has rendered Hegel's ontology untenable today.[25]

This complete historicisation of Hegel's metaphysics is both unfortunate and mistaken. Taylor defends Hegel's account on the grounds of its plausibility. He claims that in certain historical conditions we can, for example, see the necessity of monarchy as a derivation of the Idea.[26] But this interpretation lends itself to the criticisms of liberals and Marx, noted above. Namely, that Hegel's account of

---

19. C. Taylor, 'Interpretation and the sciences of man', *The Review of Metaphysics* XXV (1971), pp. 3–51 and 'Neutrality in political science', in P. Laslett and W. G. Runicman (eds), *Philosophy, Politics and Society*, 3rd ser., (Oxford, 1967), pp. 25–57.

20. C. Taylor, 'Atomism', in A. Kontos (ed.), *Powers, Possessions and Freedom* (Toronto, 1979), pp. 39–61.

21. C. Taylor, *Hegel and Modern Society*, (Cambridge, 1979), p. xi.

22. *Ibid.*, pp. 125–34.

23. *Ibid.*, pp. 154–9, 167–8.

24. *Ibid.*, pp. 100–24. See too his 'What's wrong with negative liberty', in Alan Ryan (ed.), *The Idea of Freedom* (Oxford, 1979), pp. 175–93.

25. Taylor *Hegel*, p. 539 *et seq.*

26. Taylor, *Hegel and Modern Society*, pp. 80–1, 97.

history and society amounts to a confidence trick, falsely reconciling humanity to reality they ought to reject. At best, it is little more than the conservative belief in the value of tradition.

Such is the conclusion of Raymond Plant's study. Like Taylor, he sympathises with Hegel's metaphysics and his desire to create a new communal existence.[27] However, he discerns a prototype of the legitimation crisis, said by Taylor to be affecting contemporary society,[28] within Hegel's own account of the State.[29] He argues that philosophically Hegel may succeed in re-describing industrial society so as to overcome the alienation of the poor and oppressed. But practically the problem persists, because the possibilities of exploitation continue to exist if structural changes affecting the actual working of society are not made.[30] The implication is that the resources for promoting such change are not present in Hegel's theory, a view to which Taylor also adheres. This doubt accounts for the note of despair which pervades the conclusion of Taylor's magisterial work and its sequel, which explicitly tackles the theme of *Hegel and Modern Society*. For the appeal to the common good is no longer coherent, if it ever was, once society has become too fragmented for shared meanings to prevail. In Taylor's opinion, Hegel provides a penetrating diagnosis of our ills but gives no hope of a cure.

In the final section of this paper I shall dispute this thesis, arguing that the possibility of creating community feeling does not depend, for Hegel, on pre-existing values. Rather, it requires making the rational actual through the correct appreciation of how our individual needs, both present and future, relate to those of our fellows.

III

The means of creating the Hegelian *Sittlichkeit* resides in his conception of rationality, which we saw is the key to Hegel's interpretation of the relationship between the individual, civil society and the State. Hegelian rationality is not the modern post-Kantian critical view, whereby 'ontological' assertions must be justified by prior 'epistemological' assertions about human knowledge, but has more in common with Aristotelian practical reason. This is the essence of the Hegelian claim that philosophy is a self-developing whole, whose justification

27. R. Plant, *Hegel*, 2nd edn, chs 8, 9. Plant, like Taylor, has also attempted to bring a communitarian view-point to bear on a number of our present dilemmas and criticises the approach of contemporary analytical philosophers who tackle them in a neutral and individualistic manner. *See* his *Community and Ideology* (London, 1974) and *Political Philosophy and Social Welfare* (London, 1980), chs 9–10.

28. R. Plant, 'Growth, legitimacy and the modern identity', *Praxis* I, (1981), pp. 111–25.

29. Plant, *Hegel*, chs 6–8; 'Hegel on identity and legitimation', in Z. A. Pelczynski (ed.), *The State and Civil Society*, pp. 227–43.

30. R. Plant, 'Hegel and political economy', Parts 1 and 2, *New Left Review* I/103 and 104, 1977, esp. p. 113. *See*, too, Cullen, *Hegel's Social and Political Thought*, pp. 100–14 and Avinieri, *Hegel's Theory of the Modern State*, p. 154.

resides in its presentation. As was shown in the first section, it consists of the threefold mediation of Particular, Universal and Individual, each of which is necessary to the other. Liberal theory tends to regard the individual as the locus of all value, our cognitive powers being the source of meaning in the world. This assumption is not substantially challenged by either neo-Hegelian communitarians or neo-Marxist radicals. Both assume that the legitimacy of a given community rests upon the individual's autonomous acceptance of the norms which validate it. Hegelian rationality, by contrast, works in quite a different manner, on the basis of a mediation between first principles and the datum of experience. Thus, the concept of the common good is not to be arrived at by attempting to devise ideal speech conditions or procedures whereby we might all agree, but by its pursuit as the middle element of our individual and social goals. Or rather, as what is implied by the very possibility of our having individual and social goals, as we assuredly do. A theory of the common good or, more properly speaking, of common goals or ends of human fulfilment, derives therefore from its pursuit.

A practical example will help elucidate this point. Modern liberals exclude policies based on some assumption of what is good for society as a whole, because they believe no such goal can ever be authoritatively decided upon. Political decisions must therefore be neutral between ideals of the good.[31] But this does not entail that there are no grounds for agreement on common programmes. For instance, a commitment to environmental planning legislation derives, in their view, from its net benefit to all members of the community.[32] Matters of public interest are held to prevail over the particular interest certain individuals might have in evading them. Thus, a clean-air law, which is in the net interest of all, overrides the particular interest a factory owner might have in breaking it in order to make a quick profit.

Unfortunately political decisions are rarely as clear-cut as this. It might be deemed to be in the public interest to have a policy severely restricting building in places of natural beauty. Yet from time to time the incentive to infringe it for various groups will be high. It may even be argued, to build an airport say, that it is in the public interest to go against the general ruling. In the liberal model, such decisions are arrived at by a process of bargaining. But although in circumstances where the different groups wield equal amounts of political power this might produce some compromise solution, it could not identify what aspects of the issue are of common concern. In its simplest form, the straight majoritarian vote, the wishes of a substantial minority – presumably those who would end up living next to the runway – could be excluded without any consideration of why they might merit special weighting.

---

31. For example, R. Dworkin, 'Liberalism', in S. Hampshire (ed.), *Public and Private Morality* (Cambridge, 1978), p. 127.

32. *Ibid.*, pp. 141–2. My discussion here follows on from that William Connolly, 'The public interest and the common good', in *Appearance and Reality in Politics* (Cambridge, pp. 119 and H. L. A. Hart, 'Between utility and rights', in Ryan (ed.), *The Idea of Liberty*, pp. 77–98.

There are therefore three objections to a politics based on a putatively 'neutral' definition of the public interest. (i) By not taking the strength of feeling of different groups into account, minorities with a good case (those who live next to a proposed airport in this example) may be consistently outvoted. (ii) This is because any preference-aggregation method fails to distinguish mere preferences from real interests: for example, a desire for easier mobility and trade by building an airport from permanent attachments to natural beauty. (iii) Liberals argue that if something is a collective good it is ipso facto an individual good. Thus, if natural beauty is valuable for all, people will respect it as a matter of course. The difficulty lies in the illicit move from 'everyone gains by preserving the environment' to 'each person gains by preserving the environment.' Without compulsion, it often pays better to be a 'free-rider'. For example, you could develop this particular site and use the money to go and live somewhere even nicer.

By contrast to this liberal conception of the public interest, the communitarian notion of the common good embodies a shared morality that provides a motivation to pursue collective goals which the liberal account cannot sustain. Concern for the public interest, devoid of any moral obligation, is for instrumental reasons alone. If a situation should arise where there is a greater incentive to pursue self-interest rather than the public interest, then there would be no motivation for doing the latter. In such circumstances, to reverse a famous idealist phrase, force rather than will becomes the basis of the State. The government cannot appeal to a set of norms that are held to define responsible behaviour. For it is, in principle, open to each citizen to decide for himself what his obligations to society are. Therefore, one can oppose the use of almost any public resource, since one could always claim that one's interest in an alternative way of life was potentially restricted. Nor does the caveat that such decisions show 'equal concern and respect' to all points of view remove this difficulty.[33] Indeed it compounds the problem of deciding which viewpoints are admissible or not. Consequently, any policy risks appearing arbitrary, to some at least.

The mistake is to believe that our rights and duties to others can be identified in complete ignorance of what values make life satisfying and worthwhile. The general requirement to respect nature cannot be justified in terms of facilitating the pursuit of purely personal goals. It needs to be seen as part of a general view of the quality of life for members of society as a whole. The development of healthy social relations depends on understanding the ways in which our needs and desires relate to those of others. Our preferences must be valued as contributions to the plurality of common goods which together make for a valuable social life, offering the maximum number of options to each individual member.

In the absence of a shared code of morality capable of harmonising the particular interests of different individuals, some guide is needed for the formation of preferences akin to that offered by the Hegelian syllogism. Hegelian reasoning is not neutral between different plans of life, since it specifies particular goods

---

33. Dworkin, 'Liberalism', pp. 14, 42.

as being common to and necessary for all such plans. It cannot be arrived at in isolation from the lives people actually lead but derives from the pursuit of those goods basic to both individual and social goals and by relating them to the requirements of human flourishing more generally. In the case of environmental legislation, it means recognising that more is at issue than a resource the value of which only reflects the particular life plans and aspirations of those who seek to use it. Its status is mediated by virtue of its being a place of beauty, a source of life and recreation and so on. These are universal qualities of human life in general, taking on a variety of forms in the different lives of different individuals and societies. Thus, the content of any policy would have to be one which took these basic goals of human flourishing into account to the extent that no single one of them was ignored.

The rationality which the Hegelian State presupposes is not to be linked to some specific historical state of affairs or dependent upon an immanent Idea of Progress, therefore. The development of the moral concepts and cultural and institutional arrangements which make the politics of the common good intelligible is necessarily a process within history, but with many twists and turns. At times, societies have attempted to substitute a different sort of politics but always have been led back to identify with a set of common standards and practices that, when not willed, have tended to be enforced. But allegiance to the common good is not arbitrary. It has its own rationale as being implicit in living a life orientated towards not identical goals but to self-realisation within a society of others pursuing a similar goal. Thus, the sphere of individual subjectivity, realising itself in particular goods, is not overcome but simply mediated by the Universal. To return to the reflexion with which this paper began, it is in this sense that civil society is not abolished but mediated in ethical life by politics, which is the essence of the State. The division of labour and the greater complexity of human needs and the means of their satisfaction is a fact of life of advanced economies. Politics remains indispensable, not just to adjudicate between different lifestyles but also to come to self-consciousness of what leading a life involves. We require an awareness of others to have a sense of ourselves. If this awareness was nothing but a simple group identity there would be little scope for the reflective and self-conscious adoption of goals which is the basic element of forming a life plan.[34] Such reflexive self-consciousness comes only with the mediating middle element of the Universal or common good, which imposes a consideration of what is involved in not just one's own individual life in a particular society but also in all similar projects.[35]

---

34. Hegel regarded this reflexive understanding of others as the essential difference between the imposed unity of the classical Greek community and the view of community required for the much more diverse conditions of modern society. *See* A. Walton, 'Hegel: individual agency and social context', in Lawrence Stepelevich and David Lamb (eds), *Hegel's Philosophy of Action*, (Atlantic Highlands, NJ, 1983), pp. 75–92.

35. These ideas are developed further in my 'Hegel and liberalism', *History of European Ideas* 8, (1987), pp. 693–708.

Conclusion

The *Philosophy of Right* ends not with the State but with World History. The State is a hard-won example of a form of political organisation which is built upon the rationale of the politics of the common good. Adapted to the circumstances of the age, it was far from being a blueprint for all time. In our own time, we have the choice of drawing upon those aspects of our culture that can provide the materials for a new form of common life, of which a number exist even in today's fragmented societies; or we may choose not to do so and live in a world based on checks and balances on self-interest and rocked by intermittent outbursts of religious and political fanaticism. Either way, as Hegel quoted from Schiller, 'history is the world's court of judgement' and we will reap the fruits of our endeavours.

Chapter Five

What is Living and What is Dead in Croce's Interpretation of Hegel?

Croce's appreciation of Hegel was always as ambivalent as the title of his famous study suggests. Indeed, although related to two of the major nineteenth-century exponents of Italian Hegelianism – Bertrando and Silvio Spaventa – his first encounter with Hegel had been one of almost total rejection. As he wrote to the philosopher Donato Jaja in 1892, 'I believe that the fundamental principles, and especially, the method, of that system are entirely erroneous; and the damaging consequences of this error will become plain when applied to particular disciplines'.[1] However, the study of Marx and the influence of Giovanni Gentile and Antonio Labriola led him to review his earlier position; in 1906 he translated the *Encyclopedia* and wrote the accompanying book *What is Living and What is Dead in the Philosophy of Hegel*. Thereafter, Croce, who had already completed his *Aesthetic* (1902) and the first addition of the *Logic* (1905), was increasingly to present his own philosophy as a sustained commentary on, and development of, Hegel's philosophy. Therefore, an examination of his classic study of Hegel provides an important insight into salient features of Croce's own philosophical system and its later development.[2]

Croce begins the book with a discussion of what he believes to be still 'living' in Hegel – the dialectic. Croce argues that the critique of Kant had led Hegel to his great discovery of the 'concrete universal' and its unfolding through the dialectic (pp. 5–7, 34).[3] Croce rebuts the idea of Hegel's 'optimism'. Neither the bad nor the ugly are denied; what Hegel sets out to do is to discover their role in human self-consciousness. The dialectic leads to the abolition of false dualisms and establishes the true relationship between the idea and reality, so that the real is seen to be the rational and *vice versa* (pp. 40–2). For Croce this insight leads to 'the exaltation of history':

---

1. Letter quoted in E. Garin 'Appunti sulla formazione e su alcuni caratteri del pensiero crociano', in *Intellettuali italiani del xx secolo*, Roma, 1974, p. 6.

2. For a more detailed study of Croce's philosophy, *see* my *Liberalism and Historicism: History and politics in the thought of Benedetto Croce*, Cambridge University PhD dissertation, 1983, especially ch. 1, from which the material for this article is largely drawn.

3. All references in the text, unless otherwise stated, are to *Ció che é vivo e ció che é morto nella filosofia di Hegel*, in *Saggio sullo Hegel*, 4th edn, Bari, 1948, pp. 3–143. All translations are my own.

History, the life of the human race, the facts which unfold in time, cease to be conceived as something separate and indifferent with respect to the essence of things, to the idea, or even worse as belittling or obscuring the idea (p. 46).

He praises Hegel's description of the movement of reality as 'Bacchic delirium'. Croce is fully aware of the nature of the dialectic as something not to be treated with unintelligent rigidity but as 'feel', as a means for conceptualising reality. It breaks with formal logic to enter the stream of life in which 'philosophy seems mad because it breaks down abstractions and lives that life in thought' (p. 21). Consequently, it is a madness which is 'supreme wisdom', whilst the real madmen are those who 'play the fool with the empty words of semi-philosophy and take formulas for reality' (p. 21).

It comes as some surprise, therefore, that having devoted the first three chapters to what he saw as the 'life' of the dialectic, Croce should spend the rest of the book accusing Hegel of making this very error of playing the fool with empty words and semi-philosophical formulas. For, he argues, it is the imposition of an *a priori* scheme on reality that is the source of the 'dead wood' of the system. Croce believes Hegel fails to resolve the dualism in his thought between 'is' and 'ought' and accuses him of 'panlogism', of falsely integrating 'being' into 'thought', the crux ('il punto critico') being the famous passage from idea to nature (p. 128).[4] This move leads Hegel to make two fundamental errors: the false application of the dialectic to the 'nexus of distincts' and a 'philosophical' account of history.

With regard to the first error, Croce follows Aristotle in holding there is a 'scala naturae' within reality from matter to spirit, which is not just a classification scheme of reality (p. 60). He regards this scale as forming what, following the Neapolitan philosopher Giambattista Vico, he calls an 'ideal eternal history, traversed in time by all particular histories' (p. 58). Croce contrasts this view with the Hegelian 'synthesis of opposites' (that is, as in the triad being, non-being, becoming). Whilst in the former account of a 'nexus of distincts' the three elements in this triad are all 'concrete', in the latter account of a 'synthesis of opposites' the two elements that are brought together and synthesised are 'abstract' without the third. Croce believes that Hegel makes (in the *Logic*) the mistake of treating such 'distinct' moments of the dialectic synthetically, so that the levels of thought from art, to religion and then to philosophy, and of society from the family, to civil society and then to the state, are treated as elements within a triadic synthesis (pp. 64–6). Against this approach, Croce argues that these distinct levels can never be said to be abolished but are eternal moments of spirit:

Spirit is development, history, and therefore being and non-being together, becoming, but spirit *sub specie aeterni*, which philosophy considers, is ideal

---

4. The passage referred to is in the *Encyclopedia of the Philosophical Sciences*, vol. I, para. 244. Croce devotes the whole of ch. 10 to this problem.

eternal history, outside of time: it is the series of the eternal forms of that giving birth and dying, which, as Hegel says, is never born and never dies (p. 62).[5]

The tricky question of whether Croce is correct or not in his interpretation of Hegel need not bother us here.[6] However, it is important for an understanding of Croce's thought that he should have rejected any such perfect sublation of the preceding phases of spirit into absolute spirit. This rejection excludes from his philosophy any possibility of the false absorption of all the phases of spirit into objective spirit, or the state, which was the inspiration behind the ideas of certain nationalist and totalitarian propagandists, most notably his one-time collaborator and philosopher of fascism Giovanni Gentile.[7]

As a result of this critique, Croce attempts to reconstruct the Hegelian dialectic as a circular unity of the distinct moments of spirit. He reinterprets the Hegelian phenomenology as the circular activity of spirit between its distinct moments. Abstractly considered, these moments are the eternal forms of the beautiful (intuition), the true (logic), the useful (practice) and the good (morality). In Croce's account, spirit passes from one form to the other 'not because of the contradictions intrinsic to each of these forms in their distinction, but because of the intrinsic contradictions in reality itself' (p. 63). According to Croce, the passage from art to philosophy is not from an inferior to a superior phase of spirit; 'the antithesis does not arise from the bosom of the superseded level [...] but by a necessity basic to its very nature which is to be at the same time art and philosophy, theory and praxis'. Thus, intuition rises to philosophy but, in a similar manner, spirit becomes:

dissatisfied with philosophic universality and thirsts after intuition and life, it is no longer philosophic spirit, but has already become aesthetic spirit, which begins to fall in love once more with some vision and determinate intuition (p. 63).

According to Croce, instead of seeing the progress of spirit as this dialectical movement between its distinct moments, Hegel regards it as a phenomenological movement from error to truth. However, Croce argues that this final conclusion is a presupposition that Hegel has arbitrarily incorporated into his system from the start (p. 75).

This contention motivates Croce's assault on Hegel's philosophy of history, his second supposed error, as the 'metamorphosis of particular concepts into philosophical errors' (ch. 7). Croce holds that history gives rise to philosophy when

---

5.   He develops this argument in ch. 5, in which he discusses Hegel's *Logic*.

6.   G. R. G. Mure argues forcibly that this is not the case, e.g. *An Introduction to Hegel*, Oxford, 1940, ch. 8, paras 6, 6.1. 7 and *A Study of Hegel's Logic*, Oxford, 1950, ch. 1, para. 2.1, although I believe that his comparison with Kant and Aristotle is more telling than he intended (*Study*, chs. 20, 21). *See* Croce's appreciative comments on Mure's view of his revision of Hegel in his review of these books, 'Un critico inglese della logica di Hegel', in *Indagini sul Hegel*, Bari, 1952, pp. 92–7.

7.   I have developed this argument in 'Croce, Gentile and Hegel and the doctrine of the Ethical State', in *Rivista di studi crociani* XX, 1983, pp. 263–81 and XXI, 1984, pp. 263–81.

one passes from an historical concern with facts to the theoretical presuppositions which lie behind the historian's choice of facts (p. 89).

> A philosophy of history, understood not as the elaboration for this abstract philosophy, but as *a history of a second degree*, a history obtained via that abstract philosophy, is a contradiction in terms. (pp. 90–1)

The same 'over-philosophising' which led Hegel to abolish the all important 'distinction' between the different moments of spirit leads him to replace empirical fact with *a priori* speculation and abolish the history of the historian altogether (p. 95). Although, as his discussion of the dialectic shows, Croce was well aware of the importance of history for philosophy in Hegel, he insists that what is involved:

> is not therefore the logical element, the interpretation of intuitive facts [...] indispensable for any historical work; it is, instead, a ready-made history, which only needs to be dressed up with names and dates (pp. 92–3).

Croce remains loyal to his earlier adherence to Herbart's criticism of Hegel.[8] For Herbart, the real is formed out of a plurality of simple elements in the manifold groupings of which our experience is founded, the unity being a secondary product of the more fundamental plurality. This view derives from the importance given in his method to the *datum* of experience. This thesis motivates Herbart's and, via Herbart, Croce's attack on Hegel as an 'abstract' metaphysician. Croce claims that while for Hegel the rational must be real, for Herbart it is the converse, the real must be rational. This perspective, adopted by Croce in the 1880s and 90s, explains why he criticises the Hegelian idea as the false deduction of the ground of the many from the one rather than the inference of the one from the many. Yet, it was the Hegelian formula that 'What is rational is real and what is real is rational' that was to form the keystone of Croce's own philosophy of 'absolute historicism'.[9]

Croce's appropriation of this Hegelian formula rests, once again, on his claim to rescue the living from the dead in the German's philosophy. Some consideration of Hegel's own argument is necessary at this point, to appreciate the nature of Croce's critique. Croce's criticism of Hegel is based on the relationship of the logical and the temporal progress of the idea from phase to phase through the forms of nature and spirit. In a sense his criticism misfires, since the three-fold mediation of idea, nature and spirit is precisely what makes the immanent interpretation of Hegel's thought as unfounded as its transcendent–metaphysical opposite.[10] Far from denying the contingent, Hegelian philosophy seeks to show

8.　*Cf.* B. Croce 'La storia ridotta sotto il concetto generale dell "arte"', in *Atti dell 'Accademia Potaniana* XXIII (1893), Memoria no. 7, 1–32 and in *Primi Saggi*, 2nd edn, Bari, 1927, pp. 3–46, discussed in my *Liberalism and Historicism*, pp. 6–12.

9.　*Hegel's Philosophy of Right*, trans. T. M. Knox, Oxford, 1952, p. 10. I have rendered Croce's translation of this phrase. For the importance of the Hegelian motto for Croce's thought *see Indagini sul Hegel*, pp. 10–11 and my discussion in Chapter Six of this volume.

10.　*See Encyclopedia*, vol. I. para. 187, *Zusatz*, and Croce's comment in *Saggio sullo Hegel*, p. 137.

the absolute as present within it and necessary to it. Hegel requires the finite objective world of fact as an essential element in the life of speculative thought itself. Each of the three elements of the syllogism is necessary to the other. But the whole edifice of Hegelian reasoning does rest on the fundamental assumption of the essential identity of idea and spirit, which is realised through its mediation and self-realisation in nature. As Hegel expresses it in the *Phenomenology*:

> In my view, which can be justified only by the exposition of the system itself, everything turns upon grasping and expressing the True, not only as *Substance* but equally as *Subject*. At the same time, it is to be observed that substantiality embraces the universal, or the *immediacy of knowledge* itself, as well as that which is being or immediacy *for* knowledge.[11]

Since reality is not just substance but active subject as well, a perpetually re-enacted process of self-realisation, the result includes the process and hence cannot abolish it but must remain adequate to it – this is the essential meaning of spirit's power of over-reaching.[12] The philosophy of history is therefore essential to philosophy as such: it is not simply a ladder of the Wittgensteinian kind, to be thrown away when science comes on the scene, but really and rationally an aspect of it. The nature of this circularity, of a philosophy which is a self-developing whole, whose justification resides in its presentation, is of course the crucial question with regard to Hegel's philosophy. For such circularity lays Hegel's philosophy wide open to the type of critique deployed by Croce – namely, that this conception of philosophy makes Hegelian thought a self-endorsed system, which can afford to be radically open to all contingent experience only because whilst facts are allowed to confirm the system they are systematically forbidden to refute it.[13]

In certain respects this criticism fails to do justice to the sheer ambition of Hegel's philosophy and its claim to comprehensiveness, which is both its greatest merit and its chief weakness. In the *Logic*, Hegel had radicalised Kantian rational autonomy so that it ceases to remain finite and human and has become an attribute of spirit alone. The ground of this contention lies in Hegel's claim that the content of his philosophy is Christianity.[14] Philosophy requires an existential basis that must be considered ultimate, and hence religious in significance. Indeed, he argues, religion as revealed through history is the existential base of philosophy.

11. G. W. F. Hegel, *Hegel's Phenomenology of Spirit*, trans A. V. Miller, Oxford, 1977, para. 17.

12. On this, *see* E. Fackenheim *The Religious Dimension in Hegel's Thought*, Bloomington, Indiana University Press, 1967, pp. 98–9, 106–7 and Duncan Forbes' 'Introduction' to Hegel's *Lectures on the Philosophy of World History: Introduction*, trans. H. B. Nisbet, Cambridge, CUP, 1975. All references in the text to this edition of the work are indicated *LPhWH*.

13. This is more or less the charge made by M. Rosen in *Hegel's Dialectic and its Criticism*, Cambridge, Cambridge University Press, 1982.

14. For the importance of this claim in the genesis of Hegelianism, *see* W. H. Walsh, *Metaphysics*, London, Hutchinson University Library, 1963, pp. 133–53.

The self-development of spirit traced in the *Phenomenology* and the *Logic* is necessarily paralleled in the philosophy of world history, since the Hegelian claim to comprehensiveness lies precisely in its openness to the contingencies of the actual world. The core of this claim is a philosophical confrontation with historical Christianity. This argument can be illustrated with the following quotations from the introduction to the 'Second Draft' of the *Philosophische Weltgeschichte* (1830). The philosopher approaches history with the assumption that 'reason governs the world, and that world history is therefore a rational process' (*LPhWH* p. 28). The idea is reason revealing itself and is identified with the revelation of God to humanity:

> The *world spirit* is the spirit of the world as it reveals itself through human consciousness; the relationship of man to it is that of the single parts to the whole which is their substance. And this world spirit corresponds to the divine spirit which is the absolute spirit. Since God is omnipresent he is present in everyone and appears in everyone's consciousness; and this is the world spirit. (*LPhWH*, pp. 52–3)

Given the idea is identical with the self-revealing deity, 'philosophy itself' is intimately tied to the 'philosophy of world history' (*LPhWH*, p. 53).

Thus, Hegel's philosophy is committed to the task of advance from partial revelation of God through Christ to complete comprehension of God (*LPhWH*, p. 36). God has revealed Himself through the Christian religion: that is, He has granted humankind the possibility of recognising His nature, so that He is no longer an impenetrable mystery. The fact that knowledge of God is possible also makes it our duty to know Him, and the development of the thinking spirit which the Christian revelation of God initiated must eventually produce a situation where all that was at first present only to the emotional and representational faculties can also be comprehended by thought. Whether the time has yet come for such knowledge will depend on whether the ultimate end of the world has yet been realised in a universally valid and conscious manner (*LPhWH*, p. 40).

The penetration of the depths of godhead on the level of philosophy must parallel that on the level of history. Just as, in the former, justification is to be found within the presentation of the system itself, in the latter the validity of the thesis depends upon history itself (*LPhWH*, p.29).[15] Thus, the actual existence of a specific historical world – essentially the bourgeois Protestant world – is, as Emile Fackenheim has remarked, the cardinal condition for the Hegelian philosophy to be. That does not mean that either philosophy or history is a closed process in fact but simply that, whilst the philosopher cannot 'leap over Rhodes', philosophy is the 'rose in the cross of the present' – the meeting point of the eternal in the temporal. For history to be construed as a meaningful process it must be closed in idea even whilst being unfinished in fact.[16]

---

15. Compare *Phenomenology*, para. 785, para. 808.

16. *See* Forbes, 'Introduction' and R. Plant, *Hegel: An Introduction*, 2nd edn, Oxford, 1983, ch. 10.

Croce's critical appraisal and appropriation of the Hegelian linking of philosophy and history can now be brought into focus. Croce fully appreciated the significance of the religious dimension in Hegel's thought:

It is a (I would say the only) profoundly irreligious philosophy, because it is not content to oppose itself to religion, or to place religion alongside itself, but resolves religion into itself and substitutes itself for it. And so, from another point of view, it can be called the only highly religious philosophy, because its task is to satisfy the need for religion in a rational manner, which is the highest of all human needs (p. 48).

Croce elaborates his analysis of this aspect of Hegel in an appendix added to the 1912 edition of his study on 'The concept of becoming and Hegelianism'.[17] In this essay, Croce defines the true concept of progress as the dialectical movement of particular and universal, in which the first is continually adding to and changing the latter. He construes this thesis in terms of a philosophical Christianity:

The symbol of humanity is neither God nor man but the God-Man, Christ, who is the eternal in the temporal and the temporal in the eternal: History from which it is superfluous to demand the future, since it already contains the future within it (p. 160).

Spirit and history are thus linked together in a process of becoming. Through thought, we possess truth whilst at the same time changing it, creating new truth. Truth to be found, discovered, must at the same time be possessed. In this way, transcendence is denied and there is just humankind's self-discovery through history:

There is no divine logic beyond human logic: but human logic, the true human logic, is divine. The distinction between the two logics is not philosophical, but theological, or a residue of theology in philosophy (p. 163).

In his own philosophy, Croce seeks to take forward the Hegelian project in a radical manner so as to offer a humanist and secular alternative to Christianity. This goal is to be achieved by seeing in human history a secular equivalent to salvation and eternal life in the hereafter. In this respect, Croce's criticism of Hegel is that he has failed to go far enough in his reduction of philosophy to the manifestation of spirit in history. If history is seen as an open-ended process, then there can be no fulfilment, the realisation of the eternal within the temporal must be an on-going project. Indeed, the eternal only is truly immanent to the extent that there is no end point in which it is fully realised. Thus, Croce keeps to his view that Hegel is guilty of 'panlogism' (p. 153). However, he now develops his own historicist doctrine. He argues that both 'moments' – the eternal and the temporal – must be seen as intertwined in time. He links this argument to his 'nexus of

---

17. Croce, *Saggio sullo Hegel*, pp. 145–72.

distincts'. For Croce, the dialectical unity of the levels of spirit, which are empty of all content but that which spirit provides in the course of history, is the solution to the Hegelian problem of progress:

> The true concept of progress must therefore adapt itself to two opposite conditions, the joining at every moment of the true and the good, and the putting in doubt at each new moment without however losing that which has been gained, of a perpetual solution and a perpetual resurging problem for a new solution: it must avoid the two opposed unilateral solutions of a final and obtainable end, and of an unobtainable end, of a *progressus ad finitum* and a *progressus ad infinitum* (pp. 159–60).

Croce incorporates this identification of philosophy and history as the unity of spirit's progressive self-realisation into his view of philosophy as the methodology of history. The central problem, as conceived by idealism, lies in the nature of the objectivity of a world that is only experienced subjectively and which, it is argued, derives its meaning through subjective experience. Self-knowledge in this way becomes the path towards truth. Philosophy conceived of as the method of history is the logic of this movement of self-elucidation. Croce, returning, significantly enough, to Vico's criticism of the Cartesian cogito, regarded philosophy as a progressive movement of self-discovery, whereby the stream of existence itself constitutes its own meaning. The Cartesian ontological position thereby gets a significant twist. The ontic meaning is no longer transcendentally constituted but is held to come into being and to develop through humankind in historical existence. It is through human thought and action upon the world that the real is perceived as rational and the rational real.

Croce criticises Hegel for regarding his own philosophy as the culmination of this historical process, whereby humanity proceeds through stages of self-reflection to the stage of universal self-reflection – a teleological account that he then imposes on the actual historical record. In its place, Croce proposes a view of history as the history of human thought and action in which no such final stage is assumed or reached. Our rational appropriation of reality is always a 'historical judgment' in which the universal and the particular are brought together as we evaluate our historically given circumstances and consider how to act. Yet, such judgments are always partial, not least because they are bound to the concepts and context of a given time and place; and through thinking about the world and judging it, we act upon it in ways that alter it in unpredictable ways that become in their turn the material for future history. In the process both the world and the content of our concepts of it change.[18]

Following Hegel, Croce regards his philosophy as giving expression to a religious and specifically Christian insight and he regularly employs religious language in his philosophical writings, frequently invoking Providence and Grace,

---

18. This argument was developed most fully in B. Croce, *La storia come pensiero e come azione*, Bari, 1938.

and even talking of immortality.[19] Yet, as he makes clear in a famous essay of 1942 on 'Why we cannot not call ourselves Christians',[20] he conceives the truth of Christianity to be poorly served by any notion of a transcendent God outside human thought and action. The 'profound revolution' wrought by Christianity had consisted in awakening the 'moral conscience' within individuals by making us responsible for our personal salvation through the performance of God's will. However, he thinks that belief is better captured by his humanist historicism than the teachings of the Church. For salvation and morality involve attending to the circumstances in which we find ourselves and the impact our conduct has on human history through its effects on the people around us. The pursuit of a celestial paradise constitutes an immoral escape from the world and its tribulations. We apprehend the eternal and attain true immortality in acting responsibly towards those others whose lives we affect and in who we consequently continue to live.[21] Human beings live on through playing a responsible part in the stream of human history.

Nevertheless, it can be questioned whether Croce has thereby side-stepped the problems he had identified in Hegel's philosophy, as he claims. As we saw, his distinct moments are the 'pure' concepts of the good, and beautiful, and so on, which lack content precisely because they are 'pure'. Spirit has been rendered completely immanent so as to be identified with the dialectic of human thought and action in history, which alone can give meaning and content to these 'concepts'. Croce's philosophy seems to involve either cultural relativism, the belief that beauty, truth and morality simply are what they are deemed to be in different times and places, or a blind faith in the inherent rationality and progress of human history. Indeed, much of his subsequent philosophical writing seeks to navigate between these two positions in the struggle to avoid any attempt to evolve transcendental, ahistorical criteria of judgement.[22]

Croce's own philosophy, therefore, arises out of this attempt to liberate what he regards as the living from what he deemed to be the dead in Hegel's thought. On the one hand, Croce appreciates the nature of the Hegelian dialectic sufficiently to make it his own. He also fully understands its religious context and its links to a philosophy of history via which *Geist* becomes fully self-conscious. However, he seeks to detach the dialectic from both these aspects of Hegelian thought. Instead,

19. *See*, for example, B. Croce, 'L'individuo, la grazia e la provvidenza', *La critica* XVIII, 1920, pp. 123–5.

20. B. Croce, 'Perché non possiamo non dirci "Cristiani"', *La critica* XL (1942), pp. 289–97.

21. These points emerge clearly from his epistolary exchange with Mario Curtopassi, which forms part of the background to his essay. *See* Giovanni Russo (ed.), Benedetto Croce, Maria Curtopassi, *Dialogo su dio: carteggio 1941–1952*, Archinto, 2007, and my review R. Bellamy, 'Christian at heart', *TLS*, 4 February 2009.

22. This problem is confronted most clearly in one of Croce's last writings on Hegel – an imagined dialogue with the German philosopher first published 1949 as B. Croce, 'Una pagina sconosciuta degli ultimi mesi della vita di Hegel', in *Indagini sul Hegel*, pp. 3–28. Croce's wavering between relativism and an immanent teleology is explored in Chapter Six of this collection.

he aspires to offer a secular version of Hegel's thesis, whereby individual human beings are not, as he believes Hegel had argued, creatures of some transcendent puppet master – spirit, the idea or God – gradually unfolding a divine plan in the world, but the architects of their own destiny, giving meaning to the world through their own developing thought and action upon it. On the other hand, he credits Hegel with the discovery of the 'concrete universal', the true absolute in which the finite and the infinite are necessary as such to the 'philosophy' which overcomes them. Yet, he also sees these two moments as being in constant, creative tension with each other. Humans apprehend the rational in the real through thought, yet that promotes them to act upon reality, changing it and creating a new context for thought that prompts new actions. In a similar manner, he also regards the different branches of human knowledge and activity as distinct, if related, aspects of the human spirit, which ought not to be confused with each other or treated as different stages of human self-consciousness. Once again, he believes Hegel's error lay in regarding it as possible to have a definitive synthesis between the universal and the particular, and of the transcendence or absorption of supposedly lower into higher forms of activity or social organisation. By contrast, as we saw, Croce's nexus of the distinct moments of spirit is an attempt to do justice to the plurality of human accomplishments and to retain the openness of history. The content of the basic concepts of human thinking is supplied through human thought and action, which is historically conditioned yet the product of individual free will and creativity rather than the unfolding of some immanent guiding principle.

Croce's sympathetic critique yields a genuinely humanist and liberal reading of Hegel that is shorn of its metaphysics. In certain respects, Croce's enterprise prefigures a number of more recent attempts to retrieve the method of the German philosopher by detaching it from his overarching philosophical system.[23] An evaluation of the accuracy of the criticisms of Hegel that motivate this enterprise lies outside the scope of this article. The chief aim has been to show how Croce's own views derive from this critique, representing an attempt to develop the living within the Hegelian programme without relying on its supposedly dead components. However, the coherence of this project has been questioned. For, in rightly renouncing attempts to articulate the meaning of history as flawed, it appears to rest nevertheless on an unarticulated faith in the meaningfulness of each individual's contribution to that history. As we shall see in considering Croce's political writings in the next chapter, that faith was to be sorely tested by the momentous historical events of the twentieth century which he was fated to live through – not least the First World War and the rise of fascism, both of which he opposed as irrational and illusory.

---

23. The key work in this contemporary endeavour is Charles Taylor's, *Hegel*, Cambridge, 1975, especially ch. 3.

Chapter Six

A Modern Interpreter: Benedetto Croce and the Politics of Italian Culture[1]

In his classic study of intellectuals, Zygmunt Bauman distinguishes between modern legislators and post-modern interpreters.[2] According to Bauman, intellectual legislators offer a preconceived model of social order based on supposedly constant and universal precepts of human nature, justice and social organisation. They contend that their 'scientific' methods and forms of reasoning give them access to a superior and more objective knowledge of the world and its values than non-intellectuals can possess. They claim the authority, therefore, to arbitrate between differences of opinion and to provide criteria for the whole range of human activity, from definitions of artistic taste and moral judgment to accounts of validity in the natural sciences. He associates this group with the philosophes and the so-called 'Enlightenment project'.[3] By contrast, interpreters only harbour universalistic ambitions within their specific domain or culture. Bauman links this type of intellectual with the post-modern view of the world as possessing an infinite number of models of order arising out of the various spheres of life and different communities, each with their semi-autonomous set of practices. Rather than imposing a universal order upon these diverse provinces of human endeavour, the interpreter seeks merely to explicate the meanings they instantiate and to facilitate communication between them.[4]

Behind these two images of the intellectual lie two corresponding conceptions of the relationship of knowledge to political power. Bauman argues that the legislator had great appeal for, and was to a large degree encouraged by, the increasingly centralised and bureaucratic states of the eighteenth, nineteenth and early twentieth centuries.[5] These possessed both the resources and will to implement the legislator's technocratic social vision. In principle, the legislator's ideal was both democratic and emancipatory. The republic of reason, where all claims are treated openly, equally and impartially, was to replace the kingdom of custom and convention, where privilege held sway under the cover of obscure precedents and traditions.

1. I am grateful to Alan Cromartie and Jeremy Jennings for comments on an earlier version. Research for this paper was supported by an ESRC grant ROOO222402 on 'Intellectuals and Political Culture'.

2. Z. Bauman, *Legislators and Interpreters: On modernity, post-modernity and intellectuals*, Cambridge: Polity Press, 1987.

3. Bauman, *Legislators and Interpreters*, pp. 2–4.

4. *Ibid.*, pp. 4–5.

5. *Ibid.*, p. 2.

In practice, however, this ideal has always proved utopian. Instead, a recalcitrant population has had to be disciplined by an elite acting in its supposed best interests. Recently, however, the legislator has gradually given way to the interpreter as societies have grown in complexity and plurality, thereby lessening the powers of the state to manage social life, on the one hand, and diminishing the prospects of a unified and universal public sphere, on the other. Superficially, interpreters seem less elitist and more populist than legislators. They look for the orderings implicit in the understandings and practices of ordinary people rather than attempting to reorder them according to a more rational schema of their own devising.[6] But the 'best' interpretation can be as contentious as the 'true' or 'rational' ordering of the world. Avoiding any such claims, however, leads to either a conservative and relativist strategy, which permits oppressive traditions to go unchallenged, or an emotivist subjectivism, which allows for as many interpretations as can be successfully asserted. With substantive criteria jettisoned, rival interpretations can be evaluated only by either the stylishness of their presentation or their apparent, short-term, pragmatic utility. Neither position leaves room for criticism or reform. Meanwhile, if intellectuals no longer provide an external legitimation of these practices deriving from superior and objective knowledge, then their own activity becomes but one more self-validating and autonomous profession cut off from, and with no special authority over, the rest of social life. From a valued advisor to princes, the intellectual risks becoming either a court jester or an ivory-tower academic dependent on state or private charity.

Bauman places in an historical and sociological perspective many of the problems and criticisms that typically arise when intellectuals engage with politics. As legislators, they risk condemnation for being elitist social engineers or demagogues; as interpreters they get attacked as populists pandering to the lowest common denominator, as fawning or decorative dilettantes concerned merely to amuse, or as conceited and irrelevant Olympians, who stick to their academic specialism and remain aloof from the affairs of the world. Moreover, he shows that how intellectuals respond to these dilemmas has more to do with their social role and epistemology than with their ideology *per se*, though the latter reflects the former to some extent.

Though more nuanced than this brief summary can suggest, Bauman's account is none the less too neat. This article challenges one feature in particular – the missing figure of the 'modern' interpreter. If Bauman grants that most interpreters are to some degree legislators,[7] he overlooks the whole Hegelian tradition's attempt at an interpretative defence of modernity that revealed its intrinsic rationality.[8] These modern interpreters prefigured much of the post-modern

---

6.   *Ibid.*, pp. 4, 197.

7.   *Ibid.*, pp. 6, 194–6.

8.   *See* R. B. Pippin, *Modernism as a Philosophical Problem: On the dissatisfactions of European high culture*, Oxford: Blackwell, 1991 and his *Idealism as Modernism: Hegelian variations*, Cambridge: Cambridge University Press, 1997.

critique of the Enlightenment's supposed abstract universalism; but they proposed to put in its place not the mere historical contingency of the post-modernist but a concrete universalism that located the rational within the real.[9] As such, they claimed to avoid the legislator's insensitivity to cultural differences and particular circumstances without falling into the equally problematic historicist relativism of the post-modern interpreter.

Benedetto Croce provides an interesting case study of this missing position. A contemporary of Max Weber and George Simmel, he shared their awareness of the constraining as well as the emancipatory potential of modernity – not least because he lived to witness both fascism and Soviet socialism as the embodiment of certain aspects of its downside. Like them, he sought a more philosophically modest and historically concrete appreciation of liberalism and modernism, which parallels attempts by post-modern thinkers to uncouple these movements from the type of programmatic thinking he, too, associated with the Enlightenment. But he was also made all too aware of the aforementioned drawbacks of a non-foundational and historicist stance – its potential degeneration into conservative relativism, subjectivism or the purely 'academic'. As we shall see, his was a highly self-conscious attempt to defend an engaged and critical political role for the philosophical interpreter operating in advanced (if not post-) modern times. I shall start by outlining Croce's historicist philosophy of interpretation, commenting on the parallels and differences between his thinking and that of post-modern interpreters. I shall then explore how this theory both informed and was influenced by his practice as an intellectual, noting how he was led to review his position as he found himself falling into the various dilemmas of the interpreter's stance outlined above.

The historicist philosophy of a modern interpreter

Croce consistently tried to steer a path between what he regarded as the Charybdis of empiricist and materialist theories, such as the prevailing versions of utilitarianism, positivism and Marxism, and the Scylla of transcendentalism, initially identified with contemporary scholastic and Catholic doctrines and in later years with Gentile's 'actualist' version of idealism.[10] Like post-modern interpreters, he associated these two positions with intellectual legislation. The distinctiveness of his interpretative stance lies in his attempt to overcome their respective failings rather than simply jettisoning them.

Croce's attack on empiricism and materialism centred on attempts by socialists and democrats of the positivist school to construct a rational, scientific and humanist social morality on the basis of supposed universal social laws and human

9. For an example of the post-modernist's relationship to German idealism, *see* Richard Rorty's discussion in *Contingency, Irony and Solidarity*, Cambridge: Cambridge University Press, 1989, pp. 4–9.

10. For details of the evolution of Croce's views, see my *Modern Italian Social Theory: Ideology and politics from Pareto to Bobbio*, Cambridge: Polity Press, 1987, ch. 5.

tendencies, such as the ability to receive sensations and to reason about them. The goal of such schemes was to produce an enlightened age of humanity, committed to liberty, tolerance, equality and fraternity. He caricatured this aspiration as 'the Masonic mentality,' an attitude he traced to the French *philosophes* and British thinkers such as Godwin or Bentham who were influenced by them.[11] His criticisms of this alleged mentality parallel many aspects of the post-modernist critique of the Enlightenment, including its arguably selective and tendentious view of that movement. Like others in the idealist tradition, Croce contended that our desires and impulses are moulded by human consciousness rather than creating it. Moreover, such consciousness is social as well as individual, the product of communal norms and practices. Thus, the core values of the Masonic religion of humanity are not universal but have to be understood and evaluated contextually. He thought it impossible to generalise from one context to another, since the character and importance of toleration, equality and so on varies greatly between different types of society. Attempts to devise universal declarations of human rights or principles of justice were misguided, therefore. Such projects simply reified an empirical example or class of examples of certain historical understandings of these values or principles. Not only do different circumstances have their own peculiarities, they also (and more crucially from his perspective) present themselves differently to different individuals and cultures. People reason in ways that reflect their distinctive beliefs and priorities. Liberty, say, as seen through the eyes of citizens of the ancient *polis* simply is not the same concept as the freedom of modern traders in an economic market. The 'Masonic mentality' was doubly confused, therefore. Not only did it mistake analytical categories useful for grouping similar types of empirical phenomena, such as forms of democratic regime, for normative criteria, it also overlooked the very different normative assumptions underlying superficially similar human practices. At best, Croce believed the 'Masonic mentality' encouraged sloppy thinking by making it appear that actions and policies could be easily pigeonholed within certain preset categories. At worst, however, it fostered the desire to shape human affairs according to these categories. Either way, ideals that were little more than parochial prejudices were imposed on a far more complex reality.

Croce adopted a somewhat different tack against transcendental appeals to 'pure reason,' an attitude he identified less with the Kantian strand of the Enlightenment than with Platonism.[12] Here, too, there are post-modern echoes, with his assault on the 'cloud-loving', 'friends of the transcendent' being not unlike their criticisms of 'Platonic' and 'rationalist' aspirations to discover the ideal behind the real. Croce identified six defining features of this approach,

---

11. Croce expressed these criticisms in numerous places. A good programmatic statement is his 'La "mentalità massonica"' (1910), in Croce, *Cultura e vita morale: intermezzi polemici*, 3rd edn, Bari: Laterza, 1955, pp. 143–50.

12. For a similar tendency to regard Kant's (like Hegel's) attempt to combine rationalism and empiricism as vitiated by his continuing 'Platonism', *see* Rorty, *Contingency, Irony and Solidarity*, pp. 31–5 (and on Hegel, p. 26).

rejecting each of them.[13] First, he considered the emphasis on some ultimately unifying truth, ideal, value or principle lying behind the messy reality of everyday life as a denial of the distinctiveness of separate spheres of human endeavour. One of the cornerstones of Croce's philosophy was his insistence on the distinctions between aesthetic, logical, 'economic' (instrumental/practical) and ethical activity. He contended that those who sought truth or utility in art, for example, had simply misunderstood and to some degree perverted the nature of artistic creativity. These four areas involved incommensurable value systems reflecting diverse modes of reasoning, with art the realm of intuition, truth of logic, action of will, morality of judgment. Foreshadowing Max Weber,[14] he argued that what was beautiful need not be true, that a tension frequently arose between the good and the useful and so on. Moreover, these were 'pure' categories that historically were subject to considerable variations as to content. What appeared beautiful, true, useful or good in one context need not be so in another.

Second, Croce accused proponents of this position of searching for a 'fundamental problem'. He maintained that an infinite number of philosophical problems were thrown up in the course of human history. Though linked through being part of the historical process, they could not be construed as aspects of a single problem. Nor was any problem more basic than the others, even if each was in some, usually unfathomable, sense based on what had gone before and formed the basis for what followed. We encountered these problems in responding to the particular demands and challenges thrown up by the various activities we happened to pursue. We thought philosophically in contextualising the problem within the practices and modes of thought that shape a way of life. Even the problems of God or the nature of reality were, for Croce, particular problems that changed through history.

Third, Croce argued that belief in a 'fundamental problem' led to the further error of a vain search for a definitive philosophy. Like the two aforementioned features, the desire for a complete and conclusive systematisation of everything was a denial of the openness of history and lived experience. It harked back to theological modes of thought and a view of metaphysics as the 'resolution of the mystery of the universe, knowledge of the ultimate reality, revelation of the noumenal world'.[15] He maintained that though every philosophy aimed at a definitive answer to the problems presently confronting it, new problems requiring novel solutions were raised in the process. Instead of a definitive system, Croce argued, philosophers offered at best a series of systematisations of their thought, which tracked their attempts to tackle the problems arising from their earlier theories

---

13. Croce also reiterated this position on many occasions. The key articles in this regard are Croce, 'Filosofia e metodologia', which appears as an appendix to his *Teoria e storia della storiografia*, Bari: Laterza, 1917, pp. 136–48, and his reply to criticisms of this piece, 'Contro i sistemi definitivi', republished in *Cultura e vita morale*, pp. 201–9.

14. M. Weber, 'Science as a vocation', in H. H. Gerth and C. W. Mills (eds) *From Max Weber*, London: Routledge, 1948, pp. 147–8.

15. Croce, 'Filosofia e metodologia,' p. 137.

and new experiences. However, Croce was careful not to present this procedure as leading to ever-closer approximations to some eternal and single truth, though he confessed he had been attracted to this notion in his earliest writings. Instead of either a static or a progressively evolving system, he saw his own philosophy as, at best, a framework in continuous elaboration. It developed piecemeal by providing provisional solutions to the specific series and groups of problems that interested him at particular times. Thus, he wrote books on aesthetics, logic, Vico, Hegel, Dante, Shakespeare and so on, but not a systematic treatise providing an answer to all possible problems or the fundamental problem.

The remaining three features Croce associated with 'transcendental' or 'metaphysical' points of view relate respectively to their notion of the philosopher's role, culture and language. The fourth feature was the 'metaphysicians' habit of treating the philosopher as,

> a kind of Buddha or 'awoken one', who sees himself as superior to others (and to himself in those moments when he is not a philosopher), because, thanks to philosophy, he believes himself now liberated from human illusions, passions and tumults.[16]

Such figures aimed to be 'pure' philosophers, concerned with the abstract and general questions that lie behind and above the complicated particularities of everyday life. Their culture and training, the fifth feature he identified, was consequently a rarefied one, concerned solely with the books of other philosophers dealing with similarly 'big' questions. Philosophising degenerated into a reflexive commentary on a circumscribed canon of other philosophers. Those thinkers, such as Machiavelli and Vico, who engaged with more particular and supposedly less important issues, when recognised as philosophers at all, were relegated to a minor league. Finally, their philosophical discourse, the sixth feature associated with this mode of thinking, became similarly rarefied, being either aridly systematic and schematic or high-flown and rhetorical, depending on the particular bent of the philosopher concerned.[17]

Croce's critiques of empiricist and transcendental modes of philosophising involved a clear rejection of the intellectual as legislator. In different ways, the 'enlightened', 'Masonic' *philosophe* and the 'Buddha-like' 'metaphysician' claim knowledge of the underlying nature of reality, be it in certain natural forces or a basic principle. It is this claim that entitles them to validate or not beliefs and practices of all kinds, times and places and to prescribe a model social order. As he noted in a review of Benda's *La trahison des clercs*,[18] if the positivist's treachery stems from 'the sophism of attributing absolute value to empirical concepts [...] and confusing them with spiritual categories', so that a given nation or class

16. *Ibid.*, p. 144.
17. *Ibid.*, pp. 147–8.
18. Croce, 'Il tradimento degli intellettuali' (1928), in *Pagine sulla guerra*, 2nd edn, Bari: Laterza, 1928, pp. 348–50.

becomes the carrier of Truth and Justice, that mistake cannot be avoided by seeking to separate the intellectual 'clerisy' from the 'laity'. Rather, this strategy compounds the error by either cutting intellectuals off from all contact with the world or, more usually – given this separation is almost impossible – leads them to seek to subordinate the earthly city to their preferred version of heaven. Like post-modern interpreters, he faults both positions for paying insufficient attention to the localised common sense of ordinary people and to the concrete differences that distinguish the spheres, traditions and practices within and between societies.

Little wonder that, in setting out his own immanent philosophy of 'absolute historicism', much of what Croce had to say mirrors elements of post-modern theories of interpretation. Croce rejected the form of historicism he termed 'panlogism', which sees history as what post-modern thinkers have called a 'grand narrative', involving the immanent working out of a master principle.[19] Croce denied the possibility of a universal history based on constant natural or social forces, as in Marx; unchanging human passions, as in Hume; or some metaphysical idea, as in Hegel. Rather, his appeal to history was 'absolute' in the sense of being concerned with the thought of human agents acting in concrete historical circumstances.[20] Philosophy he characterised as the 'methodological moment of historiography' or 'historical judgment'.[21] Methodology is used here in a somewhat broad and largely non-empirical sense as the opposite of 'metaphysical'. Crocean historical methodology has two elements. On the one hand, historical judgment involves contextualising action through an empathetic understanding of the concepts and thought that lie behind it. By contrast to the judgments of 'masons' and 'metaphysicians,' historical judgment cannot transcend borders, boundaries or periods. It is always particular to the location, sphere and age within which it is exercised. As he put it in a famous example, an historical understanding of Neolithic man depends on our capacity to 'mentally make ourselves Neolithic'. If that proves impossible, then all we can do is describe and catalogue Neolithic artefacts.[22] We have 'chronicle' not 'history'.[23] Likewise, our own action has to be seen as being oriented by the norms implicit in the on-going practices and traditions in which we are engaged. Historical judgment defines our present activity and provides the source of values that motivate action.[24] On the other hand, Croce did not wish to suggest that we were simply creatures of custom and incapable of breaking free from prevailing conventions. Quite the contrary, he

---

19. J.-F. Lyotard, *The Postmodern Condition*, Manchester: Manchester University Press, 1984 offers the *locus classicus* of this argument. Croce's culprits are much the same as the post-modernists.

20. For his mature exposition of this thesis, *see* the essays in Croce, *Il carattere della filosofia moderna*, 2nd revised edn, Bari: Laterza, 1945, chs I and IX (postille 2).

21. Croce, 'Filosofia e metodologia', pp. 136–7. *See also* the second (1909) edition of the *Logica come scienza del concetto puro*, 2nd edn Economica, Bari: Laterza, 1971, pp. 84–93, 121–31.

22. Croce, *Teoria e storia della storiografia*, p. 119.

23. Croce, *Teoria e storia della storiografia*, ch. 1.

24. Croce, *La storia come pensiero e come azione*, pp. 33–4.

contended that to think about either the past or our present situation was always to rethink those circumstances in ways that fostered new action. We engaged in what contemporary proponents of interpretation often characterise as an 'internal' critique. To write about Shakespeare, say, was both to think through Shakespeare's creative process and to develop one's own aesthetic ideas. Similarly, current action always involved placing oneself within the historical stream but only as a matter of preliminary orientation. Although 'products of the past' and 'immersed within it,' we created new action through 'thought, which does not break the relationship with the past' or pretend we are somehow 'outside' it but 'ideally soars above it and coverts it into knowledge'.[25] Not only was 'all history contemporary history,' as he famously observed,[26] but also all contemporary thought and action was historical, in being both part and a development of a historical form of life.[27]

Unsurprisingly, the picture of the intellectual resulting from this conception of philosophy as historical methodology shares many of the attributes of Bauman's 'interpreter'. Croce believed we reasoned through interpreting and hence reinterpreting (or as he put it 're-presenting') the meanings implicit in the practice in which we are engaged or the communal tradition of which we form a part. Philosophical interpretation not only defines the character of the problem we are tackling and the practice to which its solution contributes but is also the means whereby we understand the endeavours of others and render our own intelligible to them. Thus, Croce accompanied each of the volumes of his *Philosophy of Spirit* with a history of earlier treatments of aesthetics, logic, ethics and historiography and presented his own argument as an interpretation of previous views of these fields. At the same time, it was through writing such histories that he sought to explain his enterprise to others, to induct them into these various branches of knowledge and make them aware of their distinctive criteria and methods.

Interpreters must be specialists but they are not a special cadre. There can be no general philosophy of everything that abstracts universal principles from the particular activities of different people in different times and places. Rather than a distinct meta-profession, philosophy is an aspect of all human activity. The 'historical philosopher' cannot distance himself from the world and 'feels himself ineluctably taken up in the course of history, at one and the same time object and subject of history'.[28] In an essay of 1930, Croce ventured he had literally 'killed off' the traditional figure of 'The Philosopher' who:

---

25. Croce, *La storia come pensiero e come azione*, pp. 33–4.
26. Croce, *Teoria e storia della storiografia*, pp. 3–6.
27. Croce, *La storia come pensiero e come azione*, pp. 33–5.
28. Croce, 'Filosofia e metodologia', p. 144.

ignores history, art and poetry, politics, law, human passions, who reads neither the novel of life nor the novels written about it; and who nevertheless believes that he, who has grasped the supreme principle, not only is qualified to discourse on these matters, but that, in discussing them raises, transforms and validates them having given them, in effect, and from the outside, his stamp of approval.[29]

Instead, everyone is an intellectual interpreter to some extent, even if some are more self-conscious and thorough than others. For 'every man is (within his sphere, however narrow or wide it may seem) a philosopher, and every philosopher is a man, inextricably linked to the conditions of human life, which cannot be transcended by any means'.[30] So conceived, philosophers do not enjoy any superior status as the purveyors of a profounder or more 'enlightened' kind of knowledge. They speak the 'prose' of ordinary men and women, not the poetry or mystical runes of an elite academic caste. In characteristically provocative manner, he even suggested that 'a powerful advancement of philosophical culture' ought to lead to the disappearance of all Chairs of Philosophy as 'all the scholars of human affairs, jurists, economists, ethicists, literature specialists, in sum all scholars of historical matters, become self-conscious and disciplined philosophers'.[31]

If the above makes Croce an interpreter, how does he differ from post-modernists? His place in the modernist camp arises from the attempt to unite rather than to replace philosophy with history in ways that preserve as well as criticise elements of both empiricist naturalism and rationalist transcendentalism. From the former, Croce took his insistence that effective practical action had to be based on a thorough knowledge of the historical context in which the agent operated. He also believed that, at a 'purely' practical level, we acted in a largely instrumental manner and in accord with our passions. From the latter, he derived the view that the 'facts' of these circumstances were in part a product of how the agent perceives them. Though our reasoning about action is shaped by local conventions and circumstances, however, it is none the less intersubjectively intelligible and reflects certain universal criteria of rationality. His proposed unity of historiography and philosophy aspired to combine the two views by showing how our reasoning is grounded in, but is not simply a reflection of, a transcendent rationality and an objective reality. Rather, there is an interplay between the two. We are autonomous, reflective and rational agents acting in concrete cultures and circumstances. The actions of others are thereby recognisable as reasonable or unreasonable responses to given conditions – history could not be written otherwise. Yet what makes them such requires a thick description, since there are no general rules of thumb determining how people ought to act in all conceivable situations.[32]

---

29. Croce, 'Il Filosofo,' in *Ultimi saggi*, Bari: Laterza, 1935, p. 90. On this piece, *see* the incisive article by Norberto Bobbio in his *Italia civile: Ritratti e testimonianze*, Florence: Passigli editore, 1986, pp. 69–93.

30. Croce, 'Filosofia e metodologia', p. 144.

31. *Ibid.*, p. 145.

32. On the above, *see* Croce, *La storia come pensiero e come azione*, pp. 11–14.

Combining empiricism and rationalism, universalism and social relativism, instrumental and autonomous agency created various tensions. These are apparent from the changing interpretations he gave to the Hegelian motto that 'What is rational, is real, and what is real, is rational',[33] which held a central place in his historicist doctrine. The German term rendered above as 'real' is '*wirklich*' and derives from the German verb to act, '*wirken*'. By playing on the double sense of '*wirklich*,' either as a given reality or as what is made actual by action, it is possible to argue either that history *per se* is rational, or that it becomes rational through its actualisation. Croce tended to vacillate between various versions of these two positions before attempting to unite them. Thus, at times he gave the appearance of making individuals seem the tool of either an unfolding transcendent principle or evolving material forces,[34] even if he articulated this thesis in quasi-Weberian terms as a Calvinist-like faith that, in following their vocations, they were contributing in some important, if necessarily obscure, way to the ineffable and ultimately benign working of Providence.[35] Though Croce had a puritanical devotion to the notion of self-justification through work in and for itself,[36] this providentialist argument had little appeal for others, even if it did resonate with some during World War I. However, the more activist view held other perils, given his concern to escape a sort of transcendental subjectivism, on the one hand, and pragmatism, on the other. The former was a danger of Gentile's 'actualism', which reduced all action to the 'pure act of thought'; the latter of Marxian theories of praxis, which risked making whatever worked right, and confused empirical and normative categories. Moreover, both attitudes, as we have seen, are clear risks of the interpreter's view that has dropped all universal and objective criteria of truth and rationality.

It was only in his essays from the mid-1920s that Croce confronted these difficulties head-on in his 'ethico-political' view of history.[37] Here, he acknowledged the normative implications of his conception of human action as being the product of historical interpretation. The thesis that history was the history of liberty, because the result of the reflective action of situated autonomous agents, entailed universal claims about human reason – but ones, he maintained,

---

33. G. W. F. Hegel, *Philosophy of Right*, trans. T. M. Knox, Oxford: Clarendon Press, 1952, p. 10.

34. He even misquotes the Hegelian aphorism in his *Cio 'che e 'vivo e cio 'che e 'morto della filosofia di Hegel*, in *Saggio sullo Hegel e altri studi*, Bari: Laterza, 1913, p. 41. For an example of the tendency to treat individuals as cyphers of spirit, *see* Croce, *Teoria e storia della storiografia*, p. 87, where he characterises history as the work 'not of the empirical and unreal individual, but of that truly real individual which is spirit eternally individualising itself'. *See*, too, *La filosofia della practica: economia ed etica* (1909), 2nd edn, Bari: Laterza, 1915, pp. 174–5.

35. *See* his essays of 1920 'L'individuo, la grazia e la provvidenza,' and 'La provvidenza', in *Frammenti di etica*, republished in his *Etica e politica*, 2nd edn economica, Bari: Laterza, 1973, pp. 92–4, 94–7.

36. This austere devotion to work in and for itself, emerges clearly from Croce's autobiographical *Contributo alla critica di me stesso*, reprinted in *Etica e politica*, pp. 309–84 and even more so his unpublished work diaries discussed in G. Sasso, *Per invigilare me stesso: I Taccuini di lavoro di Benedetto Croce*, Bologna: Il Mulino, 1989.

37. *See* the essays gathered together as *Elementi di politica*, reprinted in *Etica e politica*, pp. 171, 307.

that could only be sustained and elaborated interpretively, through an appreciation of the historical process.[38] Thus he defended the normative superiority of modern liberal institutions over such alternatives as the fascist state not in *a priori* terms but through writing their history and showing how they were produced by and promoted the attempt to realise this ideal of reflexive, free action. Croce was forced to work through these tensions because of his role as an intellectual within Italian culture. In the next section, therefore, I shall describe the evolution of the views described above.

Croce and the politics of cultural interpretation

Marxist, fascist and certain radical discussions of Croce's work have typically argued that he held an Olympian and detached attitude to politics. However, Croce was highly sensitive to such attacks. As we have seen, Croce was himself critical of the 'pure', 'ivory-tower' philosopher and deeply concerned to perform a useful social role and address concrete practical problems. This defensiveness emerges clearly from his account of his role as founder and editor of the review *La critica*. Surveying its first twelve years, he recalled how:

> For years I had suffered almost continuously from a conflict between what I was doing and what I felt, though confusedly, that I ought to be doing; a division between my practical and my theoretical self, the latter reading and writing, the former idling or seeking satisfaction in various scattered and disconnected ways; between a kind of studies devoid of any real utility and the voice of conscience upbraiding me and urging me on towards another goal. But as I worked at *La critica*, there grew up within me a calm conviction that I was giving the best that I had; that I was engaged in politics, in the broad sense of that word, doing the work at once of a student and of a citizen; so that I need no longer blush, as I had often blushed in the past, on meeting a politician or a socially active fellow citizen.[39]

However, he believed intellectuals should not confuse philosophy with politics – that was to fall into one or other of the philosophical errors that lead to becoming a 'legislator'. Instead, he sought to influence Italian political culture through a critical interpretation of its underlying values and ways of thinking. Upholding certain cultural and philosophical ideals had political ramifications but these, he insisted, were different from advocating particular policies or engaging in party politics. As he remarked of Antonio Labriola's admonition of indifference when deciding to devote himself to antiquarian research on Naples rather than working for the socialist cause, the 'thinker's toil' was 'political in its own way, within its proper sphere'.[40]

---

38. For example, Croce, *La storia come pensiero e come azione*, pp. 47–51.

39. Croce, 'Contributo alla critica di me stesso', reprinted in *Etica e politica*, pp. 334–5.

40. Croce, 'Come nacque e come morì il Marxismo teorico in Italia 1895–1900', reprinted in *Materialismo storico ed economia marxista*, 3rd edn economica, Bari. Laterza, 1978, pp. 274–5.

Croce's argument faces the obvious objection that the 'broader' conception of politics cannot be fully distinguished from the 'narrower'; that there is no distinct 'sphere' belonging to political culture that can be separated from ideological and policy matters. How did he respond to this charge? The key lay in his proposed unity of philosophy and history examined in the last section. Croce's aim was to render Italians conscious of the modern ethos informing their country's institutions. He saw his histories of Italian literature since unification, of sixteenth- and twentieth-century Italy, of the Kingdom of Naples and nineteenth-century Europe, and his numerous other studies, on the one hand, and his Philosophy of Spirit and the publication of the classics of modern philosophy, on the other, as contributing to this goal. The first offered an historically informed interpretation of the character of Italian society and politics, the second a philosophical account of the forms of agency and reasoning underlying them. Taken together, they provided not 'an' but 'the' interpretation of the nature of the new Italy and of the contemporary social reality to which it belonged. As such their status was, as he ultimately put it, 'metapolitical'. They constituted the framework of cultural values within which political action took place. This claim naturally constrains the types of legitimate or feasible political regime or policy but supposedly allows for a wide range within those parameters.

Thus, Croce's project was a quintessentially 'modern' one of revealing the inner rationality of social reality but was elaborated via the interpretation of the motivating ideals on which contemporary Italian society depended for its allegiance and successful reproduction. Its success, however, depended on integrating the two elements identified above and showing how each supported the other, so that the capacity for interpretation associated with the second was seen to be, in some sense, both a product and productive of the social and political practices embodied in the first. Though Croce's general programme remained remarkably consistent throughout his career, with its broad outlines sketched out in a personal work plan of 1902,[41] he only gradually found a satisfactory way of reconciling the two aspects of his theory. This process of clarification is instructive, since it traces his attempts to confront the main pitfalls of the 'interpreter's' stance. As we shall see, he had to counter various dangers: over-emphasising the second element and apparently justifying a form of Nietzschean voluntarism, whereby all was up for creative reinterpretation; or the first element, and appearing a conservative who simply advocated acceptance of the *status quo*; and finally of combining them in a purely pragmatic way that made it seem success was its own justification. It was only the challenge of fascism, which appeared to present all three dangers, that produced a successful synthesis. The various phases of his career as an intellectual offer an illustration of the strengths and weaknesses of the role of intellectual interpreter, therefore, and highlight the advantages of the modernist version. I shall briefly explore each of them in turn.[42]

41. Croce, *Memorie della mia vita: Appunti che sono stati adoprati e sostituiti dal 'Contributo alla critica di me stesso'*, Naples: Istituto Italiano per gli Studi Storici, 1966, pp. 25–32.

42. The following draws on and to some extent revises my earlier analyses of Croce's politics in 'Liberalism and historicism: Benedetto Croce and the political role of idealism in modern Italy

Croce's initial desire was to combat the positivist, materialist and theological currents in contemporary Italian culture. He believed these were all forms of determinism that had led his compatriots to ignore the importance of human will and ideals in motivating action. As a result, Italian society lacked the vitality it had possessed during the *Risorgimento*. His aim was to revive that spirit in a new guise. In essence, his target was intellectual legislation in all its forms. The program of *La critica* was an appropriately spirited attack on 'all attempts to put the "world in short pants" and persuade adults to return to childhood'.[43] The enthusiastic reception given to this radical clarion call is well illustrated by Giuseppe Prezzolini's ecstatic review of Croce's *Aesthetic* in his Florentine journal *Leonardo*:

> Art, from the narrow minded, vulgar and almost primitive criterion of the exact reproduction of things, increasingly affirms itself as a personal vision; and the nascent conscience of the ideal transformation of these objects forms within the artist the ever stronger desire for unreal worlds and fantastic creations – whence the aesthetic, beyond an absolute relativism, comes to place the autonomy of the imagination as its foundation, and to throw away as narrow habits the useless classifications of the old rhetoric and styles. So says the recent philosophical study of B. Croce.[44]

Croce's advocacy of the artistic 'Man-God,' to quote the title of Prezzolini's piece, seemed additionally confirmed by his long article praising Carducci as 'more than a poet', whose *Hymn to Satan* was a celebration of human history,[45] and his initial admiration for the flamboyant poetry of d'Annunzio, whose chief concern was to fashion his life into a work of art.[46] Indeed, Croce found himself courted by all the various critics of *italietta* or 'little Italy', whose dissatisfaction with the reformist liberals and social democrats who dominated Italian politics he appeared to share. Thus, praise for Sorel, whose books he prompted his own publisher to translate,[47] linked him with the revolutionary syndicalists and anarchists, whilst support for Alfredo Oriani, a relatively unknown writer who turned Italy's abortive colonial ventures into the continuation of Italy's national

1890–1952', in A. Moulakis (ed.), *The Promise of History*, Berlin/New York: de Gruyter, 1986, ch. 6 and in 'Between economic and ethical liberalism: Benedetto Croce and the dilemmas of liberal politics', *History of the Human Sciences* 4, 1991, pp. 175–95. Though influenced by the fundamental studies by Norbert Bobbio, 'Croce e la politica della cultura' and 'Benedetto Croce e il liberalismo', both in *Politica e cultura*, Turin: Einaudi, 1955, chs 7 and 13, I have modified Bobbio's periodisation and am less hostile than he is to Croce's historicist reading of liberalism.

43. Croce, 'Introduzione', *La critica* I, 1903, p. 3.
44. G. Prezzolini, 'L'uomo Dio', *Leonardo* I, 1903, pp. 3–4.
45. Croce, 'G. Carducci', *La critica* I, 1903, pp. 14–15, 21, 31.
46. Croce, 'G. D'Annunzio', *La critica* II, 1904, p. 100.
47. Croce, 'Review of G. Sorel, *Saggi di critica del marxismo*, Palermo, 1903', *La critica* I, 1903, pp. 226–8 and 'Cristianeismo, socialismo e metodo storico', *La critica* V, 1907, pp. 317–30.

mission,[48] associated him with the new imperialists. Apart from a shared distaste for the prevailing 'Masonic mentality', however, Croce's views were ideologically and philosophically some distance from the imperialists. 'A liberal and radical democrat',[49] Croce found what he called the 'decadent imperialism' of d'Annunzio and others deeply distasteful.[50] Moreover, he believed their attempts at a poetic invocation of a new Italian Empire were irrational and simply failed to connect with the realities of the Italian situation and its best traditions.

From about 1908 onwards,[51] therefore, we find Croce emphasising the providential and historicist element of his theory. 'Individuals', he noted in a famous article on 'Faith and Programmes',

'no longer feel [...] part of a greater whole, obedient to and co-operating within it, and deriving their value from the work they perform within it. Good individuality, which affirms itself only though this link, has given way to the bad individuality which believes it can affirm itself by breaking this link and lording it on its own'.

As result, there had been a general collapse of social unity and 'the great words that express this unity: King, Country, City, Nation, Church, Humanity have become cold and rhetorical'.[52] Reviving such feelings, however, could not be accomplished by any specific policy or party programme. These last were best seen as practical responses to specific problems. What was needed was a faith in the value of performing the duties of one's calling and co-operating with others, and this only came from a more general perspective on the world: namely, the belief that rather than seeking 'to create new worlds', individuals must 'continue to work upon the old, which constantly renews itself'.[53] They must hold to the conviction that 'life consists in disinterested work, that the individual manages an inheritance from the past to be passed on enriched to the future, that man is nothing as an abstract individual and everything in so far as he harmonises with the whole'.[54] As ever, theory and practice remain distinct. Practically, individuals must act simply as the particular situation demands, taking each problem as it comes and operating in a largely pragmatic and instrumental manner. Theoretically, however, they should draw consolation from the historicist faith in the ultimate rationality of history and, in this way, see their actions as contributing to an unfolding and meaningful process.

---

48. Croce, 'Alfredo Oriani', *La critica* V, 1907, pp. 1–28.

49. Croce designates himself in these terms in an autobiographical note of 1902 in Croce, *Memorie della mia vita*, p. 21.

50. 'Dannunzianesimo' and imperial decadence became synonyms in Croce's terminology.

51. That is, from the first essays later collected in Croce, *Cultura e vita morale*. The first part of this book (coinciding with the first edition of 1914) is the richest source for this second phase; the second part (which contains essays dating from Croce's debate with Gentile of 1916 over actual-ism and his subsequent break with Gentile over fascism from 1922) provides crucial material for the third phase.

52. Croce, 'Fede e programmi', 1911, in *Cultura e vita morale*, p. 163.

53. *Ibid.*, p. 162.

54. *Ibid.*, p. 166.

Positively, Croce's argument was intended as a sobering counter to wild schemes for remaking society according to the grand plan or private whim of either an individual or group. Negatively, however, it rather assumed one's duty in any particular situation was clear, as was the character of the tradition to which one was supposedly contributing. Croce studiously avoided this last issue, though. Our trust in Providence had to be blind. As a result, he came perilously close to justifying either passive resignation to one's lot or a somewhat crude pragmatism, whereby whatever worked was historically justified. Both attitudes were evident in his writings on World War I.

Croce had fiercely opposed Italy's entry into the war on the grounds that such proposals were motivated by exactly the kind of thinking he wanted to combat: 'decadent irrationalism',[55] in the case of the imperialists, or 'Masonic' programmatic thinking, in the case of democrats seeking an alliance against authoritarianism.[56] Later he would even describe the war as 'a kind of war of "historical materialism" and "philosophical irrationalism"'.[57] He argued, rightly as it turned out, that Italy was unprepared both economically and militarily. Once Italy was engaged, however, he dutifully supported the war effort. So far as the combatants were concerned, he adopted the passive position noted above and preached acceptance. 'The individual,' he wrote,

> is called upon to participate in the mystical passion of the making of Reality, and therefore in the perpetual struggle, which from the daily conflict extends to the armed struggle or war, and he cannot arrogate to himself to change the divine laws of the world but must only defend the cause of the people of which he forms a part, and maintain to the utmost the post which his particular conditions have assigned to him, with faith that from his work, loyally and rigorously fulfilled, will come the greatest good.[58]

The war itself, by contrast, he interpreted in line with the pragmatist position as a matter of pure Realpolitik. States, as practical instruments, were to be regarded simply in terms of their force and power. Success proved their superiority. Thus 'the present war' was

> a fight to which the German people, well aware that life is the right and duty of the strongest and most capable, have invited the other peoples, because the trial of facts reveals who is best prepared or best disposed to give the imprint to the new historical epoch.[59]

---

55. Croce, 'D'Annunzio e Carducci', 1915, in *Pagine sulla guerra*, pp. 55–9. This judgment grew even harsher in retrospect: *see* Croce, *Storia d'europe nel secolo decimonono*, 1931, 4th edn economica, Bari: Laterza, 1981, pp. 297–303.

56. Croce, 'Contro l'astrattismo e il materialismo politici', an article of 1912 that was revised and reproduced in 1915, reprinted in *Pagine sulla guerra*, 29–38 and in *Cultura e vita morale*, pp. 182–90. *See also* 'Contro il secolo decimottavo', 1916, in *Pagine sulla guerra*, pp. 107–11.

57. Croce, *Storia d'Italia dal 1871 al 1915*, 3rd edn economica, Bari: Laterza, 1977, p. 267.

58. Croce, 'Ritorno sulle postille precedenti', 1916, in *Pagine sulla guerra*, p. 132.

59. Quoted in D. Coli, *Croce, Laterza e la cultura europea*, Bologna: Il Mulino, 1983, pp. 147–8. Unfortunately the reference given is incorrect. For similar sentiments, however, *see* 'Lo stato come potenza', 1916, in *Pagine sulla guerra*, pp. 74–88.

Croce condemned those intellectuals who confused their patriotic duty in the practical realm with their theoretical commitment to truth and morality, so as to argue *a priori* that their own side was the repository of all that was good and their opponents of all that was evil.[60] He had suffered personally from such attitudes, being vilified for his continued admiration for German thinkers and poets.[61] However, his argument rested less on the belief that truth and morality could be upheld and more on the conviction that they only emerged *post facto* through the judgment of history itself. It was the very attempt to pronounce on these matters that was wrong, since all one could do was one's practical duty whilst adopting those methods and tools, whatever their provenance, which seemed best suited to the task at hand.[62]

If Croce avoided the *trahison des clercs*, therefore, it was at the expense of boxing himself into conservatively endorsing the *status quo* and even suggesting might was right. Confronting fascism revealed that neither position was acceptable. For he now found his erstwhile collaborator, Giovanni Gentile, apparently exploiting both these arguments to justify the fascist state. On the one hand, Gentile contended the fascist ethical state was a response to the Crocean call for social unity. It aimed to give each individual his or her place in the broader scheme of things, asking no more than that they perform their allotted task.[63] On the other hand, he infamously maintained that, since there could be no distinction between material and moral force, the fascists' seizure of power proved their moral superiority.[64] Croce was quick to reply that it was one thing to perform the duties allotted by history, quite another to presume that they could be rationally distributed according to some governmental plan. He had accepted fascism as a practical rather than a moral necessity, that latter judgment being equally a matter for history to decide.[65] These responses are clearly weak, though. It was insufficient to argue that liberal institutions were simply pragmatic responses to historical circumstances or a matter of how we traditionally do things if others could offer an alternative reading of Italian history to buttress successful alternative proposals. He needed to demonstrate the normative superiority of the liberal perspective.

It was in this context that Croce came to identify his historicism with the defence of liberalism. This argument still involved asserting that the intellectual's role was distinct from party politics as such. Gentile's case for fascism, he maintained, was the product of 'too much political philosophy' – an extension of philosophy from

---

60. Croce, 'L'entrata dell'Italia in guerra e i doveri degli studiosi', 1915, *Pagine sulla guerra*, pp. 51–4.

61. Croce, '"Germano. lia": Intervista', 1915, in *Pagine sulla guerra*, pp. 68–74.

62. Croce, 'La moralità della dottrina dello stato come potenza', 1916, in *Pagine sulla guerra*, pp. 90–1.

63. G. Gentile, *Che cosa è il fascismo: Discorsi e polemiche*, Florence: Vallecchi, 1925, p. 50.

64. Gentile, *Che cosa è il fascismo*, p. 36.

65. *See* the newspaper 'interviews' of 1923 and 1924, republished in Croce, *Pagine sparse*, 2nd edn, Bari: Laterza, 1960, vol. II, pp. 475–86.

its role as a faith or general orientation to a specific programme.[66] However, he now specified how this philosophical faith addressed the nature of reality as such and had a universal relevance for all human beings. For it consisted in nothing less than the idealist conception of history 'which because it is dialectical, is liberal, and recognises, with the necessity of struggle, the role and necessity of all the most diverse parties and of the most diverse men'.[67]

Four related features distinguished Croce's argument from the modern legislator's claim to have discovered the underlying forces moving human beings and society. First, the historicist view of the world was a critical and limiting idea rather than a philosophically inspired political programme. Second, it was an ethos rather than a doctrine. One could not abstract a clear set of general principles or axioms from this theory that might guide action in all times and places. Rules and reasons were particular to and embedded within the specific practices in which one was engaged. Within modern liberal societies, however, these practices were necessarily infused with a certain spirit that supported critical enquiry, discussion, competition and autonomous action. In particular, the historicist mind-set reflected the ethos of contemporary economic and political behaviour as embodied in markets and democracy respectively. Third, as we saw in the last section, thinking philosophically was something all agents did when they reflected critically on the context in which they found themselves. However, Croce argued that what was universal was the process of critical reflection, not the action that necessarily followed from it. Different individuals possessed different dispositions, priorities and attachments, which would lead them to evaluate the same circumstances differently. Finally, and in line with the above, the intellectual's role consisted in promoting a certain approach to life: namely, that implied by the historicist theory, and of revealing how it was implicit within the institutions of modern society, but not, qua intellectual, in entering the political lists.

These four features form a package and can be found to a lesser or greater degree in all his writings of the post-1924 period as he gradually turned his historicism into a philosophy of liberty. Thus, the first emerges in his definition of liberalism as a 'conception of life' that is 'metapolitical, above the formal theory of both politics and, in a certain sense, ethics as well, and coincides with a total conception of the world and of reality'.[68] As rival philosophies, therefore, democracy, socialism and fascism were to be rejected for their positivism and/or transcendentalism. However, the liberal view positively encouraged the presence of different parties offering rival programmes for resolving the various problems of the time. Indeed, it affirmed 'the necessity of leaving, as far as possible, free play to the inventive and spontaneous forces of individuals and social groups, because one can only expect mental, moral and economic progress from these

---

66. Croce, 'Contro la troppa filosofia politica' and 'Ancora filosofia e politica', both 1923, *Cultura e vita morale*, pp. 238–47, 248–52.

67. Croce, 'Contro la troppa filosofia politica', p. 245. *See also* the more extended discussion in 'Liberalismo', 1925, pp. 283–8.

68. Croce, 'La concezione liberale come concezione della vita', 1927, in *Etica e politica*, p. 235.

forces'.[69] The second feature enters here. Croce strongly dissented from those, such as the economist Luigi Einaudi, who argued that liberalism was only compatible with a free-market economy and a particular form of democracy.[70] He argued that socialist and authoritarian measures could often be appropriate in given circumstances. The historicist approach required problems be approached one by one with due reference to context, with different solutions being evaluated for their ability at a given time to foster the liberal ethos. It was in this spirit that Croce had supported socialism in the 1890s, as making the conditions and capacity for autonomy available to workers, and fascism in 1920–22, to prevent a breakdown of disorder in which he believed all freedom was endangered. These were necessarily contestable judgments, though Croce never went back on either of them. However, as the third feature suggested, that people would and could contest them was central to liberalism as he conceived it, since all were likely to interpret the needs of the present somewhat differently. Indeed, he now characterised the whole of history as the 'ethical-political' clash of rival ideals that different groups struggled to realise.[71] Freedom was expressed through this eternal process, however, not in progressive realisations of any particular conception of liberty.

Finally, when philosophers supported a given party programme they were like any other citizen. The 'philosophical cretinism' of Gentile and his fellow fascist intellectuals lay in their attempt to turn particular practical judgments into dogma. As his famous 'Protest' against Gentile's *Manifesto of Fascist Intellectuals* insisted, the intellectual's duty was 'to raise equally all men and all parties to a higher spiritual level, so that, with ever more beneficial results, they fought the necessary battles'.[72] The place of intellectuals was as members of the 'party of culture' and proponents of the 'metapolitical' view of liberalism.[73] In other words, their duty was to enthuse everyone with a commitment to being active, autonomous participants within a liberal society. However, such enthusiasm came about not through inculcating abstract formulae but resulted from 'the possession of a tradition, which had become an emotional disposition and moral and mental habit'.[74] History played a crucial role in forming such sentiments by revealing the liberal character of the *Risorgimento*.[75] Croce called his historical works 'my best and most lasting "political activity"' for this very reason.[76] For it was through them that he offered his compatriots an interpretation of modern Italy that was at the same time an account and a defence of his liberal philosophy.

69. Croce, 'Liberalismo', pp. 284–5.

70. Croce, 'Liberismo e liberalismo', 1928, in *Etica e politica*, pp. 263–7.

71. Croce, 'Storia economico-politica e storia etica politica', 1924, in *Etica e politica*, pp. 225–34 and *La storia come pensiero e come azione*, pp. 47–51.

72. Croce, 'La protesta contro il "Manifesto degli intellettuali fascisti"', 1925, in *Pagine sparse*, vol. II, p. 488.

73. Croce, 'Liberalismo', p. 285.

74. Croce, 'La protesta contro il "Manifesto degli intellettuali fascisti"', p. 490.

75. Croce, 'Liberalismo', p. 285, 'La protesta contro il "Manifesto degli intellettuali fascisti"', p. 490.

76. Croce, 'La politica dei non politici', 1925, *Cultura e vita morale*, p. 292.

Conclusion

In a famous essay on intellectuals, Norberto Bobbio has compared Croce with Gramsci and argued that whereas the one practised 'the politics of culture', the other engaged in 'cultural politics'.[77] In other words, Croce defended the political conditions necessary for intellectual activity rather than attempting to use culture in order to promote a certain kind of politics. Bobbio's analysis is correct to the extent that Croce harshly criticised those, such as Gentile, who identified culture with government policy and the support of partial political interests, and believed that the state could be designed according to some philosophical blueprint. He thought politics and culture were both weakened by such attempts to identify the one with the other. Grandiose cultural schemes to 'make Italians' too often neglected the more prosaic practical political task of 'making Italy' and devising workable economic, social and institutional policies. At the same time, cultural values were perverted and deformed by placing art or truth at the service of a particular regime. None the less, Croce believed individuals would only accept the necessity for continual political struggle and concrete, problem-solving, political action when they adopted a certain philosophical perspective. Moreover, it was the political duty of intellectuals to spread such ideas, showing how they informed the practices and institutions that framed their fellow citizens' activities. In other words, the politics of culture had to be linked to cultural politics in order to promote an appropriate political culture. As Croce noted in the epilogue to his *History of Nineteenth Century Europe*, the moral ideals of liberalism were unlikely to make much sense to those who did not feel part of the liberal tradition from which they arose.[78] Indeed, defining and upholding the 'politics of culture' can be achieved in interpretative terms only via 'cultural politics' – in Croce's case by interpreting Italian history in order to exemplify, promote and elaborate liberal values. The combination of the two makes Croce a 'modern' interpreter, for it involves seeing the universal and rational values of culture as part of the real historical world of practical politics. As his own career shows, it is also doubtful if any attempt to defend such aspirations of Western political culture as respect for diversity and individual autonomy can avoid mixing both historical and universal claims regarding their current significance for our lives.

---

77. Bobbio, 'Croce e la politica della cultura'. *See also* Bobbio, *Il dubbio e la scelta: Intellettuali e potere nella società contemporanea*, Rome: La Nuova Italia Scientifica, 1993, pp. 164–7.

78. Croce, *Storia d'europe nel secolo decimonono*, 1931, p. 316.

Chapter Seven

Idealism and Liberalism in an Italian 'New Liberal' Theorist: Guido De Ruggiero's *History of European Liberalism* and the Crisis of Idealist Liberalism[1]

Idealism as a respectable liberal metaphysic is generally regarded as having died a none-too-dignified death with the First World War and the rise of authoritarian regimes in the 1920s and 30s, with which, in many people's eyes, it was deeply and damningly ideologically involved.[2] This makes it rather curious that Guido De Ruggiero's *History of European Liberalism* – a work written from a definite idealist standpoint – should have become and maintained its position as a standard text on the subject.[3] Much more than a timeless statement of liberal ideals, however, its value inheres in its analysis of the crisis of liberalism in the interwar period. Written in 1924, it became a manifesto of the liberal (that is, non-communist) anti-fascist movement, being a response both to the end of the cosy bourgeois world of nineteenth-century Europe, with which both idealism and liberalism are usually identified, and the desertion of large sections of the liberal political class to either fascism or socialism. The book's worth as liberal theory can only be appreciated, therefore, if it is seen as an attempt to redefine the tenets and traditions of liberalism in the light of the highly charged political situation of the 1920s.

1. This article is based on research funded by the ESRC, under its Postdoctoral Research Fellowship Scheme. Its contents are the responsibility of the author and do not necessarily reflect the views of the ESRC. I am grateful to Raymond Plant, Quentin Skinner, Jonathan Steinberg and participants in a seminar I organised on 'The Liberal Tradition' for their comments on an earlier version of this paper.

2. The classic statement of this view is L. T. Hobhouse, *The Metaphysical Theory of the State*, London, 1918. A similar opinion expressed by J. B. Baillie in *Studies in Human Nature*, London, 1921, p. vii, aroused the wrath of De Ruggiero in *Filosofi del Novecento*, 3rd edn, Bari, 1946, p. 3.

3. References are to the Collingwood translation *The History of European Liberalism*, Oxford, 1927. Described by him as 'a great book', he believed 'no book known to me since T. H. Green has, I think, made so fine a theoretical contribution to liberal doctrine, and this is far more complete and far more highly organised than anything of Green's'. Letter of Collingwood to De Ruggiero 18 November 26, Collingwood Mss. Bodleian, Oxford, Folder 27. His fear that its idealism would limit the book's market in the English speaking world appears to have been unfounded, as it seems to have a place in the bibliography of any treatment of the subject.

Idealism and the *Risorgimento* liberalism of the Italian Hegelian tradition

Born in Naples on the 23 March 1888, De Ruggiero's cultural formation was entirely within the southern Italian Hegelian tradition and his political philosophy can only be understood with reference to it.[4] The Neapolitan Hegelians (Francesco De Sanctis and Silvio and Bertrando Spaventa) sought to interpret the *Risorgimento* – the movement of national unification – in terms of the Hegelian ethical State, and used it to justify their activities in favour of a united Italian state as an expression of the collective will of the Italian people against the largely foreign-backed monarchical regimes of the time.[5] As Silvio Spaventa wrote:

> The end of our revolution, as of every revolution was precisely that of making possible the unfolding of that new life which we felt within us and which was closed within our thoughts, destroying the obstacles and impediments which restricted it to this august sphere of the individual conscience, and to put it into action in the universal conscience of society.

The true state – its ethical force – lay in the people constituted as a nation:

> It is nationality which restores this living consciousness of the State, because it is the intimate reflexion of its own material in which human association is brought about, that is to say the complex of the universal and distinctive characteristics of a people.[6]

However, the resulting Italian state was far from reflecting the fully rational Hegelian constitution. For a start, Italy lacked the cultural cohesiveness implied by the Hegelian *volkgeist* – those shared practices and cultural values that make the transition from civil society to the ethical State a possibility. The problem was twofold: first, cultural divisiveness existed both between the educated classes and the largely uneducated majority and between the different Italian territories; and, second, economic division existed both between the industrial north and the agricultural south and between large landowners, small proprietors, the big industrialists and the workers. The state was thus fragmented into different groups each locked, in Hegelian terms, in their own particularity, through the lack of a common culture to mediate between them. In a famous phrase the Italian state existed, it remained to create the Italians.[7]

---

4. For biographical information, *see* E. Garin, *Intellectuali Italiani del XX Secolo*, Rome, 1974, pp. 105–36 and G. Calo and L. Salvatorelli, 'Guido De Ruggiero', in *Accademia Nazionale dei Lincei*, Quaderno 13, Rome, 1949.

5. *See* S. Landucci, 'L'hegelismo in Italia nell'eta del *Risorgimento*', *Studi Storici* 7,1965, pp. 597–628 and S. Onufrio, 'Lo "Stato etico" gli hegliani di Napoli', *Nuovi Quaderni del Meridione* 5, 1967, pp. 76–90, 171–88, 436–57. The rest of this paragraph summarises my 'Croce, Gentile and Hegel and the doctrine of the Ethical State', *Rivista di Studi Crociani* 20, 1983, pp. 263–81 and 21, 1984, pp. 67–73.

6. B. Croce (ed.), Silvio Spaventa, *Dal 1845 al 1861, lettere, scritti. documenti*, 2nd edn, Bari, 1923, pp. 20, 149.

7. I explore this central theme of Italian thought in my *Modern Italian Social Theory: Ideology and politics from Pareto to the present*, Cambridge, 1987.

This catalogue of problems which bedevilled the new Italian nation was epitomised in the 'southern question' and hence was unavoidably at the centre of the Neapolitan Hegelians' thinking. They were disdainful of the solutions proffered by the '*meridionalisti*' – men such as Pasquale Villari, Giustino Fortunato and Gaetano Salvemini – who came from the positivist tradition and looked for a solution via extension of the franchise, a federal system of government and redistribution of resources towards the south.[8] They rejected such initiatives as fundamentally unsound because based on an atomistic view of society that reduced the individual to an empirical unit governed by a particular set of needs and desires and egoistically seeking their satisfaction. Rather than a programme for more meaningful participation, they saw the studies of Mosca and Pareto as providing confirmation from within the positivist camp of their own view that ordinary people would be at the mercy of elite groups, who could manipulate the individual's perception of his interest through control of the organs of power.[9] As a result, modern Italian politics had been characterised by the sort of political brokerage identified with Giolitti's policy of *trasformismo*. To this they opposed the Hegelian notion of individuality, dependent upon a shared moral and cultural tradition capable of embodying both individual and collective goals. The difficulty was how could this be created in a society in which cultural and economic divisions seemed to close individuals within a liberal individualist ethos, cutting them off from their fellow citizens.

The problem was one of political identity and two strategies developed to solve it, represented respectively by the two main philosophers of the second generation of Italian Hegelians: Benedetto Croce and Giovanni Gentile.[10] They took it upon themselves to revise Hegel in a radical manner, in an attempt to create at one and the same time an Italian culture and an Italian people. Both, in their different ways, sought to provide via their philosophical and historical studies a cultural tradition capable of reintegrating man's practical activity into his search and need for a framework of meaning, value and certainty. However, whereas Croce's philosophy largely continues the Hegelian project of reconciliation to the world, seeing humanity in the last instance as the servant of Providence, Gentile sought to appropriate the power of Spirit to humankind.[11] It is to this latter development of the Italian Hegelian tradition that De Ruggiero – Gentile's star pupil – belongs, though he took it in a liberal rather than the fascist direction of his mentor.

8.   For a history of the whole southern movement, *see* R. Villari, *Mezzogiorno e democrazia*, Bari, 1979.

9.   For example, B. Croce's articles 'È necessaria una democrazia?' and 'Il partito come giudizio e come prejiudizio', in *Unità* I (1912), reprinted in *Cultura e vita morale - intermezzi polemici*, 2nd edn, Bari, 1925, which gives a comprehensive account of the idealist view of politics in this period.

10. On Croce, *see* my 'Liberalism and historicism – Benedetto Croce and the political role of Idealism in Italy c.1890–1952', in A. Moulakis (ed.), *The Promise of History*, Berlin/New York, 1985 and E. E. Jacobitti, *Revolutionary Humanism and Historicism in Modern Italy*, Yale, 1981. On Gentile, *see* H. S. Harris, *The Social Philosophy of Giovanni Gentile*, Urbana, 1960, whose account I largely follow.

11. The best record of their differences was the early debate begun by Croce in *La Voce* of 1913, reprinted in A Romano (ed.), *La Voce 1905–14, La cultura italiana del '900 attraverso le riviste*, vol. 3, Torino, 1960, pp. 595–605, 608–625 and 630–8. *See* my *Modern Italian Social Theory*, ch. 5, for an extended discussion of the debate drawing on the Gentile–Croce correspondence and H. S. Harris *The Social philosophy of G.G.*, pp. 19–22, for an account more sympathetic to Gentile.

The First World War

In the years prior to and including the First World War, De Ruggiero's thinking more or less converged with that of Gentile.[12] Gentile's 'actualism' represents the subjective extreme of idealism, in that the present activity of reflective awareness is regarded as the absolute foundation on which all else depends. The act of thinking is the 'pure act' that creates the world of human experience.[13] As De Ruggiero expressed it in his first major book, *Contemporary Philosophy* of 1912:

> The world of thought is actuality, concreteness, search and achievement, aspiration and attainment. This new conception of the world as the world of our struggle and labour must supplant the old conception of the world as a natural whole which is simply the creation of our imagination, arising from the accumulation of our past experiences and the expectation of new experiences.[14]

Human thought exists only in our acts and the social world we create with others through the transformation of reality. Consciousness of self emerges from the practical activity of the will, of human *praxis*, as it shapes the natural world. In common with Hegel, he sees the most concrete example of this as being a sense of nationality – the cultural baggage we necessarily carry around with us to have any sense of personal identity at all.[15] But De Ruggiero went beyond Hegel and turned actualism into a philosophy of radical liberation and his liberalism must be seen in the light of it. Two themes dominate De Ruggiero's definition of liberalism. First, the view of liberty as the individual's capacity for unfettered development and self-expression and, second, the need to situate human freedom in the institutions and culture of liberal society, conceived of as the embodiment of human will.[16] De Ruggiero believed that a community could evolve spontaneously out of human activity if only it was given the opportunity to develop freely. It was the vision of society built on human will and involving the participation of all its members. This was the attraction of the First World War, for it seemed to obviate the need for a mediating, pre-existing culture to focus and define the individual's actions. It met the dual ends of a total mobilisation of the people and centring their action upon the core concept of the nation. It was, in the words of practically everyone

12. *See* G. Sasso, 'Considerazioni sulla filosofia di De Ruggiero', in *De Homine* XXI, 1967, pp. 23–70, for a comparison of Gentile and De Ruggiero's philosophy showing the substantial influence of Gentile throughout all De Ruggiero's writings. De Ruggiero's paper 'La scienza come esperienza assoluta', in *Annuario della Biblioteca Filosofica of Palermo* II, 1912, pp. 229–339, essentially reproduces the themes of Gentile's first outline of his actualism in 'L'atto del pensare come atto puro', in *Annuario* I, 1912, pp. 27–42.
13. H. S. Harris, 'Gentile', *Encyclopaedia of Philosophy* III, New York, 1967, pp. 281–5.
14. Guido De Ruggiero, *Contemporary Philosophy*, trans. R. G. Collingwood and A. Howard Hannay, London, 1921, p. 375.
15. De Ruggiero, *Contemporary Philosophy*, pp. 16–18.
16. De Ruggiero, *European Liberalism*, pp. 357–63 and 'Liberalism', in *Encyclopaedia of the Social Sciences* vol. 9, London, 1933, pp. 435–41.

advocating entry into the war in Italy at the time, to be the completion of the *Risorgimento*, giving the nation a spiritual unity to complement its political unity.

De Ruggiero put these ideas together in a long article of 1916 on 'Italian thought and the war'.[17] He began with a declaration of the central tenet of actualism, that 'the understanding of life can and must make itself felt in its turn as life, and no longer as the mirror image of life.' He saw the war as the embodiment of this ideal. Everyone, whether they had wanted the war or not and whatever their reasons for becoming involved, was equally engaged in the practical exigencies of fighting. This gave their particular actions a higher significance, as contributions to the national war effort. He attacked the view, made popular by Croce, that the war was the war of historical materialism. The ideologies of the pre-war world, democratic, nationalist, socialist and liberal, he argued, had indeed been dominated by the narrow sphere of self-interest. But the war had changed that and had revived people's sense of their ability to act as an autonomous agent, not in service to certain set desires which the system of production was designed to satisfy. The ethic of the war was the 'idealism of action', endowing such values as heroism, nobility, patriotism and fellowship with a force they had lost. They were no longer parts of an outmoded rhetoric to cover up essentially selfish motives but derived their meaning from a common struggle: 'the individual is reborn, no longer in the contingencies of his egoism, but in the universality of his being, in the purity of his humanity, in the unity of his race'. De Ruggiero's nationalism was therefore far from being based on an uncomplicated allegiance to an already existing community or political unit; indeed, he largely despised the run-of-the-mill nationalists, such as Enrico Corradini. His argument was that participation in the war created national feeling. In the very different circumstances of the post-war world, however, this was revealed as being largely contingent on the special circumstances engendered by armed struggle and he was forced to examine what made such a commitment unlikely under the liberal-democratic regime of modern Italy.[18] This analysis was carried out in the role of political commentator for a number of newspapers – in particular *Il Resto del Carlino* and later *Il Paese* – and in two books on English politics that resulted from his stay there in late 1920 to mid 1921 and which motivated his shift to a new liberalism.[19]

---

17. Guido De Ruggiero, 'La pensée italienne et la guerre', *Revue de Metaphysique et de morale* 23, 1916, pp. 748–85.

18. *Ibid.*, pp. 751, 762, 764, 756–61, 769, 770–1.

19. The articles are almost completely collected in Renzo de Felice (ed.), Guido De Ruggiero, *Scritti Politici, 1912–26*, 1969. De Felice's long introduction, pp. 1–76, is the best analysis of De Ruggiero's political thought but *see* also Francesco de Aloysio, 'Note su Guido De Ruggiero politico nel periodo della nascita e dell "avvento del fascismo"', *Rivista storica del socialism* 23, 1960, pp. 725–45, which is an important corrective to E. Garin, *Intellettuali*, pp. 105–36. The two books are *L'Impero britannico dopo la guerra*, Firenze, 1921 and 'La formazione dell' impero britannico', in D. Donati and F. Carli (eds), *L'Europa nel Secolo XIX*, vol. I, Storia Politica, Padova, 1925, pp. 477–513.

The Two Red Years (1919–20)

The war clearly had not produced anything like the national, to say nothing of the moral, unity sought for by Gentile and De Ruggiero. Officially victors, the Italians' defeat at Caporetto was far from redeemed by the success of Vittorio Veneto. The war had been far beyond Italy's means as a nation and the years 1919–1920 were probably, with the exception of 1943, the period of greatest social and political agitation in modern Italian history. Industrial expansion had been totally sustained by the state's war effort, which could hardly afford it in the first place, so that the post-war period witnessed a sharp decrease in demand and concomitant industrial unrest. This was better organised than ever before, union membership having dramatically increased. At the same time, there was widespread agrarian unrest amongst agricultural workers and small proprietors, again better organised than before by associations formed amongst ex-combatants. Yet, if these different groups achieved a modicum of success in their own areas, their efforts were far from being co-ordinated. The introduction of proportional representation in the 1919 elections had greatly increased the number of seats held by socialists and the Catholic 'Popular Party' but neither group had what could be called a coherent political line. For a start, the socialists alienated a large section of the peasant class, eager to buy land, by committing themselves to land nationalisation; whilst the *popolari* were an extremely heterogeneous group held together by the tenuous bonds of religion. The only attempt to give this unrest a decidedly political orientation – the factory council movement organised by Gramsci and *L'Ordine Nuovo* in Turin – had failed miserably due to its isolation from any similar action. For De Ruggiero, the pressing problem was how to organise these different groups.

The war had seemed to unite two seemingly antithetical demands – the spontaneity of action, as a free creative liberation from the past, and the spirit of order, of doing one's duty in the post assigned to you by the needs of the war, whether as officer or common soldier.[20] In the post-war crisis, spontaneous action seemed to exist in plenty but there was nothing which could be called a common conception of society to give it direction and purpose. But De Ruggiero – in contrast to Gentile – looked upon these different movements as signs of health, believing that 'liberalism is [...] spirit and therefore an eminently organising force'. He saw no need therefore 'to counter the liberal political mentality with an organic and organising mentality'.[21] The war, he believed, had proved this and he contrasted as examples of what he meant the concepts of economic co-operation and a trust. A trust is a protectionist arrangement, whereby a more powerful element dominates

---

20. De Ruggiero, 'La pensée italienne', pp. 770–1. For the contrasting views of Croce and Gentile, *see* G. Gentile, *Guerra e fede. Frammenti politici*, Naples, 1919 and B. Croce, *Pagine sulla guerra*, 2nd edn, Bari, 1928. Croce recorded his dissent from De Ruggiero's (and Gentile's) opinions in a review of his article in *La Critica* 15, 1917, pp. 130–2, which, as he explained in a letter to Gentile, he regarded as expressing the dangers of actualism (A. Croce (ed.) *Lettere a Gentile*, Milano, 1981 no. 770, 10 January 1917, pp. 533–4.)

21. De Ruggiero, 'Il tramonto del liberalism', *Il Resto del Carlino*, February 1917, *Scritti*, p. 174.

the others, depriving the system of the stimulus of competition and innovation. This was organisation in a bad sense, as represented by Germany during the war. Co-operation, however, was a libertarian concept that conserved the smaller forces, enabling them to participate freely in the system – an organic unity.[22] He saw the industrial unrest in a favourable light as a move away from the organisation of the trust imposed by the big industrialists to a new type of organisation emerging out of the nascent workers movement. It was not just a protest against bad pay and working conditions but something more positive:

> [...] an affirmation of conscience, of personality. The great modern industrial movement has created the new physiognomy of work, has given to work a conscience adequate to itself. But the material conditions in which work is carried out are inappropriate to the development of this conscience.

The labour of the workers was nullified by the weight of the accumulated labour of the past concentrated in capital; that of the peasant by landed property; the work of the clerk by an impersonal bureaucracy. Wage-labour alienated the worker from the products of his labour. The war had aggravated the situation by increasing the concentration of capital in the hands of 'a small brigade of a few great financers and a few great industrialists'. The workers were simply seeking 'to leave the amorphous state of a mass and to acquire their own personality by virtue of their productive activity'. What was required was a new synthesis of labour and capital, which must lighten the weight of the latter on the former by attacking monopolies and involving these new forces. He therefore looked for:

> A daring programme of industrial and agrarian legislation; which looks beyond the already constituted particular interests, to where these fuse with other new ones, in a supreme interest in the conservation of social life, which would be equally to the advantage of all.[23]

De Ruggiero's interpretation of this movement hinges on an essentially Hegelian view of the nature of modern society. Labour is crucial in De Ruggiero's actualist philosophy for the development of human self-consciousness and personality. It involves the objectifying of the human agent's will, giving substance to his material and spiritual needs. Indeed it creates them, since they are not biologically determined givens but formed and organised through the domination of nature. As this control increases and society develops, no single individual can satisfy all his or her needs and we are forced to co-operate with others. A network of mutually beneficial productive relationships develops, which forms the basis for a new harmony in modern society. The growth of individuality is frustrated, though, when the products of our labour are alienated to someone else. This is exacerbated by factory conditions in which one's relation to the

---

22. De Ruggiero, 'Il trionfo del liberalismo', *Il Tempo*, 23 January 1919, *Scritti*, pp. 196–200.
23. De Ruggiero, 'Tendenze', *Il Resto del Carlino*, 28 April 1919, *Scritti*, pp. 236–9.

productive process as a whole is difficult to perceive. The individual in capitalist society still works to satisfy his or her own needs and desires and is thus enclosed in the sphere of self-interest. As a result, there had been an unfair accumulation of capital in the hands of a few and the consequent enervation of the labour of the mass of the workers. But the workers' movement, in De Ruggiero's appraisal, was not simply motivated by need; in fact, living conditions had improved greatly since unification. Its importance was that it went beyond need, was an organised expression of the individual worker's solidarity with others, and thus represented a concomitant diminishing of individual particularity. The influence of George Sorel's interpretation of contemporary proletarian movements in the light of early Christian millenarianism is important here, for it helped Italian intellectuals to regard the industrial struggle in semi-religious terms as 'taking up the revolutionary movement of the *Risorgimento*', thereby creating a link to the earlier problematic of the Neapolitan Hegelians.[24] De Ruggiero's thinking in this respect has obvious affinities with that of Gramsci and, in particular, of the 'revolutionary liberal' Piero Gobetti – both ideologues of the Turin factory council movement.[25] But he accused them of substituting a narrow class interest – that of the workers – for that of society as a whole; and, in the case of the Communists, of imposing it on the workers themselves via the party bureaucracy. For De Ruggiero, an unbridgeable divide existed between human free will and 'scientific' laws of social and economic development, which Marxism inevitably resolved via the party in the direction of the latter. He believed the workers' movement, allowed freely to develop, would transcend class and lead to identification with membership of the whole national (and ultimately international) community.[26] What he was proposing was a new work ethic of human brotherhood which would, in the long run, contain and triumph over every struggle:

> It would be pointless [he was to write in 1940] to speak of the economic subject of work, as spontaneous, inventive and constructive activity if this subject was not understood as moral personality, as the autonomous source of energy. Similarly it would be empty to speak of the solidarity of work if man does not grasp in his moral conscience the more profound and intimate sense of the bonds which bind him to other men.[27]

---

24. On Hegel, *see* *Philosophy of Right* paras 189–208 and R. Plant, *Hegel: An Introduction*, 2nd edn, Oxford, 1983, ch. 9. For De Ruggiero's ideas, *see* his *Problemi della vita morale*, Catania, 1914, pp. 55–60.

25. On this point, I agree with de Aloyisio's criticism of Garin's view that De Ruggiero was a follower of Salandra at this time – a position held by Croce if anyone. ('Note su G. De Ruggiero', pp. 727–8). On Gobetti, *see* G. De Caro 'Da Energie nove a la rivoluzione liberale', *Nuova Rivista Storica* 1961, pp. 568–82. De Ruggiero contributed three articles to Gobetti's *Rivoluzione Liberale*, examined below, from 1922–4. For Gramsci's attitude, *see* the fine analysis of J. Femia in his *Gramsci's Political Thought*, Oxford, 1981, pp. 139–51.

26. *See* De Ruggiero, 'Discussioni socialiste', *Il Resto Carlino* 17 July 1919 and 'Lo Stato socialista', *Il Paese* 2 August 1921, *Scritti*, pp. 274–8, 380–4.

27. Guido De Ruggiero, *Il concetto del lavoro nella sua genesi storica*, Il filo di arianna n. 20, Roma 1947, p. 42.

The problem for practical politics was thus to secure the conditions for this ethic to develop, a programme which had more in common with Gramsci's proposals for a new hegemony than he would have cared to admit. His distinctive contribution to the contemporary debate derived, however, from the influence on his thought of English new liberalism and the philosophy of Hobhouse.

New liberalism Italian style, and the struggle against fascism

The appeal of Hobhouse's philosophy for De Ruggiero was the manner in which he built his reconceptualisation of a liberal society on the basis of a new concept of the individual.[28] Hobhouse follows Mill and Green in seeing individuality not as the cultivation of self-interest but the development of character or personality. Now if, he argues, man's end is not the pursuit of pleasure *per se* but the realisation of his nature, then society can be seen not as the arena of competing individuals but as a co-operative pursuit of self-realisation. Liberalism, as Hobhouse redefined it, is thus 'the belief that society can safely be founded on [the] self-directing power of personality [and] that it is only on this foundation that a true community can be built.' It was the vision of a society based on the possibility of the spontaneous fulfilment of the capacities of all its members. Liberty, however, is not 'impulse', but 'rational self-determination' towards the good. He brushes aside a potential conflict between different individuals' freedom for self-development, seeing self-realisation as a rational process implicitly oriented towards the common good. Following T. H. Green, he argues that 'full development of personality is practically possible not for one man only but for all members of the community.'[29]

Humans are a social animals and our conception of the good is necessarily defined in and through the practices we engage in with others and which embody the development of reason in both the individual and humanity as a whole. Now Hobhouse, famous for his attack on Hegel and Bosanquet in *The Metaphysical Theory of the State*, is clearly not interpreting this process in conventional idealist terms.[30] The essence of his criticism of the Hegelian doctrine of the State is that a putative real will of the individual is identified with the customs and practices (the general will) of an actual state. Hobhouse liberalises idealism by arguing that our freedom is prior to any particular set of social arrangements and consists in our ability to chose and frame them for our own ends. The basis for community is thus the rational perception that my self-development is intimately related to that of

---

28. I am here more or less paraphrasing De Ruggiero's own account of Hobhouse in *European Liberalism*, pp. 155–7, where he passes his famous judgement on the work as 'the best formulation of the new English Liberalism of the twentieth century' combining 'the teaching of Mill and Green in a modernised form' (p. 155). Justification for an idealist reading of Hobhouse's *Liberalism* is provided by Stefan Collini, *Liberalism and Sociology – L. T. Hobhouse and Political Argument in England 1880–1914*, Cambridge, 1979, ch. 4.

29. L. T. Hobhouse, *Liberalism* (1911), Oxford, 1964, pp. 66, 80–1, 69, 67–8.

30. *See* Stefan Collini, 'Hobhouse, Bosanquet and the state: philosophical idealism and political argument in England 1880–1918, *Past and Present* 72, 1976, pp. 86–111.

my fellows, that each individual's particular good is found in the common good.[31] Hobhouse argued that the existing distribution of wealth and power prevented the development of such a consciousness. By not just redistributing wealth but power as well, so that individuals participated in the management of their place of work, the local community and central government, he hoped to foster an organic conception of society based on co-operation and mutual aid. He thus appears to invert the Hegelian concept of the State as the unfolding of reason downwards from Spirit to humanity, to see it as the rational perception of common human goals amongst individuals. The teleology, however, is implicitly the same, being based on the belief that there is a natural 'line of development', which mediates and harmonises individual wills.[32] As I shall argue below, his position is therefore difficult to sustain without some of those self-same presuppositions concerning the nature of actual communities which he so attacked in Hegel and Bosanquet.[33]

'New liberalism' so defined had obvious attractions for De Ruggiero though. It seemed to provide a revision of the Idealist conception of community in the direction he was seeking: namely, as the product of individual effort, and involving a legislative programme adequate to his interpretation of the workers' movement. As we saw, he regarded the accumulation of wealth and power in the hands of a few industrialists and landowners as the principal bar to the development of a new political consciousness amongst workers.[34] Hobhouse argued that since any particular action in the productive process is necessarily done in co-operation with others, it is wrong to award any single individual a disproportionate amount of the social product. There was, therefore, a minimum wage required for any individual contribution, which could only be increased by personal effort to the maximum 'industrial value of the individual'. This in turn becomes an argument for the co-operative ownership and management of industry by workers and capitalists. Hobhouse's argument develops out of his notion of the common good as the combination of individual and social goals and its feasibility was dependent on this perception being actually present in the minds of members of society. In this way, he strongly distinguished his 'liberal socialism' from the bureaucratic 'official' socialism of the Fabians, on the one hand, and vulgar Marxist 'mechanical' socialism, on the other: 'It must come from below, not from above, [...] it must emerge from the efforts of society as a whole to secure a fuller measure of justice and a better organisation of mutual aid [...]'.[35]

It was precisely in these terms that De Ruggiero wished to see the social unrest of the early 1920s and hence justify 'new liberal' policies in Italy. There was some

---

31. L. T. Hobhouse, *The Metaphysical Theory of the State*, London, 1918, pp. 71, 60–1.

32. Hobhouse, *Liberalism*, pp. 70, 69.

33. Stefan Collini, *Liberalism and Sociology*, pp. 147–70, 235–40, shows how Hobhouse's argument is based on his account of Progress and that after World War I this becomes more idealist in nature than otherwise.

34. *See* De Ruggiero, *Il concetto del lavoro*, 'Capitale e lavoro'.

35. Hobhouse, *Liberalism*, pp. 88–109.

irony in this – Hobhouse's tract of 1911 had been written in the wake of 'the People's Budget', with the progressives in the Liberal Party in the ascendant. The war and the coalition government seemed to present a very different spectacle and De Ruggiero was reduced to singling out Asquith's *Paisley Policy* of 1920 for the dubious role of the post war 'Summa' of new liberal politics. He approved in particular of Asquith's rejection of 'State Socialism', aiming at direct public management of industry, for the 'liberal socialist' programme of 'public control':

> the formation of mixed commissions of capitalists, technocrats and workers with the remit to examine not simply questions of pay, but be responsible for the overall supervision of the industry. The State would also be represented as curator of the interests of the consumers.[36]

This programme constituted 'a real co-partnership of capital and labour'. Marx was correct in seeing capital as accumulated labour but wrong to seek to abolish it altogether. If the nineteenth century had seen the concentration of capital in a few hands so that workers were justified in seeing the war of capital and labour as part and parcel of class struggle, the logic of labour was itself undermining this opposition, via the development of worker co-operatives and limited companies.[37] He distinguished his attitude on this issue both before and after World War Two from the 'liberal socialism' (*liberalsocialismo*) of Carlo Rosselli and Guido Calogero. His own doctrine of 'social liberalism' (*liberalismo sociale*) was not the liberalising of a socialist economy but the establishment of the social conditions for liberalism to flourish.[38] The core of new liberalism as he interpreted it was thus Hobhouse's fleshing out of Green's notion of the common good in the organic conception of society. The essential element was that individuals should be free to rationally frame their life plans – 'What the English designate with the expression: equality of opportunity' – and that a certain amount of state regulation was necessary to secure this. Once achieved, this by itself would issue in mutuality of respect and social harmony. Thus, liberalism in England had broken out of the old individualist formulas 'to reaffirm its spiritual worth':

> Which is not in the atomistic opposition of individual to individual but the full organic unfolding of a superior spiritual individuality [...] The principle of the State, of the organic nature of life, is not therefore, repugnant to liberalism, rather it constitutes its most evolved expression.

---

36. De Ruggiero, *L'Impero britannico dopo la guerra*, pp. 59–62.

37. De Ruggiero, 'I presupposti economici del liberalismo', *La Rivoluzione liberale* I, n. 2, 19 February 1922, pp. 6–8; 'La politica inglese in Italia', *Il Paese* 2 March 1922; 'In tema di colla-borazione', *Il Paese* 17 June 1922, all in *Scritti*, pp. 472–6, 521–5.

38. Guido De Ruggiero, 'La lotta politica – liberali e laburisti', *La Rivoluzione liberale* III (1924), n. 13–14, 25 March – 1 April, p. 51 and 'Liberalismo sociale e liberal-socialismo', in *Il ritorno alla ragione*, Bari, 1946, pp. 240–5.

This higher unity was a spiritual rather than a naturalistic or material entity, 'an affirmation of self':

> From this fact issues not just the positive and constructive work, but also the critical role of liberalism, which in the face of the danger of an oppressive servility threatened both from top and bottom, before the brutal mechanism of economic forces which attempt to nullify all the dignity and nobility of human labour, critically reaffirms the autonomy of spiritual values, the sense of human personality, the self-same rights of individualism, which are not crushed, but realised in its organic conception.[39]

In De Ruggiero's opinion, the post-war crisis in Italy was therefore primarily the result of the operation of 'classical liberalism'. Classical liberalism saw man as an individual producer whose co-operation with others was freely entered into by all parties and open to renegotiation. Freedom of contract, it was held, ensured the responsiveness of society to its members. De Ruggiero criticised this view both because he believed the freedom it claimed necessary for it to work did not exist and because it put forward a theory of the individual he found repugnant. A society which conceives itself as essentially a mechanism for the satisfaction of individual interests would be spiritually empty and have no basis on which conflicting interests could be reconciled. As a result, it was likely to become polarised between rich and poor and the inherent tensions would flare up once economic growth could no longer be maintained at a level to make such a conception of society a going concern.[40] This, for De Ruggiero, was precisely what had happened in post-war Italy and he found proof of it in the sectional division of society between fascism and socialism. In a number of articles written on his return to Italy he bitterly attacked the desertion of the liberal cause.[41] Luigi Einaudi, the leading advocate of *laissez-faire* liberal economics in Italy, was a special target of his criticism. He is amazed by Einaudi's interpretation of the fights between fascist and socialist organisations in Bologna as a struggle between the freedom of the worker to choose his own work and State socialism. The apparent liberty held out by Einaudi was little less than slavery for the workers who were only demanding:

> One of the fundamental postulates of liberalism: equality before the owning classes [...] For the sake of a purely formal liberalism, for a merely decorative nationalism, by breaking up the workers organisations, we are squandering the richest national energies, dissipating its solidest capital, we are sacrificing the most real liberty which is the liberty of all men to make themselves fully men.[42]

---

39. De Ruggiero, *L'impero britannico dopo la guerra*, pp. 57–8.

40. De Ruggiero, 'I presupposti economici del liberalismo', 'Orientamenti', *Il Paese* 30 July 1922; 'Il trionfo della tecnica', *Il Resto del Carlino* 19 December 1922, in *Scritti*, pp. 535–9, 595–600.

41. De Ruggiero, 'Il concetto liberale', *La nostra scuola* 16–31 March 1921, in *Scritti*, pp. 365–71 (prefaced to his book on English politics as a statement of his ideas on liberalism, it earned the book sequestration by the authorities). 'Decalogo Spicciolo', *Il Paese* 2 April 1922; 'Servitù o libertà', *Il Paese* 13 June 1922; 'Krumiraggio liberale', *Il Paese* 20 June 1922; 'Liberali!', *Il Paese* 15 October 1922, in *Scritti*, pp. 482–6, 510–4, 526–30, 585–7.

42. De Ruggiero, 'Servitù o libertà', *Il Paese* 13 June 1922, in *Scritti*, p. 511.

However, those liberals who appeared to make overtures in the direction of the socialists were simply seeking to pacify an incipient workers revolt. 'Filo-socialism' as he called it 'was nothing but the vulgar effect of fear' which revealed its true colours in the wholesale desertion of previously self-styled liberals to fascism in 1922.[43]

Fascism, far from being the solution to the contemporary crisis, was symptomatic of it. The problem was one of authority, not in the sense of law and order, but of self-government:

> The force of the State is but the resultant of the forces which converge in it. Give to the great masses the clear concrete sensation, that the State is not outside or against them, and that they obey the State because they feel they are obeying their own law, [and] they feel in being governed not servitude, but an autonomous act, a means of self-government.[44]

Of course it was in precisely such terms that Gentile justified Fascism – what distinguished De Ruggiero's theory from his doctrine? Gentile argued that Fascism was the true Liberal Party, continuing the tradition of the Neapolitan Hegelians and completing the *Risorgimento*. The *squadristi* carried on the process of regeneration begun during the war, combining moral and material force, theory and action, in revolutionary violence. The liberal state had failed to unite will and power; Fascism had filled the vacuum with the moral force of the cudgel (*manganello*). This was the genuine expression of liberalism, the achievement of complete freedom via the subjection of nature to man's will, making it an instrument of his ends and thus spiritualising it. The revolution over, the Fascist Corporate State organised the moral will of the people within the political force of the State. The unions or 'syndicates' represented the corporate personality of the worker which, together with the employers' organisations, were in turn to be organised within the framework of the national personality – the State. As a result, the individual pursuing his private interest came via the Corporation to a consciousness of the general interest.[45] Gentile's argument here seems to be little more than a mechanical exposition of the Hegelian State in which individuals do not enter the political arena directly but via associations, corporations and so on. Hegel had believed that the classes of society were so sharply differentiated from each other that the notion of direct participation in politics was a non starter, since self-interest could never generate a sense of the general interest. It was necessary, therefore, to have a degree of corporate autonomy in public life in which the groups would regulate their own particular forms of life. He believed, however, that at a higher level the individual would become aware of the interrelatedness of the 'system of needs', that all labour is social as well as individual and that consciousness of this fact

---

43. De Ruggiero, 'Il concetto liberale', p. 367. The liberal party, he argued, was the continuation of the liberalism of the nineteenth century only in the same sense that 'a deposit of coal is the continuation of a forest', 'Liberali!', p. 586.

44. De Ruggiero, 'Il problema dell'autorità', *Il Paese* 8 December 1921, in *Scritti*, p. 423.

45. Giovanni Gentile, *Che cosa è il fascismo. Discorsi e polemiche,* Florence, 1925, pp. 29–33, 41–63, 65–94, and H. S. Harris, *The Social Philosophy of G. Gentile*, pp. 167–82.

would promote the development of a community awareness within civil society.[46] This was a perception open to the representatives and bureaucrats who formed a universal class through their direct allegiance to the State, rather than all members of society. For De Ruggiero, Gentile had obviously trivialised the Hegelian analysis by simply creating the differentiation which Hegel believed existed in his day and identifying the will of the individual somewhat arbitrarily with that of the Fascist State. The individual under totalitarianism has no will of his or her own at all. Gentile restricts the individual to seeking his or her private interest in that of his or her group since there is no incentive for any one to transcend it. This is the function of the State authority. Thus, the Corporate State can in no sense be called a higher form of self-government since individual interests are manipulated rather than allowed to develop freely.[47]

De Ruggiero regarded the Corporate State as the logical development of classical liberalism's image of the individual and society. The mechanical reduction of human individuality to a number of self-referential desires was plausible enough whilst the ideological hegemony of bourgeois values made the belief in a homogeneity of interest in capitalist society a workable ideal. But the ultimate legacy of the industrial revolution had not been the simple domination of a particular class and set of ideas over all others. When the political viability of capitalist society was called into doubt then liberal individualism came to create a very different style of politics, the very reverse of liberal values. Respect for the value of the individual could not be sustained on the basis of the model of the individual it proposed. Since all that was required was the satisfaction of certain narrowly defined interests this could be achieved just as well via the technical or bureaucratic state. The Fascist Corporate State was thus little more than the institutionalisation of Giolittian *trasformismo* – the control of political life by a mixture of intimidation and bribery by a number of *clientele*.[48] But the problem of how to develop a sense of common interest in a society deeply imbued with an ethic of possessive individualism remains as intractable for De Ruggiero as it was for Gentile – he surely has simply chosen to ignore it. De Ruggiero's naive belief in the natural supremacy of liberal values are in marked contrast to Gramsci's contemporary reflections in the *Prison Notebooks* on the difficulty of mobilising revolutionary consciousness within the proletariat, the relationship of consciousness to social structure and the consequent role of the party and intellectuals in organising the masses. In the place of analysis, De Ruggiero simply exhorted intellectuals to perform, to adopt Gramscian terms, the 'traditional' role of keeping liberal ideals alive and remain open to the overtures of the working class.

46. Hegel, *Philosophy of Right* paras, 189, 260, 301, 302, Charles Taylor, *Hegel and Modern Society*, Cambridge, 1975, pp. 438–49; Plant, *Hegel*, ch. 7.

47. De Ruggiero, 'La dialettica del camaleonte', *Il Paese* 8 October 1922; 'Nuova letteratura Cavouriana', *Pagine Critiche* 1 August 1926, in *Scritti*, pp. 572–5, 658–67.

48. Guido De Ruggiero,'Intorno al Fascismo', *Il Resto del Carlino* 14 February 1922; 'L'avenire del Fascismo', *Il Paese* 13 Sept 1921; 'Il Fascismo e la lotta agraria', *Il Paese* 5 November 1921; 'Memorie inutile', *Le Battaglie del Mezzogiorno*; all in *Scritti*, pp. 450–4, 389–92, 402–6, 615–9; 'Il liberalismo e le masse', *La Rivoluzione liberale* II (1923) n. 12, 1 May 1923, p. 49.

The History of European Liberalism

These, then, are the themes which get their fullest elaboration in *The History of European Liberalism* of 1924. The book is divided into a historical treatment of liberalism in the main European countries and a theoretical examination of liberalism in the light of this. The most telling of the historical sections is undoubtedly that on Italy. He begins by attacking the legacy of the liberal Hegelians – the 'Historic Right' who ruled Italy in the years immediately following the *Risorgimento* and who had been claimed by Gentile as precursors of fascism. Because Italian unity had not been the creation of a genuine national movement the State had become highly authoritarian in character:

> Raised to power not through a spontaneous development of liberal ideas in the minds of individuals, but by a virtual act of conquest sanctioned by a merely nominal plebiscite, this party confined liberty to the narrow political caste which took actual part in public life, and even, in its highest theoretical expressions, came to identify liberty with the State itself. [49]

The goal of liberalism though is not any State 'but the State as the organisation of liberty'. Italian politics had, unfortunately, failed to move in this direction and continued under the 'Left', who took over the government, to be a system used by the ruling class for their own restricted ends. This process culminated in the political management of Giolitti and was made worse rather than better by the extension of democracy:

> The fault of this art of government was that behind an impressive facade of liberalism and democracy it concealed a decadent governing class and a non-political populace. The social convulsions that followed the war revealed the illusion, stripping off the pretence and laying bare what had previously been papered over. It then appeared how far the Italian people were from having assimilated modern liberalism, with its opposed but complimentary elements, individual liberty and State organisation.

De Ruggiero's analysis of the situation is in marked contrast to his fellow liberal idealist and anti-fascist Benedetto Croce. His *History of Italy* was a veritable panegyric to Giolitti's political acumen, whose hated policy of *trasformismo* is praised by Croce as proof of his talent at uniting the country. He too laments the divisions in society resulting from the materialisation of spiritual values but sees no possibility for mediating between these groups besides political prudence. The class divisions consequent upon industrialisation had weakened the value system of traditional society in which individual's place in society derived its meaning with reference to a cosmic order inherent in the nature of things. The adoption of compromise and tinkering with the political system was consequent upon the impossibility – after the initial success of bourgeois individualism – for any one

---

49.   De Ruggiero, *European Liberalism*, pp. 326, 327, 329, 339, 342.

section of society to universalise its claims to form a common community of values. Hegelian philosophy had been the supreme modern attempt to provide such a structure in seeking to interpret the differentiation of society as an emanation of *Geist* in history. Croce somewhat stubbornly sought to hold this notion, perversely interpreting whatever disasters history threw up as the workings of Providence and exhorting his countrymen to do likewise. But, as De Ruggiero pointed out, such a view was tantamount to utter passivity and resignation to one's lot. Reviewing Croce's book, he blamed this philosophy for the separation of culture and politics, which had, in his view, precipitated the current crisis. Having turned politics into 'mere administrative techniques, not fed by the springs of conscience and knowledge', Croce's moral condemnation of fascism lacked all conviction. It was rather the mouthing of 'commonplaces of a not totally forgotten rhetoric'.[50] The rise of fascism had shown that the pragmatic approach of compromise, co-operation and fairness had been insufficient to cope with the rival claims of different groups. De Ruggiero sought to fill this lacuna via an appeal to a new liberalism based, as in Hobhouse, on the personality of man: 'The energy which the Italians will in the future bring to their reaffirmation of human personality will be the measure of their ability to participate in the entire life of modern liberalism'.[51]

De Ruggiero shares with traditional liberalism the belief in the all-importance of individual autonomy. The social and cultural worlds are products of human creativity rather than emanations from antecedent conditions independent of the individual's will and desire. At the same time, he did not want to suggest that the set of practices that emerge at any one time is entirely arbitrary, a chance agglomeration. He was concerned to see the historical process as essentially rational, yet in a radically different perspective to Hegel's. For the rationality is no longer that of Spirit but of the conscious ends that individuals set themselves in making history. Yet this thesis immediately posed a problem for him. He argues in Kantian manner that the individual's freedom consists 'in the capacity and ability to pursue a moral end' and that liberalism presumes:

> that this capacity belongs to every man as man and is not the privilege of a few. Every man must therefore have his opportunities through the removal, so far as possible, of obstacles to his development, yet without the substitution of another's work for his own.

But in so saying De Ruggiero is immediately faced with the classic problem of what is to count as development. Like J. S. Mill, he seems to have assumed that individuals would naturally choose to develop in nonconflicting ways by opting for 'higher' and non competitive pursuits, such as reading poetry, rather following 'lower' pleasures that led to conflicts over scarce resources. Faced with their failure to do so, he ended up fulminating against 'the caprice of individuals

---

50. Review of B. Croce, *Storia d'Italia Rivista Storica Italiana* XIVI, 1929, p. 312. *See also* Croce's review of *European Liberalism*, in *La Critica* XXIII, 1925, pp. 305–6.

51. De Ruggiero, *European Liberalism*, p. 343.

[...] squandering their chances of a higher and worthier freedom; so that Society is right to intervene'. However, he had no basis for saying which interventions were legitimate and which were not. He had hoped that an industrial society that allowed free development beyond class interest would be able to produce a moral community based on a conscious interpretation of its own activities. The 'social environment' was to be freely fashioned to give full expression to human personality. He attacks the Marxist notion of laws of human development. Socialism has been but a stage in the realisation of the creative powers of the workers which liberalism overcomes, in a 'higher individualism', the complete spiritualising of the world. Yet unless individuals actually do choose a 'higher' and mutually enhancing form of individualism, then De Ruggiero finds himself in a dilemma. He cannot simply hope that all forms of individual freedom will ultimately prove harmonious. As he himself remarked: 'Freedom exists so far as it is exercised, so far as it faces the increasingly complex demands of life', so that 'without an inferior freedom, an elementary school of character, no truly free personality can ever emerge into the light'.[52] Individual freedom cannot be conceived as if the constraints of the physical world and the need to recognise the freedom of others did not exist. Rather, a social and political theory of freedom involves offering a normative account of those constraints in order to appreciate both the conditions for and the legitimate limits on individual autonomy

As he noted on several occasions, it is the fact that individuals engage in a plurality of different and not always compatible kinds of social activities and relationships that make the view that social order is simply a matter of efficient and expert administration ultimately unsatisfactory and renders politics unavoidable to adjudicate between competing ends. Nevertheless, De Ruggiero and Hobhouse sought to depoliticise the conflicts that can arise between the different interests and ideals held by free individuals by appealing to a subject which was prior to any real individuals and was just the idea of the free individual as such, able to will and choose whatever ideals or interest he or she wished. Individual will, the realm of value, stands outside the existing world of fact so that a sense of community derives from the rational perception by the individual from a point which transcends his or her particular situation of the necessary harmony of individuals wills. The Hegelian motto that 'What is rational is actual and what is actual is rational' did not mean the perception of reason in the world, as Croce had argued but, De Ruggiero's actualism reasserting itself, its 'actualisation'.[53] Yet how is the individual in such a situation to have any basis for identification with the projects of his or her fellows, since these attachments are surely themselves socially produced?

In common with Hobhouse, he sees community arising from the comprehension of the interrelatedness of all social activity, but he does not want to adopt the conservative stance of simply endorsing things as they stand and extolling the

---

52. De Ruggiero, *European Liberalism*, pp. 343, 350–7, 358, 388–9, 393–5, 355.

53. De Ruggiero, *Il ritorno alla ragione*, pp. 14, 29.

merits of 'our station and its duties'. Part of the problem was that the basis of such a conception even in its conservative form did not exist. The fragmentation of society into different occupational specialisms meant that individuals not only felt no direct contact between their role and that of others, but were often dissatisfied with them as well. A factory worker who has a dull and boring job to do is not necessarily going to be any more reconciled to it by having a share in management and a liberal individualist strategy of simply increasing his pay and reducing his hours to be left alone to do what he wants with his spare time may well appear to be the most rational course he can take. Withdrawal and protection from society – a liberalism based on rights, the *bête noir* of idealist philosophers, is likely to appeal most once the constitutive bonds of community have broken down. Community cannot be created out of individual development alone, without the ties of human interaction which sustain and develop it. Talk of the development of human capacities only makes sense in idealist terms in the context of the shared practices of society which bring them forth. The activities people engage in, from forming friendships to eating and working, are not done indifferently but with a sense of meaning to the extent that societies embody a framework of values appropriate to each task – of for example loyalty, etiquette and application in the instances given above.[54] But De Ruggiero was seemingly trying to create this out of nothing – in such a situation the ethical State does indeed become the imposition of a presumed 'real will' on the existent wills of the people.

The years under fascism were spent pondering this problem, producing in 1946 a series of essays suitably entitled *The Return to Reason* calling for a revival of the utopian tradition of political thought. What was required, De Ruggiero argued, was a language which transcends the present, enabling us to transform it. Humans need a framework of beliefs with the scope and function of religion but without falling into the error of substituting other-worldly for this-worldly goals. But 'the ideal needs of the human spirit' are rather difficult to define and, not surprisingly, De Ruggiero got little further than extolling their necessity. As it was, the post-war world looked little different to that before fascism. His revised liberalism had little success except amongst intellectuals within the 'Party of Action'. The politics of the day was divided to an even greater extent between the rival ideologies of capital and labour and more characterised by political jobbery than ever before.[55]

---

54. Similar points with regard to Kant, Rawls and Hobhouse are made by Michael Sandel in *Liberalism and the Limits of Justice*, Cambridge, 1982, pp. 133–74 and Gerald F. Gaus, *The Modern Liberal Theory of Man*, Beckenham, 1983, pp. 257–61, 270–4.

55. *European Liberalism* was reprinted in 1941, leading to De Ruggiero losing his chair at Rome and his arrest in 1943 for his activities in the 'Party of Action'. *Il ritorno alla ragione* of 1946 consists of articles written during this period, developing the arguments of *European Liberalism* (pp. vi-viii and preface to third edition 1943, of *European Liberalism*). In 1943 he became Rector of Rome University and was Minister of Education in the Bonomi adminstration (June–December 1944). He died in Rome on 29 December 1948.

Conclusion

De Ruggiero's amalgam of idealism and liberalism make a curious combination in the modern world, not because they are a hybrid mixture but because both belonged to a period and a moral consensus which had passed. Via idealism, De Ruggiero had attempted to revitalise liberalism as a theory capable of commanding our allegiance but could only do so in terms of a cultural tradition which the social changes with which liberal theory was associated had largely undermined. The philosophy of liberation he espoused was itself the product of liberal individualism, though in radical form. Far from offering an idealist solution to the crisis of liberalism, his political philosophy was itself a product of that crisis.

Part Three

Croce *contra* Gramsci

Chapter Eight

Gramsci, Croce and the Italian Political Tradition[1]

Gramsci's huge reputation amongst influential sections of the British left rests on the belief that he reformulated classical Marxism so as to produce a political strategy that was both revolutionary and democratic and hence suited to the task of achieving socialism in the West. Recently, Stuart Hall went so far as to claim that 'Gramsci gives us [...] the means with which to ask the right kinds of questions about the politics of the 1980s and 1990s', providing 'an understanding of the profound transformation which is now underway in Western liberal-bourgeois societies' and a sense 'of the task of renewal which socialism and the Left now has before it'.[2] I will argue that this view of Gramsci's work fails to take into account the degree to which his ideas were constrained by the concerns and language of the Italian politics of his time, in ways which make him of limited use for socialists today. To a large extent, Gramsci has to be regarded as an Italian thinker, addressing a peculiar set of social and political problems and arguing within a distinctive cultural tradition that can be neither totally assimilated to Marxism nor satisfactorily extended to the analysis of contemporary Western societies. I will illustrate this thesis via a comparison of Gramsci's theory with the political and historical ideas of Benedetto Croce. For Gramsci inherited from Croce, and the Italian political tradition more generally, a political agenda and a conception of politics that seriously limit our ability to employ his theory to guide either revolutionary action in the present or the organisation of any socialist society of the future.

---

1. An earlier version of this paper was delivered at the Convegno su A. Gramsci: Un teorico della politica in un 'paese della periferia', held at the Gramsci Institute, Turin, on 10–12 December 1987. I am grateful to the other participants, particularly Franco Sbarberi, for their comments on that occasion. I have also benefitted from the advice of Bruce Haddock, Quentin Skinner, Martin Clark, Stephen Gundle, Darrow Schecter and the anonymous referees for *History of Political Thought*, where this chapter was first published.

2. The first quote comes from S. Hall, 'Gramsci and us', in his *The Hard Road to Renewal: Thatcherism and the crisis of the left*, London, 1988, p. 162; the last two can be found in a special supplement of *Marxism Today* commemorating the fiftieth anniversary of Gramsci's death (*Marxism Today* Gramsci supplement, 31 April 1987, p. vii). In the same issue, Martin Jacques pointed to Gramsci as 'the most important single theoretical influence' on the journal (p. iii). Hall develops his reading of Gramsci in more detail in an earlier article 'Popular-democratic vs authoritarian populism: two ways of "taking democracy seriously"', in A. Hunt (ed.), *Marxism and Democracy*, London, 1980, pp. 157–85. The Hunt collection contains articles by Colin Mercer and Anne Showstack Sassoon that make analogous claims concerning Gramsci's lessons for the western left, and similar arguments – articulated with varying degrees of sophistication – can be found in almost every English-language study of the Italian thinker, even the more ostensibly 'historical' analyses.

The *Risorgimento* and the Italian political tradition[3]

The social and political problems confronting Italian politicians and theorists following unification were twofold. First, there were the cultural and economic divisions existing between both the different Italian territories, particularly the developing north and the underdeveloped south, and the educated classes and the unschooled masses. Second, and largely as a result of these differences, there was the tension between 'legal Italy', the set of liberal institutions resulting from political unification, and 'real Italy', the fragmented social reality of divergent regional traditions, economic attainment and polarised classes: a tension epitomised for contemporaries in the 'southern question'.

The *Risorgimento* bequeathed a distinctive intellectual legacy to the Italian thinkers seeking to remedy this situation. Both the Giobertian Catholic-Liberals and the republican democrats inspired by Mazzini had professed essentially eschatological ideologies, in which the unification of Italy was conceived of as the realisation of a national identity. Both movements had placed great emphasis on the role of the people as carriers 'of this national consciousness – they constituted the 'real' nation in contrast to the largely foreign-backed and merely 'legal' regimes then governing the various parts of the country. Whilst effective as a means of legitimising the revolt against the *de facto* governments of the time, it had profound drawbacks as a practical strategy, since the Italian people lacked the cultural and social cohesiveness these theories assumed.

The liberals within the Moderate Party appreciated the nature of this dilemma rather better than the Mazzinians, and it was their solution – the unification of Italy by Piedmont – which ultimately set the tone of Italian politics. Gioberti's formulation of this policy following the dashing of his hopes in the failed revolutions of 1848 proved particularly influential. In language explicitly adopted by Gramsci later, he argued that the 'formative principle of nations' consisted of 'what the ancients called hegemony [*egemonia*]':

> that species of primacy, of supremacy, of majority, which is neither legal nor juridical, properly speaking, but consists in the moral efficacy, that amongst many similar provinces sharing the same language and nationality, one of them exercises over the others.[4]

If, he continued, 'every national hegemony entails, at least at the beginning, dictatorship', in order to unite politically the various components of the nation, its

3. This section draws on and modifies R. Bellamy, *Modern Italian Social Theory: Ideology and politics from Pareto to the present*, Cambridge, 1987, ch. 1.

4. V. Gioberti, *Del rinnovamento civile d'Italia*, Paris and Turin, 1851, pp. 203–4. For a considera-tion of Gioberti's influence on Gramsci, *see* A. Asor Rosa, *Scrittori e popolo*, Rome, 1979. It is indicative of their uncertain grasp of the historical context of Gramsci's writings that most English-language commentators follow Perry Anderson, 'The antinomies of Antonio Gramsci', *New Left Review* 100, 1977, pp. 15–20, in tracing the origins of his use of this concept exclusively to the debates of the Russian social-democratic movement from 1883 to 1917.

legitimacy derived from the 'national-popular' will. Thus, Piedmont's unification of the peninsula by force of arms alone and the imposition of Piedmontese institutions on the rest of the country were justified by the belief that its temporary domination would allow the development of an uncoerced moral unity stemming from the people's growing sense of a common nationality.[5]

The Neapolitan neo-Hegelian apologists of the Historic Right, the Cavourian party which governed Italy immediately after unification, refined Gioberti's thesis.[6] They viewed the relationship between force and consensus, state and nationhood in parallel terms to his. Whereas Hegel had regarded the state as the product of the national *Volkgeist*, his Italian followers reversed this formula and argued that the ethos of nationality had to be created within the political organisation of a centralised state. Only uniform procedures and strong central government could prevent regional particularism reasserting itself and dividing the new kingdom. A crucial ambiguity concerning the relationship of politics and ethics thereby entered into Italian political discourse, with Machiavelli supplementing Hegel in their thinking. The Florentine thinker, according to de Sanctis's influential interpretation,[7] had separated the political means from the ends they served, appreciating that the two operated according to different logics. In so doing, Machiavelli had not argued that only the means counted; merely, that one judged political methods by their efficacy and appropriateness, reserving moral judgment for the goals for which they were employed. 'Knowledge' and 'will' were the prime political virtues, attaining moral status only when they served to promote good ends. The state added 'moral force' to mere 'political force' when it succeeded in concentrating the energies of the entire nation by disciplining all its members in the performance of their patriotic duty. If a Prince was required to unite the country with the 'legitimate' force of good government, this achievement would only prove durable if the new rulers could foster the 'republican' consensus of the people. The entry of the Piedmontese armies into Rome at the very moment de Sanctis composed his famous chapter seemed to him to mark the end of the first stage, that of force; the problem was whether the second stage, that of consent, could be achieved – or, to echo d'Azeglio's famous phrase, whether having 'made Italy' the liberals were capable of 'making Italians'.

It is important to note that, in spite of the Hegelian influence, de Sanctis's view of Machiavelli was oddly Kantian. He sharply condemned 'vulgar' Machiavellianism for analogous reasons to those employed by Kant against the 'political moralist': namely, that it subordinated ends to means. In his view, Kant's 'moral politician' represented the true essence of Machiavelli's doctrine. On de

---

5. Gioberti, *Del rinnovamento*, pp. 271–3.

6. The Neapolitan neo-Hegelians included writers such as A.C. De Meis, F. Fiorentino, Bertrando and Silvio Spaventa and F. de Sanctis. De Sanctis and Silvio Spaventa, especially, were both influential politicians, Spaventa becoming the official spokesman of the Right following their fall from power. For details of this group *see* G. Oldrini, *La cultura filosofica napalelana dell'Ottocento*, Bari, 1973.

7. F. de Sanctis, *Storia della letteratura italiana*, 1872–3, Milan [1964], II, ch. 15.

Sanctis's interpretation, Machiavelli appreciated that it paid not merely to appear virtuous but to be so. Both political expediency and morality coincided in such a statesman, with law being judiciously applied gradually to place all citizens in a condition to act morally without forcing them so to do. De Sanctis's theory differed, therefore, from the more full-blooded Hegelianism of thinkers such as Bertrando Spaventa, who aimed at the creation of an 'ethical state' which was not a 'force which draws to itself all the individuals and remains external to those who it draws' but 'unites them to the extent it is immanent in the whole understanding, in all the activity of the individual'.[8] Although de Sanctis gave the state a tutelary function, he distinguished the force of the law from the moral consensus of the citizen body. Unfortunately, Italian politicians and intellectuals did not always resist the temptation to treat the laws of the state as representing the rational will of its members rather than the goals of its rulers, confusing Spaventa's ideal with reality.[9] In this circumstance the force of the state became confused with the consent of its subjects.

Even de Sanctis acknowledged that Machiavelli's theory required certain vital amendments to yield the *Rechtstaat*, notably with regard to individual rights. Yet popular participation and guarantees of individual liberty remained conspicuously absent from the Right's programme; the southern situation, in particular, encouraged them to adopt bureaucratic and coercive measures to moderate and control individual claims.[10] The state, as they conceived it, had an undeniably progressive function in building the infrastructure and legal framework required for liberal capitalism. This involved measures to improve communications (they fell from power on the issue of a nationalised railway network); the establishment of a single internal market and the standardisation of currency, patent laws and weights and measures; a secular education system, with particular emphasis on primary schools; and, of course, laws securing property against social threats from below. These policies were pursued in a benevolently paternalistic fashion, with the aim of moralising the populace into an acceptance of bourgeois hegemony, but went hand in hand with an attitude towards public order of a potentially authoritarian kind. Initial resistance to unification, particularly in the south – where the Piedmontese lost more troops suppressing the bandits than in fighting the Austrians – resulted in a severe penal code, giving the executive wide-ranging 'preventative' powers, which effectively criminalised criticism of the regime under a blanket denunciation of 'subversive' activity. The Right, and the liberal elite more generally, claimed to speak for the nation, but economic and social

---

8. B. Spaventa, *Studi sull'etica di Hegel*, Naples, 1869, pp. 153–4.

9. For an analysis of the dominance of this view within Italian public law, *see* P. Costa, *La stato immaginario: metafore e paradigmi nella cultura giuridica italiana fra ottocento e novecento*, Milan, 1986.

10. The following remarks follow R. Romanelli, *L'Italia liberale* (1861–1900), Bologna, 1979 and R. Vivarelli, *Il fallimento del liberalismo: studi sulle origini del fascismo*, Bologna, 1981, ch.1. For a discussion of the place of the 'southern question' in Italian history, *see* M. Salvadori, *Il mito del buongoverno: la questione meridionale da Cavour a Gramsci*, Turin, 1960.

change generated dissenting popular movements on both sides of the ideological spectrum, which eventually undermined liberalism as a political force. With the fall of the Right from power in 1876, Italian politics underwent a marked moral decline. Governments alternated between the manipulation of 'consent', by granting favours to important local *clientele*, and the application of force, in which police powers were used to the full in response to the growing 'social question'. Despite an initial liberal revolt at the abuses made by the so-called left under Crispi and his successors, these methods remained substantially unreformed during the Giolittian era. Italian politics retained a pronounced Machiavellian flavour, making the passage to fascism in the face of mounting social unrest all-too-palatable a solution for the ruling liberal classes.

This historical excursion into the language and nature of Italian politics provides the all-important context needed to comprehend the problems Gramsci saw himself as addressing and the terms in which he understood them. Depending on the views of the thinker concerned, fascism was interpreted either as the culmination or the resolution of the divide between state and nation/society, 'legal' and 'real' Italy. Both schools of thought were driven to extend the modern Italian political tradition through a reinterpretation of the *Risorgimento* and the weaknesses and strengths of the groups involved in its implementation. Indeed, fascists and anti-fascists alike claimed to be inaugurating a 'second *Risorgimento*' capable of completing the first.[11] The fascist intelligentsia, in particular Gentile, justified fascism as the 'moral force' of the 'ethical state', which creates consensus through its coercive action – the realisation of Spaventa's ideal and the programme of the Historic Right. Croce's writings post-1924 and Gramsci's reflections in his *Quaderni del carcere* sought to challenge this view. They shared the opinion that the success of fascism attested to a lack of moral will or national consciousness amongst the Italian people. It represented the victory of unalloyed political force. In offering a remedy for this state of affairs, they provided an analysis of the actions of the liberal elite in the making of Italy which was intended to serve more as a model for political action in the present than as a disinterested study of the past (in fact both denied such a history was either desirable or possible). Despite their different evaluations of this historical record, their accounts shared the following three elements:

1. A historicist conception of reality and human action, in which the 'ideal' must be adequate to the 'real', transforming existing conditions through a correct appraisal of them, and finding the political means suited to the achievement of attainable moral ends.

2. The belief that a distinct intellectual class acted as the mediators between the 'real' and 'ideal', promoting political change and organising the cultural and political transformation of the masses.

---

11. *See* A. Garosci, 'Primo e secondo risorgimento', *Rivista storica italiana* LXVIV, 1962, pp. 27–40 and S. J. Woolf, '*Risorgimento* e fascismo', *Belfagor* XX, 1965, pp. 71–91.

3. The hope that this process would result in the bringing together of 'legal' and 'real' Italy in, to employ a Gramscian term, a 'historical bloc' of congruent ethical and economic/political elements.

The next two sections explore respectively Croce and Gramsci's interpretations of Italian history. In each case, I shall first outline their version of the three features elements listed above, and then show how their different understandings of them shaped their divergent views of the *Risorgimento*, the creation of the liberal regime and its subsequent collapse into fascism. As we shall see, Gramsci's theory emerged from a critique of Croce's that intensified rather than resolved many of the ambiguities of the Italian political tradition. A further section then compares their views of the relationship between the state and civil society. Once again, the ways they conceived of this relationship and its centrality within their theories of politics mirrored its pivotal role within the Italian political tradition. I shall argue that whereas Croce retained de Sanctis's somewhat Kantian divide between politics and ethics, force and consent, 'legal' and 'real' Italy, Gramsci sought to overcome this dualism through a reworking of the ethical state tradition appropriated by fascist thinkers. I will conclude by arguing that Gramsci's Italian road to socialism proves unsuited in both its methods and its goals for contemporary democratic socialists. It rests on assumptions and proposes solutions that reflect the intellectual aporias, the social conflicts and the democratic weaknesses of 1920s and 30s Italy. Contestable even then, his strategy proves empirically flawed and normatively unappealing when applied to the developed democracies of advanced capitalist societies.

Croce: history as the story of liberty

The antinomies of modern Italy were incorporated into the very structure of Croce's political philosophy, in which he sharply distinguished the economic from the ethical aspects of human activity. According to his original formulation,[12] practical acts belonged to the realms of the 'useful' and the 'good'. These 'pure concepts' were indeterminate, their content deriving from spirit's unfolding in human history. Croce argued that these subdivisions were so related that the first preceded the second. Thus, human beings performed actions with regard to their apparent utility in given circumstances, and by a dialectical process these were revealed by their contribution to historical development possibly to have been 'good', viz. conducive to spirit's progress, as well as 'useful'. Croce separated politics from morals. Returning to Machiavelli, he maintained that politicians examined the suitability of the means with regard to their 'economic' viability alone, wisely confining ethical questions to the judgment of history.[13] This 'economic-political' view was underwritten by his historicist belief in the ultimately benign workings

---

12. For example, B. Croce, *La filosofia della practica: economia ed etica*, Bari, 1909.

13. B. Croce, 'Per la interpretazione e la critica di alcuni concetti del marxismo', 1897, in *Materialismo storico ed economia marxistica*, Bari, 1978, p. 98 n. 1.

of Providence. However, politically this resignation to history led him perilously close to identifying whatever succeeded as ipso facto moral as well. This danger became particularly evident during the First World War and the fascist seizure of power, both of which he saw entirely in terms of an idealist version of the doctrine of natural selection.[14] The undesirability of seeming to conflate political force with moral force became painfully obvious once Croce moved into opposition to Mussolini. Confronted by fascist apologists who claimed his authority for the activities of the new regime, Croce was obliged to clarify and amend his ideas. It is this phase of his thinking, post-1924, in which he developed his 'ethico-political' theory of history that I want to study here. As announced above, I shall start with the role within his theory of the three elements outlined earlier, and then turn to his deployment of them in his account of modern Italian history.

Croce's view of liberalism as a 'meta-political' doctrine, co-extensive with the progressive development of spirit within human history,[15] flowed from his understanding of the first element he shared with Gramsci – the historicist view of reality. In Croce's earlier formulation of his historicism, in the *Teoria e storia della storiografia* (1912–15), he had identified the individual with spirit, so that history was seen as 'the work of that truly real individual, which is spirit eternally individualising itself'.[16] Thus, the individual was but the particular act whereby spirit realised itself. In Hegelian manner, he regarded all 'real', successful, actions as necessarily 'rational' developments of the Idea. In 'ethico-political' history, by contrast, Croce gave primacy to the ideals individuals set themselves as makers of history. This revision posed a problem, since it appeared to deny his original contention that the real entities in history were not human beings but their acts, seen as the product of an unknowable demiurge. He found a solution in Hegel's thesis that both points of view were valid ways of describing a single process, 'the Idea' and 'human will' being the 'warp and weft in the fabric of world history', whereby 'the Idea as it expresses itself through the medium of the human will or of human freedom gives rise to the entire ethical life of nations'.[17]

According to Croce, historical knowledge served as a preparation for moral action by yielding an awareness of the dispositions of spirit within us and the world, of the 'ideal' within the 'real'. However, it was 'indeterminate': the responsibility for new action lay with the individual alone. As he summed it up in a famous passage:

---

14. On the First World War, *see* his collection of articles, B. Croce, *Pagine sulla guerra*, Bari, 1918. His response to fascism can be traced via the newspaper articles reprinted in B. Croce, *Pagine sparse*, Bari, 1943, pp. 371–406. For a fuller discussion, *see* R. Bellamy, 'Liberalism and historicism: Benedetto Croce and the political role of Idealism in Italy', in A. Moulakis (ed.), *The Promise of History*, Berlin and New York, 1985, pp. 69–119.

15. B. Croce, 'La concezione liberale come concezione della vita', 1927, in his collection *Etica e politica*, Bari, 1973, p. 235.

16. B. Croce, *Teoria e storia della storiografia*, (1917), Bari, 1943, p. 87.

17. G. W. F. Hegel, *Lectures on the Philosophy of World History: Introduction*, trans. H. B. Nisbet, Cambridge, 1975, p. 71.

We are products of the past and we live immersed within the past which presses upon us from all sides. How then can we move to a new life, how can we create our new action, without putting ourselves above the past if we are within it, and it is us? There is only one way out, that of thought, which does not break the relationship with the past but ideally soars above it and converts it into knowledge.[18]

The liberal ideal, interpreted as the capacity for self-directed action by posing ideals for oneself rather than being subject to determination by biological and material forces, became the motivating force of history. According to Croce, all history was the history of liberty, even if a consciousness of this process had only become evident during the Renaissance and the Reformation and flowered as the unifying principle of society with the development of Romanticism during the nineteenth century – the liberal era. The whole of history could be interpreted as a never-ending struggle to realise human freedom through the transformation of the world and the creation of the institutions and artefacts of human society. 'Those aspects of social life still not permeated by liberty represent [...] the material of future problems'.[19] However, he was not advocating a species of voluntarism. The 'ethical' remained conceptually distinct from the 'economic' but practically inseparable from it. The only valid ideals were those grounded in the 'real', so that liberty took on different forms throughout the course of history. His perspective had shifted from that of the liberal establishment post-unification, back to the more activist stance adopted by them during the *Risorgimento*.

The second element, that of intellectuals as a mediating class, Croce adapted from the Italian political scientist Gaetano Mosca. Substituting Mosca's 'political class' for Hegel's 'world historical individuals', Croce argued that the active elements in any society came from the members of the 'middling rank'. As he put it, 'The creators of [political and social] institutions are the political geniuses, and the aristocrats or political classes which give them life and who in turn are created and supported by them'.[20] This group could not be identified with the bourgeoisie, since they formed an ethical rather than an economic class. Neither 'rulers' nor 'ruled', they mediated between the two, linking the 'legal' state with the 'real' nation within a single ideological framework. Change occurred not through the circulation of interest groups, as Mosca claimed, but as a result of the elaboration and circulation of ideals. Intellectuals, therefore, were the most important component of this group, since their activity shaped the climate of ideas which formed the customs and manners of the polity. In this respect, Croce offered his own philosophy as a 'religion of liberty', suited to the maintenance of the liberal institutional order. As for the masses:

---

18. B. Croce, *La storia come azione e come pensiero*, (1938), Bari, 1978, pp. 33–4.

19. *Ibid.*, pp. 47–51, 224, 227–8.

20. B. Croce, 'Storia economico-politica e storia ethico-politica', 1924, *Etica e politica*, p. 231.

one cannot expect that the truths, discovered by thinkers and made the common patrimony of culture, will easily penetrate them, but one must do one's utmost by educating them, to put them in a position, on the one hand, to increase the ruling class with ever fresh forces, and new co-operators and elements and, on the other hand, to bring them gradually into harmony with it; and, when and where that does not occur, to treat them with the political shrewdness that the occasions demand, so that they do not destroy the social order, that is to say civilisation.[21]

This passage, written at the height of his opposition to fascism, attested to the continuing ambivalence of his position. Croce sought to create an open elite, capable of ruling via a common culture. However, when consent broke down, force had to be applied.

As a result, the third element – the creation of a historical bloc – could not be definitive for Croce, the realisation of the ethical state that brought 'legal' and 'real' Italy together. The two were in permanent tension. The state still represented the economic/legal order, therefore, which in neo-Kantian fashion offered the necessary means for allowing the pursuit of ethical ends. But the distinction between the two realms remained even more drastic and potentially conflictual in Croce's version than it was in Kant's. Although he expressed the thoroughly liberal conviction concerning the 'necessity of leaving, so far as possible, free play to the spontaneous and inventive forces of individuals and social groups',[22] he resisted any attempt to elaborate upon what sort of institutional order would best suit this purpose. He regarded such endeavours as utopian, rights doctrines in particular necessarily degenerating into setting up particular ends as universal. Liberty consisted in humankind's ceaseless creativity throughout history. Belonging to the ethical realm, no temporary political regime – no matter how authoritarian – could ever touch it. The state operated in the economic realm alone, coercing human beings *qua* irrational non-moral agents when they failed to curb their passions and put their own interests above those of society. The dialectic of the useful and the good, force and consensus, remained omnipresent throughout history. Each ethical epoch found expression in a given economic order, with the coercive aspect increasing during transitional or uncivilised periods.

Having outlined the three elements as they figure within Croce's political thought, we can now turn to their application in his account of the liberal era: most particularly in his *Storia d'Italia dal 1871 al 1915* (1928) and his *Storia d'Europa nel secolo decimonono* (1932). Croce viewed the liberal period as a fortuitous coming together of a political and economic revolution, which found expression in the nationalist movements, in particular, as the conscious attempt to construct a new age based on the 'religion of liberty'. As he stressed in a famous

---

21. B. Croce, 'Principio, ideale, teoria: a proposito della teoria filosofica della liberta' (1939), in his collection *Il carattere della filosofia moderna*, Bari, 1945, p. 109.
22. B. Croce, 'Liberalismo', *La Critica* XXIII, 1925, p. 126.

debate with the free-market economist Luigi Einaudi, and repeated in the opening pages of his history of nineteenth-century Europe, the liberal ideal should not be identified with any of the methods which, in given historical circumstances, may have been appropriate for its realisation. The link between liberalism and democracy or the free market was 'a relationship between [...] a regulative concept and its actualisation, in which the force of the ideal, of the regulative concept, exists in its presence, the efficacy which it displays within the actualisation, with which it never completely coincides'.[23] The crisis of liberalism derived from a failure to perceive this relationship. Only two regimes had achieved an appropriate equilibrium between the 'ideal' and the 'real', the July Monarchy in France and Giolittean Italy. Significantly, both of them had culminated in a return to force to curb social disorder. Whilst Croce acknowledged that Britain had been the home of liberalism in the nineteenth century, he regarded this circumstance as mere good fortune, resulting from a relatively stable economy. The ideas of English liberals, which he associated with various kinds of utilitarianism, reflected their essentially economic, as opposed to ethical, origins. Generally, the linking of liberalism with the material improvements of the period was to prove disastrous.

Croce interpreted Giolitti's most successful period of government, from 1901 to 1910, as the product of a delicate balance between the 'economic' and 'ethical' forces. Giolitti had found a suitable 'political formula', to employ Mosca's terminology, capable of disarming the social tensions which had characterised the late 1880s and 1890s by gradually absorbing the new elites from the emergent working classes into the political class. The suffrage reforms of 1911–12, which Mosca – clearly the inspiration behind Croce's remarks – had at the time opposed, along with the other Conservative liberals with whom Croce sympathised, became Giolitti's most consummate piece of statesmanship. *Trasformismo*, far from encapsulating the endemic corruption of the Italian political system, was reinterpreted by Croce as a term of approval, the key to Giolitti's achievement:

> having freed the term from the pejorative meaning which was initially attached to it, and because every time that the antinomy between conservation and revolution is transcended and weakens and seems to vanish there follows a drawing together of extremes and a unifying transformation of their ideals.[24]

Giolitti's policies of discreet social and political reform disarmed the socialists, placing 'Marx in the attic', and converting them to the 'liberal method'. Finally, this golden epoch was underpinned by a humanist philosophy adapted to the needs of the age, Croce's own 'philosophy of spirit'. Through his magazine, *La Critica,* Croce claimed to have worked a cultural revolution, defeating the dominant positivist and Marxist theories of the earlier, more turbulent period, and replacing them with a liberal idealism capable of filling the spiritual gap left by the decline of orthodox religion. Thus, he characterised the whole liberal era as a hegemonic system in the Gramscian sense, based on cultural consent and in which:

---

23. B. Croce, *Storia d'Italia dal 1871 al 1915*, Bari, 1977, p. 8.
24. *Ibid.*, p. 205.

democracy exists between the ruling group and the groups that are ruled, to the extent that [economic development and therefore] legislation [which expresses that development] favours the [molecular] passage from the ruled to the rulers.[25]

What went wrong? In Croce's opinion, the relatively recent nature of the Italian liberal tradition meant that its ideals were easily mistaken for its transitory achievements. When these came under strain as the general down-turn of the economy brought a slowing-up of the pace of reform, so that a degree of popular self-restraint was called for, liberalism itself came under attack. Various 'irrational' and 'materialist' ideologies began to flourish, notably in the form of nationalism and a more aggressive socialism, culminating in the First World War ('a sort of war of "historical materialism" or of "philosophical irrationalism"', as he now described it).[26] The 'economic' became mistaken for the 'ethical', and so moral consensus gave way to material conflict.

Croce glossed over the social and political limitations of Giolitti's reformism, his election-rigging and the guaranteed majority provided by his use of patronage to keep the southern deputies (the *ascari*) in his pocket. His clientelistic practices undid whatever good might have ensued from his various concessions, since they had the effect of both closing off and, eventually, de-legitimising the parliamentary arena, ultimately encouraging extra-parliamentary forms of protest and political conflict. By ignoring this issue, Croce had hidden from view the central problem of liberal Italy: namely, why the Italian political elite had turned to fascism rather than institutional means to contain and diffuse the social tensions attendant on a modernising economy.[27]

Croce's thesis, explicitly stated only in the preface to the 1947 edition, that fascism was merely a parenthesis in Italian history, has been criticised as a sleight of hand. Denis Mack Smith, in one of his characteristic interventions that Italian historians love to hate, looked upon this device as a ploy to avoid inconsistently denying that even fascism had a certain rationality, a vital role to play in history's progress and the unfolding of liberty.[28] I have already pointed out that Croce's later historicism did not simply endorse all past acts in the way this criticism implies. Even at the time of the fascist seizure of power, when he still held to his economic-political view of history, Croce had been careful to distinguish fascist force from the moral end of a return to liberal consensus which he hoped it would achieve. Returning to Machiavelli, he had argued, in a review of Chabod's edition of *Il Principe*, that 'the true political *virtus* is force'.[29] On another occasion, he stated:

25. A. Gramsci, *Quaderni del carcere*, edizione critica acura di V. Gerratana, 4 vols, Turin, 1975, p. 1056.

26. Croce, *Storia d'Italia*, p. 267.

27. For the historical background underlying these criticisms I am indebted to P. Comer, 'Liberalism, pre-fascism, fascism', in D. Forgacs (ed.) *Rethinking Italian Fascism: Capitalism, populism, culture*, London, 1986, pp. 11–20.

28. D. Mack Smith, 'Benedetto Croce: History and politics', *Journal of Contemporary History* VIII, 1973, pp. 41–61.

29. B. Croce, Review of N. Machiavelli, *Il Principe* ed. F. Chabod, *La Critica* XXII, 1924, pp. 313–15.

If the liberals have not had the force and virtù to save Italy from the anarchy in which it lay, they must bewail the fact and recite their mea culpa, and meanwhile accept what is good from any quarter that it may come from.

However, he consistently denied that fascism 'could be anything else than a bridge for the restoration of a more severe and more authoritarian liberal regime'. Since only liberalism expressed the 'ethical' element within human history:

> fascism ought to give up its attempt to inaugurate a new epoch [...] The fascists, if they realise how inescapable is the return to a liberal regime, will save their own system as a strong, salutary element in future political struggles.[30]

Croce started opposing fascism when party ideologists, notably Gentile, took up his 'economic-political' thesis in a radical manner and argued that consensus was essentially reducible to force.[31] As Gentile argued in a famous passage:

> Every force is moral force because it always addresses the will, and whatever method of argument is used – from sermon to cudgel – its efficacy cannot be other than that of entreating the inner man and persuading him to consent.[32]

On this outrageous view, the fascist squads had attained the consensus of the Italian people through their 'holy violence'. From here it was an easy step to the assertion of an essential identity between the will of the individual and that of the fascist 'ethical state', so that 'the maximum liberty always coincides with the maximum force of the State'.[33] Croce's rejection of this sophistry was undoubtedly genuine (so that he cannot be labelled a fascist). Significantly, Gentile claimed parentage for his theory in Bertrando Spaventa, whereas Croce looked to de Sanctis. Yet, Croce went no further than his mentor in providing ways for resolving the tension between state and society, force and consensus. Not surprisingly a similar ambiguity lingers in his most powerful contemporary critic – Antonio Gramsci.

Gramsci and Italy's passive revolution

Gramsci acknowledged that his political theory had strong affinities with Croce's ethico-political interpretation of history:

> Croce's thought [...] has energetically drawn attention to the importance of cultural facts and of thought to historical development, to the function of the

30. B. Croce, 'Intervista', *Giornale d'Italia* 27 October 1923 and 9 July 1924.

31. *See* Mussolini's famous speech 'Forza e consenso' in *Gerarchia* II, March 1923, reproduced in E. Santarelli (ed.), *Scritti Politici*, Milan, 1979, pp. 227–8. Croce's reply, examined in the final section, can be found in the article 'Il senso politico', in *Etica e politica*, p. 178.

32. G. Gentile, 'Il fascismo e la Sicilia' (1924), in *Che cosa e il fascismo?*, Florence, 1925, p. 50.

33. *Ibid.*, pp. 31–50.

great intellectuals in the organic life of civil society and of the State, to the moment of hegemony and of consensus as a necessary form of the concrete historical bloc.

Gramsci observed that the importance of Croce's work was demonstrated by the fact that, contemporaneously, 'the greatest modern theorist of the philosophy of praxis', *viz*. Lenin, had developed Marxism in a similar direction.[34] Debate has raged amongst Gramscian scholars over the compatibility of the Leninist and Crocean elements in Gramsci's theory, an issue related to the relative weight he accorded to the 'base' or 'superstructure' as a determinant of political change. A comparison of the Sardinian's views with those of Marx and Lenin necessarily falls outside the scope of this paper, given that my principal aim is to illustrate the degree to which he continued to address the themes and problems of the Italian political tradition, albeit in a distinctive manner. Whether the novelty of his contribution arose from or spawned a better or worse understanding of Marxism must be left for others to decide. For my purposes, it suffices to say that Gramsci believed himself to be working within a broadly Marxist conception of politics and history and to be applying these ideas to the Italian situation. I will examine his critique of Croce's ethico-political doctrine in order to show the extent to which this project involved adopting the language and ambiguities of Italian political culture.

Gramsci identified three phases within the revolutionary process, corresponding to the three common elements he shared with Croce outlined at the end of the first section of this chapter. The first element consisted in his historicist contention that knowledge of the 'objective' historical conditions for revolution could only occur when economic forces favoured it. Like Croce, Gramsci regarded historical knowledge as a necessary preliminary for political action: 'the existence of the objective conditions, of possibility or of freedom is still not sufficient: one must "understand them" and know how to use them'.[35] Hence 'a great history book is one which in the present helps the forces in development to become more self-conscious and therefore more concretely active and energetic'.[36] To discover when circumstances were propitious for inciting 'a collective national popular will', one needed 'an historical analysis (economic) of the social structure of the given country and a "dramatic" representation of the attempts made across the centuries to promote this will and the reasons for the successive failures to do so'.[37]

Gramsci claimed that this sort of investigation was conspicuously lacking from Croce's account of Italian history. The speculative nature of Croce's approach had led him to separate human thought and action from real 'flesh and blood' individuals, turning them instead into epiphenomena of a metaphysical entity

---

34. Gramsci, *Quaderni*, p. 1235.

35. *Ibid.*, p. 1338.

36. *Ibid.*, pp. 1983–4.

37. *Ibid.*, p. 1559.

– spirit.[38] Ideas made sense only when studied in relation to the social patterns in which they were embedded. In being oblivious to the dynamic relationship between the process of thinking and the real material world, Croce had missed the true essence of history as the progressive elaboration of economic structures, corresponding to (if not causally explained by) the available productive forces.

I hope I have shown that this interpretation slightly misrepresented Croce's later historicism. By seeing the objective historical conditions as an intrinsic part of spirit's development, Croce could hardly ignore them. Indeed, Croce had insisted that the role of the political class lay in providing an appropriate 'ethical' understanding of economic and social relations. Nevertheless, Gramsci's view goes further, reflecting a Marxist concern with the relations between 'base' and 'superstructure', even if he interpreted this relationship in a less deterministic manner than many other commentators.[39]

Gramsci's second phase, the political organisation of a 'subjective' historical consciousness amongst the masses by intellectuals, partly paralleled the second common element he shared with Croce's theory. Gramsci similarly believed that intellectuals performed a mediating role between leaders and led, by providing a moral perspective capable of uniting them. However, whereas Croce had regarded the intellectuals as the disinterested servants of spirit, Gramsci maintained that they must represent the needs and aspirations of the economically progressive class of the moment, formerly the bourgeoisie and now the proletariat. Only when this class had achieved an awareness of their historical position within the productive process could they transcend the 'economic-corporative' perspective and construct an ethical system capable of incorporating all classes.

Gramsci argued that the 'traditional' role adopted by Italian intellectuals since the Renaissance, as purveyors of universal verities, had secured their political impotence. They remained apart from the people, 'something detached, hanging, in the air, a caste'. In consequence, 'a national intellectual and moral bloc' had never evolved, and the Italian people had suffered the domination of foreign culture as well as of foreign arms. They had never developed 'a new secular and humanist philosophy' capable of mass appeal, so that 'popular culture in Italy is still in the condition created by the Counter-Reformation'.[40] Croce's own philosophy, which he had intended to fulfil the function of just such a 'secular religion', had remained the preserve of the intellectual elite. Moreover, the independent stance adopted by 'traditional' intellectuals was ultimately unsustainable, with them ending up as the passive tools of the ruling class. Thus, Croce might act like a 'lay Pope' but 'the most significant character' of his philosophy resides in 'his links with senators Agnelli and Benni'. Gramsci gave to the concept of the intellectual a wholly new meaning.[41] 'Organic' intellectuals, as he termed them, acknowledged

---

38. *Ibid.*, p. 1238.

39. For a fuller defence of this view, *see* Bellamy, *Modern Italian Social Theory*, pp. 121–31 and J. Femia, *Gramsci's Political Thought*, Oxford, 1981, ch. 3.

40. Gramsci, *Quaderni*, pp. 2116–20.

41. *Ibid.*, p. 1516–17.

their membership of a particular social group and 'gave it homogeneity and an awareness of its true function not only in the economic sphere, but also in the social and political spheres as well.[42] They served to bridge the gap between the economic base and civil society, the arena of consensual hegemony, making workers aware of the possibility of organising the economic structure in alternative ways.

Gramsci shared the Leninist belief that the workers' leaders who emerged spontaneously from within the capitalist productive process would necessarily embrace reformism. The political party enabled them to break this attitude. It provided an alternative institutional context within which they could operate, slowly incorporating their fellow workers and building up the socialist society of the future in embryo. However, Gramsci did not adopt the notion of the vanguard party, directed by an elite. 'Organic' intellectual leadership entailed the self-education of the masses, so that 'every leap towards a new "broadening" and complexity of the intellectual strata is linked to an analogous movement of the simple mass'.[43] In addition, the intellectual relationship existing between them developed through a process of mutual dialogue, in which 'every teacher is always a pupil and every pupil a teacher'.[44] Intellectuals and the masses complemented each other, for 'the popular element "feels", but does not always understand or know; the intellectual element "knows", but does not always understand and especially "feel"'.[45]

This pedagogical work of the party did not preclude preparing for the final phase, the organisation of 'military forces' for the revolutionary seizure of power and the creation of a new historical bloc – the third common element of Gramsci and Croce's theories. If the complexity of civil society within western democracies made it necessary to engage in a protracted 'war of position' to gain the allegiance of the masses, it did not obviate the need, when the time was ripe, for a 'war of movement' or revolutionary action of the usual type, to topple the capitalist state.[46] The triumph of a new ethico-political order could occur only with the destruction of the old economic structure and the pattern of social relations which it supported.

Gramsci criticised Croce for ignoring this third stage by excluding the French Revolution from his portrait of the liberal era. Yet how could one disregard:

> the moment in which an ethico-political system dissolves itself and another is elaborated in fire and with iron? in which a system of social relations falls apart and decays and another system rises up and affirms itself? and instead placidly assume as the whole of history the ethico-political moment of cultural expansion?[47]

---

42. *Ibid.*, pp. 1513.
43. *Ibid.*, p. 1386.
44. *Ibid.*, p. 1331.
45. *Ibid.*, p. 1505.
46. *Ibid.*, pp. 122–3, 1612–13, 865–7.
47. *Ibid.*, p. 1227.

By not investigating the origins of liberal Italy, Croce had been able to gloss over the weaknesses of the liberal system. It had blinded him to the constraints placed upon Giolittean reformism through the unwillingness of the Italian liberal classes to share any substantial portion of their power with subaltern groups. His belief that political change occurred through a process of gradual 'transformism' had simply provided a spurious legitimation of a corrupt practice. It had turned the procedures of bourgeois politics into a model for all time, conveniently forgetting that they had only been established following a period of violent upheaval. Yet, as we have seen, Croce cannot be accused of ignoring the moment of force, of 'pure politics' as Gramsci termed it. His histories deliberately portrayed the hegemonic moment of Italian liberalism because it was this achievement he sought to defend. For Gramsci, however, the fatal flaws of the liberal settlement arose from the failed nature of the revolution which had brought it about. In order to survive, this economic and social order had generated the class tensions that were eventually to destabilise it and make a coercive resolution necessary and inevitable.

Gramsci illustrated his alternative reading of the three elements of the Italian political tradition via a detailed discussion of the *Risorgimento*.[48] He refined his argument by making an important distinction between two ways in which a social group asserts its supremacy: 'as "domination" and as "intellectual and moral leadership"'.[49] Following Gioberti, he argued that 'political hegemony' combined the two elements. Gramsci believed that because of a lack of intellectual leadership, unification had been largely imposed from above by the representatives of a narrow class interest: namely, the Moderate Party composed of Cavour, the followers of the Piedmontese monarchy and the agrarian elites. The only possible alternative, the Mazzinian radical-democrats in the Action Party, had remained very much a subaltern group, whose 'abstract' and 'international' viewpoint and lack of organisational skills had inhibited them from making a decisive contribution to the national movement. To succeed, they would have needed to offer 'an organic programme of government which reflected the essential demands of the popular masses, above all of the peasants'. A project of agrarian reform, in particular, could have won the allegiance of both the peasantry and intellectuals from the middle and lower strata, who would have felt then that they represented a workable alternative to the Moderates. This policy would have created a 'liberal-national formation' capable 'at the very least of giving to the *Risorgimento* a more markedly popular and democratic character'.[50] Instead, their advocacy of religious reform mirrored the Italian intellectuals' characteristic divorce from the concerns of the people, for 'not only did it not interest the great rural masses, but on the

48. Valuable examinations of Gramsci's interpretation of the *Risorgimento* are provided by G. Galasso, *Croce, Gramsci e altri storici*, Milan, 2nd edn, 1978. pp. 116–72; P. Ginsburg, 'Gramsci and the era of bourgeois revolution in Italy', in J. Davis (ed.), *Gramsci and Italy's Passive Revolution*, London, 1979; and W. Adamson, *Hegemony and Revolution: A study of Antonio Gramsci's political and cultural theory*, California, 1980, ch. 6.

49. Gramsci, *Quaderni*, p. 2010.

50. *Ibid.*, p. 2013.

contrary rendered them open to incitement against the new heretics'.[51] Although individual radicals such as Ferrari, Cattaneo and Pisacane recognised the need for popular support, their advice went unheeded. The opportunity was lost because the Mazzinians were worried that a genuine mass movement might lead to a terror, as in 1793, or that the Austrians might exploit the peasantry for a Vendée-type counter-revolutionary offensive. Gramsci acknowledged that historical precedents existed for both alternatives but he argued that if the peasants had been offered an amelioration of their conditions they would have actively supported the cause of unification. This mass base could have enabled the Party of Action to resolve the 'military problem' of raising sufficient troops to repel the Austrians without external aid via a 'revolutionary levy' and the formation of peasant militias. When such a possibility offered itself, such as the 'Five Days' insurrection in Milan in 1848, Mazzini flinched from taking it, for the reasons given above, and capitulated to the help proffered by the Piedmontese forces. Indeed, on the one occasion when they succeeded in gaining the initiative, during Garibaldi's invasion of Sicily, the Mazzinians ended up brutally crushing peasant uprisings against the barons.[52]

Gramsci claimed the Party of Action's approach reflected a longstanding failure on the part of the urban bourgeoisie to engage with the rural peasantry, going back to the time of the medieval communes, a pattern which was repeated at a different level in the modern north–south divide. In both cases, the bourgeoisie consolidated their power not by allying with the more dynamic sections of society but by compromising with the established agrarian elites. Their practical ineffectiveness resulted in the Mazzinian group's absorption into the Moderates and their acquiescence in the purely formal unity imposed by Piedmont. A pattern was thereby set for the subsequent development of liberal Italy, with 'transformism' continuing the process of 'decapitation' of the elites of potentially disruptive social forces and their temporary 'annihilation'. As Gramsci remarked, such a mixture of bribery and police repression, employed with varying degrees of finesse, characterised the methods of political control adopted by the various liberal regimes, particularly in the South, up to and including fascism. The latter simply indicated the limits of liberal 'legality' in the face of mounting organised social unrest in both the towns and the countryside following the First World War.[53]

Gramsci's critical account followed the three-stage model of revolutionary action examined earlier. He noted what the 'objective' social forces allowed, and criticised the Mazzinians for failing to develop a political programme capable of exploiting this situation by organising a 'subjective' awareness of them sufficient to have enabled a transition to the 'military' phase, and with it a completely different economic structure. Instead they had allowed the Moderates, who at least formed an 'economic-corporate' group, to take the initiative. In so doing 'the educated class' had not fulfilled its 'historical function': namely, 'that of leading the popular

51. *Ibid.*, p. 2046.

52. *Ibid.*, pp. 2012–13, 2048–54.

53. *Ibid.*, pp. 2024, 2035–46, 1767–8.

masses and developing the progressive elements within them'. Throughout his study, Gramsci compared the Mazzinians with the French Jacobins, who had built a 'national-popular' mass movement on the basis of urban-rural alliances. They had succeeded in 'leading', representing not just the immediate interests of the existing bourgeoisie, a moderate and exiguous class, but 'the revolutionary movement in its entirety, as an integrated historical development'. Consequently:

> they did not only organise a bourgeois government, that is make the bourgeoisie the dominant class, they did more, they created the bourgeois State, they made the bourgeoisie the leading national class, hegemonic, that is they gave the new State a permanent base, they created the compact modem French nation.[54]

The contrast with the Italian radicals could not be greater:

> They said they set themselves the task of creating the modem State in Italy and they produced a bastard, they aimed to encourage a diffuse and energetic ruling class and they did not succeed, to include the people within the State and they did not succeed.[55]

Gramsci's historical reflections were intended to serve the political needs of the present. First, they revealed the incomplete nature of Italy's bourgeois revolution and pointed to the deficiencies of the liberal order. By showing how the bourgeoisie in Italy had achieved power without becoming properly hegemonic, Gramsci provided a reason for the failure of liberalism to become a consensual system that had been absent from Croce's analysis. The 'wave of materialism' bemoaned by Croce pointed to a more deep-rooted 'crisis of authority'. For:

> If the ruling class has lost its consensus, that is, is no longer 'leading' [*dirigente*] but only 'dominant', living by pure coercive force, this means precisely that the great masses have become detached from their traditional ideologies, and no longer believe what they used to believe, etc [...] The crisis consists precisely in the fact that the old is dying and the new cannot be born; in this interregnum a wide variety of morbid symptoms appear.[56]

Cries for the restoration of moral regulation reflected deep-seated tensions in the social order, which Croce's account had failed to address. Croce's 'religion of liberty' could never operate as a successful hegemonic project because it failed to reach down to the economic reality on which any new culture must build.

Second, Gramsci's history offered guidelines for how to proceed towards a future proletarian revolution. It underscored the need for an effective political organisation, linked to the aspirations of the 'historical' class, and capable of expressing them at a 'national-popular' level. Gramsci surmised that the failure of the Turin factory movement of 1919–20 had shown that although the substructural

---

54. *Ibid.*, p. 2029.
55. *Ibid.*, p. 2053.
56. *Ibid.*, p. 311.

preconditions for a revolution existed, it was necessary to organise the proletariat against the superstructural sources of class power within civil society and the state as well. He arrived at this solution by grafting the Crocean insight concerning the need for a revolutionary movement to engage in ethical-political struggle on to the Marxian thesis that the forces of production formed the primary determinant of social development. In contrast to Croce, Gramsci believed that the ethical-political contest between rival social groups formed part of the more fundamental confrontation between capital and labour at the level of production. It was in the resolution of this latter conflict that communism claimed to be genuinely hegemonic, combining cultural and political initiatives with a programme for transforming the economy as part of a fully integrated revolutionary strategy.

Once more Machiavelli was invoked as the theorist of Italian unity, this time in the guise of the first Italian Jacobin. Whereas the Florentine had looked to a Prince to revive the Renaissance city states, modem Italians required the Party. This 'Modern Prince':

> must be and cannot but be the proclaimer and organiser of an intellectual and moral reform, which also means creating the grounds for a subsequent development of the national-popular collective will towards the accomplishment of a superior and total form of modem civilisation.[57]

Croce had called Marx 'the Machiavelli of the proletariat' on the grounds that both thinkers were realists who wisely separated politics from morals.[58] By contrast, Croce regarded Jacobinism as the use of force in the service of an abstract ideal.[59] Although Gramsci's 'new Machiavelli' was once more curiously Kantian in nature, his interpretation tended in the opposite direction to de Sanctis's and Croce's: 'the Prince takes the place of the deity or the categorical imperative within human consciences, becoming the basis for [...] a complete secularisation of the whole of life and of all relationships and customs'. Gramsci's Machiavelli joined politics to morals through economics. The party's intellectual and moral programme was intimately tied to a policy of economic reform, 'indeed the programme of economic reform was precisely the concrete means by which every intellectual and moral reform presents itself'.[60] For, it was the 'economic' force of the party as the developer of national energies, most particularly in the area of production, which provided the basis for its moral superiority. In this fashion the Communist Party would repeat the pattern of the French Revolutionaries, acting as the historical agents of the proletariat much as they had ushered in the era of the bourgeoisie. As a result, the project of 'making Italians' would be completed at last and the triumph of a transformed 'real' Italy would render 'legal' Italy an anachronism. For:

---

57. *Ibid.*, p. 1560.

58. Croce, *Materialismo storico*, p. 98. Croce made this judgment with direct reference to de Sanctis's interpretation of Machiavelli.

59. Croce, 'Il senso politico', p.181. In pre-prison writings Gramsci had also held this view.

60. Gramsci, *Quaderni*, p. 1561.

A class which presents itself as capable of assimilating the whole of society, and is at the same time really capable of expressing this process, brings to perfection this [ethical] conception of the State and of law, which have become redundant by exhausting their function and having been absorbed into civil society.[61]

A number of remarks are in order concerning Gramsci's proposed political strategy. Gramsci believed that the proletariat could build an alternative hegemony in the civil society of bourgeois capitalism, in much the same way that the bourgeoisie had wrested social power from the feudal aristocracy prior to assaulting the *ancien régime* states in the eighteenth and nineteenth centuries. Part of this thesis rested on the assumption that capitalism was in crisis and the historical trend was towards communist modes of production. Although most of his admirers acknowledge Gramsci's failure adequately to theorise the role of ideology in the processes of production and exchange and his poor understanding of the economic resilience of capitalism, it is worth remembering that his much praised political analysis hinged on the mistaken supposition of capitalism's terminal decline. However, I wish to criticise the main political assumption behind his theory. Gramsci did not see how the bourgeois-democratic state engineers the active consent of its citizens through its procedures. The 'war of position' strategy, whereby hegemonic control of society can be won prior to an assault on the state, depends on the relative autonomy of civil society. Whereas this precondition largely prevailed in the case of the *ancien régime*, the same cannot be said of the states of modern industrial western nations. For a start, today's states are far more powerful and better organised than those of the eighteenth and early nineteenth centuries: not only do their bureaucratic structures stretch into large aspects of economic and social life but they also have highly efficient forces of coercion at their disposal. Both features can block counter-hegemonic projects more effectively than under earlier regimes. More important, bourgeois democracy itself channels potential opposition into supporting and upholding the state, disarming radical demands for a new form of socialist state.

It is not surprising that Gramsci should have offered no real appreciation of how parliamentary democracy serves as the main source of bourgeois hegemony under western capitalism by masking economic divisions behind a judicial equality in the state. After all, Italian liberals had largely ignored this route. The divergence of state and society was at the heart of the 'crisis of authority' threatening the liberal regime in Italy. The problem had been encapsulated by the liberal democrat Guido De Ruggiero in 1921:

This crisis can only be resolved by the gradual absorption into the state of those forces [the socialist masses] which now express themselves outside it. Only then will we have a strong state – thus enabling us to reduce the immense armies of police that we have today.[62]

61.   *Ibid.*, p. 937.

62.   Guido De Ruggiero, 'Il problema dell'autorita', *Il Paese*, 8 December 1921, reprinted in R. de Felice (ed.) *Scritti politici 1912–26*, Bologna, 1963, pp. 421–2. For an account of De Ruggiero's politics, *see* R. Bellamy, 'Idealism and liberalism in an Italian "New Liberal" theorist: Guido De Ruggiero's *History of European Liberalism*', *Historical Journal* XXX, 1987, pp. 191–200, reproduced as Chapter Seven in this collection.

De Ruggiero's was a relatively isolated voice, however. Croce's passive support for fascism was far more typical of the liberal establishment. Having witnessed the rise of the fascists, Gramsci's belief that a political party 'carries out in civil society the same function as the State carries out in political society'[63] was not unreasonable. But the post-war Italian Communist Party has found this impossible to achieve under a successful parliamentary regime and has been driven ineluctably towards reformism.[64]

Croce, Gramsci and the nature of the state

Having reached the revolutionary conclusion of Gramsci's theory, the 'regulated', truly hegemonic and stateless society of the future, I wish to return briefly to the comparison with Croce. For although Gramsci's thesis in a sense repeated the Marxist vision of a withering away of the state, it was a particularly Italian variation of this theme – the creation of a perfected ethical state.

Croce, in polemic with Gentile, maintained that the state in the strict sense could only mean the government and bureaucracy and the forces of authority. If the Hegelian theory of the ethical state had any meaning at all, then it must include moral life in general which 'embraces the men of government and their adversaries, the conservatives and the revolutionaries, and the latter perhaps more than the others, because they open the paths to the future and procure the advancement of human society'.[65] The state in the strict sense was thus a purely political and, in Croce's terminology, 'economic/utilitarian' concept, the realm of force. Civil society was the truly moral sphere, within which the clash of opposing ideals took place and agreement was consensual. Croce thereby ethicised economic and social relations, making the state the inevitable organ of political force which, given the passional and irrational aspects of human nature, always had to be present in one form or another. The organisation of civil society and the degree of state intervention it required to remain stable reflected the prevailing historical conditions.

Against fascist ideologues, Croce maintained that the ethical state, which incorporated both state and civil society, only possessed 'moral force' to the extent it reflected the 'force of circumstances'.[66] As these changed, moral and political struggle ensued and one could not pre-ordain which political system would turn out to be the most appropriate. Liberalism was not to be identified with a particular social and political order. Rather, it reflected the human ability to utilise different types of social organisation, including the communist, as the occasion demanded so as to increase human liberty through the domination of the natural environment.[67]

---

63. Gramsci, *Quaderni*, p. 1522.

64. *See* M. Clark and D. Hine, 'The Italian Communist Party: between Leninism and social democracy', in D. Childs (ed.), *The Changing Face of Western Communism*, London, 1980, pp. 112–46, for an account of the PCI's dilemma.

65. B. Croce, 'Lo Stato e l'etica', 1924, *Etica e politica*, pp. 187–8.

66. Croce, 'Il senso politico', p.178.

67. B. Croce, 'Liberismo e liberalismo', 1928, *Etica e politica*, pp. 263–7.

The state was a necessary evil, which, in Kantian manner, stepped in to bridge an ever-present gap between the ideal and the real, employing greater or lesser force to the extent that this was required. The distinction between state and society, force and consensus remained unbridgeable and in constant tension.

Thus, Croce's theory set up a duality between ethics and economics and avoided ever discussing how they might be successfully mediated at a practical level without contradiction and conflict. Might was always necessary yet always, in appearance, wrong. Only history resolved the conflict between the force and consent. Whilst this failure to discuss the mediating function of politics undermined the practical application of his theory, it enabled him to escape the worse mistakes of Gentile. For, it was Gentile's belief that the force of the state and the consensus of society could be combined in the fascist ethical state. The corporate structure of the totalitarian state supposedly organised the dispersed wills of atomistic individuals into a collective national will. In this way, the consciousness of the individual became submerged in the universal consciousness of the state and the liberty of individual citizens was harmonised with the authority of the state.[68]

Gramsci's resolution of the Crocean antinomy within both the revolutionary party and the socialist society of the future paralleled Gentile's theory of the ethical state. Gramsci's famous distinction between the 'two grand superstructural "levels"' of civil society and the state restated the Machiavellian conception of government as a mixture of force and consensus in terms of Croce's distinction between the ethical and the political. Just as Croce conceived of the one in terms of cultural activity and the second as force, so Gramsci argued:

> These two levels correspond on the one hand to the function of 'hegemony', which the dominant group exercises throughout society, and on the other hand to that of 'direct domination' or command, expressed through the State and 'juridical' government.[69]

However, Gramsci retained the Marxian belief that the primary determinants of social evolution were the forces and relations of production. The ethical power of the state, therefore, consisted in raising 'the great mass of the population to a particular cultural and moral level, a level (or type) which corresponds to the needs of the productive forces for development, and hence to the interests of the ruling classes'.[70] Unlike the liberals, fascist ideologues had appreciated the need for such a move. In essence, fascism represented a reactionary hegemonic response to the current crisis of capital accumulation. Gramsci presented communism as

---

68. The briefest summary of Gentile's account of fascist doctrine is his *Origini e dottrina del fascismo*, Rome, 1929. Unfortunately, there is no single clear statement of his ideas. I have offered an overview of his theory in Bellamy, *Modern Italian Social Theory*, ch. 6.

69. Gramsci, *Quaderni*, pp. 1518–19. Gramsci's analysis should also be compared to the other great modern Italian social theorist of force and consent, Vilfredo Pareto. *See*, for example, the *Trattato di Sociologia Generale*, 3 vols, Florence, 1916, para. 2257.

70. Gramsci, *Quaderni*, p. 1049.

a 'progressive' counter-hegemonic project, the terminology and design of which deliberately mirrored that of fascism.[71]

Croce's inability to overcome the antinomy between state and civil society arose from his perpetual postponement of the achievement of the kingdom of ends, so that the ideal remained permanently separated from the real. By contrast, Gramsci contended that 'one can imagine the State-coercion element exhausting itself as more conspicuous elements of the regulated society (or ethical State or civil society) gradually affirm themselves'.[72] Influenced by Taylorism, Gramsci believed that modern industrial production was inherently 'totalising', encouraging 'collective' forms of organisation.[73] Since the individual was but the sum of the social and economic relations of which he formed a part, these new conditions produced a new type of person, 'the collective man'. The state had an 'educative and formative role' in this regard, 'to create new and higher types of civilisation, to mould the "civilisation" and morality of the most vast popular masses to the requirements of the continual development of the economic apparatus of production, and therefore to elaborate even physically new types of humanity'.[74] Gramsci appreciated that the fascist corporatist theorists claimed to be doing just this. However, theirs was a 'regressive' form of totalitarianism. For even if it represented a necessary adaptation of bourgeois rule to modern industrial conditions, it was 'bureaucratic' and coercive in nature because it was based on the subordination of the most dynamic element in the new process – the proletarian factory worker. Fordism and fascism were new forms of capitalist expropriation. By attaining a total control of production and consumption, the capitalist classes aimed to escape the logic of the law of the falling rate of profit.[75] Against this attempt, the 'total' perspective inculcated by the Party, the embryo proletarian state, was 'progressive' because expressive of the needs of the fundamental class. As the arm of the proletariat, the Party-state removed the 'unhealthy' aspects of the new productive methods by curtailing the exploitative relation between worker and employer through public ownership of the means of production. So organised, common interests would prevail over particular ones, and the 'new order' could rest on consensus rather than on force. The divisive and repressive ideology of a ruling group would be replaced by 'a "cultural-social unity" whereby a multiplicity of dispersed wills, with heterogeneous aims, are welded together with a single aim, on the basis of an (equal) and common conception of the world'.[76] Thus, the Party-state had an initially coercive role in the transitionary period towards the rational organisation of production relations. The Party's politics must be 'totalitarian',

---

71. The following analysis has been inspired by F. Sbarberi, *Gramsci: un socialismo armonico,* Milan, 1986, ch.5.

72. Gramsci, *Quaderni,* p. 764.

73. *Ibid.*

74. *Ibid.,* p. 1565–6.

75. *Ibid.,* pp. 1228, 800.

76. *Ibid.,* p. 1331.

ensuring that 'the members [...] find in [it] all the satisfactions they previously found in a multiplicity of organisations'.[77] Even regional dialects must disappear and a common national language take their place.[78] However, the element of force would fade away as the norms regulating these relations became internalised. Laws achieved this change by being both 'punitive' and 'educative'. Hence:

> The State[...] is an instrument of 'rationalisation', of acceleration and Taylorisation, it works according to a plan, rewards, incites, solicits, and 'punishes', because, once the conditions are created in which a determinate way of life is 'possible', the 'criminal action or omission' must have a punitive sanction, with moral implications, and not merely be judged generically as dangerous.[79]

The worker became freer by virtue of following a rational plan of life, embodied in the collectivity, as opposed to his or her 'animal' or 'primitive' instincts.[80] Since dissent from the new productivist culture was punished by public opinion as much as the law, individuals ultimately controlled themselves, the system gradually became self-regulating, and the state was reduced first to a mere 'night watchman' and finally withered away into a regulative administrative apparatus.

As Gramsci correctly noted, the fascist resolution of the conflict between 'real' and 'legal' Italy had been 'the integration of civil society in all its forms into the single organisation of the party state',[81] and he clearly aimed to follow the same route. Both schemes in turn followed the trajectory of the Piedmontese state in the unification of Italy. There is no reason to believe that the authoritarianism first of liberal Italy and then of fascism would not have been further refined under Gramsci's proletarian new order. A democratic and pluralist socialism would have to find an alternative strategy for integrating state and society.

We need not dwell on the weaknesses of Gramsci's argument. The historical record belies his optimism in the liberating potential of integrated work processes for the many-sided development of the individual. In this area at least, self-realisation and co-operative production have tended to conflict rather than to complement each other. Those who worked on the Fiat assembly line, rather than theorised about it, appreciated how the new techniques achieved the maximum integration with the minimum of individual autonomy. Gramsci's theory seems concerned with overcoming *anomie* rather than alienation. His belief that one could make the rational and the real into one raises even more serious doubts. The Fichtean attempt to overcome the Kantian dualism in a rigidly organised 'organic' state based on reason has been classically criticised by Isaiah Berlin and I need not

---

77. *Ibid.*, p. 800.
78. *Ibid.*, pp. 1377–8, 2314.
79. *Ibid.*, p. 1571.
80. *Ibid.*, pp. 2160–1.
81. *Ibid.*, p. 2058.

repeat his arguments here.[82] Gramsci gave this notion a new twist by assimilating it to a behaviourist utopia in which 'rational' and 'efficient' were one and the same. In so arguing, Gramsci made the mistake of confusing the choice of ends with the practical means of attaining them. We may be able to agree that there is only one rational route to a given goal, but a variety of moral goals remains rationally possible so long as human beings have the capacity for reflection and interpretation.[83]

The state does not just serve a coercive function, it has the positive purpose of both protecting individuals from the coercion of others and of serving as an arena for political debate about the distribution of resources and the priorities of the social union binding together its constituent members. As such, it must be responsive to civil society whilst remaining separate as a controlling entity in its own right. Although Croce had a potentially more pluralistic conception of politics, he did not have a notion of the state as the guarantor of the plurality of society. According to his 'metapolitical' version of liberalism, only the infinite progress and creativity of history as reflected in human ingenuity ensured that no particular state would be definitive.[84]

Gramsci's account of the relationship between state and civil society suffers from similar deficiencies. He showed no awareness of the role the state plays in protecting the diversity of society by upholding the rule of law and the rights of individuals. Instead, he regarded such mechanisms as products of a class-divided society, which requires ways of restraining conflict. However, the state has an enabling as well as a coercive function, which cannot be realistically replaced by a common system of moral beliefs within a society of any complexity. Even if we assume perfect agreement on social values, without a similarly perfect knowledge about the interests of all our fellow citizens the most altruistic of people can still commit misinformed acts of harmful interference with the lives of others. In the rather more likely event that such consensus is absent, then debates about the priorities of society and its proper management will be unavoidable. In either case, there will be a need for a constitutional framework protecting individuals against the invasive incursions of others and providing the ground rules of public discussion.[85]

---

82. I. Berlin, 'Two concepts of Liberty', in *Four Essays on Liberty*, Oxford, 1969, pp. 149–50.

83. For a fuller discussion of this point, *see* S. Lukes, 'Taking morality seriously', in T. Honderich (ed.), *Morality and Objectivity*, London, 1985, pp. 105–9.

84. N. Bobbio, 'Benedetto Croce e il liberalism', in his collection *Politica e cultura*, Turin, 1955, pp. 211–68, makes this criticism particularly well.

85. *See* S. Lukes, *Marxism and Morality*, Oxford, 1985 and N. Bobbio, *Which Socialism?*, Cambridge, 1988 for a discussion of these problems of socialist organisation.

Conclusion: Gramsci today

In recent years, a number of figures on the left have employed Gramscian ideas to understand the rise of the 'new right' in Britain and to formulate proposals for a counter-hegemonic socialist strategy. This article suggests that Gramsci's theory will be inadequate for both tasks. The social-democratic welfare states of post-war Europe cannot be compared to the far more fragile Italian liberal regime. Its collapse in 1922 stemmed largely from the failure of parliamentary institutions to develop into a forum for competing groups and parties in a manner which diffused social conflict by connecting state and civil society in a consensual manner. This failure in turn can be accounted for by the narrow view of the state held by most Italian liberals, who had no commitment to, or understanding of, parliamentary democracy, except as an extension of transformist politics. Contrary to the jeremiads of the left and the boasts of the right, the robustness of liberal institutions within today's Britain have clearly placed severe limitations on the Thatcherite revolution. Indeed, the left's belated discovery of and successful appeal to those 'formal' liberties ignored by Gramsci attests to the continued strength and ideological power of the liberal democratic state. The prospects for hegemonic projects by either left or right, which can somehow render state institutions redundant, or reduce them to the status of a mere 'night watchman', seem equally slim. Moreover, the plurality of economic and cultural groups within the developed capitalist countries defy inclusion within a single world view capable of containing and harmonising them all. This result could only be obtained by mass indoctrination and considerable coercion. Such a policy can hardly be equated with the stand of the progressive left in defence of multiculturalism. Finally, in the post-Fordist era, the factory can no longer offer a plausible model of integrated social relations.

It is ironic that Gramsci, who lived in one of the most politically backward nations of Western Europe, should have become for many people today the principal Marxist theorist of the parliamentary regimes of advanced industrial capitalist countries. In fact, his writings contain no adequate theorisation of bourgeois democracy. Instead, as this article has shown, he addresses problems which do not concern us and employs assumptions we cannot share. We can only diminish his status as a powerful analyst of the crisis of Italian liberalism if we transpose him to the inappropriate terrain of contemporary Britain.

Chapter Nine

The Italian Origins of Gramsci's Thought: The *Pre-Prison Writings*

Gramsci's status as a canonical figure within the tradition of Western Marxism has often led to an overly schematic reading of his work. Gramsci has been credited with the formulation of a strategy for communist parties operating within the developed states of the West that was both revolutionary and democratic. As such, his ideas have appeared to offer a radical alternative to social democracy on the one hand and the autocratic party bureaucracies of the countries of 'actually existing socialism' on the other. This view drew support from and provided legitimacy for the Eurocommunist movement of the 1970s and early 1980s, especially its chief protagonist – the Italian Communist Party (PCI). The largest communist party outside the Soviet bloc, its historical links with Gramsci, who was promoted throughout this period as the PCI's chief ideological inspiration, greatly strengthened the credibility and prestige of the Euro-Gramscian thesis. However, in the aftermath of the collapse of Communism in Eastern Europe and the former Soviet Union, this thesis has lost its allure. Many, if not most, of the main proponents of Eurocommunism have ended up disavowing Marxism altogether, with even the PCI abandoning its Communist past and transforming itself into the Party of the Democratic Left. Thus, paradoxically this attempt to stress Gramsci's relevance has ended up by seeming to deprive him of any contemporary interest at all.

Fortunately, this negative judgement need apply only to one school of interpretation of his thought. Whilst the Eurocommunist view of Gramsci contained a kernel of truth, it also distorted central aspects of his thinking. In spite of Gramsci's deep commitment to the unity of theory and practice, this reading of his writings divorced the first from the second and applied his ideas to events and movements which he neither knew nor could have anticipated. The original context of the crisis of liberal democracies at the end of the First World War, the Russian Revolution and the rise of fascism was exchanged for the very different world that emerged from the Second World War. Above all, the distinctively Italian dimension of his ideas became lost from sight. There was always a certain incongruity about the fact that the supposed champion of a revised Marxism suited to the advanced economies and political systems of the West came from a peripheral region of one of the West's least industrialised nations and most fragile liberal democracies. One of the advantages of approaching Gramsci through the pre-prison writings rather than the *Prison Notebooks* is that the original intent and frame of reference of his ideas are harder to avoid. For most of the key concepts of the *Notebooks* can be found in the early texts. In particular, the emphasis on what

Gramsci came to call 'hegemony' or ideological power, which forms the most distinctive feature of his Marxism, figures implicitly throughout his analysis of the contemporary Italian State and his views on the organisation of the fledgling Communist Party of Italy (PCd'I), as it was then known. Seen within this Italian context, however, such characteristic Gramscian themes as the relative autonomy of political from economic struggle and the role of will and education in the formation of a revolutionary consciousness take on a rather different significance from that attributed to them by much of the traditional scholarship. Instead of providing the basis for a Marxist strategy suited to advanced capitalism, they can be seen to refer to the rather different problems posed by a somewhat earlier stage of development of the modern nation state.

Born in Ales, Sardinia on 22 January 1891, Gramsci was able to reflect on the failings of the Italian state from an early age. Owing to its peripheral status, Sardinia shared the lot of southern Italy as an economically and politically marginalised region. Throughout his writings, Gramsci displayed a mixture of profound affection for the traditions and culture of his native region, mixed with outrage against the injustices and chronic poverty that characterised the life of the majority of its inhabitants. However, Gramsci never fell into the sentimentalism that frequently marks provincial nationalism. A hunchback, probably as a result of contracting Pott's disease, he suffered from the local superstition towards any one or thing that was different and often felt rejected as a consequence. He appreciated at first hand, therefore, the narrow-mindedness that sometimes characterises folk cultures. His political education began early when his father, a local government official, fell victim to the endemic corruption of Italian political life. Having aligned himself with the losing faction in the 1897 election, Francesco Gramsci was suspended from his post in the registrary office and subsequently charged with embezzling electoral funds and sentenced to five years' imprisonment. The financial difficulties this caused the Gramsci family forced the eleven-year-old Antonio temporarily to suspend his school studies and work in an office until, three years later, his parents could afford to send him to secondary school in the Sardinian capital of Cagliari. There he lived with his elder brother Gennaro, who was an active member of the Italian Socialist Party (PSI) and introduced Antonio to socialist literature and circles. At this time, however, Sardinianism was more important to him than socialism and the most significant influences on him were the writers grouped around the Florentine journal *La Voce*.

The editor of this remarkable review, Giuseppe Prezzolini, had gathered together a highly diverse set of contributors linked largely by a common dissatisfaction with contemporary Italy. They felt Italian unification had been doubly incomplete. First, there were the cultural and economic divisions existing between both the different regions of the peninsula, particularly the developing north and the underdeveloped south, and the educated classes and the unschooled masses. Second, and largely as a result of these differences, there was the tension between 'legal' Italy, the set of liberal institutions resulting from political unification, and 'real' Italy, the fragmented social reality of divergent regional traditions, economic attainment and polarised classes. Both these problems were epitomised in the 'southern question', to which (as Gramsci later recalled) *La Voce* devoted a special issue on 16 March 1911. According to the contributors to this issue, who included the main members of the so-called 'southern school' of intellectuals, unification had subordinated the south politically, economically and culturally to the needs of the north in ways that had merely served to exacerbate the region's relative backwardness and suppress its distinctiveness. In particular, they argued that the centralised political system of the new state had given rise to a 'transformist' politics based on patronage and compromise between local elites and clienteles. These groups effectively blocked any reform of the social and economic inequities from which they derived their power and hindered the involvement of the masses in political life, who vented their frustration in widespread lawlessness and brigandage.

The chief goal of the *vociani* was to integrate Italy socially and culturally as well as politically in ways that built upon rather than suffocated the nation's regional strengths and popular energies. Their views of this common aspiration differed widely, however. Although Prezzolini had recently come under the influence of the Italian idealist philosopher Benedetto Croce, who also helped the journal financially, the contributors were an eclectic bunch, ranging from the elitist proto-futurism of Giovanni Papini to the democratic positivism and free-trade arguments of the southern specialist Gaetano Salvemini. Much of this eclecticism fed into Gramsci's later Marxism and is particularly in evidence in his earliest articles. He took from Prezzolini an appreciation of the political and educative role of culture, from Croce a concern with the role of human will in the fashioning of history, from Papini a certain iconoclasm, and from Salvemini a respect for the detailed empirical analysis of problems and a profound understanding of the links between the transformist political system, the import tariffs protecting certain landed and industrial interests and the social and economic decline of the south. From the movement as a whole, he took the desire to build a new state commanding the active allegiance of all sections of Italian society.

Although Gramsci was sympathetic to socialism, it took some time before he incorporated these Vocean elements into a distinctively Marxist and socialist perspective. In 1911 he won a scholarship to the University of Turin. At first he was alienated by this proletarian city, identifying it with the industrial north's subjugation of the predominantly agrarian south. Angelo Tasca and Palmiro Togliatti, who were also students in Turin and through whose friendship he became active in the PSI, both described him as still being more of a Sardinian nationalist than a socialist at this time. His Sardinianism even carried into his studies, as Gramsci became interested in the prospect of working on Sard dialects with the pioneering socio-linguist Matteo Bartoli. Significantly, he overcame his slight antipathy to socialism only when, returning to Sardinia for the elections of 1913, he began to see how socialist politics was capable of linking the concerns of northern workers and southern peasants. In the first elections held under near universal franchise, the local landowners had been unable to secure their vote without the collaboration of the mainland power brokers. Gramsci quickly appreciated that the socialists offered the most effective counter to this strategy and participated actively in the PSI campaign, signing the pro-south anti-protectionist petition that they supported and that was later published in *La Voce*. On returning to Turin, he joined the Party.

His newly acquired socialist principles mixed with rather than replaced his earlier Vocean allegiances. Moreover, the two were not entirely compatible. For example, one of his first initiatives within the local Party was to sponsor the adoption of Gaetano Salvemini, a frequent critic of the PSI, as a parliamentary candidate for one of the Turin electoral districts, as an act of solidarity between the northern proletariat and the southern peasants. Salvemini turned down the offer, so the plan was never attempted, but it would almost certainly have generated a conflict with the national Party had it been implemented. The potential tension between Gramsci's Voceanism and his socialism is similarly evident in the first article he published in a national newspaper, on 'An active and functional neutrality'. The PSI had been one of the few socialist parties successfully to maintain the Second International's opposition to worker participation in an 'imperialist' war after the outbreak of hostilities in 1914. Gramsci's piece developed out of an editorial in the Party journal *Avanti!* by Mussolini, then a leader of the maximalist wing of the PSI, who had cast the case for intervention in a new revolutionary light. Responding to the rebuttal of this argument by his comrade Angelo Tasca, Gramsci contended that 'absolute neutrality' risked degenerating into mere passivity. Such an attitude could not satisfy

> revolutionaries who conceive of history as the creation of their own spirit, made up of an uninterrupted series of lightning raids on the other active and passive forces in society, in an attempt to create the most favourable conditions possible for the final raid [the revolution] (p. 5).[1]

Now that the war was engaged, the Party had to be ready to exploit the revolutionary possibilities that might present themselves in this new situation. Like Mussolini, Gramsci shrewdly recognised the weakening of the liberal state and opportunities for mass mobilisation likely to arise from intervention.

A number of points of Gramsci's analysis are worth underlining, for they reveal how early some of the key themes of his thought emerged. First, the article illustrates Gramsci's independence of mind. 'Interventionism' was one of the major heresies for the PSI, particularly amongst those on the left of the Party, and Mussolini was ultimately expelled for this reason. It was characteristic of Gramsci that he did not falter from holding unpopular positions. Second, equally heretical was his emphasis on the role of ideas and the human will – a view that led to him being accused of 'voluntarism' at the 1917 PSI conference in Florence. The revolutionary wing of the Party typically adopted a more 'orthodox' Marxism that stressed the internal dynamics of the historical process and the necessary collapse of capitalism under its own contradictions. Gramsci, by contrast, argued that such

1. All page numbers in the text refer to the translations of the articles mentioned in Antonio Gramsci, *Pre-Prison Writings*, Richard Bellamy (ed.), trans. Virginia Cox, Cambridge, 1994, for which this chapter served as the Introduction.

vulgar versions of historical materialism encouraged an attitude of submission to the prevailing economic and political system, noting that reformists also generally embraced a vulgar positivism. Third, and as a corollary of his more idealist Marxism, he stressed the need to educate and organise the collective will of the masses, preparing them for the coming revolution through the dissemination of new values that gave them a critical purchase on their current situation and galvanised them to action. Fourth, he linked the achievement of the revolutionary goal with the creation of a new type of state. Indeed, he described the Party as

> a State *in potentia* which is gradually maturing; a rival to the bourgeois State, which is seeking, through its daily struggle with this enemy, and through the development of its own internal dialectic, to create the organs it needs to overcome and absorb its opponent (p. 4).

Even at this early stage, Gramsci had begun to formulate what was to become one of his most distinctive doctrines – the strategy of preparing for the revolutionary seizure of power by building a counter-state within the structures of civil society, via a plethora of Party-run organisations. Finally, although Gramsci embraced the cause of international socialism, he insisted that the PSI must remain at present relatively 'autonomous'. In the medium term, the Party had to concentrate on those special circumstances of the Italian situation that determined its '*particular, national* characteristics' and committed the Party 'to assuming a specific function, a particular responsibility in Italian life' (p. 4). This insistence on the 'Italian road to socialism' followed on from his undogmatic Marxism, which rejected the schematic generalisations of orthodox Marxists and allowed him to comprehend the peculiarities of the Italian state. Gramsci elaborated all these points as his thought matured.

Ill-health and growing political commitments led Gramsci to break off his studies in 1915 and he began to devote himself full time to journalism for the socialist press – one of the traditional routes to advancement within the PSI. His writing was incredibly varied, ranging from theatre reviews and general cultural criticism to commentary on daily local, national and international events. The outbreak of the Russian revolution in February 1917 gave a tremendous stimulus to his thinking. He regarded it as confirming his anti-deterministic interpretation of Marxism, revealing the 'real and undying Marxist thought' to be that which 'continues the tradition of German and Italian idealism' and was uncontaminated 'by positivist and naturalist incrustations' that often sullied Marx's own writings. As he put it in a famous article of the time, it was 'A revolution against Karl Marx's *Capital*', that showed 'the canons of historical materialism are not as iron-clad as [...] it has been thought' (p. 40). Far from occurring as part of the natural process of social evolution, as the positivist interpreters of Marx claimed it would, he argued that the revolution had sprung from the organisation of the people's will and social consciousness to a sufficient level to be able to take advantage of the revolutionary opportunity when it had arisen. It is important to note that Gramsci's position was not quite so voluntarist as it first appears. He was not denying that

166 of 342 Croce, Gramsci, Bobbio and the Italian Political Tradition

revolution could occur only under the right structural conditions, merely that these in themselves were insufficient to bring about social and political change. For revolution to occur, it was necessary both to know these conditions and to have the capacity to exploit their potential. Economic facts constrained but did not mechanically determine politics; it was necessary for people 'to understand [...] and to assess them, and to control them with their will, until this collective will becomes the driving force of the economy, the force which shapes reality itself' (p. 40).

The education and cultural preparation of the proletariat played a correspondingly central role in Gramsci's thinking. As he put it in a famous article on 'Socialism and culture', 'every revolution has been preceded by a long process of intense critical activity, of new cultural insight and the spread of ideas through groups of men initially resistant to them' (p. 10). The state education system served the mass of people extremely badly, with Italy having some of the highest illiteracy rates in Europe – rising to as much as 70 per cent in parts of the south. However, Gramsci was not greatly impressed by the attempts of the labour movement to remedy this through organisations such as the Popular Universities. He believed that these bodies failed to relate the knowledge they imparted to the needs and practical concerns of the workers. Culture, in Gramsci's view, entailed much more than the mere acquisition of esoteric information. It involved self-knowledge and with it self-mastery: 'the attainment of a higher awareness, through which we can come to understand our value and place within history, our proper function in life, our rights and duties' (pp. 9–10). In accord with his reinterpretation of Marxism, Gramsci saw education as enabling the masses to take conscious control of the forces moulding their lives and to make the most of the emancipatory potential of existing material conditions. Once again, however, the superficially voluntarist and libertarian nature of this argument needs qualifying. For Gramsci firmly believed the Marxian thesis that the liberation of the individual could come about only with the emancipation of the proletariat and with it the whole of humanity through the overthrow of capitalism and the creation of a communist society. Thus, he insisted that revolution would be achieved only by the individual's overcoming his or her rebelliousness and joining the collective will of the mass movement of the proletariat. Hence, he stressed discipline as being the necessary complement to freedom, going so far in his later writings as to treat the Party line as a moral imperative that all workers had a categorical duty to follow.

In spite of these authoritarian implications, Gramsci's linking of education to self-emancipation sought to guard against the intellectual and political élitism into which even the socialist intelligentsia had a tendency to fall. Intellectuals had to avoid adopting a 'traditional' paternalistic attitude and seek to act 'organically' and aid the ordinary person's self-awareness of his or her situation by teaching people to teach themselves. He even regarded attempts to popularise ideas by expressing them in a simplified form as condescending. In an article on 'Why we need a cultural association' and a related letter to Lombardo Radice about his short-lived 'Club of Moral Life', Gramsci outlined the sort of educational organisation he had in mind. History played a vital role in his programme, since he maintained that an understanding of the cultural and social influences that form us was at the heart of the self-understanding necessary for our gaining control over our lives. The historicist idealism of Croce and the 'actualist' doctrine of Gentile, whose pedagogical theories were particularly well developed, greatly influenced Gramsci's ideas in this respect, and he urged his comrades to study their writings and those of their followers. Although he had an interest in certain aspects of the contemporary *avant-garde*, being an early enthusiast for the plays and stories of the Sicilian writer Pirandello and sympathising with some of the experimental elements of the Soviet *Prolekult* movement, many of his favourite authors and not a few of his views – such as his emphasis on the 'classics' and the benefits of 'sweating at' grammar – would be considered traditionalist now. However, it needs to be remembered that the writers he admired, such as the great literary historian and philosopher respectively of the late nineteenth century, Franceso de Sanctis and Bertrando Spaventa, and their contemporary followers and continuers, Croce and Gentile, were in the process of constructing a cultural tradition, rather than merely defending an existing canon. Although Croce later joined the liberal and Gentile the fascist establishment, at this time they were outspoken critics of the low level of contemporary Italian cultural life, which they, like the *vociani*, related to the corruption of the Italian political system. Gramsci shared their contempt, merely radicalising their analysis.

Vocean themes continued to shape his socialism after the war and the Russian revolution. The pieces on 'Cocaine' and 'Football and *scopone*', for example, not only show his skill as a journalist in drawing out the wider significance of everyday occurrences and practices but also a Vocean desire to *épater les bourgeois*, manifested in his almost puritanical loathing for what he regarded as the degeneracy of the Italian bourgeoisie and the society they had created. His more detailed discussions of Italian politics, such as 'Class intransigence and Italian history', 'Three principles and three kinds of political order' and 'Men, ideas, newspapers and money', show the influence of Salvemini in particular, with Gramsci even espousing the arguments of free-market economists such as Luigi Einaudi and Vilfredo Pareto, who saw protectionism as the chief source of the nation's failure to evolve into a fully fledged parliamentary democracy. Like them, he believed the Italian state reflected an admixture of capitalist and quasi-feudal social and economic relations, the dire effects of which were summed up in the south's economic dependence on the north and the political dependence of northern elites on southern clientèles. To a large extent, therefore, Gramsci still saw himself as participating in the general project of the anti-Giolittian intellectuals – that of renewing Italy via a new cultural identity suited to its present social and political conditions – and as broadening that enterprise to include and promote the interests and aspirations of the working class. However, unlike them, he believed that only socialism could provide this new culture, for it was 'the one ideal which unites the Italian people'. Moreover, as 'the tangible representation of this unity, of this new-consciousness, of this new world', the task of building this new order fell to the Socialist Party and its supporters (p. 29).

The weekly journal *L'Ordine Nuovo*, which Gramsci founded with Umberto Terracini, Tasca and Togliatti in May 1919, was initially a continuation of this policy of cultural politics, similar in style to an earlier attempt of Gramsci's to create a socialist *La Voce* in the single issue *La Città Futura*. However, it soon became something far more important in Gramsci's eyes: namely, the intellectual voice of a revolutionary movement – the Factory Councils that grew up in Turin over the next few months. The Councils evolved out of the 'internal commissions' that had emerged within a number of engineering and metal-working factories around 1906 and become widespread during the war. Although function and composition varied, they were essentially a small elected body of workers designed to handle everyday problems of discipline and arbitration and to implement national wage agreements at a local level. At this stage, they were seen as part of the national union machinery and, in an agreement between the metal-workers' union FIOM and the employers' federation in Turin, they became incorporated into the official labour-relations mechanism there in April 1919. However, the Russian revolution led many to interpret the Councils in a different light, seeing them as an Italian equivalent of the soviets. Although in practice Lenin's position on the soviets was ambiguous, given that they were often dominated by the Bolsheviks' rivals, the Socialist-Revolutionaries and Mensheviks, he hailed them in *State and Revolution* and other writings as a model of the new socialist politics and as contemporary equivalents to the form of democratic organisation Marx had praised in his analysis of the Paris Commune. As a result, Gramsci, in common with most other foreign sympathisers, saw the soviets as the most distinctive feature of the Russian revolution. They were the means whereby the Bolsheviks had not merely seized power but altered its nature, by creating a new type of political organisation. In Gramsci's eyes, the soviets, or rather their native counterparts the Factory Councils, offered a model for the reconstruction of the Italian state.

As he related in the article 'The programme of *L'Ordine Nuovo*', the paper switched from being 'a review of abstract culture' to become 'the journal of the Factory Councils' in June 1919, following 'an editorial *coup d'état*' in which Togliatti and Gramsci ousted Tasca (p. 181). The need for this *coup* resulted in large part from Tasca's close links to the trade unions, which had put up most of the original finance. For reasons explained below, the unions regarded the development of the Councils into semi-autonomous bodies with some ambivalence. Gramsci, by contrast, viewed this movement away from the traditional labour organisations as marking a significant departure on the part of the workers from reformist to revolutionary action. Therefore, he aimed to encourage it. Drawing on his theory of the role of education and culture, he argued that rather than seeking to hand down 'cold, intellectual artefacts', the educational and cultural task of the journal must now be to help the workers articulate and build on their 'feelings, desires and passions', revealing the dramatic events in which they were engaged 'as moments in a process of inner liberation and self-expression on the part of the working class' (p. 181).

Initially, Gramsci enjoyed great success. The 'Two Red Years' of 1919–20 resulting from the economic crisis and political upheaval after the First World

War, together with the expectations aroused by the Russian revolution, created an environment in which it was widely felt that revolution was just around the corner. By the end of 1919, his ideas had been adopted by the Turin branch of FIOM and the local section of the PSI and the circulation of *L'Ordine Nuovo* had reached 6,000 copies. The formation of Factory Councils frightened the employers into a lock-out in March 1920, provoking a general strike in April which explicitly aimed at political control of industry and involved over 200,000 workers. Ultimately a failure due to concerted action by employers and the government, the strike nevertheless heightened the prestige of the *L'Ordine Nuovo* group – particularly as the PSI and CGL refused to back it. In September 1920 a breakdown in negotiations over a new national wage in the engineering industry led to the occupation of factories throughout northern Italy. The Prime Minister, Giolitti, decided to play a waiting game and did not intervene. Meanwhile, the factories carried on production as the workers began an experiment in self-management based around the Councils. Gramsci's theory of workers' democracy was partly a response to and partly an attempt to shape these events.

Gramsci looked on the Councils not only as a means for workers' control of industry, but as the basic unit of a totally new form of democratic state that reflected the interests and activities of the true producers of economic wealth, the proletariat. Linking his account in characteristic fashion to the unification of Italy, he argued that the industrial system of Turin and Piedmont would act as the model and agent of the proletarian revolution, in much the same way as it had for the bourgeois *Risorgimento* (p. 138). Ultimately, however, the Councils would serve to unify humanity as a whole. In Gramsci's eyes, the Councils overcame the divisions between capital and labour of the bourgeois state, giving the workers the responsibility and self-discipline to work with each other for the benefit of all, rather than just for themselves. He believed participation within them would have an educative function, making the worker aware of his or her station and its duties within the organisation of production as a whole. He envisaged the Councils as forming part of a whole network of similar bodies, feeding into territorially based ward, urban and regional Councils, including delegates from all crafts and workplaces and connecting up with a parallel system for peasants and other rural workers. In this way, every stage of the production process would be connected within a single global political and economic system.

> English *coal* will merge with Russian *oil*, Siberian *grain* with Sicilian *sulphur*, *rice* from Vercelli with *wood* from Styria [...] in a single organism, governed by an international administration which supervises the wealth of the whole world in the name of the whole of humanity.

For Gramsci, therefore, the Factory Council constituted merely

> the first step in a historical process which will culminate in the Communist International, no longer as a political organization of the revolutionary proletariat but as a reorganization of the world economy and the whole human community, both on a national and a world level (p. 167).

The role of the Party and the unions within this set-up was far from clear. Gramsci argued that both had 'grown up on the terrain of bourgeois democracy' and, although they led the working class within this system, 'they do not supersede the bourgeois State' (p. 164). Instead, the Councils had developed on the revolutionary terrain of the factories, where class struggle was engaged in earnest and where, as we have seen, Gramsci believed a new form of proletarian state was in the process of formation. The Councils would revolutionise the Party and unions rather than the other way around, therefore, the latter being necessary only in the transitional phase when the Councils were still operating within the bourgeois system. Consequently, he maintained that the Party and unions 'should not project themselves as tutors or as ready-made structures for this new institution'. Instead,

> they should project themselves as the conscious agents of its liberation from the constraining forces concentrated in the bourgeois State. They should set themselves the task of organizing the general (political) external conditions in which the process of the revolution can move forward at the maximum possible rate and the liberated productive forces extend themselves to the full (p. 167).

Needless to say, neither the reformists in the CGL, nor the abstentionists and the maximalists in the PSI, gathered around Bordiga and Serrati respectively, were very pleased with the subordinate position Gramsci had allotted them. Once again, he found himself accused of syndicalism, although he strongly denied the charge.

Gramsci's somewhat utopian vision of the new order involved a number of tensions. A radical model of bottom-up democracy, it was nevertheless hierarchically organised and the relationship between the different levels was never fully clarified. Gramsci implied, for example, that the Councils and their derivative structures could be organs both of worker self-management and a mechanism for administering a unified economic plan: but he did not explain how they could effectively be both at the same time. A similar difficulty arose in his view of the relationship between the Party and the Councils. On the one hand, he thought the Councils had to feed into the Party in an almost spontaneous fashion. He criticised the German SPD, for example, for creating tame Councils 'from above'. On the other hand, he regarded the existence of a strongly disciplined Communist Party as indispensable during the transitional period of the 'dictatorship of the proletariat', although he believed the Party had to win control over the Councils by its 'prestige' rather than by seeking directly to supplant them. Even the proletarian army, necessary for the final seizure of power, was to emerge fully formed out of the Councils, with every factory supplying 'one or more regiments [...] with its own NCOs, its own liaison services, its own officer corps and general staff' (p. 99). Here too, he appears to have believed that the mere fact of delegation resolved the tension between liberty and control within his theory, removing any authoritarian element from the discipline of the officers.

The coherence of Gramsci's position rested largely on the holistic ontology that underpins most 'organic' theories of the state. He assumed, in other words, that within a communist society the different activities of the productive process, which he came close to identifying with the entire life of the community, would be inherently complementary and harmonious. Whilst Gramsci derived much of this view from Marxist sources, particularly Lenin's ideas on 'dual power' and Rosa Luxemburg's conciliar communism, his organicism was also influenced by the 'ethical state' tradition of the Italian neo-Hegelians, especially Gentile, and by the Italian syndicalists, both of which ultimately fed into fascist corporatist doctrines. The prime inspiration for Gramsci's doctrine, however, was the new forms of factory organisation. The Fiat works had introduced the innovatory 'scientific' management techniques and assembly-line production methods pioneered by F. W. Taylor and Henry Ford in the United States. Gramsci never unequivocally endorsed these procedures but he was clearly fascinated by them and published a series of articles supportive of 'Taylorism' in *L'Ordine Nuovo*. Like many other Marxists of the period, he saw them as maximising and simplifying industrial production and disciplining the workforce in ways which made the system largely self-regulating, thereby paving the way for workers' control of industry. Unlike the young Lukacs or later Hegelian Marxists, he remained relatively oblivious to the alienating and reifying aspects of modern technology. He seems to have been more concerned with overcoming anomie by having the worker assimilate the norms he believed, in quasi-Durkheimian fashion, to be inherent to the integrated work processes of industrial production.

As Gramsci later insisted in the *Prison Notebooks*, his organicism was 'progressive' in conception – rather than 'regressive' like the fascist versions – because he saw little need to impose this order from without. The Party and intellectuals were merely to facilitate its emergence. This liberal interpretation of his theory proves plausible, however, only if we accept Gramsci's contention that the new order would generate its own objective morality, and that this ethic would be capable of rationally co-ordinating the self-realisation of individuals in a mutually enhancing way. Unfortunately, the empirical evidence suggests otherwise. Some human activities, such as playing in an orchestra or team games, do possess these characteristics, but not all. The economic focus of Gramsci's theory led him to pigeon-hole the individual according to his or her role within the productive process, with no account given of its relation to other aspects of human life. Yet, co-operative production based on an increased division of labour is more likely to diminish than to enhance human fulfilment, except in a very restricted sense. Gramsci tended to ignore this problem by associating the growth of freedom with greater productive efficiency. However, an increase in collective productivity does not necessarily entail any increase in the opportunities or autonomy of individual workers – a boring repetitive job remains such under any circumstances. Once outside the economic sphere, Gramsci's organic thesis runs into these sorts of difficulties even more frequently, since clashes between competing goals are likely to occur more often. Within a society of any complexity, allowing for a fair degree of individual diversity, the hypothesis that all human activities will prove naturally and rationally assimilable to a single moral framework becomes correspondingly less and less plausible. However, without this optimistic assumption, Gramsci's Council theory risks requiring the totalitarian social engineering of which organic conceptions of the state are traditionally accused.

Unlike Lenin, Gramsci was saved the embarrassment of having to face up to these theoretical limitations of his scheme by never having to implement it. Giolitti wilily sought to defuse the tension brought about by the occupation by setting up a committee to study the problem and promising a parliamentary bill on industrial democracy. These measures gave support to the reformists, whilst in any case the various revolutionary factions remained ambivalent about a movement they had neither initiated nor controlled. At a meeting in Milan held from 9 to 11 September, the CGL and PSI voted by 591,245 to 409,569 with 93,623 abstentions to restrict the action to gaining official recognition of union control in the plants. In spite of resistance to this policy by FIOM and the *L'Ordine Nuovo* group, the workers finally vacated the factories between 25 and 30 September and returned to working for their employers on 4 October. Although Gramsci had come to realise that the restriction of the movement to Turin and the north rendered it too isolated to achieve the revolution, he was bitterly disappointed by the defeat and placed the blame squarely on the incapacity of the Party to take the initiative. He now shelved discussion of the future society for the more pressing task of organising the revolutionary forces in the increasingly hostile atmosphere created by the rise of fascism.

In retrospect, 1919–20 marked the highpoint of the revolutionary situation in Italy and was soon followed by a reactionary backlash, culminating in the fascist seizure of power in 1922. In accounting for this setback, Gramsci was led to develop a far more complex account of the nature of the bourgeois state than many of his Marxist colleagues. The orthodox position, represented by Bordiga, regarded fascism as a straightforward expression of the ruling capitalist class. Since bourgeois democracy was merely a fig-leaf for capitalist oppression of the working class, they contended its suppression and replacement by a fascist regime simply signified an intensification of the class struggle brought on by the imminent collapse of capitalism. Instead, Gramsci sought to relate fascism much more specifically to certain distinctive characteristics of the class structure, economy and political system of Italy. On this analysis, of which 'A study of the Italian situation' provides the most developed statement, fascism was associated with states belonging to the capitalist periphery, such as Spain, Portugal and Italy. Such countries had relatively undeveloped and weak economies, and had therefore been disproportionately affected by the inter-war depression. They also possessed far fewer political resources than advanced capitalist nations such as Britain. Here,

the State apparatus is far more resistant than it is often possible to believe; and, at moments of crisis, it is far more capable of organizing forces loyal to the regime than the depth of the crisis might lead one to suppose (p. 297).

In typical peripheral nations, however, the political forces are less efficient, so that economic crises tended to lead immediately to a crisis of the state. Finally, he linked this weakness of peripheral state structures to the existence of 'a broad band of intermediate classes', composed of white-collar workers, small shopkeepers, small landowners and so on, located 'between the proletariat and capitalism' (p. 298), itself a consequence of the low level of industrial development.

In Italy, these factors had been exacerbated by the regional concentration of what industry there was in the north and the failure of the bourgeoisie either to recruit mass support for liberalism or to achieve ascendency over the rural landowners. The resulting politics of compromises and economic protectionism for vested industrial and agrarian interests, typified by Giolitti, had gradually disillusioned the petite bourgeoisie. Squeezed between large-scale capitalism and the proletariat, they had felt increasingly marginalised. Fascism was the expression of their frustration. As such, it was not as easily assimilable to the interests of the bourgeoisie as many Marxist analysts had supposed. So long as the fear of creeping proletarianisation that motivated many of those in the fascist movement vented itself in attacks on labour organisations, it was compatible with the interests of the large financial, industrial and landed groups. However, the petit-bourgeois mass base of the fascist movement felt equally threatened by these major groups, since it became clear that capitalist stabilisation could only be achieved by policies, such as the concentration of capital, that were as inimical to them as they were to the workers. Thus, far from seeking to secure the bourgeois state, as some liberals initially hoped, fascism aimed to replace it with a quite different kind of régime and to oust the established ruling class. There were 'two fascisms', therefore, that of the movement itself and that of the big capitalists and landowners who sought to exploit it for their own ends. In his various articles on fascism, Gramsci charts the unfolding tensions between these two aspects of fascism as Mussolini was obliged to purge the fascist Party of its original cadres and merge it with the existing structures and personnel of bourgeois class power in order to consolidate his régime. Gramsci came to believe that the primary task of the Communist Party had to be the exploitation of this tension in order to win the non-proletarian masses to the revolution.

Gramsci's views on the composition and function of the Communist Party evolved along with his understanding of fascism. The Communist Party of Italy resulted from the secession from the PSI, at its Seventeenth Congress in Livorno in January 1921, of certain left-wing maximalists and the communist factions gathered around Bordiga and the *Ordine Nuovo* group. The split resulted from the growing disillusionment of these groups with the PSI's tepid support for revolutionary action and its failure to expel the reformists and implement the '21 points' required by the Comintern. However, it divided the Italian labour movement at a crucial time, considerably weakening its ability to respond to the rise of fascism. By December 1921 the Comintern was putting pressure on the PCd'I and PSI to patch up their differences and form a 'united front' at trade union and party level. Bordiga, the leader of the Party, found any collaboration with the Socialists anathema, and was supported in this stance by most of the membership, including Gramsci. Bordiga argued that the fascist movement was a symptom of the crisis of capitalism and hence brought the revolutionary confrontation nearer. In this circumstance, the working class required decisive leadership from a vanguard party. He considered co-operation with a reformist PSI would inevitably sap the PCd'I's ability to provide such direction. Bordiga's position remained PCd'I policy until 1923, gaining official endorsement at the Party's Second Congress in Rome in March 1922, where his Rome Theses were passed by a large majority.

As we have seen, however, Gramsci came to adopt a subtler view of fascism, and a new leading group, far more open to the Comintern united-front policy, began to form around him and Togliatti. His stance was further strengthened by his period in Moscow as the PCd'I representative, from June 1922 to December 1923, although he opposed the Comintern's tendency to dictate to member parties without consideration of their particular national situation and refused moves to make him the PCd'I's General-Secretary instead of Bordiga. Nonetheless, on returning to Italy in 1924 after election as a deputy, he quickly assumed the Party leadership. He saw the crisis precipitated by the murder of the Socialist deputy Giacomo Matteotti in June as the culmination of the tension between the 'two fascisms' and an opportunity that the Party had to exploit, if need be by joining with other opposition parties. He maintained that it was vital that the Party claim the peasants and the petite bourgeoisie from the Catholic Popular Party (PPI) and the fascists, respectively. Drawing on Soviet discussions of the 'agrarian question' and the Comintern's call for the 'Bolshevisation' of communist parties through the building up of cells, Gramsci sought to reorientate the PCd'I organisation around the formation of 'worker and peasant committees', which would form the basis of a future network of Councils. Gramsci also continued to emphasise the importance of education. He advocated the creation of a Party School and insisted on the need for 'democratic intellectuals' to break the ideological hold of figures such as Giuseppe Fortunato and Benedetto Croce. Although Gramsci was committed to a centralised Party structure, he considered it important to obtain the active consent of the membership through mass democratic organisation. Consequently, he was alarmed by the increasingly bureaucratic imposition of Party discipline within the Soviet Union, voicing his doubts in the letter to Togliatti of October 1926. He steadily consolidated his own control of the PCd'I, however, and the Third Congress of the PCd'I of January 1926 approved the 'Lyons Theses' drawn up with Togliatti by 90.8 per cent, decisively defeating the Bordiga faction.

Essential to Gramsci's discussion of both fascism and the Party was his recognition of the relative autonomy of the political and ideological power of the state from the economic structure. Although he would only explore the full implications of this thesis with the elaboration of his conception of hegemony in the *Prison Notebooks*, many of its main features are already present in his early journalism and occasionally he even uses the term. In particular, he had already begun to distinguish the revolutionary strategies required in the developed states of advanced industrial Western countries from those suited to the less complex states of peripheral Western nations such as Italy. He had also begun to contrast both with the tactics Lenin had been able to adopt in the even more fragile state system of Russia.

In this regard, it is important to note that the concept of hegemony or gegemoniya had a long history in the Russian labour movement, going back to the writings of Plekhanov. Within this tradition it had been used to refer to the need to form a revolutionary awareness and political will amongst the proletariat that went beyond their narrow corporate interests; but it did not have the additional meaning Gramsci gave it to describe the mechanisms of ideological consensus within a developed political system. Lenin had adopted the term from the Russian Social Democrats and it was employed in the external documents of the Third Communist International, from which source Gramsci almost certainly picked it up. However, the term also has an Italian lineage in the writings of the nineteenth-century philosopher Vincenzo Gioberti, who used it in an analogous manner to signify the 'moral primacy' one province within a national grouping might exert over others, a thesis he related to the unification of Italy by Piedmont. Moreover, the essential features of the concept were clearly present in Gramsci's early writings on the role of education and culture in the organisation of a socialist consciousness. Characteristically, Gramsci assimilated the Russian-Comintern usage to the Italian. Although he had yet to employ Vincenzo Cuoco's notion of a 'passive revolution' to describe how the Italian bourgeoisie had come to rule Italy without gaining the consensual adherence of the population that only came through establishing a cultural and hegemonic ascendency, this thesis was implicit within his analysis of the contemporary Italian state. He believed that it was imperative that the proletariat did not repeat the liberals' mistakes. In promoting a second and truly revolutionary *Risorgimento*, it was necessary for the Communist Party to gather to it all the oppositional forces within the country. To achieve this goal, Bolshevik means had to be incorporated within the Giobertian end of achieving a national moral supremacy over the Italian people. Developing his argument in the essay 'Some aspects of the southern question', he insisted that 'for the proletariat to become the ruling, the dominant class, it must succeed in creating a system of class alliances that allow it to mobilize the majority of the working population against capitalism and the bourgeois State' (p. 316). This entailed getting the allegiance of the peasants and petite bourgeoisie and counteracting the intellectual influence of the Church and liberal thinkers such as Croce.

On the evening of 8 November 1926 Gramsci was arrested in defiance of his immunity as an elected deputy. The prosecutor at his trial in May 1928 called for his imprisonment on the grounds that 'We must stop this brain from functioning for twenty years.' The phrase was to prove ironic. In the tradition of his hero Machiavelli, withdrawal from politics forced him to engage in continuous reflection upon it. Like Machiavelli, however, he was no abstract system builder and the thirty-three exercise books that make up the *Prison Notebooks* are the fruit of a decade as one of the principal actors in the political life of his country and the socialist movement. The prime virtue of reading the *Notebooks* through the *Pre-Prison Writings*, therefore, lies in providing the appropriate practical and theoretical context for understanding his work. What emerges from these early writings is a Gramsci as much concerned with the creation of a modern nation-state as with its overthrow, and who was particularly preoccupied with explaining the peculiarly illiberal and fragile nature of the bourgeois regime in Italy. In the aftermath of the fall of communism post-1989, it is his analysis of peripheral capitalist states rather than his attempts to build a Communist Party that continues to absorb our attention.

Chapter Ten

A Crocean Critique of Gramsci on Historicism, Hegemony and Intellectuals[1]

Gramsci's debt to Croce is well known and was fulsomely acknowledged by him. All the most distinctive aspects of his thought owe certain central features to the Neapolitan philosopher, from the function he allotted to human consciousness in his version of historical materialism to his conceptions of hegemony and the role of intellectuals.[2] Indeed, in certain crucial respects, Gramsci saw his own philosophy as a 'settling of accounts' with Crocean philosophy, an 'Anti-Croce' that completed and superseded his compatriot's historicist doctrine.[3] Most commentators have duly noted these influences and criticisms. However, they usually do so in order to endorse Gramsci's own claim to have pinpointed and resolved the lacunae and contradictions of Croce's thought.[4] This article reverses this perspective by presenting a Crocean critique of Gramsci.

Gramsci's reputation largely rests on his having incorporated a broader understanding of ideological power into Marxism than either most Marxists or their critics had hitherto standardly allowed.[5] He then employed this account to explain the resilience of Western liberal democracies and devise a revolutionary strategy suited to overcoming their defences and building the communist alternative. Recently, post-Marxist theorists have wanted to draw on Gramsci's ideas in order to explore forms of social and political domination arising from culture, gender and other sources that are allegedly non-, or only tangentially, economic- or class-

1. Research for this paper was supported by an ESRC grant ROOO222402 on 'Intellectuals and Political Culture'.

2. As Gramsci observed, Croce had 'energetically focused attention on the importance of cultural facts and thought in the development of history, on the function of the great intellectuals in the organic life of civil society and the State, on the moment of hegemony and of consensus as a necessary form of a concrete historical bloc'. V. Gerratana (ed.), A. Gramsci, *Quaderni del carcere*, Turin: Einaudi, 1977, p. 1211.

3. Gramsci, *Quaderni*, p. 1234.

4. This is true even of those books that reveal a higher than usual engagement with Croce's writings, e.g. J. V. Femia, *Gramsci's Political Thought*, Oxford: Clarendon Press, 1981, ch. 3; M. Finocchiaro, *Gramsci and the History of Dialectical Thought*, Cambridge: Cambridge University Press, 1988, ch. 1; B. Fontana, *Hegemony and Power*, Minneapolis: University of Minnesota Press, 1993, ch. 2. The best Italian studies have generally involved a scholarly tracing of the influences of Croce on Gramsci, though even these tend to adopt a Gramscian perspective, e.g. E. Garin, *Intellettuali del XX secolo*, Rome: Editori Riuniti, 1974, ch. 12.

5. For an early recognition of this importance from, in some ways, a surprising quarter, *see* L. Althusser, *For Marx*, trans. B. Brewster, London: Verso, 1990, p. 114, n. 29.

based, in origin if not in effect.[6] They have developed new theories of democracy centred primarily on struggles for recognition and only secondarily and derivatively on the issues that preoccupied Gramsci, namely, the control and ownership of the means of production. Given that the crux of Gramsci's critique of Croce was that he failed to relate ideological to economic and class power, a comparison of the two thinkers provides an indirect exploration of the coherence of such arguments. As we shall see, many of Gramsci's arguments misfire, with Croce not so much ignoring the socio-economic dimension of ideological domination as reversing the connection between the two so that the former becomes an aspect of the latter rather than, as Gramsci argued, the other way around. Though Croce is frequently portrayed as a conservative and 'Olympian' idealist, he offered a rival programme to Gramsci's that had tremendous appeal for young dissident intellectuals of the time, such as Pietro Gobetti.[7] In a number of respects, the recent post-Marxist reading of Gramsci can be regarded as an implicit return to this Crocean radical alternative.

Gramsci made three related criticisms of Croce. First, he contended that Croce's idealist historicism remained 'speculative' and 'transcendental' rather than grounded in the 'real' forces of history. Second, he argued that Croce consequently focused on the 'hegemonic' moment, overlooking its basis in class domination. As a result, he treated liberal norms and practices as universal rather than as particular to a certain stage of economic development, ignoring not only their origins in class struggle but also the flaws that had both given rise to fascism, on the one hand, and would lead to and be transcended by communism, on the other. Finally, he believed Croce had adopted the 'traditional' 'Olympian' stance of the disengaged philosopher, without appreciating that the practical effect of this position was to legitimise the *status quo*. These charges against Croce's views of historicism, hegemonic struggle and intellectuals will here be examined and rebutted in turn. As Gramsci acknowledged, at least in certain notes, his critique had to overcome the difficulty that, in every case, Croce made explicit statements defending positions that were apparently quite contrary to those Gramsci attributed to him. Indeed, he maintained it was to some extent necessary to engage in a Crocean critique of Croce.[8] Gramsci's crucial criticism was in this respect the first, for it was Croce's supposed failure to adopt as 'absolute' a historicism as he claimed that led to his other purported errors.

---

6. The key text in this regard is E. Laclau and C. Mouffe, *Hegemony and Socialist Strategy: Towards a radical democratic politics*, London: Verso, 1985.

7. The radical Croce is well brought out in E. E. Jacobitti, *Revolutionary Humanism in Modern Italy*, New Haven, CT: Yale University Press, 1981.

8. Gramsci, *Quaderni*, p. 1238.

Historicism

Gramsci argued that 'the opposition between Croceanism and the philosophy of praxis is to be found in the speculative character of Croceanism.'[9] Croce had battled against transcendental and theological modes of thought of a 'religio-confessional' character but, in every other respect, they remained deeply embedded within his philosophy.[10] As a result, 'history became a formal history, a history of concepts, and in the ultimate analysis a history of intellectuals, indeed an autobiographical history of Croce's own thought, a history of coachman flies.'[11] Thus the agents of Croce's histories were 'boned "figures", lacking skeletons and possessed of flacid, feeble flesh'.[12] Unlike certain later commentators,[13] Gramsci nevertheless cleared Croce of the main fault of 'idealist' historicism, that of viewing philosophies as giving birth to further philosophies and ideas to other ideas, with both being the products of some ultimate principle, Spirit or the Idea, working itself out through human history.[14] This was transcendentalism of the 'religio-confessional' kind Croce had rejected. As he observed, Croce's success lay in not conceiving philosophical thought as 'a development from thought to thought but as thought of historical reality.' However, if Croce had correctly insisted on the necessity 'in the perennial stream of events to devise concepts, without which reality could not be understood', he had failed to appreciate the inescapable fact 'that reality in movement and the concept of reality, even if they can be logically distinguished, historically have to be conceived as inseparably united'.[15]

Grasping the force of this criticism involves seeing Gramsci's critique of Croce as more than a straight contrast between idealism and historical materialism. Thus, Gramsci accepted Croce's counter-charge that certain types of Marxism were also 'speculative' and 'theological' in the worst sense, turning the economic substructure into a 'hidden God', whereby the forces of production evolved according to an inherent logic of their own.[16] For example, he attacked Bukharin on just these grounds in the *Quaderni*.[17] However, he regarded Croce's insistence that this view was inherent to Marxism as a deliberately perverse manoeuvre that belied his own debts to Marx. Indeed, he perceptively noted that, in a number of respects, Croce's own thought was an idealist reworking of Marxism of a kind that had sometimes been attributed to himself: namely, a voluntarist position that

9. *Ibid.*, p. 1224.
10. *Ibid.*, pp. 1225–6.
11. *Ibid.*, p.1241. (The term 'coachman flies' is a reference to La Fontaine's fable 'Le coche et la mouche', in which a fly perched on the back of a coach is convinced that the vehicle is ascending the hill as a result of its efforts.)
12. *Ibid.*, p. 1238.
13. *See* note 4.
14. Gramsci, *Quaderni*, p. 1134.
15. *Ibid.*, p. 1241.
16. *Ibid.*, pp. 1211, 1226.
17. *See*, e.g. *ibid.*, pp. 1445, 1402–3.

saw history as the product of human will and consciousness alone.[18] Gramsci saw his project in large part as retranslating Croce's theory back into Marxist terms by relating the ideological struggle to the conscious and revolutionary exploitation of social and economic circumstances. He desired a 'materialism perfected by the work of idealist philosophy', which appreciated that 'the existence of objective conditions [...] is not yet sufficient: it is necessary to "know" them and know how to use them. And to want to use them.'[19] In other words, 'reality' grounded but did not determine human thought and action. History consisted of the ever-more-conscious mastery of this 'reality' as humanity economically transformed nature and created increasingly efficient and hence emancipatory forms of production and social organisation. By contrast, Gramsci believed Croce denied the existence of any such 'external' or 'objective' reality. As a result, he was caught uneasily between sneaking 'theology' back in as some sort of covert ideal force or demiurge, Gramsci's interpretation of Croce's 'spirit', and simply failing to see the true grounding of ideas in material conditions, so that we got the 'flesh' without the 'bone'.[20]

In what follows, I shall argue that Croce attempted the very strategy Gramsci assumed impossible – that of avoiding any 'external' grounding at all. His counter-claim was that a true historicism dealt solely with the historical worlds created by human thought and action and could do so without falling into either of the pitfalls identified by Gramsci. Indeed, these traps arose from the very notions of 'reality' and 'objectivity' that Gramsci believed were necessary to avoid them.

Gramsci rightly identified the key to Croce's historicism in his identification of 'philosophy' with the 'historical methodology' or 'judgement' he believed we employed when tackling 'particular problems'.[21] It was these features that Gramsci saw as signalling a more 'realist' idealism of the kind that had initially attracted him. Indeed, he perceptively singled out an article on 'Philosophy and methodology' as a turning point in Croce's elaboration of this view.[22] Appended to the Italian edition of his *Theory and History of Historiography* of 1917,[23] this

---

18. *Ibid.*, pp. 1232–33, where he also notes his early 'Crocean' tendencies in articles such as 'The revolution against *Capital*' of 1917. Though he does not cite it, Giovanni Gentile made a parallel observation in a review of the 1917 edition of Croce's articles on Marx (G. Gentile, 'Il marxismo di Benedetto Croce', *Il Resto del Carlino*,14 May 1918).

19. Gramsci, *Quaderni*, p. 1338.

20. *Ibid.*, pp. 1240–1. Gramsci employs 'bone' and 'flesh' to refer respectively to the economic 'base' and the ideological 'superstructure' in *ibid.*, p. 437.

21. *Ibid.*, p. 1210. *See also* p. 1239, where he advocates employing this view to interpret the development of Croce's own philosophy.

22. Gramsci does not refer to this article by name but he frequently paraphrases key dicta from it, clearly indicating that it provides the source of his interpretation of Croce's mature philosophy, e.g. *ibid.*, pp. 1239, 1240.

23. B. Croce, 'Filosofia e metodologia', in *Teoria e storia della storiografia*, Bari: Laterza, 1917, pp. 136–48. *See also* his reply to criticisms of this piece, 'Contro i sistemi definitivi', republished in B. Croce, *Cultura e vita morale: intermezzi polemici*, 3rd edn, Bari: Laterza, 1955, pp. 201–9.

piece coincided with Gramsci's most avowedly 'Crocean' period.[24] As Gramsci observed, Croce was motivated in large part by the desire to distance himself from Gentile's 'actualism'. Thus, the chapter was organised around a refutation of what he regarded as the key defining characteristics of 'metaphysical' or 'transcendent' conceptions of philosophy: namely, the belief in 'a fundamental philosophical problem', the related view that there must be 'a definitive philosophy' which provides its solution, and the assumption that all particulars and distinctions are manifestations of a single unitary principle.[25] However, Croce's attempt to rid philosophy of these conceptions had more far-reaching consequences than Gramsci appreciated.

Croce argued that individuals were moved to philosophise not in the abstract or in general but in relation to the particular problems that confronted them in their daily lives. Not only were many of these problems of very different kinds, they also presented themselves to people in highly diverse ways within different cultures and periods. No common, basic or universal principle, set of human needs, essence or facts of the matter underlay the various ways people reasoned and acted. For different ways of conceptualising both the world and human nature provided contrasting criteria as to what their essential characteristics might be. Nor was it possible to somehow reach behind or go beyond these various time-bound and circumstantial descriptions of the world or nature, by employing either some pure empirical method or a rarefied mystical or wholly logical mode of thought that might allow one to apprehend an eternal and unchanging Truth or Reality. Every person's present thinking and activity was conditioned by the past thought and action of those who had influenced the values and practices within which he or she worked and would, in its turn, condition that of others as well as his or her own in the future. To this extent, all judgement was 'historical', and all history 'contemporary', because it connected past and future by reflecting and revising certain prevailing attitudes and pursuits.[26]

This subsequent elaboration of received ways of conceiving and doing things ought not to be seen either as producing ever-nearer approximations to the Truth or as the embodiment of evolving elaborations of the Truth, either in general or on a specific issue. Conventions, traditions, systems of thought, no matter how complex and sophisticated, were simply a haphazard accumulation of responses to various issues. No single design or general or universal principle underlay them. Following Vico and Marx, Croce had a deeply practical sense of philosophy as a set of tools that had gradually been elaborated for tackling particular problems and which were refined and occasionally discarded as new problems emerged. To the extent philosophers had any general task, it consisted of making apparent both the

---

24. Gramsci, *Quaderni*, p. 1233.
25. I discuss this article more fully in my 'A modern interpreter: Benedetto Croce and the politics of Italian culture', *The European Legacy: Towards New Paradigms* 5, 2000, pp. 845–61, reproduced here as Chapter Six.
26. Croce, 'Filosofia e metodologia', pp. 137–8, 140, 148 and *Teoria e storia della storiografia*, ch. 1.

contingency and the historical diversity of theories and the actions they spawned. Thus, Croce treated his own studies into aesthetics, logic and practical ethics as simply interventions in contemporary debates, fashioned through discussion of particular poets and writers and reflecting a certain lineage, which he scrupulously traced in the historical sections that accompanied each volume of his *Philosophy of Spirit*.[27]

It is important to see that in debunking philosophies orientated towards promoting Truth, Justice or Reality, Croce was not putting forward an alternative way of viewing these notions, such as advocating relativism or denying the world existed outside human mental states. It is the belief that he must be that has led Gramsci and many other commentators astray. Rather, he simply doubted if any philosophical purpose could be achieved by pursuing them as such and trying to devise criteria by which they might be arrived at. He obviously accepted people employed 'true', 'just', 'natural' and so on when making practical judgements of right or wrong relative to some way of doing things. However, in these instances these terms no longer meant true 'to the world' or to 'intrinsic human purposes' but to the norms of a particular conceptual scheme. Used in this manner, these terms were 'pseudo-concepts' or practical rules of thumb that helped group particular classes of actions together. Of importance within practical bodies of knowledge, such as the law, natural science and economics, they had no absolute status. They were simply appropriate within a given temporally and spatially located cultural context that would inevitably change as history moved on.[28] If the error of 'transcendental' philosophers was to assume a noumenal reality behind the transient world of phenomena, the mistake of a certain sort of empiricist rationalist was to reify the 'facts' of a given era or form of enquiry into universal social laws or human tendencies. An approach Croce associated with the French *philosophes* and appeals to universal human rights in particular, he caricatured it as reflecting what he called 'the Masonic tendency'.[29]

The only proper significance Croce allowed for 'true' or 'just' was that of 'historically appropriate'.[30] But since history had no intrinsic meaning, or at least not one accessible to human beings, this was simply an *ex-post-facto* observation of no normative import. Truth in this historical sense could only be captured by a philosophy of history in the grand manner, of the kind Croce thought impossible.[31] As we have seen, Croce also denied that historical change indicated 'progress'. Croce's suggestion that we view history as if it were the work of Providence can

---

27. Croce, 'Contro i sistemi definitivi', pp. 201–9. *See*, too, his later elaboration of several of these points in B. Croce, *La storia come pensiero e come azione*, (1937) 6th edn, Bari: Laterza, 1954, Part 1 chs 2 and 5, pp. 5–10, 19–25.

28. B. Croce, *Logica come scienza del concetto puro*, 2nd edn economica, Bari: Laterza, 1971, Part 1 ch. 2.

29. Croce expressed these criticisms in numerous places. A good programmatic statement is his 'La "mentalità massonica"' (1910), in Croce, *Cultura e vita morale*, pp. 143–50.

30. Croce, *La storia come pensiero e come azione*, Part 1 ch. 5, pp. 19–25.

31. Croce, 'Filosofia e metodologia', p. 148.

mislead in this respect and has to be interpreted carefully. Croce espoused an austere 'disenchanted' Providentialism of a distinctly Weberian kind. In language strikingly similar to Weber's secularised Puritan, he argued that we must follow our 'vocation' and act 'as if' history were Providentially guided, without in fact knowing if this was true or not.[32] In other words, the issues of Truth and Objectivity were simply bracketed through being 'absolutely historicised'. However, this was not a recipe for passivity, though in certain occasional writings the politically conservative Croce occasionally made it seem so. On the contrary, the key value for Croce was freedom, with history the manifestation or 'story of liberty'. By liberty he meant the human capacity for self-creation in all the various fields of endeavour that gave meaning to people's existence. He believed this capacity to be irrepressible. Since all human thought and action inevitably produced change, human affairs were in a continual state of flux.[33] As we shall see in the next section, it is liberty so conceived that offered the criterion by which he judged different social and political regimes.

In emphasising freedom, Croce was not suggesting that how we view and 'make' the world is thereby an act of will. He saw this danger as afflicting Gentile's 'actualism', on the one hand, and certain types of 'realist' politics, on the other, with fascism suffering from both forms of this malady.[34] Actualism was a radical attempt to integrate our consciousness of experience with its creation, with the 'pure' (by which Gentile meant presuppositionless) 'act of thought', the absolute foundation of the human world. Croce regarded this doctrine as an extreme, solipsistic and ultimately despotic version of transcendentalism, with the Gentilean claiming access to a personal Truth which he then sought to impose on a recalcitrant world. Croce contended the 'pure' act of thought was an inconceivable and impossible notion, since all thought assumed, even if it transformed, the theoretical and practical suppositions of the historical context. Put another way, the thoughts and actions of others provided the language or medium though which we fashioned our own thinking and acting. 'Actualism', in sum, involved a denial of history – in Crocean language it was 'anti-historicist'. In certain respects the youthful 'voluntarist' writings of Gramsci suffered similar defects and some commentators have argued he was in fact more influenced by Gentile than Croce in this period.[35] By contrast, a pure 'realism' made the opposite mistake of assuming practical success entailed some sort of theoretical vindication or gain, that 'might' was 'right'. If the actualist fell into the errors of 'theological' thinking, the realist

32. *See* his essays of 1920, 'L'individuo, la grazia e la provvidenza' and 'La provvidenza', in *Frammenti di etica*, republished in B. Croce, *Etica e politica*, 2nd edn economica, Bari: Laterza, 1973, pp. 92–4 and 94–7.

33. Croce, *La storia come pensiero e come azione*, Part 1 ch.12, pp. 48–52.

34. *Ibid.*, ch. 7, pp. 28–30.

35. R. Bellamy and D. Schecter, *Gramsci and the Italian State*, Manchester: Manchester University Press, 1993, pp. 8–11. *See also* Gramsci's youthful article 'Socialism and actualist philosophy', *Il Grido del Popolo*, 9 February 1918, in Antonio Gramsci, *Pre-Prison Writings*, Richard Bellamy (ed.), Cambridge: Cambridge University Press, 1994, p. 50.

committed the parallel mistakes Croce associated with the 'Masonic' positivist. Arguably, as we shall see, it is this latter error that afflicts the later Gramsci.

Croce attempted to avoid the problems of both these perspectives, whilst keeping certain insights from each of them. This position has led some commentators, Gramsci (as we noted) included, to accuse him of falling into one or other of the traps he was trying to circumnavigate. There are certainly times he seemed to do so but the desire to avoid these pitfalls was plain and his attempted way of doing so coherent. Croce wanted to insist on a dialectical relationship between the distinct moments of 'theory' and 'practice'. The idealists were correct in believing action was always shaped by theory, which determined how we saw the world. *Pace* Gentile, though, this theory was not an entirely personal vision. Nonetheless, we were more than mere cyphers of pre-existing communal norms and practices and could reinterpret and challenge them. Yet in putting forward our own reading of these values and activities we were constrained by the readings of others and so had to act realistically whilst thinking idealistically. For the realists were correct to suggest that action involves employing appropriate means to achieve our ends, including manipulating the available legitimating norms and occasionally compromising our ideals. Where they went wrong was in suggesting we had no ideals at all, that interests were a 'given' and that their efficient satisfaction was the only evaluation that counted. Therefore, Croce was a realist in arguing that people did not theorise in a vacuum and acted instrumentally in pursuing their goals, an idealist in contending that we were reflective actors improvising within a context that was intellectual yet no less real for that. As he put it, we were both historical products and makers of history at one and the same time, continually shifting between reflecting on the past and acting to shape the future. Thus, we were at once 'immersed in the past' and capable of rising above it through thought, 'converting it into knowledge [...] which forms the ideal premise for new action, new life'.[36]

Given this analysis of Croce's historicism, how accurate was Gramsci's critique? Gramsci argued that Croce's idealist approach provided mere 'criteria of interpretation' for historical research because his 'ethico-political' conception of history was 'independent from any conception of reality', by which he meant economic and social forces.[37] In so saying, Gramsci was echoing what he took to be Croce's back-handed compliment to historical materialism, which the Neapolitan had described in identical terms.[38] However, Croce was expressing a quite different evaluation to what Gramsci supposed. He had not meant to slight Marxism but to affirm that, like any other doctrine, it was only 'realistic' as opposed to 'theological' in so far as it was understood solely as giving 'criteria' for interpreting (and hence identifying) a given set of 'facts' rather than a thesis that

---

36. Croce, *La storia come pensiero e come azione*, Part 1 ch. 8, p. 30.

37. Gramsci, *Quaderni*, p. 1235.

38. Croce, *Materialismo storico*, pp. xii, 75.

these 'facts' somehow existed as 'facts' prior to their interpretation.[39] Seen in this light, Marxism had a practical application in identifying and shaping the interests of the proletariat, even if Marxist insights could be employed by others too for quite different purposes.[40]

Gramsci's accusation that Croce's historical agents were the disembodied brains of a select group of intellectuals not only ignored salient aspects of Croce's argument but also assumed the validity of the very ontological and epistemological positions he wished to question. Croce did not deny the 'reality' of the social and economic conditions within which people engaged, he merely argued they were ideational artefacts. Nor did he deny that history was concerned with the social relations within which people engaged. He simply contended that all we could know about our relations with either other people or the outside world was the relational aspect and this was 'internal' to the agents themselves. However, he was at one with Gramsci in believing the 'internal' 'thought' of these historical relations consisted not of the abstruse ideas of philosophers but of the 'common-sense' thinking of ordinary men and women. Moreover, as we have seen, Croce believed that though idealist in conception, effective practical action was realist in its execution. Indeed, Croce's praise of Marx as the 'Machiavelli of the proletariat' arose from his appreciation of the German's 'realism' in this sense.[41] Where Croce departed from both Marx and Gramsci was from their further argument that the capacity of an ideal to become real was a test of its 'objectivity' or 'truth'. In his opinion, this assertion conflated the fact of the world's containing the causes that justified our holding a belief with the view that some state of the world was true or made a belief true by 'corresponding' to it.

This conflation was fundamental to Gramsci's linking of theory and practice, however. It was also the source of his main differences from Croce and led him into the very 'speculative' and 'theological' modes of thought he detected in the Neapolitan. Gramsci addressed the question of the objectivity of the external world in various notes that either interspersed or accompanied his comments on Croce. We have seen that Gramsci accepted the Crocean view that 'objectivity' and 'reality' could only be human constructs that reflected the practical activity of making history. As he remarked, drawing on a famous example of Bertrand Russell's, 'East and West [...] are arbitrary and conventional, i.e. historical constructions, since outside of real history every point on the earth is East and West at the same time.'[42] Whereas Croce viewed all such constructs as linked to certain particular purposes, however, and hence as being dropped or transformed as human beings conceived other projects and history moved on, Gramsci believed human history involved progress towards an intersubjective consensus or 'concretely universalised subjectivity', which would be the mark of a society in which all legitimate human

---

39. *Ibid.*, pp. 9, 18 and 75.
40. *Ibid.*, p. 15.
41. *Ibid.*, p.104.
42. Gramsci, *Quaderni*, pp. 1419–20.

needs had been effectively met. The class struggle was, in this sense, a struggle for objectivity, where 'Objective always means "humanly objective", that which can correspond exactly to "historically" subjective', which would mean "universally subjective"'.[43] The 'cathartic moment' of revolution occurred when 'a totalitarian ideology rationally reflects the contradictions of the superstructure and represents the existence of the objective conditions for the revolutionising of *praxis*'.[44] This thesis invokes exactly the 'transcendental' notions Croce had wished to expunge from his philosophy: the ideas of a 'fundamental problem' requiring a 'definitive answer' from an all-encompassing 'system', of a validating reality behind the appearances, of a progressive teleology, whereby we gradually approach a final solution.

Most of the problematic aspects of Gramsci's argument stem from his belief that the subjective must ultimately be grounded in the objective and the rational be allied to the real. For example, this is the source of his equating truth with success, with Lenin credited with 'having advanced philosophy as philosophy in so far as he advanced political doctrine and practice'.[45] For similar reasons, Gramsci had little appreciation of what Weber called the 'ethical irrationality of the world',[46] whereby good can lead to evil and *vice versa* and few choices do not entail some loss. He assumed that differences over values and goals ultimately reflected an inadequate grasp of our historical situation and the best means of exploiting it to the full. As a result, he could also aspire practically as well as theoretically to achieving a 'total' perspective that combined both rational cognitive agreement about the state of the world and a rational ethical consensus on what goals we should pursue and how.[47] The associated exclusion of complexity and pluralism brought with it a blindness to the value of free thought and action, with liberty redefined as conformity to the real and rational will – 'the conscious and lucid assimilation of the directives to be accomplished'.[48] On all these counts, the Crocean position proved more open and democratic. These advantages over Gramsci become apparent in his alternative reading of hegemony and the role of intellectuals, to which we now turn.

---

43. *Ibid.*, pp. 1415–6.

44. *Ibid.*, p. 1244.

45. *Ibid.*, p. 1250.

46. M. Weber, 'Politics as a vocation', in H. H. Gerth and C. Wright Mills (eds), *From Max Weber: Essays in sociology*, London: Routledge, 1970, p. 122.

47. Gramsci, *Quaderni*, pp. 1051–2.

48. *Ibid.*, p. 1706.

Hegemony

Although Gramsci credited Croce with having 'focused attention [...] on the moment of hegemony and consensus as a necessary form of a concrete historical bloc',[49] he criticised his compatriot for seeing ideology as a purely 'superstructural' phenomena, unconnected to a specific and historically located socio-economic 'structure'. As a result, his 'ethico-political' perspective involved little more than 'the polemical presentation of more or less interesting philosophisms, but it is not history'.[50] Gramsci believed Croce's purely 'superstructural' approach led him to ignore, and be effectively unable to explain, the transition from one hegemonic moment to another. He cited Croce's histories of modern Italy and of nineteenth-century Europe as evidence of this failing. He found Croce's starting points of 1871 and 1815 respectively highly significant, since they excluded the formative moments of the *Risorgimento* and the French Revolution. Yet how, he asked, could one disregard

> the moment in which an ethico-political system dissolves itself and another is elaborated in fire and with iron? in which a system of social relations falls apart and decays and another system rises up and affirms itself? and instead placidly assume as the whole of history the ethico-political moment of cultural expansion?[51]

Croce simply failed to see how a 'historical bloc' combined an appropriate 'ethico-political form' with the existing 'economic and social content', with revolution occurring when the first no longer captured the second and was incapable of providing the most optimal development of the economy in ways that benefited all social classes. Two consequences resulted from this alleged oversight. First, Croce fell into the classic error of the Italian liberal intelligentsia of imagining that liberalism could be instituted in Italy via a 'passive' and largely elite-driven political revolution without a comprehensive 'national-popular' social revolution as well. The *Risorgimento* had failed to 'make Italians' because, unlike their French and English counterparts, the Italian bourgeoisie had not presented themselves as the leaders of a progressive movement for the transformation of the whole of Italian society that would benefit all classes.[52] Second, Croce adopted a purely 'speculative' analysis that treated liberal values as eternal, transcendental verities, which were unrelated to the specific interests of particular social groups at a given stage of historical development.[53]

How justified are these criticisms? Though it is true that Croce omitted the revolutionary moment from the histories Gramsci mentions, he had dealt with

---

49. *Ibid.*, p. 1211.

50. *Ibid.*, p. 1238.

51. *Ibid.*, p. 1227.

52. *Ibid.*, pp. 1209, 2029, 2053–4.

53. *Ibid.*, pp. 1227–8, 1230–1.

them in studies elsewhere: for example the early essays on 1799 in Naples[54] and of Carlo Lauberg in his *Lives and Adventures of Faith and Passion*,[55] the final chapter on the Risorgimento period in the *History of the Kingdom of Naples*[56] and the various pieces on the Poerio and others in the collection *A Family of Patriots and Other Studies*.[57] Far from seeing liberal ideals as eternal verities, he closely associated them with political forms and philosophical ideas that only emerged in the nineteenth century. Moreover, he spurned the facile progressivism of much liberal theory. Not only did each political regime set up new forms of domination but also, as he believed fascism amply demonstrated, the very worst abuses known in the past were always liable to present themselves afresh in even more oppressive ways in the future.[58] However, he did contend that the philosophical and 'metapolitical' view of liberalism that identified history with human liberty represented a permanent conceptual gain. Once attained, this insight could be read back as a way of understanding the past and planning the future, even if the practical difficulties standing in the path of the realisation of freedom had varied over time and were never-ending.[59]

Croce's focus in the two books Gramsci cited was not on the genesis of liberalism but on providing a picture of on-going liberal politics and defending it against fascist and, to a lesser degree, Marxist attacks. This defence has to be read alongside the various essays elaborating his political philosophy of the mid-1920s,[60] which were, in many respects, preparatory studies for the description of liberalism given in the historical works.[61] These essays are largely targeted against Gentile's neo-Hegelian conception of the ethical state,[62] a notion that was later reinterpreted and employed by Gramsci.

---

54. B. Croce, *Studi storici sulla rivoluzione napoletana del 1799*, Rome, 1897.

55. B. Croce, *Vite e avventure di fede e di passione*, Bari: Laterza, 1936.

56. B. Croce, *Storia del Regno di Napoli*, Bari: Laterza, 1925, ch. IV.

57. B. Croce, *Una famiglia di patrioti ed altri saggi storici e critici*, Bari: Laterza, 1919.

58. B. Croce, 'Principio, ideale, teoria: A proposito della teoria filosofica della libertà' (1939), in his *Il carattere della filosofia moderna*, 2nd edn, Bari: Laterza, 1945, pp. 115–6.

59. B. Croce, 'La concezione liberale come concezione della vita', in Croce, *Etica e politica*, pp. 235–43.

60. Gathered together as *Elementi di Politica* in Croce, *Etica e politica*, pp. 171–300.

61. Ernesto Ragionieri has argued that the *Storia d'Italia* was 'unique in not being accompanied by a group of preparatory and minor essays' (E. Ragionieri, 'Rileggendo "la Storia d'Italia" di Benedetto Croce', *Belfagor* XXI,1966, p. 125). But, to a large extent, the essays grouped together as 'Politica in Nuce' of 1924, along with those on 'Economico-political and ethico-political history' of the same year and 'Liberalism' of 1925, performed this function. Likewise, the essays on 'Liberismo e liberalismo'; Church and State; conflicting political ideals after 1870; Constant and Jellink; and the concept of the bourgeoisie, amongst others, which were added to these to form the book *Etica e politica*, Bari: Laterza, 1931, provided the conceptual basis for the *Storia d'europea nel secolo decimonono* of 1932.

62. *See* H. S. Harris, *The Social Philosophy of Giovanni Gentile*, Urbana: University of Illinois Press, 1960, ch. 7.

Croce feared this idea could be misinterpreted so as to produce a 'governmental' morality. Drawing on his thesis concerning the necessary distinctions between theory and practice, ethics and economics/politics, Croce argued that the state in the strict sense simply meant the government.[63] Like party politics more generally,[64] the state so conceived was narrowly focused on practical projects for the solution of particular problems and the meeting of certain needs and interests. As we have seen, however, the identification of the problems to be addressed and of where one's interests lay was dependent on its turn on the theories one held about the world. To this extent, all politics had a theoretical and ethical component. However, the broad ethos of a community was not itself a creation of the state or government but of civil society. It consisted not in any set of rules or principles but in the various values implicit in the way of life – the on-going practices and institutions – in which people were engaged. This ethos was not static but a contingent and historical product that developed as people tackled new problems and reflected back on the consequences of changing circumstances and activities for their inherited ways of doing things. Moreover, given that both thought and action were the products of human freedom and creativity, the paths that any society might follow were always open and underdetermined by prevailing conditions and customs. Thus the 'moral life' that made up civil society included a range of different perspectives, from both conservatives and revolutionaries, and with these latter being in many ways more important than the others 'because they, better than the others, open the paths to the future and obtain the advancement of human society'.[65]

The true ethical state, therefore, consisted of both state and civil society. Fascist attempts to colonise the second by the first were essentially imposing a governmental view on the whole of society, stifling individual initiative in the process. Croce also took up a related discussion as to whether the basis of the state was 'force' and 'will', as the fascists argued, or 'consensus', as they contended liberals believed.[66] Gentile had infamously defended this position by arguing that only 'force' offered a stable and practical foundation for the state and was intrinsically moral since 'it is always an expression of will, and whatever method of argument is used – from sermon to blackjack – its efficacy cannot be other than that of tackling the inner man and persuading him to agree.'[67] Croce rebutted this sophistry by arguing that Gentile had got matters the wrong way around, confusing 'force' with 'morality' rather than seeing that it was 'morality' that possessed 'true

---

63. B. Croce, 'Lo Stato e l'etica' (Essay 2 of his *Politica 'in nuce'*), in Croce, *Etica e politica*, pp. 187–8.

64. *See* B. Croce, 'I partiti politici' (Essay 3 of his *Politica 'in nuce'*), in Croce, *Etica e politica*, pp. 189–95.

65. Croce, 'Lo Stato e l'etica', pp. 187–8.

66. For a full discussion of this debate, *see* Bellamy and Schecter, *Gramsci and the Italian State*, pp. 137–48.

67. G. Gentile, 'Il fascismo e la Sicilia', speech at Palermo 31 March 1924, reprinted in his *Che cosa è il fascismo?*, Florence: Valecchi, 1925, pp. 50–1.

force'. Thus consent was necessarily 'forced' in the sense that it arose through all parties recognising the 'force' of each other's arguments. As such, only a state based on consent possessed true 'force'. For it alone was truly 'realistic' in its appreciation of the force of prevailing conditions as perceived by its citizens and was capable of capitalising on the strength and will of the population.[68]

A liberal regime was one premised on liberty, in the sense of providing citizens with the space to think and act differently and to negotiate an ever-changing consensus to accommodate their developing and diverse ideals and interests. The chief mechanism for preserving this possibility lay in distinguishing the state from civil society, even if the precise boundaries between the two were amongst those issues that had to be continuously discussed and adapted.[69] For example, he disputed Luigi Einaudi's claim that liberalism necessitated free trade, noting that liberals had successfully adopted socialist policies at certain times.[70] Unlike many contemporary liberals, he also denied that either liberty or liberalism could be identified with either a particular view of justice or certain juridical arrangements.[71] Philosophically, liberty was simply the creative force of history that manifested itself in the practical sphere in a moral imperative to foster the energies and autonomy of others 'by the overthrow of tyrannies and oppressions and the establishment of customs, institutions, and laws tending to guarantee such a condition'.[72] But the latter were ad hoc creations and their importance lay in 'the historical content of the concrete and weighty political requirements which they bring up for discussion and which find an expression and an affirmation in them', not in their accordance with any ideal concept of liberty. For the 'moral assent' they achieve is not to their 'abstract form' 'but to their practical efficacy in given times and places, circumstances and situations, which though it may last for a long time, is always in the nature of things conditional and transitory'.[73] Croce, then, offered a radical liberalism consisting of an agonic politics of freedom in which the mark of genuine consensus was the continuing liberty to contest prevailing rules and structures.

Though Croce believed theory always advanced through tackling particular problems he was not advocating reformism. It might well be that a range of problems led to a revolutionary paradigm shift that effectively produced a comprehensive redescription of the world. However, such changes were neither sudden acts of will, as extreme voluntarists such as Gentile made it appear, nor, as Gramsci would have it, the product of changes in 'reality'. Rather, they were the

---

68. Croce, 'Lo Stato e l'etica', p. 186 and B. Croce, 'Il senso politico', (Essay 1 of his *Politica 'in nuce'*), in Croce, *Etica e politica*, p. 178.

69. Croce, 'Il senso politico', pp. 171–83.

70. B. Croce, 'Liberismo e liberalismo', in Croce, *Etica e politica*, pp. 263–67 and Croce, 'Principio, ideale, teoria', pp. 118–19.

71. Croce, 'Principio, ideale, teoria', pp. 119–21.

72. *Ibid.*, p. 111.

73. *Ibid.*, pp. 122–3.

cumulative result of people conceiving and doing things differently in ways that gradually set up inconsistencies and incoherences in traditional views.

As is well known, Gramsci partially adopted Croce's analysis of the ethical state as involving 'political society', which he conceived as a realm of coercion or force, and 'civil society', which he saw as the sphere of hegemony or consent.[74] From a Crocean point of view, however, Gramsci's analysis subverts liberty and does so for the very reasons that the Sardinian believed marked his superiority to the Neapolitan. Like Croce, Gramsci conceived the distinction between political and civil society and the two associated forms of rule as 'methodological' rather than 'organic', since most states combined elements of both.[75] The crucial issue was the nature of their combination. However, Croce maintained that, though linked, the two could never be fully united. The one, the political *status quo*, always provided the material for critique by the other, the moral and theoretical positions developed within civil society. Politics, by its nature, was the art of the possible in given circumstances or, what was the same thing, given the prevailing views of people. Human freedom of thought, and hence of action, meant these last, though, were always in the process of change. Thus, the 'state' and 'civil society' were in a permanent condition of creative tension between each other, with freedom both the cause and the product of this condition.[76]

By contrast, Gramsci believed that the ultimate aim was to produce an 'ethical state' that abolished the state in the narrow sense by incorporating it within civil society. This position was not only a variation on the Marxian 'withering away of the state' but a neat reversal of Gentile's corporatist version of the 'ethical state', whereby civil society was to be incorporated within the fascist state. Gramsci saw this last view as representing the 'economic-corporative' phase of domination, when the primary productive class were motivated by narrow material self-interested and so failed to carry subordinate groups with them.[77] In such circumstances, consent gradually gave way to state-imposed coercion. Instead, in the 'ethical' phase of the state, the prime socio-economic group asserted its supremacy not just as 'domination' but through 'intellectual and moral leadership' as well. It achieved this ascendancy by presenting and conceiving of the pursuit and development of its interests on a 'universal' rather than a 'corporate' plane.[78] As a result, it might even make certain economic sacrifices, though without jeopardising its pivotal economic role. Gramsci believed that successful bourgeois revolutions had achieved this 'organic' as opposed to merely 'mechanical' hegemonic unity. A successful future proletarian hegemony would have to follow a parallel path. However, the proletariat would inaugurate a genuine 'ethical state' since it was a truly 'universal class' that could 'present itself as capable of assimilating the

74. Gramsci, *Quaderni*, pp. 1518–9.

75. *Ibid.*, p. 1590.

76. Croce, 'Il senso politico', pp. 171–83.

77. Gramsci, *Quaderni*, p. 1583.

78. *Ibid.*, pp. 1584, 1591.

whole of society, and [...] really expressing this process'.[79] In consequence, this group could 'propose the end of the state and of itself as the goal to be attained [...] leading to the end of the internal division of ruled and rulers and to the creation of a unitary technico-moral organism'.[80] The state's role as an instrument of economic 'rationalisation' would ultimately give way to a truly hegemonic 'regulated society' or 'state without a state' in which people shared a 'collective will' through 'a multiplicity of dispersed wills' and 'heterogeneous aims' being 'welded together on the basis of an equal and common conception of the world'.[81] Needless to say, the grounding of this 'common conception' lay in 'the world of production', 'the reference point for the new world in gestation'. As he explained:

> The maximum utility must be at the base of any analysis of the moral and intellectual institutions to be created and the principles to be diffused: individual and collective life must be organised for the maximum return of the productive apparatus.[82]

The crucial contrast between Croce and Gramsci emerges when we consider the conception of liberty adopted by the latter. Gramsci rightly noted that, for Croce, liberty meant '"movement", development, dialectic' and that the advance represented by liberalism in the nineteenth century was to have become conscious of this fact.[83] However, he then accused Croce of thereby lacking a substantive conception of what freedom meant, in terms of the tangible benefits and capacities people might hope to enjoy. Croce's dialectical conception was either empty, since all history was a manifestation of liberty, or a reification of the bourgeois liberties of a given historical period and stage of economic and social development.[84] As we have seen, though, neither of these characterisations correctly captures Croce's position. With regard to the second of Gramsci's criticisms, Croce was well aware that the definitions of liberty in terms of either a given set of rights or certain other kinds of legal or political protection were historically contingent mechanisms. Indeed, certain liberal thinkers have criticised him for over-historicising his view of human freedom in this respect.[85] Yet this historicisation of liberalism was an entailment of the dialectical account of liberty he held, whereby the inevitably constraining rules of collective life have to be continually negotiated to reflect the evolving and diverse practical choices and moral views of autonomous individuals. Freedom became, in this way, its own foundation.

---

79. *Ibid.*, p. 937.

80. *Ibid.*, p. 1050.

81. *Ibid.*, pp. 764, 734, 1330–1.

82. *Ibid.*, p. 863 and *see also* p. 743.

83. *Ibid.*, p. 1229, Croce, 'Principio, ideale, teoria', pp. 112–3.

84. *Ibid.*, pp. 1229–32.

85. Most notably N. Bobbio, 'Benedetto Croce e il liberalismo', collected in his *Politica e cultura*, Bari: Laterza, 1955, pp. 211–68.

This contention did not make Croce's position vulnerable to Gramsci's first criticism of vacuous circularity. Not only was Croce able to distinguish the philosophical account of freedom from both different theories and practices of freedom, he could also affirm that a society that defined truth and justice in terms of the free assent of individuals, even if the terms of that assent were unstable and liable to error, was undoubtedly better than one which sought to impose a putatively universally valid account of these notions on people, on the grounds of an alleged pre-established harmony with some metaphysical or material reality. This thesis motivated all his post-1924 political writings.

The latter tack, however, was precisely the one taken by Gramsci. He believed the new proletarian hegemony would remove political conflicts, which were but the product of economically derived class 'contradictions'. Liberty became redefined in this context as 'self-discipline', 'the conscious and lucid assimilation of the directives to be accomplished'. With citizens no more than 'functionaries' of a well regulated society oriented towards the common good, 'democracy' ceased to be a mechanism for constructing and deliberating either the general will or mutually acceptable agreements and turned instead into a system of communication, whereby information flowed upwards to a central planning authority which passed directives downwards.[86]

Although Gramsci has often been praised for appreciating the relative autonomy of politics, his desired 'new order' involved the overcoming of the circumstances of political disagreements and decision-making. The abolition of the distinction between state and civil society, and with it the protections for individual freedom of thought and action, flowed from this expectation. Moreover, the reasons for this supposed supersession were precisely those motivating Gramsci's critique of Croce – namely, that he took a purely superstructural approach that treated economics as an epiphenomenon of politics rather than the other way around. Yet an absence of political conflict assumes more than agreement on norms, however well grounded. Individuals must not only possess angelic dispositions but be ruled by a trustworthy human agency that is both omniscient and omnipotent as well. Only angels can be counted on always to act from the appropriate motives and principles. Moreover, the road to hell is paved with good intentions and, unless they both know the correct action to take to realise the intended results and can actually implement that action, there will be ample room for debate over means and the prioritising of ends, even if there is a general moral consensus.[87] Croce's superiority lay in recognising these practical sources of political disagreement as well as the more contentious issue of theoretical conflict.

---

86. Gramsci, *Quaderni*, pp. 1706–7.

87. On the ways politics is linked to the pluralism of values in these and other ways, *see* R. Bellamy, *Liberalism and Pluralism: Towards a politics of compromise*, London: Routledge, 1999. For the failure of the Marxist tradition to acknowledge this, *see* S. Lukes, *Marxism and Morality*, Oxford: Oxford University Press, 1985.

Intellectuals

The contrasts between the two thinkers traced so far were further reflected in their respective views of intellectuals. Predictably, Gramsci criticised Croce for failing to relate the intellectual's role to practical socio-economic activity. Like other 'traditional' intellectuals, Croce saw himself as 'autonomous and independent of the dominant social group'. Croce might act like a 'lay Pope', but 'the most significant character' of his philosophy resided in 'his links with Senators Agnelli and Benni'.[88] His attempt to distinguish 'philosophy' from 'ideology' proved impossible. It merely indicated a continuing 'speculative' and essentially élitist conception of philosophical enquiry that deprived Croce of any critical engagement with the prevailing liberal hegemony that he unreflectively endorsed.

Once again, Gramsci's criticisms prove difficult to square with certain key elements of Croce's thought. Croce was insistent that one corollary of his historicist view was to have literally 'killed off' the traditional figure of 'The Philosopher' who:

> ignores history, art and poetry, politics, law, human passions, who reads neither the novel of life nor the novels written about it; and who nevertheless believes that he, who has grasped the supreme principle, not only is qualified to discourse on these matters, but that, in discussing them raises, transforms and validates them, having given them, in effect, and from the outside, his stamp of approval.[89]

By contrast, the 'historical philosopher' could not distance himself from the world and 'feels himself ineluctably taken up in the course of history, at one and the same time object and subject of history'.[90] Moreover, as we have seen, Croce contended such philosophers did not seek solutions to the meaning of the universe or address the 'fundamental problem' employing the tools of 'pure reason' in the manner of metaphysicians. Rather, they philosophised in relation to a specific problem as it arose within their lives. Thus, they were specialists but not a special cadre. Indeed, Croce maintained 'every man is (within his sphere, however august or wide it may seem) a philosopher, and every a philosopher is a man, inextricably linked to the conditions of human life, which cannot be transcended by any means'.[91] Contrary to Gramsci's interpretation of his thesis, therefore, Croce did not think philosophers enjoyed any superior status as the purveyors of a profounder or more 'enlightened' kind of knowledge. True philosophers spoke the 'prose' of ordinary men and women, not the poetry or mystical runes of an elite academic caste.

---

88. Gramsci, *Quaderni*, p. 1515 and A. Gramsci, *Lettere dal carcere*, Turin: Einaudi, 1965, n. 210, 7 Sett. 1931, p. 451.

89. B. Croce, 'Il Filosofo', in *Ultimi saggi*, Bari: Laterza, 1935, p. 90. On this piece, *see* the incisive article by Norberto Bobbio in his *Italia civile: Ritratti e testimonianze*, Florence: Passigli editore, 1986, pp. 69–93.

90. Croce, 'Filosofia e metodologia', p. 144.

91. *Ibid.*, p. 144.

If Croce explicitly distanced himself from the 'ivory-tower' conception of the 'traditional' intellectual, he also wished to avoid the confusion of philosophy and ideology. That did not mean philosophy and scholarship had no political role. As he remarked of Antonio Labriola's admonition of indifference when deciding to devote himself to antiquarian research on Naples rather than working for the socialist cause, the 'thinker's toil' was 'political in its own way, within its proper sphere'.[92] Elaborating on this position, he observed how in his later work on his journal, *La Critica*,

> there grew up within me a calm conviction that I was giving the best that I had; that I was engaged in politics, in the broad sense of that word, doing the work at once of a student and of a citizen; so that I need no longer blush, as I had often blushed in the past, on meeting a politician or a socially active fellow citizen.[93]

True to his distinction between theory and practice, Croce wished to insist on the difference between doing and reflecting upon politics. Whilst the latter fed into the former, it provided an orientating 'faith' rather that a practical 'programme'.[94] As we noted above, Croce believed politics involved realist and instrumental forms of reasoning that were inappropriate in ethics. The philosopher's role consisted in large part in ensuring the two were not confused, for to do so was to espouse the sort of governmental morality that afflicted fascism and Stalinism. The philosophical or ethical moment not only informed, it also offered a source of criticism of the practical or political, which was always constrained by the necessities of the moment. Moreover, Croce was personally remarkably true to his own position, always carefully distinguishing his own party-political conservative liberalism from his 'metapolitical' philosophical liberalism. That the first tied him to Sonnino and then Giolitti (if not Agnelli and Benni[95]) he freely confessed but the second allowed him to criticise these positions and appreciate their historical contingency.

Croce's intellectuals were an elite but in much the same sense as Gaetano Mosca's 'political class' were.[96] Indeed, he came to assimilate the two.[97] The division of labour inevitably produced a group of cultural specialists, who had

---

92. B. Croce, 'Come nacque e come mori il Marxismo teorico in Italia 1895–1900', reprinted in *Materialismo storico ed economia marxista*, 3rd edn economica, Bari: Laterza, 1978, pp. 274–5.

93. Croce, *Contributo alla critica di me stesso*, reprinted in *Etica e politica*, pp. 334–5.

94. B. Croce, 'Fede e programmi' (1911), in *Cultura e vita morale*, pp. 181–91, though this is elaborated in a much less conservative manner in Croce, 'I partiti politici'.

95. Reviewing the passage from the *Quaderni* cited above, Croce confessed complete bemusement and claimed not even to know who Benni was. B. Croce, *Terze Pagine Sparse*, vol. 2, Bari: Laterza, 1955, p. 137.

96. On Mosca's 'political class', *see* R. Bellamy, *Modern Italian Social Theory*, Cambridge: Polity, 1987, ch. 3.

97. B. Croce, 'Review of G. Mosca, *Elementi di scienza politica*, 2nd edn, Turin, 1923, *La critica* 21 (1923), pp. 374–8.

more time for reflection than others. However, we observed earlier how Croce insisted they should be neither detached from the concerns from the world nor incapable of speaking to others. Quite the contrary, they had a civic duty to engage with both. Thus, he argued that,

> the labour of speculative thought does not remain closed in its own range but seeks there the energy required for working in the wider world, and accomplishes this not only by the communication of the logical process to others who receive it and can more rapidly cover the same intellectual ground and make it their own, but also, and above all, thanks to the conversion, in the minds of the many, of reasoned argument into self-evident truth, common sayings, proverbs, divested of all theoretical apparatus and transmuted into articles of faith, a sure guide for the soul.[98]

Not for nothing had Croce been a pioneering scholar of popular culture. Moreover, to the extent that ordinary people were to a degree philosophers as well, 'the intellectual and directing classes' also had to be open to them and to educate the masses

> with a view, in the first place, to its providing an ever-richer flow of new and fresh recruits for the directing class, as members of it and co-operators with it, and in the second place with a view to attaining a progressively harmonious relation with it.[99]

Gramsci, also influenced by Mosca, similarly portrayed the ruling class as an open elite in the double sense of being open both to the world and to ordinary people. Superficially, he also appeared more populist. After all, he thought 'all men are intellectuals' and insisted on the need for a mutual educational relationship between intellectuals and masses, in which the one offered 'knowledge' and the other 'understanding' and especially 'feeling'.[100] Yet, formally, at least, his project was not that different from Croce's: to transform the 'common sense' of the masses and to bring their views into harmony with that of the intellectual leaders. It was the substance that differed. Gramsci's intellectuals may be 'organically' situated within given social groups and their everyday activities but their aim was to inculcate a 'universal morality' that reflected certain objective requirements – namely, 'adapting "civilization" and the morality of the vast popular masses to the requirements of the continual development of production'.[101] As the repository of this superior knowledge, the Party 'takes the place of the Divinity or categorical imperative' within 'people's consciences'.[102] By offering a 'total' conception

---

98. Croce, 'Principio, ideale, teoria', p. 108.

99. *Ibid.*, p. 109.

100. Gramsci, *Quaderni*, pp. 1516, 1505.

101. *Ibid.*, pp. 1561, 1565–6.

102. *Ibid.*, p. 1561.

of the world, the members would 'find in it the satisfactions previously found in a multiplicity of organisations'. Regional dialects and local practices were to be replaced by a common language and a unified moral, social and political structure.[103]

From a Crocean perspective, Gramsci committed two cardinal errors. First, he has subjected philosophy and morality to the instrumental goals of a Party programme.[104] Second, he fell into the 'metaphysical' error of claiming to have discovered the reality behind the appearances of people's ordinary thinking, solving in the process the riddle of history. Thus it was Gramsci, rather than Croce, who adopted the stance of the 'traditional' and 'speculative' intellectual, seeking a universality and objectivity beyond the particular, situated and historically contingent thought and action of everyday life. It was also Gramsci who then used the authority of this supposedly superior intellectual position to legitimise the political hegemony of the Party over its members. A move with revolutionary intent, it could only have highly reactionary and coercive consequences.

Conclusion

In a famous article, Norberto Bobbio presented Gramsci as a theoretician of the 'superstructure'.[105] I have implicitly endorsed those Marxist critics of Bobbio's thesis who have stressed the 'structural' and class-based character of his account of the struggle for hegemony.[106] Unlike them, however, I have seen this aspect as a weakness rather than a strength, one which ultimately led Gramsci to the unwarranted negation of politics. From this perspective, Gramsci's much-vaunted appreciation of politics was purely strategic – the political arts were merely means to achieve the revolutionary end of transcending their necessity. To the extent a superstructural reading of Gramsci can be given, it depends heavily on his dialogue with Croce. As we have seen, however, Gramsci's chief concern was to criticise Croce's analysis of the autonomy of politics. Much of this critique turned on a misapprehension that Croce's position involved denying economic and social sources of domination – a view that even certain liberal critics of Gramsci have endorsed, including Bobbio. Instead, we have noted that the Neapolitan's main concern was to stress their politically derived nature. Meanwhile, for those radical democrats seeking to question the 'essentialism' of much liberal as well as Marxist thought and to explore the constitutive character of political conflict, Croce offers a more plausible and fruitful source than his Sardinian antagonist, albeit one that

---

103. *Ibid.*, pp. 800, 1377–8, 2314.

104. Croce hammered this first point home himself in reviews of the *Quaderni* as they were released in the late 1940s. *See* Croce, *Terze Pagine Sparse*, pp. 137–9, 252–3.

105. N. Bobbio, 'Gramsci and the conception of civil society', in Richard Bellamy (ed.), *Which Socialism? Marxism, Socialism and Democracy*, Cambridge: Polity, 1987, pp. 139–61.

106. *See*, e.g. J. Texier, 'Gramsci, theoretician of the superstructures', in C. Mouffe (ed.), *Gramsci and Marxist Theory*, London: Routledge, 1979, p. 71 and J. Lester, *Dialogue of Negation: Debates on Hegemony in Russia and the West*, London: Pluto Press, 2000, pp. 59–63.

many will not find wholly congenial. For it was precisely on these issues that Croce and Gramsci divided, with the one endorsing an agonistic politics of freedom and the other regarding it as a purely bourgeois phenomenon. That Gramscian criticism is echoed by many left-wing critics of difference politics.[107] Clearly this debate cannot be engaged with here but hopefully some indication has been given as to at least some of the inadequacies of this critique.

---

107. *See* Lester, *Dialogue of Negation*, chs 4 and 5.

Chapter Eleven

Gramsci and Walzer on the Intellectual as Social Critic

Intellectuals have often been criticised by left and right alike for being detached from the everyday concerns of their fellow human beings. The left usually characterise this detachment as an ivory-towered and unworldly elitism, which leads at best to irrelevance and a passive acquiescence in the oppression of their fellow citizens and at worst to a spurious legitimation of that oppression as part of the way of the world.[1] The right, not dissimilarly, typically accuse intellectuals of being snobbish and anti-populist. Even the self-styled friends of the people are said to dislike the popular culture of the masses, which they seek to displace through sinister programmes of re-education.[2] Indeed, intellectuals who engage in politics generally attract much greater criticism than those who shun it. They are accused of either betraying their role as independent guardians of the truth, by placing their talents in the service of those in power,[3] or of being dangerous utopians who oppose their own feeble rational constructions to time-honoured common sense.[4]

Intellectuals, therefore, seem caught in something of a cleft stick. If they remain outside politics, they end up being charged with aloofness and a selective blindness to injustice. If they enter the political arena, they appear condemned either to prostrate themselves before the powerful or illegitimately to impose their ideals on others. On the one hand, they stand accused of a false objectivity obtained via a refusal to dirty their hands by engaging with the often messy affairs of the world, while on the other hand they are warned against covering their hands in blood by seeking to make a necessarily imperfect world conform to their

---

1.   These criticisms are levelled by Gramsci at what he calls 'traditional' intellectuals, for example. *See* V. Gerratana (ed.), *A. Gramsci, Quadenri del carcere*, Turin: Einaudi, 1975, pp. 1514–6.

2.   For a recent example of this type of criticism, *see* John Carey, *The Intellectuals and the Masses: Pride and prejudice among the literary intelligensia 1880–1939*, London: Faber & Faber, 1992. Of course, many on the right also endorse such views.

3.   The classic statement of this view is Julian Benda, *The Betrayal of the Intellectuals*, trans. R. Aldington, Boston: Beacon Press, 1955.

4.   A view propounded to the point of caricature by P. Johnson in, *Intellectuals*, London: Weidenfield and Nicholson, 1988. Although these two criticisms are typically levelled by conservatives against intellectuals on the left, they have been expressed with equal vigour against right-wing thinkers. With regard to the first argument, Benda's main target was nationalists, whilst the second is as telling against fascist apologists, such as Giovanni Gentile, as against communist theorists. George Orwell's *1984*, New York: Signet, 1950, for example, represents a socialist's condemnation of totalitarianism as such.

abstract ideals.[5] Even those who make these sorts of criticisms may not be able to escape this dilemma. Intellectuals themselves (George Orwell and Edmund Burke come to mind as examples from left and right respectively), they risk falling into self-contradiction or bad faith. Is there, then, an acceptable form of intellectual engagement with politics? Can intellectuals play a distinctive political role without either trimming their ideals in despicable ways or indulging in the sorts of reprehensible behaviour associated with various kinds of elitism? Or was Ernest Gellner right to argue that, whether one becomes involved or not, it is practically impossible to avoid committing *la trahison des clercs* ?[6]

These issues arise to some degree or other for most moral and political philosophers. However, they have been particularly pressing for intellectuals on the left, who have often felt an obligation to speak *for* the people without necessarily being of the people, on the grounds that various barriers, both physical and psychological, have inhibited or prevented the people from speaking for themselves. In this paper, I want to address two influential attempts to confront this dilemma, by the Italian Marxist Antonio Gramsci and the contemporary American social and political theorist Michael Walzer.

Gramsci's writings have long had a special place in the hearts of Western left-wing intellectuals in this regard. Not only does his theory allot an all-important role to the intellectual within the revolutionary struggle, particularly in the West, but he also has the added advantage of being, in Walzer's wonderfully apt phrase, 'an innocent communist'.[7] For imprisonment and death in a fascist jail saved him from becoming tainted with Stalinism. However, Walzer is ambivalent about Gramsci's thought and rightly so. As he notes, Gramsci's writings can be as plausibly interpreted to suggest that Mussolini 'saved him from Stalinist orthodoxy' as that he 'deprived the left of a brave and supremely intelligent opponent of Stalinism'.[8] So although Walzer includes Gramsci within the pantheon of his Ancient and Honourable Company of Critics, he is there as much as a salutary example of the pitfalls the social critic needs to avoid as a model of social criticism at its best.

Both the merits and the drawbacks of the Gramscian approach are particularly pertinent for Walzer, since he adopts a very similar perspective to the Sardinian. Like Gramsci, he believes that the dangers of Olympian detachment on the one hand and rule by an intellectual elite on the other can best be avoided through a

---

5. Norberto Bobbio regards these as the dangers confronting what he calls the 'pure' and the 'revolutionary' intellectual respectively. *See* N. Bobbio, *Il dubbio e la scelta: Intellectuali e potere nella societa contemporanea*, Rome: La Nuova Italia Scientifica, 1993, p. 165.

6. E. Gellner, 'La trahison de la trahison des clercs', in I. Maclean, A. Montefiore and P. Winch (eds), *The Political Responsibility of Intellectuals*, Cambridge: Cambridge University Press. 1990, p. 27. As Edward Said points out, even this statement constitutes a form of betrayal, since inaction may end up as culpable of some great wrong as positive actions. *See* E. W. Said, *Representations of the Intellectual: The 1993 Reith Lectures*, London: Vintage, 1994, p. xiii.

7. M. Walzer, *The Company of Critics: Social criticism and political commitment in the twentieth century*, London: Peter Halban, 1989, p. 81.

8. *Ibid.*, p. 80.

form of immanent critique that evolves out of the prevailing views and practices of ordinary people. Unlike Gramsci, though, he does not wish to adopt a teleological view of history to ground this thesis. Gramsci's criticism of 'scientific' Marxism notwithstanding, Walzer is correct to point out that the Marxist account of history remained central to Gramsci's thinking. As a consequence, Walzer contends that elitism and what he regards as a 'false' objectivism enter via the back door, and that Gramsci's view of intellectuals has more in common with Lenin's notion of the 'vanguard party' than is often thought. However, rejecting any kind of teleology is not unproblematic either, since it potentially denies immanent critique any critical bite with regard to the *status quo*. Although Walzer seeks to escape the charge of conservative traditionalism, it is unclear that he does so. His belief that he can avoid appealing to any universal or transcultural values may be more the result of his living in liberal America instead of fascist Italy than because of any theoretical advance on his part.

The following comparison of the two thinkers focuses on three central and related aspects of their theories. The first section explores the epistemological theory underlying their conception of the intellectual and questions the coherence of a view of immanent critique that eschews any teleology. The second section develops this criticism by examining the accompanying sociological account they give of the intellectual's social role and his or her relationship to the people. The third section turns to their views on the social and political context of intellectual activity. I shall argue that Gramsci's difficulties stem from the fact that, within the Italy of his time, he felt that the intellectual had to engage in what Norberto Bobbio has called 'cultural politics' – the advocacy of a particular ideological position.[9] However, this leads to all of the difficulties described at the start of this chapter. The way to avoid them lies in intellectuals adopting what Bobbio terms the 'politics of culture'. In other words, they must militate for the conditions necessary for social criticism to occur, rather than arguing to a particular substantive view. The latter is something the intellectual may do as a citizen acting within a social and political system that allows us all to be, to some degree, intellectuals; the former represents a specific intellectual duty.[10] Walzer's problem turns out to be that he assumes the appropriate social and political pre-conditions are always present.

Epistemology

In developing his epistemological position, Gramsci attempted to distance himself from both crude positivism, which he thought characterised vulgar 'scientific' Marxism, and from idealism, most especially the branch popularised in contemporary Italy by Benedetto Croce. The nub of Gramsci's criticism was that

---

9.   N. Bobbio, *Politico e cultura*, Turin: Einaudi, 1955, ch. 2.

10. For a more detailed argument to this effect than I can offer here, but with which I basically agree, *see* A. Montefiore, 'The political responsibility of intellectuals', in I. Maclean *et al.* (eds), *The Political Responsibility of Intellectuals*, Cambridge: Cambridge University Press, ch. 11.

both Marxist economism and the Crocean doctrine of spirit involved a return to theological modes of thought, which negated the agent's freedom of choice and action.[11] In vulgar Marxism, matter replaced God as the final cause and the 'assured rationality of history' became a 'substitute for predestination, for Providence', with human beings mere pawns of some cosmic plan.[12] This Providentialism was even clearer in Crocean idealism, which had a tendency to reduce history to 'the work of that truly real individual which is spirit eternally individualising itself'.[13]

In Gramsci's opinion, both views led to either political passivity or to a pernicious élitism. Scientific Marxism either encouraged people simply to wait until the process of history brought about the revolution or turned the Party cadre into a quasi-priesthood, claiming knowledge of the natural laws of an inner reality distinct from the merely derivative experiences of ordinary believers. The masses had only to trust in the scientific prescriptions of their leaders to achieve salvation. Likewise, Crocean historicism either fostered a quietist resignation to the station and duties assigned one by spirit, or produced an Olympian detachment on the part of those philosophers who claimed a privileged access to the spiritual reality behind the material world of appearance.

Gramsci sought to avoid these faults, stressing instead the need for political action and popular participation to bring about the revolutionary goal. He believed that the respective drawbacks of each of these theories could be removed through their synthesis. Historical materialism needed to incorporate some of the idealist's insights about human consciousness. Idealism had to take into account the historical materialist's concern with the social and economic context within which ideas are formulated and operated. The resulting philosophy of praxis was a form of pragmatism that was nevertheless historicist. Truth was not a matter of the coherence of the beliefs concerned, or a general consensus on their validity, or even their correspondence to a given empirical reality, but rather resulted from an idea's practical efficacy. Ideas, as embodied in whole cultural and political traditions, both shaped and were influenced by changing social and economic conditions.[14]

Criticism, from this perspective, is always immanent critique – for there are no higher principles or unmediated brute facts to be appealed to. Reality and consciousness are intertwined in a complex way. As he remarked in a series of important notes on the 'so-called "reality" of the external world', objective 'always means "humanly objective", that which can correspond exactly to "historically

---

11. For a full discussion of Gramsci's criticisms of historical materialism and Crocean historicism *see* R. Bellamy and D. Schecter, *Gramsci and the Italian State*, Manchester: Manchester University Press, 1993, ch. 4.

12. Gramsci, *Quaderni*, pp. 1591, 1580.

13. B. Croce, *Teoria e storia della storiografia* (1917), Bari: Laterza. 1943, p. 87.

14. For a detailed account of Gramsci's theory, together with supporting evidence from the texts, *see* Bellamy and Schecter, *Gramsci and the Italian State*, pp. 99–106.

subjective"'.[15] North and south, for example, 'are arbitrary, conventional, that is historical constructions [...] And yet these references are real, they correspond to real facts, they permit us to travel by land and by sea [...] to objectivise reality'.[16] Gramsci was no relativist or voluntarist. Whilst he thought social being did not mechanically determine consciousness, he certainly believed material conditions constrained it, even whilst being in part a product of it. His point was that social and economic circumstances only determined to the extent that they were theoretically known in ways that allowed them to be practically employed. 'Mass adhesion or non-adhesion to an ideology' could be taken as

> the real critical test of the rationality and historicity of modes of thinking [...] because any arbitrary constructions are pretty rapidly eliminated by historical competition, even if sometimes, through a combination of immediately favourable circumstances, they succeed in enjoying a certain popularity.

By contrast, he held that 'constructions which correspond to the demands of a complex and organic period of history always end up imposing themselves and prevail even if their affirmation only occurs in more or less bizarre heterogeneous combinations'.[17]

Gramsci's account of the nature of human knowledge both opened up avenues for social criticism and threatened to prevent it entirely. Its liberating potential can be seen in his account of the Russian Revolution. As he famously argued, since it did not result from the development of the forces of production it was to a large degree a 'revolution against Kapital'. However, it had not been produced by spirit unfolding itself through human will and consciousness either. It came about because of the ability of the Bolshevik tacticians to mobilise the people in a revolutionary manner consistent with the material circumstances of the time.[18] The pragmatist epistemology underlying this account is brought out clearly in his observation, in the *Notebooks*, that Lenin had thereby 'advanced philosophy as philosophy in so far as he advanced political doctrine and practice'.[19]

The other side of the coin, however, was Gramsci's acknowledgement of the amazing resilience of capitalist countries. Proletarian revolution should have taken place here long ago. It had failed to do so because of what he termed the cultural and political 'hegemony', or ideological ascendency, of bourgeois capitalist values within the sphere of civil society.[20] However, the practical efficacy of capitalist ideology meant, on Gramsci's analysis, that it possessed an element of truth. Gramsci's difficulty was whether it possessed a monopoly of the truth, given that

---

15. Gramsci, *Quaderni*, pp. 1415–6.
16. *Ibid.*, p. 1419.
17. *Ibid.*, pp. 1392–3.
18. A. Gramsci, 'The revolution against *Kapital*' (1917), in Richard Bellamy (ed.), *Pre-Prison Writings/Antonio Gramsci*, Cambridge: Cambridge University Press, 1994, pp. 39–42.
19. Gramsci, *Quaderni*, p. 1250.
20. *Ibid.*, pp. 1519, 1590.

capitalist values appeared all pervasive and no appeal could be made to challenge them on the basis of either justice or historical reality. Gramsci's response was that no ideology – at least prior to the establishment of a communist society – was likely to be so complete. Until then, the intellectual hegemony of the ruling class could only be achieved to the extent they made certain concessions to the interests of subordinate classes. As a result, the ruling ideology tended to contain self-contradictory elements.[21] Moreover, whilst a mass might, 'for reasons of intellectual subordination', express overt support for a given view of the world, there were often covert signs in their actions of an alternative 'embryonic' conception of their own.[22]

The resources for criticism, then, were always available. The social critic's task was to make people see the internal contradictions within the prevailing hegemonic system of ideas as manifested in the differences between their thought, actions, and interests. Intellectuals achieved this result by developing those same bourgeois ideas. For once a contradiction arose between theory and practice, internal incoherences would become apparent in the ideas themselves. In this way, critics were able to initiate

> a process of differentiation and change in the relative weight that the old ideologies used to possess. What was previously secondary and subordinate [...] is now taken to be primary and becomes the nucleus of a new ideological and theoretical complex.[23]

From this perspective, the scientific superiority of Marxism, for example, lay in its having untangled the theoretical inconsistencies found within nineteenth-century German idealism and British political economy, as they related to the practices of industrial societies and economies, and thus laid the basis for working-class revolution.[24]

An unacknowledged progressive teleology underlay Gramsci's thesis at this point, whereby the present was somehow 'truer' and more 'developed' than the past. Why did Gramsci fall into this trap? Michael Rosen has shown how the internal logic of immanent critique is vulnerable to what he calls the '*postfestum* paradox', namely the paradox of only being able to evaluate the results of immanent critique by depending upon these same results' validity.[25] The only escape from the circularity of this argument is to assume that history involves the progressive unfolding of truth. In order to ground this belief, Gramsci ended up endorsing the very orthodox Marxism he began by seeking to modify. Although Gramsci was no doctrinaire, the standard Marxist theses concerning the gradual unfolding of

---

21. *Ibid.*, p. 461.
22. *Ibid.*, pp. 1302–3.
23. *Ibid.*, p. 1058.
24. *Ibid.*, p. 1860.
25. M. Rosen, *Hegel's Dialectic and Its Criticism*, Cambridge: Cambridge University Press, 1982. ch. 2.

different modes of production, the eventual crisis of capitalism and the status of the proletariat as the universal class embodying human emancipation ultimately ran through almost all his arguments. They provided the basis for his confidence that only a communist society would be able to provide a 'universally subjective' and 'total' vision of the world, that would be '100 per cent homogeneous on the level of ideology' without the need for either brainwashing, coercion, or social engineering of the population.[26]

Walzer's arguments are in many ways less well elaborated than Gramsci's but follow a parallel trajectory. As he explains in the preface to *The Company of Critics*:

> Over a number of years, I have been arguing (most clearly in *Spheres of Justice*) against the claim that moral principles are necessarily external to the world of everyday experience, waiting *out there* to be discovered by detached and dispassionate philosophers. In fact, it seems to me, the everyday world is a moral world, and we would do better to study its internal rules, maxims, conventions and ideals, rather than to detach ourselves from it in search of a universal or transcendent standpoint.[27]

Walzer believes that those critics who claim to discover moral principles either through divine revelation or by reference to a 'higher' reality beyond the phenomenal world, will be unable to engage with the beliefs of ordinary people. At best, their views will be irrelevant; at worst they will be tempted to reshape societies and their members to fit them.[28] Equally misguided is the attempt to invent or construct a moral system: this exercise proves similarly utopian.[29] The 'path of invention', like that of 'discovery', has the prime defect of ignoring the moral worth and complexity of the values that inform the various social practices of different societies and provide most individuals with their ethical code. In contrast, Walzer advocates the 'path of interpretation' which takes existing morality as its starting point.[30] This form of social criticism is best conducted in what, following Gramsci, he calls '"national-popular" mode', which Walzer takes to mean 'national in idiom, popular in argument'.[31] Such criticism involves critics conceiving of themselves as 'members speaking in public to other members who join in the speaking',[32] rather than as a class apart employing an abstruse language of their own.

---

26. Gramsci, *Quaderni*, pp. 1051–2.

27. Walzer, *Company of Critics*, p. ix.

28. M. Walzer, *Interpretation and Social Criticism*, Cambridge: Harvard University Press, 1985, pp. 3, 8.

29. Walzer, *Interpretation*, pp. 8–15.

30. *Ibid.*, pp. 18–32.

31. Walzer, *Company of Critics*, p. 233.

32. Walzer, *Interpretation*, p. 35.

Walzer admits that this thesis has problems of its own since, at face value, it appears to make social criticism impossible. As he notes, many reviewers of his earlier works have argued that 'if we are unable to appeal to the outside, critics inside must turn apologist'.[33] Walzer's reply is that all cultures generally contain their own critical principles. Therefore, social criticism is reflexive, like self-criticism. Although societies may not literally criticise themselves, social critics can promote 'a collective reflection upon the conditions of collective life' through their interaction with other members of the community.[34] The intellectual achieves this result by 'holding up a mirror to a society as a whole', which forces its members to confront their 'social idealism' and by enquiring whether the values which give them their self-respect 'are hypocritically held, or ineffectively enforced by the powers that be, or inadequate in their own terms'.[35]

Walzer explicitly endorses many of Gramsci's arguments concerning hegemony in this regard. He believes that the ideological legitimation that rulers (or their intellectual servants) are forced to elaborate to secure their power 'gives hostages to future social critics'. Any ideology 'strains towards universality as a condition of its success'. As a result, it 'has to embody lower-class interests' as well as those of the 'ruling-class', thereby introducing all sorts of internal tensions that the social critic can exploit.[36] Like Gramsci, Walzer notes how these internal contradictions often appear in the guise of a disjunction between social practices and people's beliefs about them. Unlike the Sardinian, however, he considers the practices more easily controlled by outside economic and political interests than beliefs, so that they frequently fail to live up to the expectations and ideals of participants within them. Critics, therefore, can point to this gap by giving voice to the often unarticulated popular understanding of how social institutions ought to be.

Walzer contends that,

> the ideal critic in this mode is loyal to men and women in trouble – oppressed, exploited, impoverished, forgotten – but he sees these people and their troubles and the possible solution to their troubles within the framework of national history and culture.[37]

It remains unclear why this should always be so, however. First, Walzer gives us no account of either what counts as morality and how we might distinguish moral beliefs from the general range of opinions, cultural practices and the like that people hold and engage in, or how we might arbitrate between differing moral systems. He appears simply to assume that societies are reasonably morally homogeneous,

---

33. Walzer, *Company of Critics*, p. ix.

34. Walzer, *Interpretation*, p. 35.

35. M. Walzer, 'Maximalism and the social critic', in *Thick and Thin: Moral argument at home and abroad*, Notre Dame: University of Notre Dame Press, 1994, pp. 42–3.

36. Walzer, *Interpretation*, p. 41.

37. Walzer, *Company of Critics*, pp. 233–4.

so that intra-societal moral disputes are resolvable in ways that those between societies are not. But a common complaint made by many oppressed groups is that 'national' morality simply reflects the point of view of the state and the hegemonic groups who control it. In this situation they either appeal to a universal morality, such as human rights, whose standards the dominant morality fails to uphold, or argue that they have a distinct moral position of their own deriving from their religion or ethnic culture or some other particular source. In such cases, argument in 'national-popular' mode will be anything but liberating. Indeed, as Gramsci fully appreciated, it might simply serve as but another dimension of the exercise of power. Walzer's contention that the national should be prioritised on the grounds of its greater 'inclusiveness' simply begs all the important questions. Why must differences stop at national boundaries, or arguments that appeal to human concerns as such not claim to be the most inclusive of all?

Second, it is similarly obscure what constitutes a good interpretation for Walzer. He seems to suggest that, as a social practice, the role of the social critic and the nature of interpretation will differ from society to society. In some it will be a matter of priests engaging in debates about sacred texts, in others of politicians discussing the constitution and so on. The sources of authority and the style of argument are subject to a high degree of variety, with what counts as a successful interpretation in one context being unacceptable in other. Consequently, the only criteria he offers are rather formal ones, such as consistency, coherence, cogency and verisimilitude.[38] The difficulty here is that what will be cogent and coherent in one style of argument is likely to prove unacceptable in another. The Platonist, for example, will look for an idea's consistency with the ideal forms, a Walzerian interpreter for its proximity to established beliefs.[39] Once again, this position suggests that any society containing more than one form of moral argument will be faced with either deadlock or the arbitrary imposition of a particular dominant view. Moreover, it leaves open the possibility that the role of social critic may not always be available, as would be the case in any system where all authority flowed from the pronouncements of a designated leader who was to be unwaveringly obeyed.

Third, to the extent that interpretation differs from mere reproduction, it is also hard to see how it could avoid involving some degree of each of the two supposedly rejected alternatives. Although Walzer is keen to show how they both involve 'interpretation',[40] the converse also holds. In certain cases, such as the scientific interpretation of experimental data, it will shade into the 'discovery' path of enquiry. In other cases, such as a dance based around a certain piece of music, it involves an element of creativity akin to his path of 'invention'. Both

---

38. *Ibid.*, p. x.

39. B. Barry, 'Social criticism and political philosophy', *Philosophy and Public Affairs* 19, 1990, p. 365.

40. 'A simple maxim: every discovery and invention [...] requires interpretation.' Walzer, *Interpretation*, p. 26.

these hybrid types of interpretation prove essential if he is to avoid the charge of conservatism. To show that people are misguided, deluded or suffering from 'false consciousness', for example, will involve some attempt to discover what people's real interests might be. To improve a moral tradition or apply it to unprecedented situations will entail a certain creative ingenuity. In each case, we will be concerned to offer the best interpretation of our traditions, not in the sense of its being the most authentic but because it incorporates the most justifiable elements.[41]

A fourth criticism arises here. Walzer wants to deny that social critics could – or should – perform either of the above mentioned tasks. Critics, he argues, need only point out people's hypocrisy, bad faith, dishonesty and the like. The prophet Amos, for example, is held up as a model social critic for the way he identified 'public pronouncements and respectable opinion as hypocritical', employed hypocrisy as a 'clue' to identifying the 'core values' of his society and used them to attack the leaders and prevailing institutions of his age.[42] At times this may be enough. But some traditions contain elements of highly dubious moral worth, concerning, say, the position of women or certain ethnic groups. Walzer acknowledges, for example, that in caste societies social meanings are likely to reinforce hierarchical distributions rather than the egalitarian ones he favours.[43] Here Walzer will be placed in a dilemma. For the critic will be unable to challenge those shared beliefs themselves or seek to alter them in any way.

As Joseph Raz has observed,[44] the thesis that existing morality can be interpreted so as to provide a moral criticism of itself proves incoherent. It implies the paradox that the prevailing morality contains both true and false moral propositions. Yet if morality is simply the existing morality it cannot be a source of moral error, only of truth. Likewise, any radical overhaul or even any change of the existing morality would imply that it was or had somehow become wrong. This proposition too is logically absurd since, once again, the only ground for moral correctness is that self-same morality. The only possible immanent moral critique, therefore, consists of pointing out false deductions from accepted premises, uncovering duplicity and the like – a point that Walzer sometimes appears to concede.

Such reasoning may not produce the radical conclusions Walzer desires, however. As Raz pointedly remarks, neither the protestors in Tienanmen Square nor their foreign supporters, with the apparent exception of Walzer,[45] based their condemnation of the Chinese government on arriving at the correct interpretation of the relevant cultural discourse. It may well be that the massacre was justified according to 'national-popular' doctrine. Critical purchase on this event derives from invoking principles that have a wider and not just a parochial relevance,

---

41. *See* Barry, 'Social criticism', p. 369, for a parallel criticism.

42. Walzer, *Interpretation*, pp. 87, 89.

43. M. Walzer, *Spheres of Justice: A defence of pluralism and equality*, Oxford: Martin Robertson, 1983, pp. 26–7.

44. J. Raz. 'Morality as interpretation', *Ethics* 101, 1991, pp. 392–105.

45. Walzer, 'Maximalism', pp. 59–60.

whereby certain forms of behaviour are condemned as simply wrong: a matter that is likely to involve adopting some aspects of one or other of the rejected paths.

Walzer attempts to answer this criticism by making a distinction between 'thick' and 'thin' moralities. A fifth difficulty surfaces at this point, however. He asserts that we can find a 'thin' universal morality in all (or nearly all) cultures, involving prohibitions against murder, deception, and gross cruelty. 'Thick' morality, by contrast, involves notions such as treachery, cowardice, and virtue that are more culturally specific.[46] Note that this claim is descriptive. On Walzer's reasoning, one can only legitimately invoke moral universalism to the extent it actually exists. Nevertheless, the argument offers a hostage to fortune that issues in a thicker universalism and a thinner particularism than Walzer desires. To do any work, universalism has to be more than purely formal – otherwise, Walzer risks the slide into relativism, the avoidance of which motivates this new twist to his thesis. However, if local cultures are to remain consistent with a more substantive universalism, they are likely to simply offer a particular 'thin' elaboration of 'thick' universal concepts, rather than differing totally from them in the way Walzer supposes.[47] Britain, France, and Italy, for example, all have recognisably liberal-democratic political systems that are informed by certain common 'universal' principles, such as a respect for human rights. Yet there are considerable differences in the political and legal procedures they adopt for realising them, which reflect important local historical differences. Thus, Walzer is undeniably correct to say the Chinese should seek to construct a democratic system suited to China rather than simply importing American institutions. But this need not involve studying Confucian or Mandarin traditions, let alone Maoist-Leninist vanguard doctrines, for an elusive Chinese conception of democracy, as Walzer proposes.[48] To the extent that democracy possesses certain intrinsic merits, it can be justified independently of the existence of any indigenous form. Its introduction merely entails adapting the democratic ideal and its associated rights to Chinese circumstances. That this task will be probably better performed by the Chinese than others, no matter how well intentioned, is, in most cases, no doubt also true. Walzer suggests that such regard for the self-determination of peoples only proves consistent for an 'interpretative' approach that respects the 'thick' local moral views of others.[49] But 'thick' universalists need not be paternalistic imperialists, as Walzer fears.[50] They can believe that China will have to embrace democratic practices of its own accord for largely pragmatic reasons, such as that

---

46. Walzer, *Interpretation*, p. 24.

47. Walzer, 'Moral minimalism', in *Thick and Thin*, ch. 1, pp. 1–19.

48. Walzer, 'Maximalism', pp. 59–61.

49. A similar argument has recently been put forward at some length by David Miller in his *On Nationality*, Oxford: Oxford University Press, 1995, ch. 4. I have criticised this position in a review of Miller's book entitled 'National socialism: a liberal defence', in *Radical Philosophy*, 80, Nov/Dec 1996, pp. 37–40.

50. Which is not to deny that they have been, usually (though not always) with disastrous results.

it will probably be more enduring and successful in that case, or because they value autonomy as an inherent aspect of democracy.

The only way Walzer can consistently adopt an interpretative morality based on a purely immanent critique is for him to adopt some form of progressive immanent teleology (as Gramsci does), whereby existing morality is seen as the evolution of some inherent principle that must gradually work through various stages with all their contradictions. Or he has to argue that existing 'thick' moral systems involve far more 'thin' universal elements than he usually wants to admit – but that these are shockingly poorly observed by many of those who claim to profess them.[51] On occasion, he appears to adopt the former course, as when he argues that the modern view of human equality 'grew out of the critique of a failed hierarchy' during the feudal era, and that progressive interpretations will culminate in the acceptance of egalitarianism.[52] This view, however, is hopelessly optimistic. Far from adopting the radical welfare and democratic-socialist measures that Walzer contends are at the heart of Western liberal values,[53] for example, the general trend is towards the ever-greater extension of the market – a development for which libertarian thinkers can provide a perfectly coherent rationale. This fact does not mean that radical views cannot be defended or libertarian ones criticised, merely that appeals to contemporary mores are unlikely to prove the best ground for conducting a debate between these positions. In contrast, Walzer's frequent complaint that many philosophers fail to recognise the degree to which ordinary people's beliefs are moral points in the direction of the second course. However, this strategy fits ill with his assertions about the variety of moralities. Either way, he cannot avoid offering some criteria for sorting out the wheat from the chaff in any tradition. Nevertheless, this process need not entail either discovering morality on another plane to that inhabited by the rest of us, or of inventing one de novo, but merely of combining the tools of investigation and construction with the interpretation of existing views in the manner suggested above.

Social role of the critic

The social role each thinker assigns to the critic follows pretty straightforwardly from their respective epistemological positions and suffers from parallel incoherencies that reinforce the criticisms of the last section. Gramsci's famous distinction between 'traditional' and 'organic' intellectuals essentially turned on the distinction he drew between those who adopt what he variously characterised as a 'transcendent', 'speculative', or 'metaphysical' point of view and those who

---

51. In a recent critique of Charles Taylor, Ronald Beiner has noted how he, too, oscillates between these two positions. *See* his 'Hermeneutical generosity and social criticism', *Critical Review* 9, 1995, pp. 447–64.

52. Walzer, 'Maximalism', p. 45.

53. Walzer, *Spheres of Justice*, p. 318.

reason historically, in the sense of 'immanent critique'.[54] Whilst the social stance of the traditional intellectual is detachment, the organic intellectual is engaged. The former 'put themselves forward as autonomous and independent of the dominant social group',[55] as operating in an eternal realm of truth that is somehow separated from the rest of the world. The latter discover the truth through examining the thoughts of common people. Whereas traditional intellectuals aspire to be a caste apart, a latter day priesthood, organic intellectuals form no special cadre. They can be found amongst all social groups, and seek to give them 'homogeneity' and an awareness of their 'function' in the social and economic system.[56]

Gramsci believed that the detachment of 'traditional' intellectuals ultimately proved untenable. Either they implicitly and perhaps unwittingly collude with the dominant regime by preaching political passivity – heaven being in the next world – or they seek to impose their version of heaven upon people in the here and now. He thought the Catholic Church provided the best examples of both these positions, though he also accused Croce of having fallen into the first and the fascist philosopher Giovanni Gentile of adopting the second.[57] Organic intellectuals, in contrast, expressly acknowledged their social connections. In many cases, this stance involved their directly supporting the dominant class. This is true of the various pundits, experts and professionals that the capitalist class creates to further and support its various activities.[58] However, Gramsci also believed that it was possible for a certain kind of organic intellectual to represent the interests of oppressed groups and encourage them to liberate themselves by developing a critical consciousness of their situation from within their own current forms of thinking and acting. It was in this manner that social revolutions came about.

Gramsci maintained that to some degree 'all men are intellectuals',[59] since any practical activity presupposed a certain conceptual schema through which people orientated themselves in the world. This consciousness generally consisted of a 'composite' of often 'disjointed' elements that had been 'deposited' by history in a rather haphazard manner, forming 'an infinity of traces [...] without an inventory'.[60] Folklore and superstitions offered good examples of this level of thought, often providing what he called the 'spontaneous philosophy' of ordinary people. As a result, the masses were frequently 'intellectually subordinate' to the ruling elites, who monopolised 'high' culture. The function of the 'professional' intellectual lay in helping the masses to go beyond its own 'common sense' understanding of its activities. In Walzerian fashion, the first stage of this process entailed providing the missing 'inventory', by bringing a certain coherence and

---

54. Gramsci, *Quaderni*, pp. 1550–1.

55. *Ibid.*, p. 1515.

56. *Ibid.*, p. 1513.

57. *Ibid.*, p. 1515.

58. *Ibid.*, pp. 1513–4.

59. *Ibid.*, p. 1516.

60. *Ibid.*, p. 1376.

logical rigour into what might be somewhat loosely connected and badly-thought-through notions. If one was to avoid the possibility of simply producing well versed as opposed to inarticulate bigots, however, it was also necessary to get workers and peasants to develop a 'critical' consciousness. This stage involved them attempting to universalise their interests and opinions in ways that addressed the concerns of others as well. Consequently, the opinions of the masses often had to be 'broadened' so as to go beyond mere parochialism or narrow self-interest. A successful hegemony was 'national-popular' rather than provincial-elitist.[61]

Walzer and Gramsci begin to part company here.[62] Whilst Gramsci accepted that we inevitably start out from the local, he maintained that one's aim must be to transcend this position and move from 'dialect' towards a language or mode of thought that can be 'a world-wide means of expression'.[63] This enterprise was necessarily socially and historically conditioned rather than a matter of individual philosophic discovery or creation.[64] It did not require intellectuals to simply instruct peasants or workers on what they ought to think. The 'educational relationship' was, he believed, a matter of mutual dialogue, with the popular element providing 'feeling' and the intellectual element 'knowledge' and 'understanding'.[65] Intellectuals, in other words, had to respond to the often unarticulated needs and values of the people in order to identify their 'real' interests, rather than assuming they could be arrived at *a priori*. Nonetheless, the ultimate result of a revolution would be the subversion of the conception of the world underlying current practices and their substitution by a new social order reflecting a quite different view.

As we saw in the last section, Gramsci regarded theory and practice as being intimately linked within a pragmatic epistemology that avoided relativism through being tied to an essentially orthodox Marxist account of history. Immanent critique and historical materialism went hand in hand. What allowed a class or group to universalise its interests was the degree to which they enabled the transformation of economic and social relations on the basis of the available means of production. Thus, the ideological hegemony exercised in the past, first by the feudal aristocracy and then by the bourgeoisie, reflected their dominant functional position in the economic system of the time. To this extent, their hold on subordinate groups and classes could be historically 'real' and hence 'rational' and so based on consent rather than coercion. Only the interests of the working class were truly universal, however, and communism represented the sole form of social and economic organisation capable of providing a genuinely 'total' conception of the world, one that could be freely adopted by all.

---

61. *Ibid.*, pp. 1376–8.

62. *See* Walzer, *Company of Critics*, pp. 84–8.

63. Gramsci, *Quaderni*, p. 1377. *See*, too, the letter to his sister in which he urges her to let his nephew learn dialect, whilst stressing that, unlike Italian, Sardinian was not a 'national' language with a 'great' literature (A. Gramsci. *Lettere dal carcere*, Turin: Einaudi, 1965, n. 23, p. 64. Walzer, in contrast, finds either a linguistic or a moral Esperanto highly improbable (Walzer, 'Moral minimalism', pp. 7–9).

64. Gramsci, *Quaderni*, pp. 1377–8.

65. *Ibid.*, p. 1505.

The scientific understanding of history offered the warrant by which the Party intellectuals were justified in moulding the new collective man. In working towards this revolutionary goal, the Communist Party could legitimately claim to take 'the place of the Divinity or the categorical imperative' within people's consciences.[66] Its role was to create 'cultural-social unity', capable of welding together 'a multiplicity of dispersed wills, with heterogeneous aims' within a 'common conception of the world'.[67] The Party's policy was to be 'totalitarian', so that 'the members [...] find in it all the satisfactions previously found in a multiplicity of organisations'.[68] Regional dialects and local practices were to be replaced by a common language and unified moral, social and political structure,[69] as 'the whole system of intellectual and moral relations' was 'overturned' in the process of 'adapting "civilisation" and the morality of the vast popular masses to the requirements of the continual development of production'.[70] Only Gramsci's largely untested belief that organic intellectuals could persuade the masses to break with their earlier attachments and ways of thinking of their own accord saved him from resorting to the coercive methods eventually employed by the Soviet state. It seems that the organic intellectual, no less than his traditional colleague, is destined to either support the *status quo* or drift into totalitarianism.

Walzer starts off from remarkably similar premises but understandably wishes to avoid Gramsci's conclusion. 'Some critics', he tells us, 'seek only the acquaintance of other critics. They find their peers only outside the cave, in the blaze of Truth'. In contrast, 'others find peers and sometimes even comrades inside, in the shadow of contingent and uncertain truths'.[71] In a similar manner to Gramsci, he assumes that those philosophers who leave the cave are likely to be unable to connect with the needs and preoccupations of their fellow human beings. If and when they elect to return it will be in the guise of legislators, who seek to impose their vision of the world upon an often recalcitrant populace. Those critics who remain in the cave, in contrast, are best characterised as interpreters who remain respectful of ordinary people's own way of seeing things. As such, he believes they are natural democrats. Critics may well be marginalised – they say disturbing things and those with power are made uncomfortable by that – but they tend not to become detached or alienated. Rather than getting a critical purchase on their society by appealing to principles external to it, connected critics always argue from within the local culture. They explore the degree to which a society measures up to its own standards, often reinterpreting those shared norms in the process by making use of their internal dynamics. By giving expression to people's 'deepest sense of how they want to live', 'false appearances' are unmasked and reforms proposed.[72]

---

66. *Ibid.*, p. 1561.

67. *Ibid.*, p. 1331.

68. *Ibid.*, p. 800.

69. *Ibid.*, pp. 1377–8, 2314.

70. *Ibid.*, pp. 1561, 1565–6.

71. Walzer, *Company of Critics*, pp. ix–x.

72. *Ibid.*, p. 232.

Walzer attempts to distinguish his approach from Gramsci's by contrasting the Sardinian theorist with his co-national and one time fellow communist, the novelist Ignazio Silone. According to Walzer, 'whereas Gramsci repressed whatever there was of Sardinia in him, Silone preserved and cherished the "traces" left by his native Abruzzi'.[73] 'At no point', he claims, 'did Silone stand free, the way the critic is commonly supposed to stand, look around, choose the best moral principles, design the ideal society, compare party programmes, decide on the strategically appropriate course of action'.[74] Instead of a 'grand theory', Silone is said to be blessed with a 'moral sensitivity' derived from rubbing shoulders with salt-of-the-earth southern Italian peasants. Rather than writing a treatise on oppression or elaborating a purportedly 'scientific' doctrine of human emancipation, he wrote novels, such as *Fontamara*,[75] which voiced the peasants' own moral indignation and aspirations. Walzer draws the moral that it was Silone's 'natural' identification with the cause of justice and his empathy and closeness to the views of the peasants that made Party discipline and Stalinism unpalatable to him and eventually led to his expulsion and exile.[76]

This contrast between Gramsci and Silone is both theoretically and factually highly questionable.[77] Gramsci had just as much admiration for the noble peasant sentiments portrayed in Silone's novels as his compatriot and remained deeply attached to his Sardinian roots throughout his life, as his *Prison Letters* amply testify.[78] However, he did not romanticise this culture. His experience as a hunchback had also given him knowledge of its downside – the superstition and hostility towards anyone or thing that was different.[79] Walzer is right to report that Gramsci often felt unloved, that he hated Sardinian backwardness and that he was occasionally suspicious of worker solidarity. What he forgets to mention is that Gramsci had good cause for these feelings. Walzer's advocacy of moral empathy cannot come to terms with the tyranny of a bigoted majority, whose moral sensitivity may have been warped by their social experience. Whilst it is true that,

---

73. *Ibid.*, p. 102.

74. *Ibid.*, p. 106.

75. I. Silone, *Fontamara*, Milan: Mondadori, 1949.

76. Walzer, *Company of Critics*, p. 106.

77. Walzer appears to be ignorant of the high degree of self-promotion involved in Silone's novels, or of his career as an informer for the fascist regime while a member of the Communist Party and subsequently with the Italian intelligence services. *See* Dario Biocca and Mauro Canali. *L'informatore: Silone, i comunisti e la polizia*, Milan: Luni Editrice, 2000; the use of this material to reinterpret the novels by Elizabeth Leake in *The Reinvention of Ignazio Silone*, Toronto: University of Toronto Press, 2003; and my review in 'Tainted heroes', *Times Literary Supplement*, 28 January 2005.

78. His letters to his family are particularly eloquent in this respect. *See*, for example, his letter to his mother of 5 March 1928, in which he affirms his keen interest in every kind of news from his native village of Ghilarza (Gramsci, *Lettere dal carcere*, n. 85, p. 184), or his encomium to Sardinian yoghurt in a letter to his sister-in-law of 7 April 1931 (Gramsci, *Lettere dal carcere*, n. 186, p. 425).

79. *See*, for example, his letter to his sister-in-law of 30 January 1933, recounting a family's cruel treatment of a retarded boy (Gramsci, *Lettere dal carcere*, n. 326, pp. 736–7).

in such circumstances, a bad theory is likely to exacerbate these prejudices even further (as fascism undoubtedly did, for example), moral exhortation on its own is unlikely to be enough to overcome them. Even if the seeds of humanity manage to survive in the barrenest of soils, they amount to little more than cries in the wilderness for human beings to act better unless aligned to a programme for the reform of social and political institutions. Walzer remarks that Gramsci's essay 'On the Southern Question', in which he sought to address the problem of uniting the struggles of peasants and workers, is 'a peculiarly lifeless document' and implies he ought to have followed Silone and written a novel.[80] But whilst (as Gramsci certainly appreciated) social reform without individual intellectual and moral reform will never be effective, the reverse is also true. Social criticism involves more than advocating changes in personal conduct – important though that is. It necessarily aims at a critique of those social and political practices that constrain and frame our action as well. Gramsci's theory may well have been a bad one but at least it provided him with challengeable grounds as to why certain practices were to be preferred to others. In comparison, Walzer's argument is thin indeed.

Cultural politics and the politics of culture

This last observation notwithstanding, Gramsci did share Walzer's predilection for linking moral with social reform, even if, in the last analysis, the first was dependent on the second. The resulting advocacy of what Norberto Bobbio has termed 'cultural politics' and the relative neglect of what he calls the 'politics of culture' provides the final similarity between the two thinkers to be examined.

Bobbio's two terms refer respectively to 'the planning of culture by politicians' and 'the politics of men of culture in defence of the conditions necessary for the existence and development of culture'.[81] Bobbio links the first with what he calls the 'revolutionary intellectual', who fights 'against the established government in the name of a new class and in order to create a new society' – a position clearly adopted by Gramsci.[82] By contrast, the second reflects the attitude of the 'pure intellectual', who opposes 'power as such in the name of absolute values such as truth and justice' – a perspective Bobbio associates with Croce.[83] He contends that this second path allows intellectuals to avoid the errors of either politicising culture or treating it as apolitical. Rather, culture can be distinguished from everyday party politics and yet possess a distinct political role as one of the preconditions of politics itself.[84] A primary weakness of both Gramsci's and, especially, Walzer's theory lies in a tendency to take the existence of this cultural framework for granted. Whilst understandable to some extent in the Italian, it is less comprehensible in the case of the American thinker.

80. Walzer, *Company of Critics*, p. 108.

81. Bobbio, *Politico e cultura*, p. 37.

82. Bobbio, *Il dubbio e la scelta*, p. 164.

83. *Ibid.*, pp. 164, 165–6.

84. Bobbio, *Politico e cultura*, pp. 34–46.

As is well known, Gramsci argued that intellectuals had to play such an important role in the revolutionary process in more developed countries because, within these societies, the coercive power of the state was reinforced by the ideological power or hegemony exercised by the institutions of civil society – schools, churches, the media, and all kinds of private associations. Revolution here would only be achieved if the struggle for hegemony had first been gained and the Party had won the hearts and minds of the masses to the cause.

Rather less remarked on is the degree to which Gramsci's argument for a cultural politics was essentially a Marxist variant of a well worn theme of modem Italian social and political theorists. Most Italian theorists of the nineteenth and early twentieth centuries had conceived the unification of Italy in terms of 'making Italians' rather than simply creating a unified Italian state. Institutional and constitutional questions related to the exercise and distribution of political power were largely ignored, with the emphasis being placed instead on the attainment of a degree of national cultural homogeneity capable of breaking down various particularist attachments to region and class. Indeed, success in the latter was generally thought largely to obviate the need to consider the former.[85]

Gramsci's analysis reflected these peculiarities of the Italian tradition. In spite of his emphasis on hegemony, he has been rightly criticised for underestimating the degree to which the liberal-democratic state can engineer the active consent of its citizens through its procedures, bureaucratic apparatus and capacity for economic and social regulation.[86] He maintained that a 'war of position' to attain hegemonic control of civil society could be distinguished from, and precede, a direct assault, or 'war of manoeuvre', on the state.[87] This strategy may have been appropriate to a state of the capitalist periphery, such as Italy, where the political class was few in number and relatively isolated and social, economic and political institutions were comparatively weak.[88] Within advanced societies, however, state and society are intertwined in too complex a way to allow such a neat distinction and the difficulty of mounting a counter-hegemony is commensurately harder. In the absence of an effective state, cultural politics may be effective and even necessary to give expression to popular demands. Within more complex political and social systems it will be hopelessly inadequate. Not only will it be much harder for the social critic to get his or her voice heard, opinions will be far more diverse and difficult to mobilise around a given 'national-popular' programme.

Even if a cultural politics were successful, however, cultural homogeneity would not render the political sphere redundant. The fact that everyone had somehow come to internalise the same set of norms and goals would not remove

---

85. For details, *see* R. Bellamy, *Modern Italian Social Theory: Ideology and politics from Pareto to the present*, Cambridge: Polity Press, 1987. Gramsci is aligned with this tradition in ch. 6.

86. *See* P. Anderson, 'The antinomies of Antonio Gramsci', *New Left Review* 100, 1976–7, 5–80, for this critique.

87. Gramsci, *Quaderni*, pp. 1566–7.

88. Gramsci's analysis of Italy as a country of the 'capitalist periphery' is contained in 'A study of the Italian situation' (1926), *Pre-Prison Writings*, especially pp. 297–8.

the need to resolve disputes over how best to realise them or the need to safeguard individuals against unwitting errors in their interpretation or implementation by others. On the far more likely scenario that a wide degree of value and interest pluralism persists, then more radical disagreements will arise. It will be necessary to think in some detail about how to ensure people can make their case, deliberate with others, reach mutually acceptable collective agreements and be protected against majority or other forms of tyranny or simple myopia or foolishness. Like other thinkers in the Marxist tradition, Gramsci regarded these standard tasks of a liberal constitutional democracy as destined 'to wither away'.[89]

That Gramsci saw no need for a 'politics of culture' is to some degree comprehensible. That Walzer similarly neglects the institutional and moral framework required for the practice of interpretation to be undertaken is less so. To a large extent, Walzer presents his thesis in the guise of an implicit and, at times, explicit critique of liberal political philosophy. The emphasis on individual rights and state neutrality, combined with the search for a universal justification for these arguments, comes in for especial criticism.[90] In contrast, he regards his own theory as being linked to collectively defined goods that the state may legitimately act to promote, on the basis of reasoning peculiar to the particular community involved. He argues that this bottom-up approach is essentially democratic, in that it appeals to popular understandings, elucidates shared values and expresses common complaints.[91]

Walzerian interpretation clearly assumes a public forum, for to be successful it must ultimately persuade people that it offers the best reading of their beliefs.[92] Unfortunately, Walzer is unwilling to explore the preconditions for persuasive as opposed to coercive or manipulative argumentation. True, a prime aspect of his argument for distinctive spheres of justice is to perfect the liberal 'art of separation',[93] particularly with regard to limiting the scope of political and economic influence. His argument, however, goes both too far and not far enough. It is excessive to the extent that it ignores the need for politics and markets to cross over spheres in order to co-ordinate disparate activities. Like Gramsci, he places the burden for this task on a national community possessed of a shared set of goals and values that provide an overarching moral framework for the plurality of different spheres. Pluralism, however, frequently undermines such agreement, or at least renders it deeply problematic – as recent debates about multiculturalism illustrate.

Walzer also overlooks the degree to which social criticism is a political activity. In this respect his views are underdeveloped in not saying anything

---

89. For a critique of the Marxist aspiration to go beyond both justice and the state, *see* S. Lukes, *Marxism and Morality*, Oxford: Oxford University Press, 1985.

90. Rawls is singled out for special criticism in both *Spheres of Justice*, e.g. pp. 79–82, and *Interpretation*, e.g. pp. 11–12, 14, 16.

91. Walzer, *Interpretation*, pp. 38–9, 64–5; 'Philosophy and democracy', *Political Theory* 9 (1981), pp. 379–99.

92. Walzer, *Interpretation*, p. 28.

93. M. Walzer, 'Liberalism and the art of separation', *Political Theory* 12, 1984, pp. 315–30.

about the principles and mechanisms, such as rights and democracy, required for a 'collective reflection' on social traditions and goods and to mediate between rival interpretations and cultures. As an American, he tells us, he does espouse a liberalism 'committed in the strongest possible way to individual rights and [...] to a rigorously neutral state', because it is 'the official doctrine of immigrant societies like the United States'.[94] However, the Chinese, as we have seen, do things differently. Walzer implies that to deprecate this fact is to engage in a form of egregious Podsnappery. We are informed somewhat hesitantly that certain 'thin' conditions may be universal to all cultures and *for that reason* ought to be met but these are not related to the practice of criticism itself. To do so might well entail conceding the thick–thin divide, as Walzer observes.[95] Yet, as we noted earlier, the consequences of not doing so seem theoretically and practically far worse. Thus Walzer too, albeit in a slightly different way from Gramsci, also divides state and civil society too sharply and indulges in cultural politics whilst neglecting the politics of culture. Somewhat optimistically, the social activity of interpretation is seen as largely autonomous from the state and, in certain circumstances, as even capable of toppling it. Once again, Tienanmen Square gives the lie to Walzer's thesis in a somewhat brutal manner.

Conclusion

The immanent critique aimed at by Gramsci and Walzer is incoherent. Both thinkers find themselves caught between viewing history as an inherently rational process, on the one hand, and cultural relativism, on the other.[96] Whilst Gramsci ultimately impales himself on the first horn of the dilemma, Walzer tends to fall on to the second. Moreover, this approach issues in a cultural politics that suffers from the very two difficulties they both wish to avoid. Either it leads to social conservatism or it turns intellectuals into political servants of the Modern Prince, seeking to engineer human souls in order to achieve a total cultural reform. By contrast, the more traditional view of the intellectual, as the upholder of universal values, proves consistent with the politics of culture. This form of political commitment requires intellectuals to enquire into the presuppositions of the critical enterprise and hence, on occasion, to distance themselves from cultures or practices that stifle such activity. They must sometimes act as Legislators, but in the classical sense of being concerned with the legal framework that makes both politics and culture possible, rather than actually ruling, as Walzer suggests this approach decrees. Only then can a collective reflection upon, and critique of, social norms take place, with intellectuals playing their part alongside their fellow citizens.

---

94. M. Walzer, 'Comment', in C. Taylor, *Multiculturalism*, Princeton: Princeton University Press, 1994, pp. 99, 101.

95. Walzer, 'Moral minimalism', pp. 11–15.

96. As Hilary Putnam has noted, this problem is likely to bedevil all attempts to historicise or immanentise morality. *See* his 'Beyond historicism', in *Realism and Reason: Philosophical Papers Volume 3*, Cambridge: Cambridge University Press, 1983, pp. 287–8.

Part Four

Positivism, Bobbio and Social Democracy

Chapter Twelve

The Advent of the Masses and the Making of the Modern Theory of Democracy

'There are in fact no masses; there are only ways of seeing people as masses.'[1]

The gradual extension of the suffrage to all adult men and, ultimately, women too during the late nineteenth and early twentieth centuries transformed the politics of Western Europe and North America. Many contemporary theorists attributed these reforms not to any improvement in ordinary people's political judgement because of better education and higher living standards, nor to a progressive appreciation of the right of all adults to be considered full citizens, but to a new social and economic reality making such measures unavoidable. Quite simply, within a mass society, political power could only be exercised with mass support. In spite of the inevitability of a widened franchise, many theorists believed deep tensions existed between the concepts of the 'mass' and 'democracy', rendering a 'mass democracy' almost a contradiction in terms. For the ideas of the 'masses' and 'mass society' were embedded within accounts of social organisation and behaviour that challenged the models of individual agency and rationality traditionally associated with democratic decision-making. Consequently, even democratically-minded thinkers found that a coherent conception of mass democracy required a radical rethinking of the norms and forms of the democratic process.[2] This chapter traces the development of the new sociological and psychological languages of mass politics and their deployment in the construction of a modern theory of democracy. As we shall see, though still widely accepted, this theory incorporates empirical and normative assumptions arising from contentious and anachronistic views of human nature and society few would wish to espouse today.

The 'masses' and 'mass society'

Originating in counter-revolutionary analyses of the French revolution, the concepts of 'the masses' and of 'mass society' became part of the new 'scientific' approaches to politics developed by pioneering political sociologists and social

---

1.   R. Williams, *Culture and Society 1780–1950*, Harmondsworth, 1971 [1958].
2.   J. V. Femia, *Against the Masses: Varieties of anti-democratic thought since the French Revolution*, Oxford, 2001.

psychologists from the 1890s onwards.[3] Underlying these concepts were more general theories of social disorganisation, disorientation and anomie occasioned by the break-up of the allegedly homogeneous and hierarchical communities typical of agrarian societies and their replacement by the quite different social relations of large-scale industrial societies.[4] On the one hand, industrialisation was said to have fostered greater interconnectedness between a wider circle of people through better communications, the growth of cities and large factories, a more extensive division of labour and so on. On the other hand, these new relations were believed to be less close-knit and more compartmentalised than the organic ties of the extended families and local communities they had supplanted. Instead of possessing a clear status with known rights and obligations within a fixed social hierarchy, the increasingly mobile individual had to assume a multiplicity of often transient roles within an ever-changing social environment. In the process, individuals lost both the coherent sense of self and the unified set of values that came through living within a more integrated society. Lacking either a stable moral framework or a strong identity, the individual had become an anonymous member of an amorphous mass.[5]

Three features of this mass condition attracted the attention of contemporary social theorists.[6] First, they highlighted the psychological aspects of involvement in the mass. Masses, they contended, were motivated by passion rather than reason. Being part of a mass made people a prey to their emotions. They became open to suggestion, highly malleable, impulsive, instinctive and even bestial. Mass behaviour was described in pathological terms and linked to various types of moral and social deviance – from supposedly abnormally high rates of crime, to drunkenness, suicide, lunacy and sexual perversion. Second, theorists associated mass society with new forms of social organisation. The state had expanded vastly, overseeing economic and social behaviour ever more closely, while the economy was dominated by huge corporations and industries. Bureaucratic methods suited to the efficient administration of complex tasks by large departments and businesses had swept through the private and public sectors. As a result, the mass individual was subject to increasing managerial regulation in all spheres of his or her life. Finally, and largely as a result of these two features, traditional elites – intellectuals, the clergy and social superiors – had been displaced by demagogues and technocratic managers.

3. L. Bramson, *The Political Context of Sociology*, Princeton, NJ, 1961, ch. 2.
4. D. Pick, *Faces of Degeneration: A European disorder c. 1848–1918*, Cambridge, 1989. For examples, *see* J. Harris (ed.), F. Tönnies, *Community and Civil Society*, [1887], Cambridge, 2001, pp. 17–21; E. Durkheim, *The Division of Labour in Society*, [1893], trans. W. D. Halls, Basingstoke, 1984, pp. 292, 304, 311; G. Le Bon, *The Crowd: A study of the popular mind*, [1995] London, 1926, p. 14; O. Y Gasset, *The Revolt of the Masses*, [1930] London, 1961.
5. L. Bramson, *The Political Context of Sociology*, Princeton, NJ, 1961.
6. G. Hawthorn, *Enlightenment and Despair*, Cambridge, 1976.

All three features were held to typify the new mass political actor – the urban and increasingly organised proletariat.[7] Uprooted from rural communities and massed into the expanding industrial towns, they were prone to strikes, riots and other forms of 'deviant' and 'emotive' behaviour, only being contained by the discipline of factory routines and mass organisations – be they unions or parties. Meanwhile, mass production and consumption had replaced high with popular culture. Educated elites had given way as the shapers of opinion and taste to populist, rabblerousing politicians, their journalistic supporters, manufacturers and advertisers. Socialism and organised labour became symptoms of the psychological and structural malaise afflicting modern societies, prompting even liberals to reconceptualise both liberalism and democracy via the new psychological and sociological political categories.[8] Reasoned deliberation to reach a consensus on the common good became an impossible ideal within a mass society. Instead, agreement had to be manufactured through controlling the masses and improving the quality of leadership.

Thus, all three features of the social theory of mass society came to be incorporated into a reworking of democracy in mass terms. In what follows, I shall trace the development of the resulting new language of democratic politics. The second section explores how social psychologists extended their analysis of mass crowd behaviour to the electorate more generally, giving both the attributes of a mob. Section three then examines an early analysis of political parties as the new mass political organisations. In each case, individual political judgement and action was claimed to have been curtailed – in the first by absorption into the irrational collective consciousness of the group, in the second by the discipline of party bureaucracy. Section four reveals how scope was nonetheless believed to exist for elites to manipulate both popular passions and the party machine. Section five then traces how these three theses were brought together to produce a denial of the very possibility of mass (or indeed any) democracy in the strict sense, thereby forcing its rethinking as a mechanism for selecting between party elites and leaders, who compete to win the people's vote by exploiting the tools of mass persuasion and organisational superiority.

Two general themes emerge from this analysis. The first notes how, rather than being scientific discoveries, each of these theses involved national variations on the more general historical experiences and intellectual trends of the time, in which a certain political culture shaped the various ideological preferences of the individual thinkers, making some theoretical moves more accessible and plausible than others. Thus, crowd theory reflected reactions within France to the French revolutionary tradition, whereby popular sovereignty frequently took the form of direct action or the plebiscitary populism of Bonapartism, as refracted through a predominantly positivist psychological approach. Élite theory was shaped by Italian clientelistic politics as perceived by a similarly positivistic social science

---

7.   R. Williams, *Culture and Society 1780–1950*, [1958], Harmondsworth, 1971, pp. 287–8.

8.   Femia, *Against the Masses.*

tradition, whilst the bureaucratisation of the state and parties in Germany rendered organisation theory particularly compelling to German theorists, even if a more historical methodology enabled it to be interpreted in more socially contingent terms than was allowed by the behaviourist explanations favoured elsewhere. Significantly, the one analysis to see mass movements as enriching and even spreading democracy drew on Britain and America, where revolutionary mass movements were lacking, though its conclusions were subsequently systematically misread by others.

These different emphases did not prevent theorists from drawing upon each other's work, making national comparisons, or – in certain cases – eventually forging a synthesis. Indeed, this became all the easier as the various arguments became codified as elements of a scientific political sociology. The second theme enters here. For this codification made later political scientists prisoners of a supposedly 'scientific' discourse, the true assumptions of which few knew and most would have rejected. Theorists were led by the pseudo-scientific logic of their arguments to conclusions at variance with their own ideological commitments, forcing them into either incoherent reworkings of their beliefs, pessimism or a volte-face. This tendency was especially true of those theorists who emphasised psychological rather than structural and organisational laws to account for mass behaviour. In their eyes, altering social structures had little purpose so long as human nature appeared unreformable and unchanging.

From crowds to mass electorates

Since classical times, theorists have criticised democracy for being less rational and efficient, whilst more prejudiced, parochial and intolerant, than rule by an enlightened elite. Neither genius nor difference could survive the democratic desire to level everything down to the same lowest common denominator. These criticisms were standardly linked to descriptions of the anarchy, destructive violence and irrationality of the mob.[9] The French Revolution reinforced such views amongst conservatives and liberals alike, from Burke and de Maistre, de Tocqueville and J. S. Mill, onwards. However, later theorists now saw the character of crowds as determined by human psychology and their growing dominance as the product of social development. Consequently, they generalised the analysis of crowd behaviour to cover all activity within a mass society – from the operations of elected assemblies and the influence of the popular press to the nature of religious worship and political activism and the production and marketing of everyday commodities. As Gustav Le Bon dramatically put it: 'The age we are about to enter will in truth be the ERA OF CROWDS [...] The divine right of the masses is about to replace the divine right of kings.'[10]

---

9.   J. McClelland, *The Crowd and the Mob: From Plato to Canetti*, London, 1989.

10.   Le Bon, *The Crowd*, pp. 15, 17.

Le Bon's *Psychology of Crowds* is by far the best known work in the field. A huge success when published, it was rapidly translated into English and German and remains in print in several languages. Fundamental for later thinkers as diverse as Sigmund Freud,[11] Robert Michels[12] and Graham Wallas,[13] it became a touchstone for the whole discipline of social psychology. If his conclusions have been remarkably little challenged, however, they rested on assumptions that are highly contestable, amounting as they do to little more than the prejudices of the day. A brilliant and prolific populariser, Le Bon simply synthesised the ideas of contemporary French and, to a lesser extent, Italian authors – notably Victor-Alfred Espinas, Henry Fournial, Gabriel Tarde and Scipio Sighele.[14] Few had undertaken much empirical research, though empiricist assertion and pseudo-scientific psychological speculation characterised their arguments. Rather, their views reflected the *fin de siècle* preoccupations with the social disorder of mass societies outlined earlier. As Susanna Barrows[15] has remarked, these views provided the often 'distorting mirror' through which theorists reflected on the growing political presence of 'the popular classes', particularly organised labour.

In the early 1880s the Third Republic had loosened restrictions on the freedoms of association, speech and assembly but was troubled by what were perceived as unprecedented levels of popular protest at the corruption of its parliamentary system. Many French intellectuals saw echoes of 1789 and the Paris Commune of 1871 in these demonstrations – both the object of an influential analysis of crowds by Hyppolite Taine.[16] Two events in particular became symbols of the susceptibility of contemporary democracy to popular uprisings and violence: the meteoric career of General Boulanger in the late 1880s and the Decazeville miners' strike of 1886.[17]

Boulanger had capitalised on disaffection with the Third Republic amongst both conservatives and workers, inspiring huge popular demonstrations in Paris in 1886 and 1887. Appointed Minister of War in 1885 because of his supposed Radical sympathies, his army reforms won him great popularity and led a nervous government to remove him from office in 1887 and send him into unofficial exile from Paris. Growing discontent with the government following the Wilson affair, when the President's son-in-law, Daniel Wilson, was revealed to have been

11. S. Freud, *Group Psychology and the Analysis of the Ego*, in James Stratchey (ed.), *The Standard Edition of the Complete Psychological Works of Sigmund Freud*, London, 1953–74 [1921], pp. 23–4.

12. R. Michels, *Political Parties: A sociological study of the oligarchical tendencies of modern democracy*, New York, 1959 [1912].

13. G. Wallas, *Human Nature in Politics*, London, 1908.

14. S. Barrows, *Distorting Mirrors: Visions of the crowd in late nineteenth-century France*, New Haven, 1981; R. A. Nye, *Gustav Le Bon and the Crisis of Mass Democracy in the Third Republic*, London, 1975.

15. S. Barrows, *Distorting Mirrors*, New Haven, CT, 1981, p. 5.

16. H. Taine, *The Origins of Contemporary France*, [1887–8] trans. Durand, 6 vols, Boston, 1962.

17. Barrows, *Distorting Mirrors*, ch. 1.

trafficking in bribes, encouraged him to enter a series of by-elections in 1888 with outstanding success, including winning Paris where a gathering of between 30 and 100,000 Parisians celebrated his victory. For the French theorists, Boulanger's power to galvanise crowds exemplified the capacity of a charismatic figure to harness mass support. Le Bon even credited him with the capacity to inspire an almost religious fervour.[18] Yet the return to Bonapartism that different groups either feared or hoped for failed to materialise. Urged to storm the Elysée rather than waiting for the general election, he lost his nerve and, fearing prosecution, fled abroad, where he committed suicide two years later.

The Decazeville strike, by contrast, was seen as an example of the destructive impulses of the leaderless, spontaneous crowd. Made famous by Emile Zola's fictional account in *Germinal* [1885],[19] Decazeville had given rise to the murder of a company official. Like Boulangism, however, it was a singular event. Despite the rising strike rate throughout the 1880s and the dramatic growth in union membership amongst industrial workers, less than 4 per cent of strikes involved violent acts and only a tenth public demonstrations. Though these strikes did become increasingly political in character, recent research has stressed their well organised and strategically rational character.[20] Nonetheless, just as the Boulanger affair eclipsed the relative stability of Third Republic politics, so this isolated episode also captured the crowd psychologists' imaginations and conjured up the spectre of proletarian violence against private property and the capitalist system.

Rightly interpreted as expressions of disaffection, these examples of popular protest became transformed into aspects of a broader social malaise brought about by the 'new conditions of existence' associated with industrial and urban life and 'the destruction of those religious, political beliefs in which all the elements of our civilisation are rooted'.[21] Crowds resulted from the deracination associated with modern urban life, the break up of family and the forcing together of the masses into a single area.[22] Seen as typical products of a transitional period between an old and a new social and moral order, they took on the same characteristics as certain other forms of supposedly 'pathological' and 'anomic' behaviour studied at the time.[23]

Significantly, criminologists were key pioneers of crowd psychology, with Sighele and Tarde the most prominent.[24] Sighele's *The Criminal Crowd*[25] was indebted to both the Italian criminal anthropologists Cesare Lombroso and Enrico Ferri, under whom he studied, and French writers such as Taine, Espinas

---

18. Le Bon, *The Crowd*, p. 85.

19. Barrows, *Distorting Mirrors*, ch. 4.

20. E. Shorter and C. Tilly, *Strikes in France, 1830–1968*, Cambridge, 1974.

21. Le Bon, *The Crowd*, p. 14.

22. *See*, e.g. G. Tarde, *Penal Philosophy*, [1890], trans. Rapelije Howell, Boston, 1912, pp. 325–6.

23. *See*, e.g. *ibid.*, pp. 323–4.

24. McClelland, *The Crowd*, ch. 6; Barrows, *Distorting Mirrors*, chs 5 and 6.

25. S. Sighele, *La foule criminelle*, [1891], trans. P Vigney, Paris, 1892.

and Tarde.[26] Sighele sought to guide the sentencing of individuals involved in destructive riots. Following Ferri, he argued the law should distinguish between the behaviour of 'born criminals', organised criminal 'sects', such as the Mafia, which they often formed, and those who were so influenced by the internal dynamics of crowds they performed criminal acts. Only the first two categories deserved the severest penalties. Though certain crowds could be made up of 'born criminals', his example being the Decazeville strikers, he thought the majority consisted of normally lawful citizens and should be treated more leniently.[27] Sighele explained crowd behaviour by reference to French theories of hypnotism. Hypnotism had fascinated medical researchers from the eighteenth century but, in the late nineteenth century, it became enmeshed in both criminal psychology and sociology via the notion of 'suggestibility'. Following the Salpêtrière school, Sighele viewed the propensity to hypnotic suggestion as indicating various degrees of moral 'weakness'. In keeping with his distinctions between different sorts of crowds, he contended only the 'criminaloid' could be influenced to commit terrible crimes.[28] However, he was vague about the mechanisms whereby crowds induced their hypnotic effect. These were more fully elaborated by Tarde.

A provincial magistrate, Tarde belonged to Sighele's target audience. However, he had also acquired a formidable reputation as a social scientist and criminologist. Tarde saw hypnotism as the 'experimental junction point' between psychology and sociology.[29] Developing this thesis in his *The Laws of Imitation*,[30] he argued that all social behaviour resulted from mutual suggestibility or 'imitation', which induced 'a kind of somnambulism'. Indeed, he contended, 'the social, like the hypnotic state, is only a form of dream'.[31] In his *Penal Philosophy* of the same year he had begun to apply this thesis to the study of crowds. Crowds were simply extreme forms of this imitative effect, all the more potent when they involved members of a similar social group – notably workers. Spurred by Sighele's work, he now developed this aspect further. Though the two agreed on many points, Tarde was apt to think any individual would fall under the spell of the crowd. Like hypnotic subjects, crowds acted 'unconsciously', with only the 'spinal cord' rather than the brain.[32] Thus, 'a spark of passion' could turn 'a gathering of heterogeneous elements, unknown to one another', into a cohesive, homogeneous mass 'which marches towards its goal with an irresistible finality'.[33] People lost all sense of personal responsibility, acting in a quite different manner from how they would have done as individuals. Even if the majority in a crowd 'assembled

26. Barrows, *Distorting Mirrors*, p. 126.

27. Sighele, *La foule criminelle*, pp. 117–22.

28. Barrows, *Distorting Mirrors*, pp. 128–9, Sighele, *La foule criminelle*, pp. 137–44.

29. Tarde, *Penal Philosophy*, p. 193.

30. G. Tarde, *Les Lois de l'imitation*, Paris, 1890.

31. *Ibid.*, pp. 77, 87.

32. G. Tarde, 'Les crimes des foules', *Archives de l'anthropologie criminelle* 1892, 7, pp. 354–5, 359.

33. Tarde, *Penal Philosophy*, p. 323.

out of pure curiosity', 'the fever of some of them soon reached the minds of all, and in all of them there arose a delirium. The very man who had come running to oppose the murder of an innocent person is one of the first to be seized with the homicidal contagion'.[34]

By reference to descriptions of mob violence such as Taine's,[35] Tarde and his contemporaries gradually mixed the hypnotic metaphor with others that stressed how crowds induced a diseased and disordered mental and physical state. So, crowds were not only prone to drunkenness, they acted in many respects like alcoholics – mentally inebriated and deprived of their reason by the heady atmosphere, they were subject to 'hallucinations' and delusions of grandeur. As a result, they lacked all restraints, giving way to pure 'instinctual' behaviour involving sexual excesses and murder. Like alcohol, membership of a crowd could 'poison' an individual, driving him temporally 'insane'. Crowd behaviour was also compared to a group sickness or an 'epidemic' – individuals were 'infected' by the collective consciousness of the crowd, which spread 'contagiously' throughout all its members until they found themselves in a mental 'fever' or 'delirium'.[36] Finally, crowds were 'savage' and 'bestial' – atavistic throwbacks to a 'primitive' evolutionary stage – 'the human animal [bête humaine]'.[37]

In these ways, crowds became portrayed as the exact opposite of the classical ideal of citizenship and democratic deliberation. Whereas citizens were traditionally characterised by such supposedly 'masculine' virtues as courage and fortitude, their discussions directed by reason, all the pathological symptoms associated with crowds, with the inconvenient exception of alcoholism, were traditionally dubbed 'feminine' traits. Like women, crowds were 'cowardly', 'instinctive', moved by 'feelings' and 'passions' rather than reason, inconstant and unpredictable, prone to hysteria, at once highly open to suggestion and alluring to others. As Gabriel Tarde observed: 'By its whimsy, its revolting docility, its credulity, its nervousness, its brusque psychological leaps from fury to tenderness, from exasperation to laughter, the crowd is feminine, even when it is composed, as is usually the case, of males'.[38] Civilisation, like reason, being male, the violence of crowds was akin to that of 'a female savage or a female faun, worse than that, an impulsive and maniacal plaything of its instincts and its mechanical habits, often an animal of the lower orders, an invertebrate, a monstrous worm whose sensibility is diffuse'.[39]

---

34. *Ibid.*, p. 323.

35. *Ibid.*, pp. 323–4.

36. For all of the above, *see* Tarde, *Archives de l'anthropologie criminelle*, pp. 359–60.

37. H. Fournial, *Essai sur la psychologie des foules: considérations médico-judiciaires sur les résponsibilités collectives*, Lyon, 1892, p. 109 ; Tarde, *Archives de l'anthropologie criminelle*, p. 358.

38. Tarde, quoted in Barrows, *Distorting Mirrors*, p. 47.

39. Tarde, *Archives de l'anthropologie criminelle*, p. 358.

Le Bon both summarised and simplified the work of these authors, turning discussion of the crowd's 'collective mind'[40] into 'the *law of the mental unity of crowds*'.[41] Likewise, he drew out in typically brazen fashion the misogynistic and racist prejudices informing these ideas, blithely asserting ('its demonstration being outside the scope of this work') how those

> special characteristics of crowds – such as impulsiveness, irritability, incapacity to reason, the absence of judgement and of the critical spirit, the exaggeration of the sentiments, and others besides – [...] are almost always observed in beings belonging to inferior forms of evolution – in women, savages and children, for instance.[42]

His own contribution lay in treating crowds no longer as aberrations that threatened the prevailing social and political order but as typifying mass behaviour within modern societies – not least the new popular democracy. Crowds, he argued, did not 'always involve the simultaneous presence of a number of individuals on one spot'. 'Thousands of individuals', including 'an entire nation', could 'under the influence of certain violent emotions' acquire the characteristics of a 'psychological crowd'.[43] Indeed, the detachment and isolation of the individual from traditional hierarchical structures and loyalties had turned the populations of mass societies into 'an agglomeration of individualities lacking cohesion' and rendered them particularly susceptible to acting as a crowd.[44]

Meanwhile, it was beside the point to talk of protecting juries and parliamentary assemblies from crowds because they operated largely in a like manner.[45] Tarde had lamented how

> Our political constitutions are primitive mechanisms compared to our own organisms, and the collective spirit called a parliament or congress is never equal in sure rapid functioning, in profound and far-reaching deliberation, in inspired intuition or decision, to the *esprit* of the most mediocre of its members.[46]

Le Bon went further – political institutions had no independent influence on behaviour. They were only effective when attuned to the nation's sentiments. Character and custom rather than law and government were the determining factors in how a people were ruled, an argument Le Bon increasingly associated with race.

---

40. Le Bon, *The Crowd*, pp. 29–30.

41. *Ibid.*, p. 26.

42. *Ibid.*, p. 40.

43. *Ibid.*, pp. 26–7.

44. *Ibid.*, pp. 238–9.

45. *Ibid.*, pp. 36, 215.

46. Tarde, *Archives de l'anthropologie criminelle*, p. 358.

Within a mass society, the masses had to be accommodated. Democracy may have had no intrinsic worth, and notions of the general will or consent might be illusory because no agglomeration of people was capable of rational deliberation,[47] but the prevailing democratic dogma held that truth and numerical superiority went hand in hand.[48] Though 'stupidity', 'not mother wit', was accumulated in crowds, mass approval and assent were necessary for any regime's legitimacy.[49] Fortunately, however, the masses could be manipulated, with crowd psychology offering statesmen a scientific guide to how to do it.[50] If Decazeville revealed the dangerous destructiveness of crowds, Boulanger had indicated their malleability. 'Primitive' and 'suggestible', crowds were highly susceptible to the arts of oratory and charisma. Unable to think for themselves, crowds were always controlled by a few leaders. Needless to say, crowds did not respond to 'pure reason' or 'ideas' but, like women, had to be 'seduced' by exaggerated appeals to their 'sentiments'. Moreover, they had no opinions of their own but only those that were 'impressed' upon them.[51] The key to political power lay in the ability to stir the popular imagination and to inspire an almost religious devotion amongst one's followers. The allure of socialism, like all successful ideologies, was in this respect fundamentally religious in character.[52]

'Electoral crowds' resembled other crowds in possessing 'but slight aptitude for reasoning, the absence of critical spirit, irritability, credulity and simplicity'.[53] Nor was there any point in restricting the electorate, given that 'in a crowd men always tend to the same level and, on general questions, a vote recorded by forty academicians is no better than of forty water-carriers'.[54] However, the electorate were as easy to manipulate as other crowds, swayed by the 'prestige' of a leader and rhetorical skills that by 'affirmation' and 'repetition' could appeal to sentiments and create a groundswell of support by the contagious effects of suggestibility.[55] Drawing a parallel that would become a cliché amongst his successors, Le Bon noted how 'statesman called upon to defend a political cause' used the same techniques as 'commercial men pushing the sale of their products by means of advertising'. Just as 'when we have read that X's chocolate is the best, we imagine we have heard it said in many quarters, and we end by acquiring the certitude that such is the fact', so,

47. Le Bon, *The Crowd*, p. 210.
48. *Ibid.*, p. 211.
49. *Ibid.*, p 32.
50. *Ibid.*, p. 21.
51. *Ibid.*, pp. 21–2, 56–9.
52. *Ibid.*, pp. 77–80, 82–5.
53. *Ibid.*, p. 201.
54. *Ibid.*, pp. 211–12.
55. *Ibid.*, pp. 141–59, 202–4.

if we read in the same papers that A is an arrant scamp and B a most honest man, we finish by being convinced that this is the truth, unless, indeed, we are given to reading another paper of the contrary opinion, in which the two qualifications are reversed.[56]

The power of 'imitation' was such that any notion pushed with sufficient vigour would soon pass amongst the populace as a received truth.

Much the same tactics also allowed leaders to dominate parliamentary assemblies.[57] Again like later theorists, Le Bon noted that a cost of needing to constantly woo the masses was the gradual extension of government. The result was financial waste, as different parts of the electorate were bought off, and the gradual restriction of liberty, as taxes were raised to pay for these measures. The consequent growth of the state also augmented the number and authority of the bureaucracy – the latter's power being all the greater because impersonal, permanent and without responsibility.[58] Mass politics thereby reinforced that other feature of mass societies, the introduction of mass-production methods into government as well as industry. Though this development drew ideological support from socialism, Le Bon maintained that it would ultimately provoke a popular reaction. Citizens would become dismayed at the corruption of politicians embroiled in bribing their local constituencies to win support. The state would become increasingly mechanical and despotic.[59] It was in these circumstances that the destructiveness of crowds became a creative force, especially when controlled by a charismatic leader possessing sufficient prestige to harness their spontaneity and energy.[60]

Reactionary and racist, Le Bon's views would find a natural audience with the far right. As the power of organised labour grew, Le Bon was to become increasingly opposed to parliamentary democracy and turn to nationalism and charismatic leadership as the means to control the masses.[61] However, his approach proved just as influential amongst both radical[62] and conservative[63] liberals. Though these later thinkers would no longer have subscribed to Le Bon's or Tarde's explanations of the actual hallucinatory effects of crowds, or even the sexist let alone racist assumptions on which they often relied, they were captivated by the metaphors and (pseudo) social l-laws to which these theories gave rise. In addition, these theorists had access to a further dimension absent from Le Bon – namely, the psychological influence of party organisation on the masses, politicians and their leaders.

56. *Ibid.*, pp. 142–3.

57. *Ibid.*, p. 215.

58. *Ibid.*, pp. 231–35.

59. *Ibid.*, pp. 235–6.

60. *Ibid.*, pp. 237–9, 150–1.

61. *See* R. L. Geiger, 'Democracy and the crowd: the social history of an idea in France and Italy, 1890–1914', *Societas* 7, 1977, pp. 47–71 – who notes a parallel change in Sighele's thinking.

62. Wallas, *Human Nature in Politics*.

63. W. Lippmann, *Public Opinion*, [1922], New York, 1965, p. 127.

The rise of party organisation

Much as the origins of crowd psychology are associated with Le Bon, so the study of political parties as mass organisations gets traced to Moisei Ostrogorski and his *Democracy and the Organisation of Political Parties* of 1902. Once again, this linkage distorts as much as it illuminates.[64] Ostrogorski was outside many of the historical experiences that shaped the new science of politics. A Russian Jew who studied with Emile Boutmy at the Ecole libres des sciences politiques, Ostrogorski was influenced by the nineteenth-century French historical school and its British followers and shared their Anglophile liberal sympathies. Thus, he was broadly Tocquevillian in seeing democracy as a social and moral phenomenon,[65] with de Tocqueville's famous call for 'a new political science for a new world' providing the epigraph for his book.[66] Rather than the constant tendencies of human nature or social structure, he emphasised ideas or 'mental tendencies' and the 'working of wills' of the main political actors, noting how these 'forces' were both shaped by and helped to shape responses to changing social and political conditions.[67]

Ostrogorski's decision to compare political parties in Britain and America was inspired by the contemporary British debate over whether Britain was succumbing to the 'American model' of 'machine politics' described by James Bryce in *The American Commonwealth* (1888).[68] Hence the book's appearance in English translation – with a preface by Bryce, who had encouraged his project – prior to the publication of the French original.[69] Ostrogorski's argument that British politics had indeed been 'Americanised' was taken by many commentators as confirming a general trend towards the domination of party organisation. However, his analysis was much more nuanced and ultimately rooted in earlier debates about the extension of the franchise, most particularly the views of J. S. Mill.

A Millean liberal, Ostrogorski shared Mill's fear that that 'the general tendency of things' within commercial societies was towards 'mediocrity'[70] – a process he associated with the growing influence of 'the masses' as 'the only power deserving the name'.[71] Like Mill, though, he saw the danger as stemming less

---

64. R. Barker and X. Howard-Johnstone, 'The politics and political ideas of Mosei Ostrogorski', *Political Studies* 23, 1975, pp. 415–29; P. Pombeni, 'Starting in reason, ending in passion. Bryce, Lowell, Ostrogorski and the problem of democracy', *The Historical Journal* 37, 1994, pp. 319–41, 163–69; G. Quagliariello, *Politics Without Parties: Moisei Ostrogorski and the debate on political parties on the eve of the twentieth century*, Aldershot, 1996.

65. Quagliariello, *Politics Without Parties*, ch. 2.

66. *See*, too, M. Ostrogorski, *Democracy and the Organisation of Political Parties*, 2 vols, trans. F. Clarke, with a Preface by James Bryce, London, 1902, vol. II, pp. 633–4.

67. Ostrogorski, *Democracy and the Organisation of Political Parties* vol. I, pp. li–lii.

68. Quagliariello, *Parties Without Politics*, ch. 3.

69. P. Pombeni, *Partiti e sistemi politici nella storia contemporanea*, 3rd edn, Bologna, 1994; Pombeni, 'Starting in reason', pp. 162–3.

70. J. S. Mill, 'Civilization' [1836] in J. Robson (ed.) *Essays on Politics and Society*, Toronto, 1977, p. 121.

71. J. S. Mill, 'On liberty', [1895], in J. Gray (ed.), *On Liberty and Other Essays*, Oxford, 1991 p. 73.

from democracy *per se* than from the social pressures to conform to the lowest common denominator. As a result, the public were increasingly guided only by people like themselves. Mass parties both reflected and exacerbated this trend. The worry was that 'persons of genius' would be unable to thrive and society stagnate in consequence. For he shared Mill's belief that 'the initiation of all wise or noble things comes and must come from individuals'. Yet Ostrogorski also followed Mill in optimistically thinking 'the honour and glory of the average man' lay in being 'capable of following that initiative'.[72] Again picking up on Mill's insight,[73] he argued that the solution lay in devising institutional mechanisms for preserving individuality and ensuring exceptional persons could voice their views and be heard – so long as they could be, the mass of people would follow.

Consequently, Ostrogorski did not accept the inevitability of mass parties. Alternative forms of democratic organisation could and should be promoted. Like many British liberals of the time, he saw Gladstone's remarkable ability to harness popular support to the Liberal Party through moral campaigns as revealing how parties could both galvanise and elevate their popular supporters though a combination of inspired leadership and a focus on crucial issues of rights and justice.[74] Parties could thereby obtain some of the ethical force of earlier campaigning organisations, such as the Anti-Corn-Law League. His aim was to advocate a return to this model against the new forms of party organisation being promoted by Chamberlain in Birmingham.

In these respects, Ostrogorski's analysis reflected both British liberal political culture, with its optimistic faith in social and moral progress,[75] and the absence in Britain of a significant revolutionary socialist party or movement that threatened the political dominance of the liberal elite and their values. Yet, Ostrogorski's work has been consistently misread. Contemporaries plundered his study for examples that they then reinterpreted according to their own theories. Later commentators have followed their lead, praising him as a pioneering 'behaviourist' political scientist[76] but regarding his reform proposals as a bafflingly 'absurd'[77] 'fantasy'[78] – totally at variance with his analysis of modern party politics. However, his importance in this story lies in his *not* being 'one of the most important originators

72. *Ibid.*, p.74.

73. J. S. Mill, 'Considerations on representative government' [1861], in J. Gray (ed.), *On Liberty and Other Essays*, Oxford, OUP, 1991.

74. J. R. Vincent, *The Formation of the British Liberal Party 1857–68*, London, Constable 1966, ch. 3; C. Harvie, 'Gladstonianism, the provinces and popular political culture 1860–1906', in R. Bellamy (ed.), *Victorian Liberalism: Nineteenth century political thought and practice*, London, Routledge, 1990, pp. 152–74.

75. I. Bradley, *The Optimists: Themes and personalities in Victorian liberalism*, London, Faber and Faber, 1980; R. Bellamy, *Liberalism and Modern Society: An historical argument*, Cambridge, CUP, 1992, ch. 1.

76. D. Butler, *The Study of Political Behaviour*, London, Hutchinson, 1958, p. 44.

77. *Ibid.*, p. 44.

78. W. G. Runciman, *Social Science and Political Theory*, Cambridge, CUP, 1965, p. 71.

[...] of political sociology'.[79] His recruitment to that role derived from the triumph of a given intellectual paradigm that he had stood outside, sharing neither its methodological or experiential assumptions: a position that allowed him to evaluate democracy's prospects quite differently.

Though Ostrogorski linked the rise of mass parties to certain features of modern societies and a related climate of ideas, he avoided both structural and psychological determinism. Social structures and ideas were independent variables, albeit with a mutual influence on each other, which developed in historically contingent ways. Ostrogorski believed the nature of both British and American parties arose from the social and economic changes that had created a mass society having been accompanied by an individualistic ethos. This combination had different origins in the two countries but in Britain had resulted from the linking of the industrial revolution with a Benthamite ideology.[80] Initially a genuinely radical doctrine, which expressed the entrepreneurial bourgeoisie's struggle for the extension of civil liberties and a more meritocratic society, diffusion amongst the masses had transformed Benthamism into a levelling and materialistic creed.[81] As a result, the organic social ties of duty and the deference of the aristocratic social order were replaced by the bonds of economic interest between buyers and sellers. When these cultural attitudes were accompanied by the decline of supportive social structures, individuals became isolated atoms who were attracted to being part of a homogenous mass. It was these circumstances rather than human psychology *per se* that was 'forcing individuals to dissolve into crowds',[82] and explained their subsequent behaviour. Just as mass production offered people generalised tastes, habits, culture and ready-made opinions that spared them from having to make up their own minds, so mass organisations gave individuals a sense of solidarity and collective purpose they seemed unable to provide for themselves. He saw the spread of evangelical religion as exemplifying this trend.

Mass parties simply mirrored this more general social transformation. Ostrogorski regarded the ideal nature of parties to be the Burkean one of being 'a body of men united, for promoting by their joint endeavours the national interest, upon some particular principle in which they are all agreed'.[83] This view reflected the early stages of a more individualistic society, in which notions of organic unity had given way to a conscious union between individuals.[84] However, the extension of the franchise had turned parties into mere electoral machines to organise the mass vote. Ostrogorski associated this change with the 'Caucus' system developed

79. S. M. Lipset, 'Ostrogorski and the analytical approach to the comparative study of political parties', in S. Lipset (ed. and abridged), M. Ostrogorski, *Democracy and the Organisation of Political Parties*, Chicago, 1964, vol. I, p. xiv.

80. M. Ostrogorski, *Democracy and the Organisation of Political Parties*, vol. I, p. 39.

81. *Ibid.*, vol. I, pp. 48, 580–1, 587.

82. *Ibid.*, vol. I, pp. 48–50.

83. Quoted in Ostrogorski, *Democracy and the Organisation of Political Parties*, vol. II, p. 652.

84. Compare T. Ball, 'Party', in T. Ball, J. Farr and R. L. Hanson (eds), *Political Innovation and Conceptual Change*, Cambridge, 1989.

by Joseph Chamberlain in Birmingham, which paralleled similar organisations in the United States, such as the infamous Tammany Hall. These new types of parties reflected the ethos of the age. Popular election of leaders and officials had produced politicians who followed rather than challenged the mass mediocrity around them. Professional politicians rather than public-spirited citizens, they saw politics as a trade from which they sought a living.[85] The parties were 'businesses', with electioneering and the pursuit of office ends in themselves rather than the means to realising certain desirable policies.[86] Though not necessarily corrupt in the sense of seeking kick-backs, they were willing to do anything to win electoral success and hence secure their position.[87] Requiring considerable funds to maintain the party machine, they became prey to sectional interests, happy to exchange favours – from honours to public-works contracts – for finance and support from business, unions or particular communities. A tendency particularly prevalent in the United States, especially in municipal elections, it led parties back into factionalism, albeit of a new kind.

The worst aspect of this new form of politics was in the realm of ideas. Ostrogorski related the Burkean notion of party to an extremely radical neo-Rousseauean idea of the social contract, in which support for any government had to be constantly re-negotiated, by debating every single issue so as to build a rational union of wills on policies of genuinely common interest.[88] Ostrogorski's ideal was not 'a social contract' but multiple 'social contracts, which follow each other in an indefinite succession'.[89] By contrast, the new parties wanted a permanent presence that allowed them to win and hold onto power – hence their need for professionals and a permanent organisation.[90] Consequently, they wished to speak for the majority on any matter that might arise. To do so, they abandoned the notion of a rational union of principle for a passive uniformity derived from peddling 'wholesale' opinions that would appeal to the lowest common denominator on any topic – no matter how incoherent the result.[91] Rather than vehicles of civic education, such parties pandered to conventional views and self-interest.[92] Independent views posed a constant threat to party ascendancy[93] so appeal was made 'not so much to reason, which analyses and distinguishes, as to feeling; by stirring up emotions which confuse the judgement and make a prisoner of the will'.[94] Citizens and politicians alike were 'demoralised' in the process,[95]

---

85. Ostrogorski, *Democracy and the Organisation of Political Parties*, vol. I, p. 593.

86. *Ibid.*, II, p. 651.

87. *Ibid.*, II, pp. 656–7.

88. *Ibid.*, II pp. 671–81.

89. *Ibid.*, II, p. 680.

90. *Ibid.*, II, p. 656.

91. *Ibid.*, I, pp. 588–9.

92. *Ibid.*, I, p. 594.

93. *Ibid.*, II, p. 656.

94. *Ibid.*, I, p. 585.

95. *Ibid.*, I, p. 585, II, p. 635.

with the latter especially becoming 'timorous' conformists unwilling to say anything that might offend a potential supporter or paymaster.[96] Democracy had ceased to have the substantive purpose of deliberating on the common good and had become a purely formal and mechanical procedure of popular endorsement.[97] Indeed the organisation mentality had infected all public duties, with personal rule and responsibility replaced by an empty 'mechanical' formalism and a deference to conventional views and practices.[98]

Ostrogorski regarded such 'organisation' parties as 'the negation of democracy',[99] removing any sense of a civic duty of citizens or politicians even to form opinions of their own, let alone to participate actively in the democratic process. Yet he believed their days were numbered.[100] Parties had begun to break up, as their members – alienated by their corrupt tendencies and essentially anti-political character – rebelled against the necessarily anodyne character of a common programme and began to militate for the various issues that interested them. A chief flaw of permanent parties was that they impeded the formation of new associations, by crystallising opinion and preventing the evolution of ideas.[101] He believed the solution lay in returning to a situation of temporary parties consisting 'of a combination of citizens formed specially for a particular issue'.[102] Such parties would be *ad hoc* and prevent the formation of a permanent cadre. Citizens would be forced to weigh up the merits of particular questions rather than accepting a ready-made package that often involved the log-rolling of inconsistent positions. Parties would have to take on an educative role of winning citizens around to a particular cause. Democracy would return to its ideal form of constructing social unity around the general will.

Ostrogorski believed his proposed 'league system' of temporary issue-based parties was 'suited to the conditions of a complex society with a multiplicity of interests', where citizens only became enthused about particular issues but found the concerns of the whole community hard to conceive of or identify with.[103] However, he also suggested a number of institutional devices for promoting this scheme, from a state-organised preliminary poll to select candidates, in which all could vote and from which party affiliations were excluded, to proportional representation for the election itself. He claimed that the resulting legislature would reflect the degree of concern people felt for particular issues of the day. Like modern political pluralists, he argued that society contained 'majorities and minorities, whose constituent elements change continually with circumstances',

---

96. *Ibid.*, II, pp. 632, 635–6.
97. *Ibid.*, II, pp. 638–9, 650–1.
98. *Ibid.*, II, p. 643.
99. *Ibid.*, II, p. 622.
100. *Ibid.*, II, p. 687.
101. *Ibid.*, II, pp. 637–8.
102. *Ibid.*, II, p. 658.
103. *Ibid.*, II. p. 681.

so that tyrannical majorities were unlikely.[104] Laws would 'no longer be the imperious decisions of a dominant majority' but

> a continual series of compromises, settled by majorities whose composition may vary from one question to another, but which will in each case present a genuine reflection of the views and feelings of the true, of the only majority that can have been constituted on the basis of the particular question.[105]

Needless to say, for Ostrogorski the 'decisive battle' was in the realm of ideas – 'the *habeas animum*'.[106] Electors had to regain the moral will to employ their judgement. Crucial to this task was the revival of the political class, for 'equality of rights' could never 'make up for the natural inequality of brains and character'.[107] Ostrogorski believed his scheme would encourage men of merit and principle to come forward because, by contrast to the party system, moral conviction and the power of reason would once again become electoral assets rather than liabilities. Yet he admitted this could not be counted on. Indeed, hardly any of his contemporaries believed it possible. Though Bryce thought his analysis of the Americanisation of the British system exaggerated,[108] almost all other commentators believed he had not gone nearly far enough. In a telling analogy, Graham Wallas likened his analysis to 'a series of conscientious observations of the Copernican heavens by a loyal but saddened believer in the Ptolemaic astronomy'.[109] Paradoxically, the only theorist who took ideas seriously was unable to get his arguments a considered hearing because they belonged to a political language that contemporaries and most later commentators regarded as at best anachronistic, at worst incoherent and, for many, incomprehensible. Wallas believed Ostrogorski had failed to grasp the lessons of the new social psychology and hence had totally unrealistic expectations of the electorate. Robert Michels was to add that he had also overlooked the historical necessity for organisation.[110] In particular, he had not seen how psychological and organisational factors combined not to undermine elites but to change their nature and give them ever more power. Instead of serving to revive democracy, therefore, Ostrogorski found himself recruited to the service of those wishing either to declare its impossibility[111] or to argue that it was only possible in the very form he sought to criticise and change.[112]

---

104. *Ibid.*, II. p. 678.

105. *Ibid.*, II. p. 715.

106. *Ibid.*, II. p. 728.

107. *Ibid.*, II. p. 640.

108. Preface to *ibid.*, I, p. xliii.

109. Wallas, *Human Nature in Politics*, p. 125.

110. R. Michels, *Corso di sociologia politica*, Milan, 1927, p. 361.

111. *See*, e.g. G. Mosca, *The Ruling Class* (Elementi di scienza politica), A. Livingstone (ed.), trans. H. D. Kahn, New York, 1939 [1896 and 1923], p. 389. N.B. Mosca, *The Ruling Class*, is a translation of the first (1895) and some of the second (1923) editions of his *Elements of Political Science*, the dates in brackets indicate the edition from which the reference derives.

112. *See*, e.g. M. Weber, 'The profession and vocation of politics' [1919] in P. Lassman and R. Speirs (eds), *Political Writings*, trans. R. Speirs, Cambridge, 1994, pp. 309–69, p. 340.

The persistence of elites

The thesis that democratic arrangements promoted rather than counteracted the rule of elites was to provide the third element of the modern theory of democracy. The notion that elites always rule was not itself novel. Indeed, as such it amounts to no more than the truism that rulers will almost always be fewer than the ruled, whatever the form of government. The originality of the democratic elite theorists arose from their reference to the new social psychology and the role of organisations, especially parties, to explain the character and basis of elite power, and from their contention that the elite was not only unaccountable to the electorate but manipulated them. They differed from the traditional elitism of a figure such as Ortega Y Gasset, who saw the rise of the masses as a populist 'tyranny of the majority', promoting a general levelling down to the lowest common denominator that replaced culture with barbarism.[113] Their contention was that elites still ruled, though their character and the sources of their power had indeed changed.

If the analysis of crowds drew on an account of French politics and the theory of parties on Britain and America, elite theory elaborated certain characteristics of Italian political life, with its chief proponents being Vilfredo Pareto and Gaetano Mosca. Pareto and Mosca quarrelled over who had originated elite theory throughout their careers. Though both aspired to producing a 'scientific' theory based on the social 'uniformities'[114] and 'constant laws or tendencies that determine the political organisation of human societies',[115] shared a positivist disregard for metaphysics and employed their theses to deflate and unmask the pretensions of democrats and socialists alike, their approach to and conception of elitism was very different.

Pareto made his name as a free-market political economist. He regarded economic and political liberalism as logical entailments of a rational-actor model of human agency. Yet he found this belief confounded during the 1890s.[116] Rather than pursuing free trade and a limited state, liberal politicians had practised 'bourgeois socialism' by employing protectionism and state monopolies to benefit certain industrial and agricultural supporters.[117] He condemned Marxism as utopian and unworkable but was initially sympathetic to 'popular socialism' as an understandable reaction to government corruption and the failings of its economic policies.[118] However, the bourgeoisie had not returned to liberal ways to reconcile

113. Y Gasset, *The Revolt of the Masses*, pp. 13–14.

114. V. Pareto, *Trattato di sociologia generale*, 3 vols, Florence, 1916, para. 69.

115. G. Mosca, *The Ruling Class* (Elementi di scienza politica), A. Livingstone (ed.), trans. H. D. Kahn, New York, 1939 [1896 and 1923], p. 6.

116. R. Bellamy, *Modern Italian Social Theory: Ideology and politics from Pareto to the present*, Cambridge, 1987, ch. 2.

117. V. Pareto, 'Socialismo e libertà', *il pensiero italiano*, Feb. pp. 227–37, in *Écrits politiques*, G. Busino (ed.), 2 vols, Geneva, 1974 [1891], vol. I, pp. 376–409, pp. 378–9.

118. V. Pareto, 'Introduction' to K. Marx, *Le capital*, extraits fait par P. Larfargue in *Marxisme et économie pure*, Lausanne, 1966 [1893], pp. 33–70, p. 70.

the workers to the advantages of the market. Instead, they had bought them off by resorting to state welfare. Since the free market remained the optimal system, the explanation for this strategy could not lie in either changes in the nature of capitalism or flaws in liberal political economy. The answer had to reside in the psychological appeal of 'non-logical' irrational ideas to the masses and the ability of elites to exploit them to win power.[119] His sociology simply elaborated this diagnosis of the nature of Italian transformist politics.

By contrast, Mosca was a constitutional lawyer and parliamentarian.[120] A member of the very bourgeois liberal class Pareto came to vilify, he remained convinced of their civic virtues and sought to revive their ethos and position. Like Ostrogorski, whose political attitudes and background he largely shared, he believed their decline and corruption arose from social and structural changes – particularly the extension of the franchise and a blurring of the separation of powers once the legislature came to predominate.[121] However, unlike Ostrogorski, he saw these developments as exemplifying sociological laws and so much harder to combat.

Pareto first outlined his theory in the early 1900s with his analysis of *Socialist Systems*.[122] Élite theory clearly emerges from this work as both an alternative to Marxism and a critique and explanation of its appeal. Class struggle is replaced by the circulation of elites, the proletariat with the mass, and a future without domination declared illusory because exploitative rule by an elite occurs under all systems, private property being but one source of power and authority. Like Le Bon, he saw socialism's attraction as akin to millenarian religion: emotional rather than intellectual. Notions such as the 'general will', the 'common good' or 'popular sovereignty' were in themselves incoherent. They simply offered a spurious legitimacy for the replacement of a capitalist by a socialist elite. Subsequent writings, culminating in the massive *Treatise of General Sociology* of 1916, outlined the socio-psychological mechanisms involved.

Pareto argued that humans were moved by a number of basic emotional 'residues'. These could then be manipulated by certain sorts of argumentation, which he called 'derivations'. Though he enumerated some 52 residues, the most important were the 'instinct of combinations' and the 'persistence of aggregates'. Adapting Machiavelli, Pareto divided political elites into 'foxes' and 'lions', depending on which of these two residues they operated upon. The first favoured the 'cunning' of those who ruled via consent,[123] the second was a conservative tendency that was more inclined to employ force.[124] These two types of political elite obtained power by recruiting support from coalitions of much more heterogeneous

---

119. V. Pareto, *Les systèmes socialistes*, 2 vols, Paris, 1902, vol. I, p. 125.

120. Bellamy, *Modern Italian Social Theory*, ch. 3.

121. Mosca, 'Sulla teorica dei governi e sul governo rappresentativo', pp. 310–26.

122. Pareto, *Les systèmes socialistes*, 1902.

123. V. Pareto, *Trattato di sociologia generale*, 3 vols, Florence, 1916, para. 889.

124. *Ibid*, para. 888.

social and economic groups possessing the parallel characteristics associated with innovative 'speculators' and investing 'rentiers' respectively. Pareto argued there was a cyclical 'circulation' of elites which went hand in hand with socio-economic cycles. Thus, foxes wooed speculators by either tacitly or actively helping them to 'despoil' the rentiers – be they small petit-bourgeois savers or major shareholders. Initially, rising prosperity would be accompanied by a calling into question of traditional morality and a consumer boom. However, both the government and the populace would begin to go into debt due to over-consumption based on credit, whilst a scarcity of capital and a lack of productive investment would lead the economy to contract. The need for restraint and saving would become apparent and a more conservative government of lions would come to the fore, backed by a rentier economic class full of the second type ('persistence of aggregates') of residues. Eventually, though, the economy would start to stagnate and people tire of leonine austerity, thereby precipitating the rise of foxes and speculators again and the start of a new cycle.[125]

Pareto claimed to be describing a universal phenomenon and mainly employed examples drawn from ancient history to demonstrate his theory's objectivity. However, the Italian context emerges as all important once he applied it to democracy in both the final chapters of the *Treatise* and the various articles written after the war, especially those later collected as *The Transformation of Democracy*.[126] Italy, he argued, was in the grip of a pluto-democracy. Parliamentary democracy offered the perfect instrument for foxish politicians to build up a clientelistic network of 'speculators'. To a certain degree, workers had common cause with the plutocrats. If the one desired increased wages and social benefits, the other wanted bigger bonuses and state subsidies. Both wished to expropriate the rentiers' surplus and raise taxes for an expanding state. However, at a certain point their paths were bound to diverge. He now feared that democracy was likely to get the upper hand over plutocracy. Clientelism encouraged *centripetal* tendencies that dispersed state power, creating what he regarded as a new feudalism of warring barons, exemplified by the conflict between organised labour and fascists. Yet, economic and social instability was encouraging *centrifugal* forces calling for a return to authority. Initially, he had anticipated a socialist seizure of power on the Bolshevik model but he was equally happy to greet the rise of Mussolini as confirming 'splendidly the predictions of my *Sociology* and many of my articles'.[127] In fact, Pareto's theory was but an ex *post facto* elaboration of his jaundiced interpretation of the Italian situation, whereby he re-described these events in terms of the categories of his theory and then read them back into all other past events as universal laws of human behaviour. However, though anti-democratic, he was not a fascist. He regarded the state as an instrument of 'spoilation' whoever ran

125. *Ibid.*, paras 2053–9, 2223–36.

126. V. Pareto, *La trasformazione della democrazia*, [1921], in G. Busino (ed.), *Ecrits sociologiques mineurs*, Geneva, 1980, pp. 917–1060.

127. V. Pareto, Letter to Lello Gangemi, 13 November 1922, in G. Busino (ed.), *Correspondence 1890–1923*, 2 vols, Geneva, 1975.

it. Had he lived, he would undoubtedly have regarded Mussolini's regime as an archetypal 'demagogic plutocracy'. His difficulty was that he had ruled out the very possibility of realising the regime he most desired – a free-market economy combined with a liberal state.

Mosca also criticised the transformist politics of the pre- and post-war liberal administrations but his analysis was quite different. He attributed elite power to societal and organisational rather than purely psychological factors. A ruling class dominated not only because they posed the personal qualities necessary for leadership in a given society but also, and 'more important and less observed', because 'an organised minority, which acts in a co-ordinated manner, always triumphs over a disorganised minority, which has neither will, nor impulse, nor action in common'.[128] The problem with mass electoral politics was not elitism *per se* but its favouring a certain kind of elite.

Mosca believed in the traditional liberal parliamentary ideal of impartial, reasoned debate amongst independent, educated representatives. Unlike Le Bon, he denied that parliaments necessarily operated with the logic of the crowd. Far from being

> a 'mob', in the sense of a haphazard inorganic assemblage of human beings [...] they contain many men of long experience of public affairs, who are thereby safeguarded against any harm that might result to less well-balanced brains from an overardent or ravishing eloquence.[129]

The difficulty was ensuring that such 'men' were indeed represented. Hitherto, this system had relied on a particular political class, the landed gentry. In his view, they had possessed both the intellectual qualities needed to administer a modern state and, most crucially, sufficient economic independence to devote themselves to public service out of a sense of duty rather than as a living.[130] Somewhat naively, he assumed they had no sectional interests of their own to promote that might conflict with those of the public at large. Yet they were a declining group and he looked to the professional middle classes as a potential replacement. A role he adopted personally, combining an academic with a political career as a deputy from 1909–1919 and a senator thereafter, including serving as under-secretary in the Colonial office from 1914–16, he was nonetheless all too conscious that his fellow politicians rarely lived up to his high ideals.[131] Thus, his aim was to identify the reasons for the poor quality of the contemporary elite and to seek possible remedies that might motivate them in ways he saw as more appropriate.

---

128. Mosca, 'Sulla teorica dei governi e sul governo rappresentativo', p. 34; *see*, too, *The Ruling Class*, pp. 50–3.

129. Mosca, *The Ruling Class*, p. 257.

130. *Ibid.*, p. 144.

131. *Ibid.*, pp. 269–70.

Mosca believed a major obstacle to reform arose from misconceptions about the nature of democracy. He argued that elites could not rule by force alone. They needed the moral legitimacy provided by a 'political formula', such as the divine right of kings or popular sovereignty, to obtain the willing co-operation of the ruled.[132] Formulas did not require any 'scientific' basis, they merely had to be accepted. However, unlike Pareto, he regarded the roots of such acceptance to be social rather than psychological. Formulas had to be appropriate to the social context in which they were employed but were not socially determined. More than one formula might be viable in any society, though not all formulas would be. In a mass society, democracy and socialism had great appeal since they offered the prospect of government by and for the people. Mosca hoped to weaken their attraction to bourgeois intellectuals in particular by providing a 'positivist' analysis of these two 'metaphysical' systems, which revealed how they enhanced rather than limited elite power.[133]

Mosca observed how in mass democracies 'the electors do not elect the Deputy, but usually the Deputy has himself elected by the electors'.[134] Universal suffrage favoured the prime factor fostering elite domination: the superiority of an organised minority over a mass of isolated individuals. Voters could not pick candidates at will from amongst themselves or propose whatever policies they pleased; within a mass electorate individual efforts were insufficient to obtain a hearing or galvanise support. As a result, the political agenda, including who might stand for election, was set by groups possessing an organisational and positional advantage: particularly parties and other political organisations; influential individuals – especially the very wealthy;[135] and incumbent governments and their appointees.[136] Instead of being constrained by popular democracy, powerful interest groups were favoured by it. The result was a clientelistic political system concerned with the trading of favours rather than disinterested deliberation on the common good. Political success now called for 'moral cowardice, lack of a sense of justice, cunning, intrigue' rather than 'independence of character, boldness and impartiality'.[137]

Mosca had initially thought the best remedy for these failings was to limit democracy. He opposed the extensions of the franchise to all adult men and women in 1912 and suggested the senate and executive be royal appointees, in order to weaken the power of the legislature. However, he regretfully acknowledged these measures were unlikely to command much support. Consequently, he turned to how democracy might limit itself. This possibility arose from his doctrine of 'juridical defence', which he began developing as early as the first edition of

132. *Ibid.*, pp. 70–2.

133. *Ibid.*, pp. 325–8.

134. Mosca, 'Sulla teorica dei governi e sul governo rappresentativo', p. 275; *The Ruling Class*, p. 154.

135. What Mosca called 'Grand Electors'.

136. Mosca, *The Ruling Class*, p.155.

137. Mosca, 'Sulla teorica dei governi e sul governo rappresentativo', p. 284.

his *Elements of Political Science*, in 1896. 'Juridical defence' consisted of the mechanisms which promoted the 'moral discipline' of people's selfish interests and hence their respect for government by law.[138] Such discipline originated from 'the reciprocal restraint of human individuals', making people 'better, not by destroying their wicked instincts, but by accustoming the individual to tame them'.[139] Mosca thought the ruling class was broader than simply the rulers – it consisted of all politically active and capable individuals. An effective form of 'juridical defence' not only established checks and balances between the governed and the governing class but also (and most crucially) between the various levels and sections of the ruling class. This system involved more than the establishment of legal constitutional constraints. Social and political power had to be dispersed in such a way that no one group monopolised them all. As he put it, the most important (and only practical) demand

> to make of a political system is that all social values shall have a part in it, and that it shall find a place for all who possess any of the qualities which determine what prestige and what influence an individual, or a class, is to have.[140]

To preserve liberty and obtain the rule of those best suited to any given task, no single political principle or class should dominate and dictate access to all sources of influence. He believed this pluralist argument provided the rationale not only for the separation of church and state but also for a division between polity and economy and, within the state, between the bureaucracy and the government, as well as a measure of decentralisation.

A pure or ideal democracy tended to ignore the need for 'juridical defence', centralising all power in the hands of an elite chosen by the single method of popular sovereignty. He criticised socialism as leading to just this situation. He thought it natural for people to believe the remedy for democracy alone not producing political equality lay with introducing economic equality via the collective ownership of the means of production. Yet, as he presciently saw, this measure could only lead to despotism. For it gave the Party elite a monopoly of both economic and political (including ideological and military) power.[141] However, within a social system in which there were many sources of influence, democracy could be redefined as a mechanism for fostering 'reciprocal restraint'. The key was to obtain a mix of different social classes and levels of political power, whilst improving the calibre of representatives. Whereas 'pure' democracy suggested rule by whoever obtained the support of the majority, he suggested democratic procedures might be compatible with different electoral systems for the senate and the lower house and strong local government in order to create counterweights to

---

138. Mosca, *The Ruling Class*, p. 126.

139. *Ibid*, p. 127.

140. Mosca, *ibid.*, p. 258.

141. Mosca, *ibid.*, p. 144.

the power of the executive with its base in the Chamber of Deputies. He developed this thesis in the second edition of the *Elements* published in 1923, the year after Mussolini's March on Rome. He maintained that social and political institutions should be designed to secure a balance between the 'aristocratic' and 'democratic' 'tendencies' within society, creating a ruling class open to below yet reasonably secure and able to perpetuate itself. Likewise, government should combine 'liberal' and 'autocratic' 'principles' to allow effective yet limited rule. The present danger lay in the combination of the democratic tendency with autocratic principles, whereby a popularly elected leader could claim absolute power.

Thus, Mosca moved from being a critic of mass democracy to defending liberal against socialist democracy. In certain respects a precursor of contemporary pluralist as well as elite theories of democracy, he was ultimately pessimistic about the former being realised in ways that might moderate the malign effects of the latter. He recognised the mechanisms he associated with 'juridical defence' would only work in propitious social conditions. In particular, he thought it necessary to have a middle class that was large enough to provide a check on both the masses and the wealthy and which could supply rivals for office who would check each other. Yet this very stratum had been decimated by the First World War and economically impoverished by the slump that had followed. That left the mass vulnerable to plutocrats and demagogues. An opponent of fascism, his worst-case scenario – democratic autocracy – was epitomised by Mussolini.

Democratic autocracy or competitive elite democracy

Mosca's dilemma was that the contemporary critique of mass democracy appeared to make democratic autocracy inevitable. To defend democracy in the terms established by the new science of politics, the elite manipulation of the masses had somehow to be made a virtue rather than a fatal flaw. This quandary is clear in the contrast between the political writings of Robert Michels and Max Weber. Both thinkers offered brilliant syntheses of the three components of mass democracy explored above – the view of the mass as an irrational crowd, the account of parties as electoral machines, and the theory of elites in their case with Germany joining Italy, France, Britain and America as the backdrop to their reasoning. Notwithstanding their common reference points and mutual influence, however, they diverged over whether democracy was futile or had to be radically rethought. Once again, these differences not only reflect contrasting ideological standpoints but also indicate how narrowly scientific and psychological approaches provided less room for rethinking democracy than more historical and organisational analyses.

By contrast to the thinkers surveyed so far, Michels began as a socialist and committed democrat. As a syndicalist activist in Germany, he had been critical of the SPD's preoccupation with 'organisation for its own sake' and its leaders' tendency to treat the party as a means to secure their own position rather than to further the revolutionary cause. However, he attributed this trend to German conditions, notably the SPD's fear of being disbanded and Germany's military and bureaucratic culture, and had not despaired of radicalising the party. His conversion to elite theory occurred after 1907 when, having been refused his 'habilitation' in Germany because of his socialist sympathies, he was helped by Weber to obtain a post in Turin. Mosca had moved there four years earlier and was to exert an important influence over his new colleague. Michels now came to regard the shortcomings of German Social Democracy as exemplifying a more universal process of elite circulation and the propensity of organisations to reinforce oligarchy.[142]

In developing this thesis in his classic study of *Political Parties*,[143] Michels drew on and synthesised various aspects of the theories examined thus far.[144] From Pareto, he took the argument that beliefs reflect certain basic 'sentiments'. He dropped both his earlier faith in the power of rational argument in favour of the socialist cause and the Marxist view that ideologies and political forms could be related to changes in the economic structure. Instead, he focused on regularities of human behaviour that were allegedly the same in all times and places. However, he also went back to Sighele, Tarde and Le Bon (who published the French edition of his book), to argue that these psychological traits reflected differences between the masses and their leaders, with the one being subject to suggestion in the manner of a crowd and the other able to influence them through their eloquence, energy and boldness.[145] From Mosca he took the thesis that party organisation fostered the growth of an elite capable of running it – as he pithily put it: 'Who says organisation says oligarchy'.[146] Moreover, organisation was inevitable. Weber had encouraged Michels to read Bryce on American 'machine' politics,[147] a source he supplemented with Ostrogorski's volumes. Developing certain of Weber's views on bureaucracy, Michels argued that large groups of people needed organising if their activities were to be co-ordinated, especially when they performed the diverse tasks involved in modern societies characterised by the division of labour. Yet, running an organisation was itself a specialised task that required technical expertise, separating the leaders from the mass. Organisations also fostered conservatism and the more general tendency for new groups to assimilate to and rejuvenate existing elites, rather than simply replacing them. Whilst Pareto and Mosca had feared the ousting of the bourgeoisie by a revolutionary elite, Michels argued that a revolutionary oligarchy proved a contradiction in terms. For it grew out of the creation of an organisation that would necessarily move the leadership away from their socialist principles.

142. D. Beetham, 'From socialism to fascism: the relation between theory and practice in the work of Robert Michels. I. From Marxist revolutionary to political sociologist', *Political Studies* 25, 1977, pp. 3–24.

143. Published in 1911, first English translation 1915.

144. D. Beetham, 'Michels and his critics', *Archives européennes de sociologie* 22, 1981, pp. 81–99, p. 82.

145. R. Michels, *Political Parties: A sociological study of the oligarchical tendencies of modern democracy*, [1912], New York, 1959, pp. 24–5.

146. *Ibid.*, pp. 401, 32.

147. L. Scaff, 'Max Weber and Robert Michels', *American Journal of Sociology* 86, 1981, p. 1279.

Michels now thought democracy not so much a sham as vain. The psychological and organisational elements of his argument reinforced each other. However idealistic, leaders would find themselves unable to overcome either the 'profound need' of the masses 'to prostrate themselves' before some outstanding figure,[148] or the manner in which power begets power.[149] Neither oligarchy nor the subjection of the masses could be overcome, for

> The formation of oligarchies within the various forms of democracy is the outcome of organic necessity [...] the objective immaturity of the mass is not a mere transitory phenomenon which will disappear with the progress of democratisation [...] it derives from the very nature of the mass as mass [...] because the mass *per se* is amorphous, and therefore needs division of labour, specialisation, and guidance.[150]

In *Political Parties*, Michels hoped that the very striving to realise the ideal of democracy, while doomed to failure, might still serve the useful purpose of enhancing the criticism and control of elites, seeing the 'great task' of social education as the raising of 'the intellectual level of the masses' to enable them 'within the limits of what is possible, to counteract the oligarchical tendencies of the working class movement'.[151] Ultimately, though, Michels found it impossible to follow Mosca in rethinking democracy as a mechanism for selecting and controlling elites. He remained true to his revolutionary past in regarding anything but a radically participatory form of democracy as no democracy. Residual left-wing prejudices also partly explain his overestimation of the established elites capacity to absorb outsiders and his assumption that organisation must always produce conservative results.[152] The collapse of the old order with the First World War and the Bolshevik revolution of 1917 were to explode both these beliefs, with Lenin and, especially, Gramsci drawing very different conclusions from the elitist literature to argue that organisation and elite leadership were crucial to a revolutionary party's success.[153] Of course, Michels could not be expected to foresee these developments, though Pareto, for one, had acknowledged they were likely if social circumstances meant that elite replacement could only occur through revolutionary action.[154] Radical biases apart, what inhibited his contemplating such scenarios as even logical possibilities were the psychological qualities he attributed to leaders and masses, whereby the leaders' sense of their own superiority

---

148. Michels, *Political Parties*, p. 67.

149. *Ibid.*, pp 205–9.

150. *Ibid.*, pp. 402, 404.

151. *Ibid.*, p. 407.

152. *Ibid.*, pp 304–7.

153. V. I. Lenin, *What is to be Done?*, [1902], trans. S. V. and P. Utechin, Oxford, 1963; V Gerratana (ed.), A. Gramsci, *Quaderni del carcere*, 4 vols., Turin, 1977, pp. 1733–4; R. Bellamy and D. Schecter, *Gramsci and the Italian State*, Manchester, 1993, pp. 132–3.

154. Pareto, *Les systèmes socialistes*, pp. 34–41.

and desire to dominate were reinforced by not only organisational factors but also the apathy and susceptibility of the masses to emotional manipulation.[155] In this account, the mass played no independent role apart from the elites who controlled them. Believing that only charismatic leadership could transcend organisational conservatism and mobilise the masses, Michels ended up supporting Mussolini.[156] Thus, elite theory transformed Michels's socialist critique into an argument for fascism as a 'scientific' necessity.[157]

Weber had encouraged Michels' study of the SPD.[158] Though he shared many of his prejudices about the masses, however, he evaluated the role played by elites and organisations in controlling them quite differently. Like Michels' analysis, Weber's can also be viewed as a synthesis of the theorists examined earlier.[159] But unlike his younger compatriot, he was not a disillusioned democrat. His concern was with the broader issue of power and its legitimation, effective use and control. Meanwhile, he regarded Michels' psychological emphasis as un-sociological, turning his attention to the role of socially produced organisational factors. Both these differences can partly be related to Weber's desire for a 'scientific' account, purged of the researcher's ideological assumptions.[160] Yet it would be wrong to infer from these criticisms of Michels that he aimed at a 'value-free' and purely 'descriptive' account of mass democracy – merely that fact and value had to be clearly distinguished. Values might simply be matters of personal choice rather than fact but the likelihood of their being realised could be empirically assessed. Weber's own interest was in the 'human type' a particular set of social relations gave rise to.[161] Taking both elite rule and mass democracy as inevitable, his focus centred on the type of leadership different sorts of democratic organisation of the masses were likely to promote.[162]

Weber followed Le Bon in seeing the masses as a feature of modern societies and the social levelling produced by the spread of markets, industrialisation and bureaucracy.[163] Even autocratic Germany had become a mass state, responsive to mass social and welfare concerns and the need for mass armies, for example. He denounced the Prussian three-class suffrage as not only socially untenable but

155. Michels, *Political Parties*, pp. 205–14.

156. R. Michels, *Corso di sociologia politica*, Milan, 1927.

157. Beetham, 'From socialism to fascism [...]'.

158. Scaff 'Max Weber and Robert Michels'; W. J. Mommsen, *The Political and Social Theory of Max Weber*, Cambridge, 1989, ch. 6.

159. D. Beetham, 'Mosca, Pareto and Weber: a historical comparison', in W. Mommsen and J. Oster-hammel (eds), *Max Weber and his Contemporaries*, London, 1987, pp. 139–58.

160. Scaff, 'Max Weber and Robert Michels', pp. 1275–78.

161. M. Weber, 'The meaning of "ethical neutrality" in sociology and economics', [1917], in E. Shils and H. Finch (eds), *Max Weber on the Methodology of the Social Sciences*, Illinois, 1949, p. 27.

162. R. Bellamy, *Liberalism and Modern Society: An historical argument*, Cambridge, 1992, pp.194–216.

163. D. Beetham, *Max Weber and the Theory of Modern Politics*, Cambridge, 1985, pp. 103–5; M. Weber, *Economy and Society*, G. Roth and C. Wittich (eds), 2 vols., Berkeley, 1978a, pp. 983–4.

politically so, given that modern state institutions presupposed equality of status – not least for military service. Indeed, he saw political equality as offering an all-important counterweight to market-produced social inequalities and as a source of national unity.[164] However, Weber also shared Le Bon's view of the mass as irrational and, as such, incapable of social action.[165] Moreover, the mass was not a social class but a condition of many members of modern societies. Emotional and imitative, concerned only with the short term, the mass were passive unless stirred up by outside stimuli. As such, they were easily swayed by demagogues. Reinforcing this tendency to demagogy was the elitist theory of the 'law of the small number', with which Weber also agreed. Yet, unlike many of the other theorists examined so far, Weber did not see these trends as necessarily destructive of democracy, so long as they were linked to certain forms of party organisation. For, he argued, mob rule and the 'democracy of the streets' were products of 'the unorganised mass', 'strongest in countries with either a powerless or a politically discredited parliament, that means above all, in countries without *rationally organised parties*'.[166] Far from undermining democracy, party organisation made it possible.

In elaborating this thesis, Weber proceeded to reverse Ostrogorski's argument. In a mass age, machine politics was inevitable.[167] Individuals no longer had the resources to wage election campaigns. Professionals were needed to raise the funds and provide the bureaucratic support needed for mass electioneering. Yet a consequence of the growth of parties was to organise the mass, constraining their mob tendencies, and to enhance not just the influence but potentially also the qualities of political leaders. Weber agreed with Ostrogorski that modern campaigning required different political skills to the notable politics of the eighteenth and early nineteenth centuries. As Ostrogorski had noted, politicians and party workers now lived 'off' rather than 'for' politics. Party bosses placed electoral success above principle, effective propaganda and campaign finance before a good argument, while party leaders had to be charismatic crowd-pleasers rather than public-spirited and independent.[168] However, he noted how the new politics nonetheless gave the mass an indirect influence on decision-making that ensured their interests were taken into account. Like Mosca, Weber argued the mass, being passive and unorganised, were recruited by politicians rather than choosing them for themselves. But to win their support, parties had to respond to their concerns. The mass might not know which economic policies were best for

---

164. M. Weber, 'Suffrage and democracy in Germany', [1917], in P. Lassman and R. Speirs (eds), *Political Writings*, trans. R. Speirs, Cambridge, 1994, pp. 80–129, pp. 87, 103–6.

165. P. Baehr, 'The "masses" in Weber's political sociology', *Economy and Society* 19, 1990, pp. 242–65; M. Weber, 'Parliament and government in a reconstructed Germany', [1918], in *Economy and Society*, appendix 2, vol. II, pp. 1459e60.

166. Weber, 'Parliament and government in a reconstructed Germany', p. 1460.

167. Weber, 'The profession and vocation of politics', pp. 318–22, 338–48.

168. Weber 'Parliament and government in a reconstructed Germany', pp. 1450, 1459; Weber, 'The profession and vocation of politics', pp. 342–3.

the country but they could feel the effects of bad policies and had the negative power to reject poor governments.[169] In addition to being charismatic, therefore, leaders had to be decisive and effective.

The crucial element behind Weber's argument was that there should be party competition. Since Weber was preoccupied with domination rather than democracy *per se*, he wished to ensure there were countervailing sources of power. Just as the efficiency and prevention of monopolies within the economy depended on market competition between firms and the entrepreneurs and managers who ran them, so the political system required the electoral contest between parties to ensure that only those politicians with a capacity for charismatic and effective leadership rose to the top.[170] Though Weber never cited Mosca's work, one can presume he knew of it – if only indirectly through Michels – he shared the Italian's view of democracy as a system of checks and balances. For example, he regarded the average MP operated as little more than lobby fodder, yet he saw parliament – especially the committee system – as capable of forcing both leaders and the administration to justify their policies through debate, curbing executive authority in the process.[171] Likewise, he saw the political system as itself a counterbalance to both the economy and bureaucracy, similarly regarding the danger of socialism being the Party's monopoly of economic and bureaucratic power.[172]

Weber's engagement with contemporary German politics runs through his analysis. Indeed, much of his argument emerged from a discussion of 'Parliament and government in a reconstructed Germany'.[173] He compared German leaders unfavourably to the British during the First World War and thought the political immaturity of the German middle class, the over-bureaucratisation of the state, the cartelisation of the German economy and the mob-like interventions of the German masses could be explained, in part, by the absence under the Kaiser's regime of either a genuine electoral contest for power or effective parliamentary scrutiny of the executive. As he put it: 'In Germany we have *demagoguery* and the pressure of the rabble *without democracy*, or rather *because of the absence* of an orderly democracy'.[174] Nevertheless, some commentators have seen his emphasis on leadership as having unwittingly prepared the ground for Hitler's democratic seizure of power, aligning him in this and other respects with Carl Schmitt.[175] Yet Weber did not share Schmitt's decisionism or his anti-parliamentarism.[176] Though

---

169. Weber, 'Parliament and government in a reconstructed Germany', pp. 1456–7.

170. Weber, *Economy and Society*, p. 288.

171. Weber, 'Parliament and government in a reconstructed Germany', pp. 1452–53; Weber, 'The profession and vocation of politics', pp. 309–69, p. 343.

172. M. Weber, 'Socialism' [1918], in *Political Writings*, P. Lassman and R. Speirs (eds), trans. R. Speirs, Cambridge, 1994, pp. 272–303.

173. Weber, 'Parliament and government in a reconstructed Germany'.

174. *Ibid*, p. 1451.

175. W. Mommsen, *Max Weber and German Politics 1890–1920*, New York, 1967, ch. 10.

176. Schmitt, *The Concept of the Political*; C. Schmitt, *The Crisis of Parliamentary Democracy*, trans. E. Kennedy, Cambridge, Mass, 1985; R. Bellamy, *Rethinking Liberalism*, London, 2000, ch. 4.

he regarded the liberal democratic virtues of rational and responsible decision-making as historically contingent practices that could never be exercised by the masses, his aim was to provide an environment in which elites would adopt them in ways that benefited the populace at large. Leadership involved 'a feeling of responsibility and a sense of proportion' as well as charisma and 'passion', the 'ethic of responsibility' as well as the 'ethics of conviction'.[177] However, his reworking of democracy and liberalism deprived them of any intrinsic substantive value. In Weber's view, democracy does not promote the popular formulation of and allegiance to the public interest. Rather, it offers a mechanism whereby elites can manipulate the masses and, through competing with each other for their support, provide mutual checks that promote the selection of suitable political leaders. By allowing rulers to be popularly removed when they fail, electoral competition ensured they responded, at least indirectly, to the interests of the ruled. Liberalism no longer concerns the equal rights of individuals so much as responsible leadership that guides, but does not subvert, efficient administration and the due process of law.

Epilogue

The rethinking of democracy that culminated in Weber essentially reversed the priorities of classical democratic theory, turning the democratic process from a means whereby the ruled control their rulers into a mechanism for legitimating and improving the quality of control exercised by rulers over the ruled. As we have seen, the crucial factor was electoral competition between elites to win the right to rule. To quote Joseph Schumpeter's celebrated redefinition, democracy was now 'that institutional arrangement for arriving at political decisions by means of a competitive struggle for the people's vote'.[178] With various elaborations, Schumpeter's popularisation of Weber's synthesis was to be accepted for the next twenty years by a majority of American and European political scientists and theorists as a realistic account of what liberal democracy could attain in mass conditions.[179]

In effect, the social attitudes and historical conditions of the 1890s–1930s had become scientifically codified so as to circumscribe the normative and practical scope of democracy.[180] Post-war analysts of the democratic process simply took as read all three elements of the 'modern theory of democracy' traced above – from the nature of the masses, to the role of parties and elites in organising and directing them. Thus, the chief constraint upon and danger to democracy was

---

177. Weber, 'The profession and vocation of politics', pp. 309–69, pp. 352–3, 357–68.

178. J. A. Schumpeter, *Capitalism, Socialism and Democracy*, [1942], London, 1976, p. 269 and, more generally, *see* chs 21–2.

179. P. Bachrach, *The Theory of Democratic Elitism*, Boston, 1967; G. Parry, *Political Elites*, London, 1969.

180. Bellamy, *Rethinking Liberalism*, ch. 5.

deemed to be the mass character of modern society. The rise of totalitarian regimes was attributed to the pathological characteristics of unorganised, amorphous masses and their susceptibility to the extremist and emotive rhetoric of charismatic leaders.[181] Consequently, the insulation of elites from mass pressure was deemed crucial to avoiding the temptations of populist demagoguery.[182] Democratic stability depended on keeping voters passive and even indifferent to politics by organising them within the party system.[183]

Theorists now put their efforts into developing the democratic elitism of Mosca, Weber and Schumpeter in order to explain what incentives existed for elites to compete effectively in the absence of an informed and active electorate.[184] This new generation of democratic elitists argued that the 'mass' tendencies of modern societies could be counterposed by 'pluralist' tendencies originating from the enhanced differentiation and diversity accompanying the spread of the division of labour.[185] As a result, there were a plurality of elites whose power rested on different social sources, such as wealth, technical expertise and community following, and who could influence different sorts of issues and sections of society. Consequently, no single elite could monopolise all forms of power and so dominate society.[186] Provided all adults possessed a vote and there were regularly held, free and fair elections, elites would be forced to compete for support from amongst a plurality of groups holding a variety of different sorts of interests. Rather than appealing through populist rhetoric to a mass majority, they would have to construct a coalition of different minorities. Elites would be obliged to bargain and collaborate with each other, with the public interest emerging from mutually beneficial compromises. Such bargaining was further facilitated by most people belonging to more than one group, mixing with different sets of people at work, in their church, with their families and so on. These cross-cutting cleavages prevented societies becoming polarised between different classes or sectional interests, allowing a consensus around certain core democratic values to emerge. Though these pluralist theorists granted that political resources are unevenly distributed, so that certain elites and interests can mobilise more easily and effectively than others, they tended to downplay the effects of this inequality for the political agenda and remained unconcerned by low levels of political

181. K. Mannheim, *Diagnosis of our Time*, London, 1943, p. 1; H. Arendt, *Origins of Totalitarianism*, New York, 1951, pp. 310–11; W. Kornhauser, *The Politics of Mass Society*, Glencoe, 1959, pp. 14–15; S. M. Lipset, *Political Man*, Glencoe, 1960, p. 109.

182. W. Kornhauser, *The Politics of Mass Society*, Glencoe, 1959, pp. 59–60, 64, 99, G. Sartori, *Democratic Theory*, New York, 1962, p. 119.

183. B. Berelson *et al.*, *Voting*, Chicago, 1954, pp. 25–6.

184. J. Plamenatz, 'Electoral studies and democratic theory', *Political Studies* 6, 1958, pp. 1–9.

185. W. Kornhauser, *The Politics of Mass Society*, Glencoe, 1959, p. 13; R. A. Dahl, *Who Governs? Democracy and power in an American city*, New Haven, CT, 1961, pp. 85–6.

186. Dahl, *Who Governs?*, p. 228.

involvement or interest.[187] Mass mobilisation was 'unnecessary' given that elite competition was sufficient to ensure minorities obtained a hearing.[188]

However, critics noted how Pareto often seemed a better guide than Mosca to the dynamics of elite rivalry and the sorts of interests they were likely to promote and attend to.[189] For example, significant economic interest groups have decided advantages in accessing elites. They can employ professional lobbyists, offer financial support at elections and exercise various indirect kinds of influence – such as threatening to invest elsewhere in the case of business, or to hold a strike in the case of unions. As Pareto noted, such groups may employ public-interest rhetoric but it often covers self-interested activity of a rent-seeking kind, as when businesses justify incentive-giving tax cuts on the grounds that the economy as a whole will benefit. Because such groups frequently use intermediaries, their role in decision-making may not be immediately evident. Far from fostering democracy, however, their activities can profoundly distort the political agenda in ways that undermine it. By contrast, other kinds of minority interest may not be considered by competing leaders if political elites fear that courting them will alienate other groups or they lack the standing or finance to gain entry to the political establishment.[190] In these cases, voter apathy may signify not content with the system but alienation from it and their difficulties in organising themselves in ways suited to exploiting the established channels. Their only alternative may be mass mobilisation and forms of protest that take them outside the formal political process, as occurred with the civil rights, anti-Vietnam, feminist and other movements from the 1960s.

These new social movements inspired some theorists to argue against the elite democracy thesis for the possibility of more participatory forms of politics.[191] They revealed the mass to operate in a more strategic and rational manner than the elite theorists had allowed, while being quite different to ordinary interest groups.[192] Even when focused on a single issue, as with the peace and green movements, or a particular group, as with the feminist and civil rights movements, their arguments have been generally framed in terms of universal principles, such as human rights, equality or some public good, rather than private interests. Instead of relying solely on professional lobbying, with ordinary members being largely passive funders of such activities, these movements have engaged in more participatory

187. *Ibid.*, pp. 80–1.

188. N. Polsby, *Community Power and Political Theory*, New Haven, CT., 1963, pp. 118–20.

189. P. Bachrach, *The Theory of Democratic Elitism*, Boston, 1967; G. Parry, *Political Elites*, London, 1969.

190. P. Bachrach and M. S. Baratz, 'The two faces of power', *American Political Science Review* 56, 1962, pp. 947–52.

191. G. Duncan, and S. Lukes, 'The new democracy', *Political Studies* 11, 1963, pp. 156–77; P. Bachrach, *The Theory of Democratic Elitism*, Boston, 1967.

192. R. J. Dalton, and M. Küchler (eds), *Challenging the Political Order: New social and political movements in Western democracies*, Cambridge, 1990; T. N. Clarke and M. Rempel, *Citizen Politics in Post-Industrial Societies: Interest groups transformed*, Boulder, CO, 1997.

activities, such as demonstrations. In so doing, they have challenged both the prevailing political consensus and the existing boundaries of institutional politics, drawing attention to the issues and groups they exclude.[193] Conservative critics raised fears that such 'unconventional' political activism produce 'excessive' demands that risk 'overloading' and over-extending government. They enlisted the standard critiques of mass politics to condemn these movements as 'deviant' and 'unreasonable', re-invoking the elite theory of democracy as a solution to the ensuing 'crisis'.[194] However, this negative characterisation has found little if any support in studies of the new politics. Like earlier elite theorists, these critics have overlooked, or in some cases been positively antagonistic to, the ways mass movements of this kind have worked to promote democracy. For example, in the late nineteenth and early twentieth centuries they were responsible for the political inclusion and continued involvement of both workers and women and, in the late twentieth century, for addressing the limitations of state-based politics with regard to tackling issues of global justice. Indeed, scholars have shown how even violent protests by so-called mobs are frequently calculated, reasonable, organised, free from demagogic manipulation and motivated by democratic ideals.[195] Far from threatening democracy, therefore, the various forms of non-institutional politics have often indicated a frustration with the democratic limitations of the party political elites – a disillusionment reflected in both the generally declining party membership and the growing dissatisfaction with politicians found within advanced industrial societies.[196]

The loss of a mass base deprives parties of a vital source of democratic idealism. Without it, they risk developing many of the failings anti-democratic elite theorists feared, becoming increasingly dominated by professional managers and reliant on the support of well organised and financed pressure groups and individuals, without acquiring the capacity for leading public opinion or framing the public interest that was hoped for by the democratic elitists. Therefore, in stressing the need for formal politics to connect to the campaigning and more participatory mass movements most relevant to peoples lives, Ostrogorski, the outsider within this chapter's story, may well prove to be not a nostalgic throwback to the nineteenth century so much as a model for how politics needs to evolve in the twenty-first.

---

193. C. Offe, 'Challenging the boundaries of institutional politics: social movements since the 1960s', in C. Maier (ed.), *Changing the Boundaries of the Political*, Cambridge, 1987.

194. M. Crozier, S. P. Huntington and J. Watanuki, *The Crisis of Democracy: Report on the governability of democracies to the Trilateral Commission*, New York, 1975.

195. E. Canetti, *Crowds and Power*, [1960], New York, 1978; G. Rudé, *The Crowd in History, 1730–1848*, [1964], London, 1981; E. P. Thompson, 'The moral economy of the English crowd in the eighteenth century', *Past and Present* 50, 1971, pp. 76–136; C. Tilly, 'Collective violence in European perspective', in H. D. Graham and T. R. Gurr (eds), *Violence in America: Historical and comparative perspectives*, London, 1979.

196. R. J. Dalton, *Citizen Politics: Public opinion and political parties in advanced western democracies*, Chatham, NJ, 1996.

Chapter Thirteen

Which Socialism? Bobbio on Marxism, Socialism and Democracy

Norberto Bobbio's *Which Socialism?* challenges socialists to reconsider the relationship between democracy and socialism.[1] The two are often assumed, on the left at least, to be inextricably linked yet, on closer examination, the connection between them contains a number of ambiguities. Theorists of both left and right have wanted to distinguish socialist democracy from liberal-democratic political systems; the view held by proponents of the free-market economy that socialist planning is incompatible with individual freedom[2] being apparently mirrored in Lenin's famous assertion that the 'democratic republic is the best possible shell for capitalism'.[3] Many socialists have traditionally contended that whilst 'bourgeois democracy' supports capitalism, 'true democracy' between social and political equals only arises once vast differences in economic power have been curtailed through public ownership of the means of production. They assert that democracy amounts to more than a means for making decisions but must be identified with the yet-to-be-realised socialist goal, when its nature will be so transformed as to make the liberal guarantees of individual rights and political liberties redundant.

Bobbio disputes this neat solution to the question of the relations between socialism, capitalism and democracy, claiming that it encourages a misplaced hostility to liberal rights among socialist, and particularly Marxist, theorists. He contends that concentration on an essentially unworkable goal for socialism, in which so-called 'bourgeois' freedoms are unnecessary, has seriously weakened socialist political practice. Arguing against the Marxist conception of politics, largely represented in Italy by the Italian Communist Party (PCI), he maintains that we must rethink the socialist end in ways compatible with the preservation of the liberal means. He therefore poses socialists with a problem not just about what style of politics to adopt but equally as to which socialism to aim for.

---

1. This chapter formed the introduction to the English translation of N. Bobbio, *Quale socialismo?*, Einaudi, 1976.

2. *See*, e.g. M. Friedman, *Capitalism and Freedom*, Chicago, University of Chicago Press, 1962.

3. Although the classic argument is Lenin's in 'State and revolution' (*Collected Works*, vol. 25, Lawrence & Wishart, London, 1969, p. 393), both Kautsky and Luxemburg (who disagreed with Soviet practice) held similar views about the transformation of politics under communism. For a full discussion of these issues *see* C. Pierson, *Marxist Theory and Democratic Politics*, Polity Press, Cambridge, 1986, chs 2 and 3. This argument was also used by Bobbio's critics, as we shall see.

Bobbio's book consists of a number of articles written between 1973 and 1976, to which various other writings dating from 1968 to 1978 have been added for the English edition.[4] Four themes run through them:

1. An examination of Marxist writings on the state, democracy and the transition to socialism.
2. An evaluation of the special contribution of Gramsci to this tradition.
3. An implied critique of the strategy of the PCI.
4. The rethinking of socialism in liberal-democratic terms.

I shall examine each of these themes in turn below, referring in the final section to the debate Bobbio's arguments aroused in Italy.

'State' and 'civil society'

Bobbio's analysis of Marxist politics centres on his examination of the concepts of state and civil society and the important innovation brought about by Marx with respect to the liberal usage of these terms.[5] According to Bobbio, the concept of politics found in the natural-law tradition of Hobbes, Locke, Rousseau and Kant turns upon a crucial distinction they made, albeit in different ways, between natural and civil society, the latter including (or being co-extensive with) political society.

Hegel broke with this line of reasoning by downgrading civil society to the status of a pre-political society distinct from the state. In performing this operation Hegel continued and united two trends within modern political thought. The first, deriving from realist theories of politics such as Hobbes' and Machiavelli's, conceived the state as a product of the rational calculation of self-interested individuals. The second, represented by Rousseau and Kant, saw the state 'as a product of reason, or as a rational society, the only one in which human beings can lead a life which conforms to reason, that is which conforms to their nature'.[6] Hegel's *Philosophy of Right* produced a synthesis and a transformation (in the Hegelian sense of *Aufhebung*) of these two processes, whereby the state was perceived as both the result of instrumental reason and as the construction of a rational society. Hegel situated the first element within civil society, for out of

---

4. The English edition, published as Norberto Bobbio, *Which Socialism? Marxism, Socialism and Democracy*, trans. Roger Griffin, ed. Richard Bellamy, Cambridge, Polity Press, 1987, contained four additional articles. The article on 'Gramsci and the conception of civil society', explored in the second and especially the third sections below, dates from 1968; all the others were presented at various conferences in the late 1970s.

5. Bobbio has provided an extensive consideration of this theme in a number of places: 'Gramsci and the conception of civil society' (translated in *Which Socialism?* pp. 139–61 – to which subsequent references to this article refer); 'Sulla nozione di "societa civile"', *De Homine 7*, 1968, pp. 19–36 and in the *Enciclopedia Einaudi*, reproduced in his *Stato, governo, societa*, Turin: Einaudi, 1985, pp. 23–42.

6. Bobbio, 'Gramsci and the conception of civil society', p. 139.

the *bellum omnium contra omnes* – which he identified not just with the state of nature but with the self-interested competition of capitalism as well – came only the compacts and agreements of the pre-state, for example private property rights and the law of contract. However, in contrast to the realist tradition, Hegel regarded these settlements as essentially unstable, emerging from the partial perspective of particular interests and hence liable to dissolve when these were not satisfied. Their inner rationale, as ethical norms providing the framework for a fully developed life, only came about in the state, understood in the second sense of Kant and Rousseau as a rational society.

Marx's conception of politics built upon a critique of Hegel's and both extended and simplified it. Commenting on his early critical re-examination of Hegelian philosophy, Marx recalled how it led him:

to the conclusion that neither legal relations nor political forms could be comprehended whether by themselves or on the basis of a so-called general development of the human mind, but that they originate in the material conditions of life, the totality of which Hegel [...] embraces within the term 'civil society', the anatomy of which, however, has to be sought in political economy.[7]

Marx followed Hegel in assimilating civil society to the natural society of the war of each against all, now transferred to the capitalist competition between egoistic producers. But he radicalised this description to assert that the agreements and principles of justice which regulated such relations had no other rationale than as a means of stabilising the class system of a given mode of production and social order. As a result, any attempt to treat these notions, as in the 'so-called *rights of man*', as universally valid principles applying to humanity as such were profoundly misconceived, for they 'are quite simply the rights of the member of civil society, i.e. of egoistic man, of man separated from other men and from the community'.[8]

As Bobbio and, more recently, Allen Buchanan and Steven Lukes have remarked, Marx was aided in drawing this inference from the somewhat narrow account of the circumstances giving rise to justice and morality in the natural jurisprudence tradition. Underlying the various theories of these precursors of liberal political thought was a highly conflictual model of human nature and the belief that these rules arose as mutually beneficial compromises for resolving inevitable disputes in conditions of relative scarcity.[9] Marx simply drew the natural conclusions from such premises with his characteristically relentless logic, commenting that in civil society therefore 'the only bond which holds [individuals]

---

7. K. Marx, 'Preface to a contribution to the critique of political economy', in *Early Writings*, trans. R. Livingstone and G. Benton, Harmondsworth: Penguin, 1975, p. 425.

8. K. Marx, 'On the Jewish question', in *Early Writings*, p. 229.

9. A. Buchanan, *Marxism and Justice: The radical critique of liberalism*, Methuen, London, 1982, pp. 162–3; S. Lukes, *Marxism and Morality*, Oxford University Press, Oxford, 1985, pp. 30–3.

together is natural necessity, need and private interest, the conservation of their property and their egoistic persons'.[10]

Marx maintained that the traditional liberal rights, together with the social system they support, arose from the material base of society. Following the 1793 Declaration, he identified them as the right to equality, liberty, security and property. For Marx, the 'right of man to liberty', interpreted in negative terms as 'the right to do and perform everything which does not harm others', 'is not based on the association of man with man but rather on the separation of man from man. It is the *right* of this separation.' This defence of freedom has its 'practical application' in the right to private property: 'the right to enjoy and dispose of one's resources as one wills, without regard for other men and independently of society: the right of self-interest'. So interpreted, rights lead 'each man to see in other men not the *realization* but the *limitations* of his own freedom'.[11]

The manner in which certain liberal theories of rights are explicitly linked to a justification of market exchanges and private appropriation regardless of the social, or even moral, costs involved undeniably provides good grounds for such criticisms.[12] But as a characterisation of rights *per se*, Marx's account is inadequate. For example, the right to liberty, outlined above, does not imply that all association with others will be harmful, so that only the individual 'restricted to himself' can be free. On the contrary, the doctrine, as classically interpreted by Mill, suggests that only a very few of the various activities we engage in harm others and warrant restriction. Marx's dovetailing of the right to freedom with private property seems equally strange, if we recall the Millian application of it to protect the political liberties of freedom of speech and assembly. Neither of these freedoms seem to have value solely for monadic, egoistic persons. Debate over issues such as censorship or euthanasia, for instance, involve rather more than the clash of egoistic wills – genuine differences concerning the nature of the good are of more importance. Nor does the right to freedom exclusively benefit the exercise of property rights even in societies based on private property. Thus libertarian thinkers, such as Nozick and Hayek, accept that a monopolist of vital resources, such as a water hole in a desert, may infringe the freedom of potential customers by charging excessively for it and thereby harming them.[13]

---

10. Marx, 'On the Jewish question', p. 230.

11. *Ibid.*, pp. 231–2.

12. See J. Dunn, *The Politics of Socialism: an essay in political theory*, Cambridge: Cambridge University Press, Cambridge, 1984, pp.4–5, for appropriate criticisms of Hayek and Nozick. As G. A. Cohen, 'Self-ownership, world-ownership, and equality: part II', in E. F. Paul *et al.* (eds), *Marxism and Liberalism*, Oxford: Basil Blackwell, 1986, pp. 78–80, has argued, libertarian arguments are especially damaging to Marxists because of the shared assumptions underlying their respective views of legitimate appropriation and the nature of rights. Even those seeking to defend Marx's position make analogous caveats to those given below, e.g. R. Keat, 'Liberal rights and socialism', in K. Graham (ed.), *Contemporary Political Philosophy: Radical studies*, Cambridge: Cambridge University Press, 1982, pp. 59–82.

13. F. Hayek, *The Constitution of Liberty*, London: Routledge & Kegan Paul, 1960, pp. 135–7; R. Nozick, *Anarchy, State and Utopia*, Oxford: Basil Blackwell, 1974, pp. 178–82.

Marx's frequently reiterated contention that the underlying cause and need for rights was the egoism and particularism of capitalist relations suggests the implied belief that they will be unnecessary in a society of selfless altruists. In itself this criterion is insufficient, since 'the road to hell is paved with good intentions' and a misinformed or misguided altruist could unwittingly inflict harm on others. The altruist may have both a different conception of the good to the recipients, or make unintentional mistakes about how best to achieve their well-being. Without perfect moral agreement and knowledge about all individuals' interests and the means of satisfying them, differences about the type of society and its management will arise and minorities may require rights to protect them from the paternalistic interference of the majority. Marx hoped to circumvent this problem by hypothesising that the super-productiveness of communist society would remove the need for such clashes.[14] Thus he sought to correct a pessimistic view of human nature with an over-optimistic account of life under communism, where a combination of altruism, abundant resources, maximum co-ordination and agreement concerning human interests would prevail.

The above considerations, recently expounded by a number of commentators, form a necessary preliminary to understanding Marx's view of the state – the main focus of Bobbio's criticisms. Bobbio argues that it was 'the antithesis to the tradition of natural law which culminated in Hegel'.[15] Hegel claimed that the state overcame the tensions within civil society by providing people with a proper understanding of the social relations governing their lives and reconciling them to abiding by the norms and customs necessary to achieve the common good. Marx objected that the Hegelian solution amounted to a confidence trick, a regressive and anachronistic attempt to bring civil society and the state together by returning to the organic harmony between the two characteristic of feudalism.[16] Under capitalism, state and society have become separated. The latter has returned to a Hobbesian condition of competing egoistic individuals motivated solely by self-referential passions and desires.[17] The state, rather than resolving this conflict, as Hegel believed, simply reflected it in transmuted form. The differentiated hierarchical political order of feudalism had given way to a concept of equal citizenship without 'distinctions based on *birth, rank, education* and *occupation*'.[18] Yet these distinctions retained their full force within society, with the result that:

> Where the political state has attained its full degree of development man leads a double life, a life in heaven and a life on earth, not only in his mind, in his consciousness, but in reality. He lives in the *political community*, where he

---

14. K. Marx, 'Critique of the Gotha Programme' in D. Fembach (ed.), *The First International and After*, Harmondsworth: Penguin, 1975, pp. 346–7.

15. Bobbio, 'Gramsci and the conception of civil society', p. 141.

16. K. Marx, 'Critique of Hegel's doctrine of the state', in *Early Writings*, p.145.

17. Marx, 'On the Jewish question', p. 221.

18. *Ibid.*, p. 219.

regards himself as a *communal being*, and in *civil society*, where he is active as a *private individual*, regards other men as means, debases himself to a means and becomes a plaything of alien powers.[19]

Although the modern state appeared to grant citizens equal rights and freedom, their exercise of these liberties remained constrained by the continuing differentials of wealth and position in society. The apparent fraternity of our political existence was illusory, being totally subordinated to the relationships of civil society. The state did not resolve but perpetuated social divisiveness: the very reverse of what the natural-law tradition had argued.

This critique of liberal politics has proved among the most enduring contributions of Marxism. Exposés of the way the inequalities of power generated by capitalist society undermine the putative equal exercise of rights within western democracies have been made with some force by socialist political sociologists.[20] Bobbio did not dispute the validity of these arguments but introduced two caveats that outraged his antagonists. First, while recognising the merits of these detailed dissections of the capitalist state, Bobbio noted the marked absence of concrete proposals as to what should replace it. Second and related to this point, he argued that, to the extent that many socialist positions derive from an uncritical view of how things could be, they remain untenable. Marxists have neglected the task of constructing a feasible form of socialism, capable of empirical scrutiny, and engaged instead in a scholastic repetition and exegesis of the classic works of the founding fathers – an occupation that has blinded them to the practical shortcomings of these texts. The wholesale rejection of the state, including 'the bourgeois democratic republic', as 'an organ of class *rule*, an organ for the *oppression* of one class by another' proves self-confirming.[21] As the history of Leninism revealed, it ends up not with the withering away of the state – only possible in improbable circumstances – but by turning the state into the very instrument of dictatorial rule Marxists claimed it to have been.

Marx argued that liberal political rights served bourgeois class interests by providing them with a veneer of legitimacy. In this respect they mirrored the function of religion:

> The relationship of the political state to civil society is just as spiritual as the relationship of heaven to earth. The state stands in the same opposition to civil society and overcomes it in the same way as religion overcomes the restrictions of the profane world, i.e. it has to acknowledge it again, reinstate it and allow itself to be dominated by it.[22]

---

19. *Ibid.*, p. 220.

20. Bobbio cites R. Miliband, *The State in Capitalist Society*, London: Weidenfeld & Nicolson, 1969 and N. Poulantzas, *Pouvoir politique et classes sociales*, Paris: Textes a' l'appui, 1968, as the best examples of the genre.

21. Lenin, 'State and revolution', pp. 387, 393.

22. Marx, 'On the Jewish question', p. 220.

The critique of the state similarly paralleled that of religion. For Marx:

The abolition of religion as the *illusory* happiness of the people is the demand for their real happiness. To call on them to give up their illusions about their condition is to *call on them to give up a condition that requires illusions*.[23]

Thus, the abolition of the state depends upon the transformation of society. To follow Bobbio's analysis, Marx's 'neat inversion of the relation between civil society and political society', propounded by liberal theory, meant that historical

progress no longer moves from society to the state, but on the contrary from state to society. The line of thought beginning with the conception that the state abolishes the state of nature, ends with the appearance and consolidation of the theory that the state itself must be abolished.[24]

What did this re-absorption of the state into society involve? Marx's writings on this issue were notoriously fragmentary, for he refused to provide recipes for the future on the grounds that such exercises were 'Utopian' rather than 'scientific'.[25] Bobbio disputes that this reticence points to any greater profundity on Marx's part than the more extensive writings of Engels and Lenin. What he did say has similar weaknesses, strengths and, above all, lacunae. Marx contended that socialism emerged from the internal development of capitalism and the conditions of exploitation and oppression that it imposed upon the working class. Change came from the formation of a revolutionary consciousness among the proletariat, due to a growing awareness that their emancipation entailed the overthrowing of capitalism.[26] Unlike the other classes, the proletariat had no vested interests to defend and hence had nothing to gain from the protection afforded by the numerous bourgeois rights. Their oppression stemmed from the very logic of capitalism and could only be ended when the development of productive forces brought about the creation of an authentic communal existence within society that rendered the bourgeois state and its false heaven unnecessary. A community of self-regulating producers would replace the capitalist relations of production based on private property, and the distinctive feature of states, the legitimate exercise of coercive force, would pass from governments to the people themselves.[27]

---

23. K. Marx, 'Critique of Hegel's philosophy of right: introduction', in *Early Writings*, p. 244.

24. Bobbio 'Gramsci and the conception of civil society', p. 142.

25. *See*, e.g. K: Marx, *Capital*, vol. I, trans. Moore and Aveling, Moscow: Foreign Languages Publishing House, 1959, Afterword, p. 17.

26. Marx, 'Critique of Hegel's philosophy of right', p. 256. Some commentators have pointed out that Marx's use of a simple rational self-interest theory of revolutionary motivation, devoid of any moral appeal, runs into 'free-rider' problems which suggest it would not work. *See* A. Buchanan, 'Revolutionary motivation and rationality', *Philosophy and Public Affairs* 9, 1979, pp. 59–82.

27. K. Marx, 'The civil war in France', in *The First International*, p. 250.

The Paris Commune, Marx believed, had demonstrated that 'the working class cannot simply lay hold of the ready-made state machinery and wield it for its own purposes'; real change required 'a revolution to break down this horrid machinery of class domination itself.[28] A transitional period of class dictatorship consolidated the transformation of society by removing the vestiges of the bourgeoisie's social power, for example, their monopoly of the technical skills and administrative positions vital for the running of the economy, and the continued prevalence of bourgeois ideology in such matters as incentives for work. The 'narrow horizon of bourgeois right' could only be finally crossed, however, either when society had become so productive or human beings so socialised that clashes over resources did not occur.[29] We have already cast doubt on the tenability of both these propositions and yet they are clearly entailed by Marx's claim that a new form of socialist democratic co-ordination renders the modern state and its associated concepts redundant.

According to Marx, in 'true democracy' 'government' gave way to 'administration' in the following two respects. First, members of the new community internalised the social norms regulating conduct within it to the extent that no enforcement of them was necessary. Second, society was similarly self-administering in deciding questions concerning the allocation of goods and the planning of production. Specialists in charge of these functions were not to be free agents, but bound by the formal instructions, or *mandat imperatif*, of the people.[30] Marx held that the division of labour, necessary for running a complex economy even under communism, was a 'business matter that gives no one domination'. All the different functions within society would be on a par with each other and appointments made on purely technical considerations, indeed technology will have so simplified the different tasks that jobs could be interchangeable and in principle performed by any of the citizens. Elections for these various posts and the making of decisions generally will have lost in consequence their 'present political character'.[31] Yet if matters could be as cut and dried as this, what purpose would elections serve?

Marxists sometimes argue that perfectly harmonious agreements could be reached given sufficient opportunities for rational debate and that this forms the essence of a democratic socialist politics. However, as Bobbio remarks, there are constraints of time, information and scale which this model does not take into account. Even with the use of computer technology, the time necessary to decide on an agenda, discuss issues and vote on them will be prohibitive, while making the relevant information available may be both costly and only comprehensible to those with specialist knowledge (two problems Marx characteristically assumed away). Finally, possible exploitation of a minority could only be avoided by a

---

28. *Ibid.*, pp. 206, 249.
29. Marx, 'Critique of the Gotha Programme', pp. 346–7.
30. Marx, 'Civil war in France', p. 210.
31. K. Marx, 'Conspectus of Bakunin's "Statism and Anarchy"', in *The First International*, p. 336.

unanimous decision. Proponents of participatory democracy maintain that involvement in the decision-making process leads people to an awareness of the nature and intensity of the preferences of others and a concomitant modification of their own. But the optimal size of such groups is fairly restricted, since only small communities possess the requisite face-to-face relations and shared interests for this system to work and, in any case, a large society would run into the time and information costs outlined above. Moreover, as we have already pointed out, conflicts between individuals do not always reflect divergent interests but also arise over genuine ethical differences concerning such questions as the nature of the good society. Even a small community may need anti-paternalist rights to protect minorities from the benevolent, but still tyrannical, impositions of a well intentioned majority opposed to or uncomprehending of their way of life.[32]

Marx's rejection of politics relied on an overly narrow conception of what makes it necessary. Summarising these problems, Bobbio notes how Marxism has neglected discussion of the political *means* for the attainment of dubious political *ends*, and ignored the question of *how* power is exercised by concentrating on *who* holds it. As a result various strategies for seizing power, and the preparation of the proletariat for this task, have dominated Marxist political practice, while analysis of the forms of government that will succeed this event are dismissed as 'bourgeois'. Most damagingly, the grounds on which the new era was to be ushered in, far from uniting socialism and democracy in a higher synthesis, seem in many respects to be deeply inimical to democratic procedures. Marx insisted that communism was not one ideal among others but inscribed within the historical process. 'Communists do not preach morality at all', he remarked in *The German Ideology*, only 'schoolmasters' base their arguments for revolution on such specious reasoning.[33] A belief in the incontrovertible nature of one's goal renders all obstacles to its attainment intolerable. While this attitude need not lead to Lenin's dismissal of all 'spontaneously' arrived at beliefs as necessarily 'unscientific',[34] it does remove one important rationale for democracy – namely that there are at the very least a plurality of ends which could be reasonably followed and that preferences need to be argued for and cannot be regarded as definitive.

Marxism's claims to a 'scientific objectivity', its antagonism to rights and its belief in a future of perfect harmony all create insuperable obstacles to the adoption of a Marxist democratic politics and encourage the belief that failure to reach the desired idyll stems from residual bourgeois egoists of various kinds, with all the

---

32. For the following criticisms of Marxist politics, I'm indebted to Keat, 'Liberal rights and socialism'; Pierson, *Marxist Theory and Democratic Politics*, ch. 1; J. Elster, *Making Sense of Marx*, Cambridge: Cambridge University Press, 1985, ch. 7; A. Buchanan, 'The conceptual roots of totalitarian socialism', in Paul (ed.), *Marxism and Liberalism*, pp. 127–44; and Lukes, *Marxism and Morality*, pp. 48–100.

33. Marx, 'Civil war in France', p. 213; *The German Ideology*, Progress Publishers, Moscow, 1964, pp. 267, 413.

34. V. I. Lenin, 'What is to be done?', *Collected Works*, vol. 5, London: Lawrence and Wishart, 1969, pp. 355, 375, 384–5.

tyrannical implications such an attitude involves. Lack of political safeguards and the continued presence of the state has meant that in 'actually existing socialist' countries, class antagonism based on differential access to property has been replaced by the oppression of one group by another deriving from differential access to state power. As Bobbio remarks, Marxists have provided no studies of 'actually existing socialism' comparable to their many analyses of life under capitalism. They have usually simply denied that the experience of these countries has any bearing on Marxist theory. Yet the continued existence of elite domination in such societies, of injustices and the violation of individual freedom through the exercise of coercive power by one group over another, needs examination precisely because it suggests, among other things, that such abuses cannot be ascribed solely to economically derived class conflict. Bobbio contends that the failure of Marxist political sociologists to address these problems is but one more indicator of the very weaknesses of the Marxist approach to politics which gave rise to them within the socialist world in the first place.[35]

Finally, Bobbio raises the problem of a Marxist theory of international relations.[36] While liberal theory has attributed war to a particular political system (principally, despotism), Marxists have generally regarded it as the product of a given economic system – capitalism and, in particular, its final, imperialist phase. Kant's proposal for perpetual peace was premised on the universal adoption of the most rational form of government, republicanism. Marx, in contrast, believed only communism would end international conflict. Yet, as Bobbio points out, war is not inherently imperialist nor does all imperialism lead to war. Thus, just as 'class hegemony' proved too crude an explanation of the state, so imperialism cannot explain all wars. In both instances, power has to be recognised as having a certain autonomy with respect to economics. This applies as much to the international arena as it does to domestic politics for, in the former, the state behaves as an individual actor among others in an analogous manner to different persons in a Hobbesian state of nature, with conflicts arising in a similar way, not only over the exploitation of scant resources but also over the nature of the good life and the best way to achieve it. The only difference is that relations between states are harder to bind by the same kinds of contractual agreements than those occurring between individuals within society. But the resulting balances of force between different national groups, for example, cannot be assimilated to the balance of classes, any more than all domestic arrangements can. Since the First World War, the willingness of workers to join with capitalists in rallying to the nation has proved a major stumbling block to the thesis of class solidarity, which the struggles of third-world countries in recent times has noticeably exacerbated. A full theory of the state cannot concentrate solely on its internal monopoly of force, therefore, but must take into account its capacity to employ force in the international arena of nation-states as well.

---

35. For details *see* S. Lukes, 'Marxism and dirty hands', in Paul (ed.), *Marxism and Liberalism*, pp. 204–23, and the items listed in n. 31.

36. N. Bobbio, 'Filosofia e politica', in *Scritti dedicati a Cesare Luporini*, Florence: La Nuova Italia, 1981, pp. 301–18.

One can well understand the provocative nature of Bobbio's argument in Italy, given the importance of the PCI as the major opposition party. However Italian communists maintain that they have developed Marxist theory and practice to a point which avoids these difficulties without degenerating into liberalism, a claim to which we now must turn.

The Gramscian conception of 'civil society'

Much of the novelty of the PCI's policies have been attributed to the distinctiveness of the Italian Marxist tradition and the ideas of its former leader, Antonio Gramsci, in particular. Bobbio's essay of 1968 on 'Gramsci and the conception of civil society' provided not only an examination of Gramsci's use of this term, but also a controversial account of the significant departures from Marx which followed from it.

Gramsci's unique place within Marxism derived in large measure from his critique of 'economism'. He argued that the economic base did not mechanically determine the superstructure; rather it placed a constraint on what forms of consciousness were possible. Marxism was but one such option, whose validity rested upon its practical efficacy and popular acceptance and was 'perishable' in changed historical circumstances.[37] This departure from the dogmatism of 'orthodox', 'scientific', Marxism produced commensurate differences in his analysis of capitalist society and the strategy communist parties needed to adopt to overthrow it. According to Bobbio, these changes are encapsulated in the innovatory interpretation he gave of 'civil society' as part of the superstructure rather than, as Marx had argued, as an aspect of the substructural base.[38]

Gramsci divided the superstructure into two levels, 'the one that can be called "civil society", that is the ensemble of organisms commonly called "private", and that of "political society" or the State'. The two levels corresponded to two different dimensions of power. The first set of institutions, which included, for example, the educational system and the media but also the whole organisation of production relations, exerted power through the framing of social norms which restrict the possibilities for action conceived of by agents. Gramsci called this 'the function of "hegemony", which the dominant group exercises throughout society'. The second level of power, 'expressed through the State and "juridical" government', only became operative once hegemony had broken down and individuals were in overt conflict with the system. Then the dominant group needed to maintain control directly and 'legally enforce discipline' through the organs of 'State coercive power', such as the police and judiciary.[39]

---

37. For a defence of this interpretation, *see* my *Modern Italian Social Theory*, Cambridge: Polity Press, 1987, ch. 7.

38. Bobbio, 'Gramsci and the conception of civil society', pp. 148–50.

39. V. Gerrantana (ed.), *A. Gramsci, Quaderni del carcere* 4 vols, Turin: Einaudi, 1975, vol. III, pp. 1518–19.

Bobbio regards Gramsci as having moved back from Marx to Hegel, who similarly included within civil society both economic relations and the first rudimentary social forms controlling them, such as corporations.[40] The parallel does not completely hold, as Bobbio concedes, for Hegel also located the judiciary and the police in civil society and only the bureaucracy and political institutions within the state. The essential point of convergence, however, was their common view that the ethical life of the community derived from the norms and customs arising from the experiences and practices of civil society.

Rather more controversial is the conclusion Bobbio draws from this comparison: namely, that Gramsci thereby gave priority to the superstructure over the base as the determinant factor of historical change. Many commentators have pointed out that Gramsci did not go so far, and merely insisted, in the fashion of Engels, that the economic base was determining 'only in the last analysis'.[41] Drawing on Marx's 'Preface' of 1859, Gramsci argued that, while the base did not mechanically determine the superstructure, it provided the 'real' conditions which a 'rational' theory should correctly capture.[42] This does not rule out the possibility of irrational ideologies continuing to hold sway over people's minds. Indeed only thus could one explain the survival of outmoded forms of consciousness and institutions and the political dominance of classes which no longer played a leading economic role.

This observation leads to a difficulty Gramsci never directly acknowledged, although much of his work implied it, *viz.* the impossibility of always clearly distinguishing the base from the superstructure. Marxists have traditionally argued that legal forms of ownership and power arise to stabilise or otherwise endorse relations of effective economic control. Despite recent attempts to defend this position,[43] it is doubtful that all legal and political phenomena occur in this manner. A great deal of our behaviour is shaped, as Gramsci appreciated, by norms and laws without any prior economic control having been established. In fact many of the entitlements, privileges and obligations people demand of others could only be made in this way. In some cases, such as the patenting of an idea for computer software or rights of inheritance, economic control and norm-governed control are simply intertwined in ways which cannot be separated, since *de jure* ownership precedes any established *de jure* control.[44]

---

40. Bobbio, 'Gramsci and the conception of civil society', pp. 149–50.

41. *See* Bellamy, *Modern Italian Social Theory*, ch. 7 and J. Femia, *Gramsci's Political Thought*, Oxford: Clarendon Press, 1981, ch. 3.

42. Gramsci, *Quaderni*, II, pp. 1422, 1338.

43. G. A. Cohen, *Karl Marx's Theory of History: A defence*, Oxford: Clarendon Press, 1978, esp. chs 3 and 8.

44. The following discussion draws on the criticisms of Cohen by S. Lukes 'Can the base be distinguished from the superstructure', in D. Miller and L. Siedentop (eds), *The Nature of Political Theory*, Oxford: Clarendon Press, 1983, pp. 103–19 and Elster, *Making Sense of Marx*, pp. 402–28.

This circumstance does not entail that these forms of political control cannot be explained by the economic functions they perform. More serious for the Marxist are those cases in which the structure and norms governing the state have no reference to the interests of an economically dominant class, or indeed to classes at all. The internal dynamics of bureaucracies or of given decision-making procedures can have a determining effect on government action, regardless of the interests of those in charge. These will operate increasingly when no one group wields absolute power. True, they can be exploited for class reasons – the periodic adoption and discarding of various types of collective bargaining procedures being a case in point. In many instances a dominant class may feel the opportunity costs of assuming direct power or using coercion outweigh the advantages to be gained. Gramsci adopted similar arguments to explain the peculiar nature of the bourgeoisie's ascendancy in Italy, which had largely been accomplished through a 'passive revolution' via hegemonic control of civil society, rather than by a direct seizure of the institutions of the state. Only the final breakdown in hegemony and the outbreak of violent class struggle following the First World War had necessitated the 'direct domination' exercised by fascism.[45] Important though Gramsci's innovations are, his theory cannot account for all the actions of states and the limits imposed by the 'invisible powers', to use Bobbio's suggestive term, of bureaucracies and the sheer mechanics of making decisions in complex modern societies. Nor does it exhaust all disputes about which goals are most desirable or how social relations should be conducted. Feminist and racial issues, for example, have been notoriously distorted by being reduced to questions of class, and Gramsci was particularly sensitive to the way nationalism and religion had a wider appeal than class interests and often overrode them.

Gramsci's appreciation of the inseparability of norm-governed economic relationships from the norms embedded within them, a state of affairs captured by his concept of hegemony, had important repercussions for his theory of political practice. Gramsci isolated two phases of the attack on bourgeois institutions: the 'war of position' and the 'war of manœuvre' or 'war of movement'. The former constituted a protracted attack on the cultural superstructure, necessary in 'the more industrially and socially advanced states' protected by the 'trench-systems' of civil society. But this did not obviate the need, when the time was ripe, for a rapid and no doubt violent 'war of movement', or revolutionary action of the usual type, to topple the capitalist leaders when they too resorted to coercion to maintain their position. The 'massive structures of modern democracies [...] merely render "partial" the element of movement which before was "all" the war, etc'.[46]

These refinements do not in themselves distinguish Gramsci from the spirit of Leninism, as some have supposed, since Lenin's advocacy of a 'violent revolution' to destroy 'the apparatus of state power which was created by the ruling class' remained perfectly suitable to Russia, where 'the state was everything and civil

---

45. Gramsci, *Quaderni*, II, p. 1229.
46. *Ibid.*, I, pp. 122–3; III, pp. 1612–13, II, pp. 865–7; III, p. 1567.

society was primitive and amorphous'.[47] They differed greatly, however, on how to organise the masses within the party, a divergence stemming from Gramsci's rejection of 'economism' and his conception of hegemonic power. As Bobbio phrases it, Gramsci gave priority to 'cultural leadership', the creation of a new proletarian moral order and conception of the world among the masses, over 'political leadership', the seizure of power by a vanguard party. Unlike Lenin, he did not believe that party cadres should 'elaborate an independent ideology' without reference to what the workers, deluded by 'bourgeois ideology', actually thought themselves.[48] The 'educational relationship', he argued, 'which exists throughout society', was 'active and reciprocal, so that every teacher is a pupil and every pupil a teacher'. Ideologies were formed on the basis of scientific laws of economic and social development. The party brought together leader and led 'organically', not 'mechanically'. Far from denigrating the 'spontaneous philosophy of the masses', Gramsci praised it. He condemned 'bureaucratic centralism' as the 'pathological manifestations' of a 'narrow clique' – a sign of 'the political backwardness of peripheral forces' – and advocated the alternative of 'democratic centralism', whereby the party's unity in the face of its opponents involved no sacrifice of internal discussion and debate.[49] While for Lenin the new moral order succeeded the revolution and a transitory 'dictatorship of the proletariat',[50] Gramsci believed the party must achieve a 'total and molecular transformation of modes of thought and being', prior to the assault on the state. The party, the 'Modern Prince' of Machiavelli:

> must be and cannot but be the proclaimer and organizer of an intellectual and moral reform, which also means creating the grounds for a subsequent development of the national-popular collective will towards the accomplishment of a superior and total form of modern civilization.[51]

Gramsci therefore gives greater attention to how the individual might be socialised *before* the revolution. But the assumptions lying behind his picture of what this 'superior and total form of civilization' will look like were no different to Marx's and shared all Marx's failings. 'The intellectual and moral reform', according to Gramsci, 'has to be linked with a programme of economic reform'.[52] As in Marx's conception, the *gemeinschafilich* relations of Gramsci's new hegemony were to be built upon the overcoming of both natural and artificially created scarcity through the productiveness of communist society.[53] 'Necessity'

47. Lenin, 'State and revolution', pp. 400, 413–17.
48. Lenin, 'What is to be done?', pp. 382–5.
49. Gramsci, *Quaderni*, II, pp. 1331, 1397; III, pp. 1633–5, 1691–2.
50. Lenin, 'State and revolution', pp. 402–4.
51. Gramsci, *Quaderni*, III, pp. 1560–1.
52. *Ibid.*
53. *See*, e.g. Marx, 'Critique of the Gotha Programme', pp. 346–7.

would be exchanged for 'freedom', so that the 'structure ceases to be an external force which crushes man' and becomes 'an instrument to create a new ethico-political form and a source of new initiatives'.[54] Gramsci assumed that, under communism, the division of labour ceased to generate class conflict and united everyone in the essentially social process of production instead. The individual's conception of selfhood would be shaped by society so that communal goals entered into his or her appraisal of self-interest and development and formed part of a 'collective will [...] through which a multiplicity of dispersed wills, heterogeneous aims, are welded together with a single aim, on the basis of an equal and common conception of the world'.[55] This 'total' perspective risks becoming totalitarian though, for even within such a socialised community of individuals, if they remain individuals in any meaningful sense, then they will engage in a variety of different types of relationship operating at a variety of levels. The relations between friends, workmates, lovers, neighbours, other citizens and strangers – all of which would presumably persist under communism – are not of the same quality and with the best will in the world cannot always be brought into harmony with each other. Regrettably, Gramsci was not wholly devoid of the intellectual hubris of any fellow Marxists who have also argued that the struggle for this final goal justifies all sacrifices required to attain it. Thus 'every act comes to be judged useful or harmful, virtuous or wicked, solely in so far as it refers to the Modern Prince itself and serves to increase or oppose its power'; so that the party 'takes the place of the deity or the categorical imperative within human consciences'.[56]

Defenders of Gramsci will argue that he arrived at his model of a holistically organised society through an appreciation of the benefits of workers' self-management in the Turin factory movement.[57] They maintain, along with other advocates of 'direct' democracy, that political participation yields agreement on social goals without sacrificing individuality. Gramsci, and indeed Marx and Lenin (in *State and Revolution* at least),[58] sought not to abolish politics but to move it into society. However, none of the criticisms adumbrated above are removed by this argument. Even if one accepts the moral virtues attributed to participatory democracy by its advocates, the various problems of scale, complexity, imperfect knowledge and understanding and so on, outlined in the last section, remain unanswered. Given these defects, the Marxist failure to elaborate a concept of the state persists as an unresolved difficulty that the PCI cannot ignore.

---

54. Gramsci, *Quaderni*, II, pp. 1051–2.

55. *Ibid.*, pp. 1330–1.

56. *Ibid.*, III, p. 1561. See Lukes, *Marxism and Morality*, pp. 86–99 for the means-end problem within Marxism.

57. *See*, e.g. A. S. Sassoon, *Gramsci's Politics*, London: Croom Helm, 1980, esp. pp. 222–31 and her 'Gramsci: a new concept of politics and the expansion of democracy', in A. Hunt (ed.), *Marxism and Democracy*, London: Lawrence & Wishart, 1980, pp. 81–99.

58. Lenin, 'State and revolution', pp. 394, 426, 473–4.

The PCI and Italy's 'third road to socialism'

The Italian communists have often acted as if Gramsci provided them with the philosopher's stone, magically reconciling their divergent claims to be both a Leninist, or at least a Marxist, party and to operate within the 'rules of the game' of a western liberal democracy. The manner in which they have reconciled these two strands has varied considerably. Whether one sees these changes as the product of contingent tactical manœuvres or as the evolution of a theoretically inspired strategy will largely depend on one's own ideological preferences.[59] I believe both elements are involved, political decisions being constrained by a particular doctrinal framework, which is in turn modified and transformed by the exigencies of participation in electoral politics.

Two particular aspects of the PCI's policy have been attributed by its leaders to the Gramscian heritage. The first, enunciated by Togliatti soon after his return from Russia in 1944, employed Gramsci's distinction between the different strategies applicable to the East and West to argue that there were 'differing roads to communism', according to historical circumstances. For Gramsci, as we saw, this belief implied neither any criticism of Leninist tactics in Russia nor the adoption of parliamentary methods in Italy. However, Togliatti started by claiming the latter and, by 1964, in his testamentary 'Yalta Memorandum', had moved close to arguing the former as well. By the 1970s the PCI's break with Soviet communism had become overt, symbolised by a series of denunciations of Russian interventions in Czechoslovakia, Poland and Afghanistan and by their joint declaration on 'Eurocommunism' with the Spanish communists in 1975.[60]

Taking up the second aspect of Gramsci's work, his emphasis on 'cultural leadership', the PCI professed to follow an alternative democratic path to socialism, distinct from both Leninism and social democracy. This policy has undergone a similar sea change. During the Cold War era the Italian road was largely assimilated to Leninism. However, in the wake of the post-Khrushchev thaw and the revolt in Hungary, Togliatti moved towards an outright rejection of revolution for a process of molecular social change through the conquest of hegemony within civil society. 'Progressive democracy', as originally conceived in 1944–7, was a 'profound revolutionary process, which, however, through the common orientation of the progressive forces, develops without abandoning the terrain of democratic legality'. By 1956, the PCI wished to insist that there would be no break with parliamentary democracy, even when they achieved power. Emphasising the fact that, due to their participation in the post-war-constituted assembly, the constitution contained a number of vaguely worded workers' and

---

59. Compare P. Piccone, *Italian Marxism*, Berkeley: University of California Press, 1983; D. Sassoon, *The Strategy of the PCI*, Pinter: London: 1981; and M. Clark and D. Hine, 'The Italian communist party: between Leninism and social democracy', in D. Childs (ed.), *The Changing Face of Western Communism*, London: Croom Helm, 1980, pp. 112–46, for different slants. Pierson, *Marxist Theory and Democratic Politics*, ch. 4, provides a useful account of the relation of the PCI's ideas to the Marxist tradition.

60. P. Togliatti, *Discorsi alla Costituente*, Rome: Editori Riuniti, 1958, pp. 40–1 and 'Elements for a Programmatic Declaration, VIII Congress of the PCI (1956), both quoted by G. Vacca, 'The "Eurocommunist" perspective: the contribution of the Italian Communist Party', in R. Kindersley (ed.), *In Search of Eurocommunism*, London: Methuen, 1981, pp. 132, 139.

welfare rights, the PCI contended that the goals underlying the republic required socialism for their realisation. They aimed to win consensus for the requisite social reforms through elections. In this way parliament 'could and must exercise an active function, both for the transformation of the country in a democratic sense and in the new socialist society'. The chief difference was that, beside current arrangements, 'forms of direct democracy can and must develop to ensure further developments and the superiority of socialist democracy' and through which the struggle for hegemony could be fought. The PCI's strategy thus moved in two directions. On the one hand, they assumed that the development of capitalism inherently led people to identify on grounds of rational self-interest with socialism, a view encouraged by the steady increase of their share of the vote until 1976. When they achieved exactly 51 per cent, the time would be propitious for the transition to socialism. The working class could exercise class power through existing institutions simply by winning a majority. On the other hand, their current exclusion from government meant that they continued the battle for hegemony in those aspects of civil society which were open to them, preparing the way for the new moral order which would follow the advent of communism. The PCI's adoption of a parliamentary road to socialism only seems compatible with a traditional Marxist view of the state if it is presumed that, once a majority has been achieved, they will also have so changed the organisation of civil society that a smooth transition to a stateless community no longer requiring 'bourgeois' structures could take place. Even so, the appeal to 'workers' rights' and a promise to retain parliament both conflict with orthodox Marxism. Moreover, the second aspect operates with a different logic from the first, since it aims to mould a common will among citizens rather than cultivating their self-interest. The two policies will only be coherent on the assumption that historical processes lead the two to coincide, since, as Rousseau showed, the 'will of all' and the 'general will' often conflict.

The PCI's practical and doctrinal difficulties arose in the 1970s because this presupposition became increasingly untenable. Both the highly fragmented economic and social structure of Italy and the diverse nature of capitalist development made a policy predicated on the formation of a homogeneous working-class majority extremely difficult to pursue. Instead, the PCI had to cultivate the support of a disparate and heterogeneous number of groups, including southern peasants and various elements of the expanding middle classes (from white-collar workers to professionals) as well as the industrial and agricultural workers of its traditional northern strongholds. By virtue of its participation within the parliamentary system the PCI was forced to act as a party of disparate interests, attempting to construct a broad enough alliance around specific policy issues to gain a majority, rather than as the voice of a particular class basing its appeal on the desirability of overthrowing the system altogether and constructing a new hegemony.[61]

---

61. For two detailed discussions of these issues, on which I've extensively drawn, *see* S. Hellman, 'The PCI's alliance strategy and the case of the middle class', in D. Blakmer and S. Tarrow (eds), *Communism in Italy and France*, Princeton, NJ: Princeton University Press, 1975, pp. 373–4, 9 and Peter Lange. 'Crisis and consent, change and compromise: dilemmas of Italian communism in the 1970s', *West European Politics* 2(3), 1979, pp. 110–32.

1968 brought the conflict between the party's two strategies to a head. It revealed the extent to which the years of relative economic prosperity had transformed Italian society, building up numerous sources of disaffection with traditional institutions. However the various movements spawned by this discontent were extraordinarily diverse in their form, function and demands, encompassing student protest, industrial unrest, and revolts both within and against existing social structures such as the family and the church. Violent and non-violent, utopian and reformist, materialist and anti-materialist currents vied with each other, often in incompatible ways. The PCI hoped to gain from this social unrest, but the movements were simply too disparate to be organised within a single party, let alone to form a new 'historical bloc' under the aegis of the proletariat.

The PCI's inability to organise these groups and its adoption of the conventional status of a party representing a coalition of interests was symbolised by the expulsion of the 'Manifesto' group in 1969, who had advocated greater grass-roots involvement in policy-making and criticised the parliamentarism of the party leadership.[62] The PCI feared that any failure to co-operate with the system on their part might lead to a reactionary backlash by the conservative forces then controlling the state apparatus, which would simply squash all protest and impede the most moderate reforms. The deepening economic crisis, which affected Italy particularly badly due to its lack of natural resources, the fate of the Allende administration in Chile and the growth of urban terrorist movements towards the end of the decade all reinforced this conviction. Instead the PCI aspired to channel the demands of the extra-parliamentary groups back into the institutional arena, styling itself as a mediator between state and society. This new role was not made any easier by the proliferation of a number of smaller parties allowed by the Italian electoral system, many on its left wing as well as in the centre. Their failure to come to terms with these groups, and hence to break the Christian Democrats' monopoly of power, ultimately led them into co-operation with the government without actually attaining ministerial office. This policy inevitably compounded the party's doctrinal difficulties, since participation within the state, particularly at the regional and municipal levels where they often had control, entailed an overt revaluation of traditional Marxist hostility to bureaucracy, the police and judiciary and so on as organs of 'bourgeois' rule.[63]

This policy of 'historic compromise' was consolidated between 1973 and 1975, when most of the articles in Bobbio's book were written. The contemporary relevance and ideological import of his analysis of the Marxist theory of the state can now be brought into focus. On the one hand, he implicitly challenged

---

62. *See* S. Hellman, 'PCI strategy and the question of revolution in the West', in S. Averini (ed.), *Varieties of Marxism*, The Hague: Martinus Nijhoff, 1977, pp. 207–18, for an analysis of these issues.

63. In addition to Lange, 'Dilemmas of Italian Communism' and Hine and Clark, 'The Italian Communist Party', *see* J. Fraser, *Society in Crisis/ Society in Transformation*, London: Routledge & Kegan Paul, 1981, for a general study of the Italian left's reactions to the crisis of the 1970s. The relevant statements of PCI policy dating from 1970 can be found in a collection of the main speeches of the then party leader E. Berlinguer, *La 'questione comunista'*, Editori Riuniti, Rome, 1975.

the coherence, in Marxist terms, of the party's simultaneous defence and use of existing state institutions and its continued call for their transformation through more participatory forms of political involvement within society. He had been particularly disturbed by the threat posed by many groups on the left to the existing institutional order, believing they risked making the mistake of the 1920s of abetting fascism through excessive criticism of the state motivated by unrealistic aspirations. Part of this fear may well have been influenced by the prominence of his own son in the radical movement *Lotta Continua* ('Continuous Struggle').[64] On the other hand, given that a choice had to be made between two kinds of socialism, he argued that only liberal socialism, which seeks a form of socialism compatible with the protection afforded the individual by the liberal state, rather than the Marxist socialist variety, which rejects the state as 'bourgeois', was feasible. Indeed the PCI's own policies pointed to this conclusion.

The 'Communist question' had a particular importance for the Italian Socialist Party (PSI), to which Bobbio was affiliated as an 'independent' member of the socialist group in the Italian senate. Historically the differences with the PCI cannot be readily assimilated to a distinction between reformism and Marxism. Even in 1921, when the communists broke away, the PSI was dominated by 'maximalists' rather than the moderates around Turati. After the Second World War, under Nenni's leadership, it was frequently more radical than the PCI, opposing, for example, the incorporation of the Lateran treaties into the constitution – something Togliatti supported so as not to alienate Catholic opinion. Indeed the pro-Soviet, anti-American stance within the PSI precipitated a schism within its ranks and the formation of a separate Italian Social Democratic Party (PSDI) under Saragat. The PSI nevertheless wished to preserve its own identity and refused to merge with the PCI following the 1948 election, fought alongside the communists, when it gained fewer votes than its partner for the first time. During the 1960s Nenni's policy changed and he engineered a brief reunion with Saragat's faction, participating with the Christian Democrat Party (DC) in centre-left coalitions from 1963 to 1972. This reorientation produced a similar degree of internal turmoil to that experienced by the PCI. In 1964 the party lost its left wing, approximately a third of its rank and file, who formed the Italian Socialist Party of Proletarian Unity (PSIUP), while the union with the Social Democrats collapsed in 1968 after a disastrous result at the polls.[65]

Bobbio's intervention addressed his fellow socialists as much as the communists therefore, since it was vital for them to put their own house in order to avoid being outflanked by the PCI. Nor was Bobbio any stranger to such polemics. In the

---

64. Bobbio offers an account of his views of 1968 and after in the 'Postfazione' to his *Profilo ideologico del '900 italiano*, Turin: Einaudi, 1986, pp. 179–83.

65. These changes have been documented by David Hine in the following articles: 'Social democracy in Italy', in W. E. Paterson and A. H. Thomas (eds) *Social Democratic Parties in Western Europe*, London: Croom Helm, 1977, pp.67–85; 'Socialists and Communists in Italy reversing roles?', *West European Politics* 1(2), 1978, pp. 144–60 and 'The Italian Socialist Party under Craxi: surviving but not reviving', *West European Politics* 2(3), 1979, pp. 133–48.

mid-1950s he had engaged leading thinkers and members of the PCI, including Galvano della Volpe and Togliatti, in an analogous debate on the compatibility of Marxism and liberalism. By the 1970s the issue had become increasingly pressing as the PCI threatened to subvert the PSI's 1960s role as government partner of the DC, especially after it gained a mammoth increase in its share of the vote, from 27.2 per cent in 1972 to 34.4 per cent in 1976, while the socialists had remained at 9.6 per cent. His book, which first appeared as a series of articles in the PSI cultural journal *Mondoperaio*, pre-empted a general change in the party's image. Though it would be wrong to identify Bobbio too closely with the Craxi leadership, since he criticised Craxi's strengthening of the party secretary's position at the expense of internal party democracy, he played an important role in the process of ideological reorientation. This change, symbolised by a red carnation replacing the hammer and sickle as the PSI emblem, involved the elaboration of a distinctive 'socialist alternative', which would clearly distinguish it from the PCI.

We have already examined the negative side of this new programme, the critique of the Marxist theory of the state. However, Bobbio's contribution to the debate should not be seen simply as party-political polemic, as a comparison with Craxi's vulgarisation of a number of similar arguments would suffice to show,[66] and it received a correspondingly serious response from spokespersons of the PCI. For, in addition to his criticisms of Marxism, Bobbio posed a number a questions concerning the more general problems facing democrats and socialists in advanced industrial societies.

The paradoxes of democracy

According to Bobbio, a minimal definition of democracy consists of the following basic 'rules of the game':

1. That all citizens who have reached the age of majority, regardless of sex, race, creed or economic condition, possess political rights and can vote on collective issues or elect someone to do so for them.
2. That everyone's vote has equal weight, counting for only one.
3. That all citizens can vote according to their own freely arrived at opinion, that is, in a free competition between rival political groups which vie with each other to aggregate demands and transform them into collective decisions.
4. That they have a free choice in the sense of having real alternatives to pick from.
5. That they are bound by the majority decision (whether relative, absolute or qualified).
6. That no majority decision can limit the rights of the minority to become in their turn, and on an equal basis, the majority.[67]

66. B. Craxi, 'Il vangelo socialista', *L'Espresso* 34, 27 August 1978.
67. *Cf.* ch. 3, p. 66.

Bobbio gives three reasons for preferring democratic government to other forms. The first, or ethical defence, derives from Rousseau's formula that liberty consists in obeying laws we have prescribed to ourselves – a condition most nearly approximated by democracy. The second, political justification, regards it as the best available protection against the abuse of power, since it shares sovereignty among the people as a whole. Finally, from a utilitarian standpoint, democracy is preferable to autocracy on the grounds that the people are the best interpreters of their own collective interests. This point, as Bobbio notes, is the most debatable, since the collective interest is not identical with the sum of individual interests. However, provided one assumes that everyone has agreed to co-operate to find a mutually beneficial solution, and that each person has a better-than-even chance of being right, then (as Condorcet proved) the majority will be more often right than a single voter in the long run.[68]

The above arguments have a distinctly Rousseauean tenor and hence might seem to provide a *prima facie* case for preferring 'direct' forms of democracy to 'indirect' or representative models. For the latter, as practised in most western countries, reduces the autonomy and sovereignty of the people by delegating large areas of decision-making and encourages self-interested voting for different factional groups, rather than a disinterested adjudication on the common good. Indeed, Rousseau himself gave the most comprehensive account of why democracy as he understood it could not work without modification within modern societies:

> How many conditions that are difficult to unite does [a democratic republic] pre-suppose! First, a very small state, where the people can readily be got together and where each citizen can with ease know all the rest: second, great simplicity of manners, to prevent business from multiplying and raising thorny problems [which empowers those 'in a position to expedite affairs']; next, a larger measure of equality in rank and fortune, without which equality of rights and authority cannot long subsist; last, little or no luxury – for luxury either comes of riches or makes them necessary; it corrupts at once rich and poor, the rich by possession and the poor by covetousness; it sells the country to softness and vanity, and takes away from the state all its citizens, to make them slaves one to another, and one and all to public opinion.[69]

For Bobbio these discrepancies are indicative of the 'paradoxes of democracy' facing us today.

The first paradox arises from our need for ever more democracy in conditions which are increasingly inimical to its functioning. The 'iron law of oligarchy' operates the larger the state becomes, so that direct democracy degenerates into the rubber-stamping of executive decisions. The second paradox derives from the

---

68. *See* B. Barry, 'The public interest', in A. Quinton (ed.), *Political Philosophy*, Oxford: Oxford University Press. 1967, pp. 112–26.

69. J. J. Rousseau, *The Social Contract and Discourses*, trans. G. D. H. Cole, London: J. M. Dent and Sons Ltd, 1973, p. 217. [Amended trans. R.B.]

growth not only in the size of the state but of its functions as well. This process leads to the development of bureaucratic structures in which power is organised hierarchically, descending from above, rather than democratically, ascending from below. Even worse, this phenomenon increases in step with the expansion of democracy itself, since the latter produces ever-greater demands upon the state, which in turn requires ever-newer mechanisms to satisfy them. The third paradox refers to the effects of technology on industrial societies, which means more and more decisions call for specialised knowledge to solve them, so that democracy is subverted by technocracy (quite the reverse of what Marx and Lenin supposed). The final paradox belongs to the contradiction between democracy and mass society. Although mass involvement potentially means more democracy, the pressures towards social conformity produced by the former undermine the sense of individual responsibility presupposed by the latter. For example, the growth of information technology potentially gives us greater access to the workings of government and could facilitate a more active and informed participation of citizens in making decisions previously left to politicians or administrators. However, it has also given the state, through the storage of private files and the use of the media, more persuasive and subtle ways of manipulating and spying on us.[70]

All of the above paradoxes reflect the double-edged nature of the processes at work in contemporary society. Summarising these effects elsewhere, Bobbio has remarked how 'state' and 'civil society' have become increasingly intertwined. While the state has been 'socialised' through the influence of great democratic control, this in turn has induced increasing intervention by the state in society:

> These two processes are represented by the two aspects of citizenship, that of the citizen qua participant and that of the citizen qua state protected subject, which often conflict with each other within the same person. For through participation the active citizen calls for greater protection from the state and thereby reinforces the very state which he or she wishes to control.[71]

State and society are thus two separate but interdependent moments of the modern social and political system. 'Direct' democracy, in so far as it aspires to absorb state functions within society through schemes for self-administration through collective decision-making, falls victim to the dialectic of modern politics. Only representative democracy, albeit in modified form, can meet this challenge.

It was this assertion which most provoked Bobbio's critics among the PCI.[72] As we have seen, a commitment to forms of 'socialist' participatory democracy remains the one distinctive element of their programme. Their dissent was

---

70. Bobbio, *Which Socialism?*, p. 72. *Cf.* also his *The Future of Democracy*, Cambridge: Polity Press, 1987, pp. 96–7.

71. N. Bobbio, *Stato, governo, societa*, pp. 41–2.

72. The debate, carried out in the journals *Mondoperaio* and *Rinascita*, organs of the PSI and PCI respectively, is collected in *Il marxismo e lo Stato: il dibattito aperto nella sinistra italiana sulle tesi di Norberto Bobbio, Mondoperaio,*, n.s., Quaderno 4, 1976, from which all quotations are taken.

particularly inflamed by the apparent agreement of one of their number, a communist journalist called Massimo Boffa, with Bobbio's remarks. Indeed, Boffa believed he had not gone far enough, for:

> [T]he abolition of every mediation between people and power [...] which is the extraordinary objective enclosed within this formulation, has led historically not only to the abolition of multiparty representation, but has also created that which paradoxically could be called 'single party direct democracy', which is precisely what one wants to avoid.[73]

To Bobbio's amusement, Boffa's article diverted much of his critics' attention away from himself. Almost all of them began by accepting the inadequacies of much Marxist thinking on the state. Instead, they wished to insist on the possibility of cutting through the paradoxes of democracy. Thus Umberto Cerroni, follower of the Marxist philosopher Galvano della Volpe, argued that it was precisely the growing intervention of the state which rendered the socialising of politics, summed up in the Togliattian formula of 'progressive democracy', so necessary. He contended that the PCI aimed at

> a socialization of power which would render possible the socialization of the economy, and which is itself made possible by this very socialization of the economy. Thus a circle forms between *a socialized politics* and a *politicized economy* which demonstrates the need for socialism at all levels of the contemporary world.[74]

However, he offered no indication of how this would come about, except to assert (quoting Gramsci) that a future when the abolition of classes would end the division of labour between rulers and ruled was inherent in the progress of history.[75]

Most of Bobbio's other antagonists similarly fell into the very trap of Marxist scholasticism, reiterating phrases from an unexamined creed, which Bobbio had complained about. Vacca went so far as to offer a mini-history of the evolution of PCI doctrine from Marx to Berlinguer as his response.[76] Ingrao, the member of the central committee most concerned to cultivate the new social movements rather than parliamentary coalition partners,[77] together with Gerratana, the editor of Gramsci's *Prison Notebooks*,[78] both made the point that equal political and civil rights carry unequal weight within a society that allows great disparities of wealth and economic power. They argued that representative democracy only functioned

73. M. Boffa, 'Le dure repliche della storia', *Il marxismo e lo Stato*, p. 79.

74. U. Cerroni, 'Esiste una scienza politica marxista', *ibid.*, p. 46.

75. *Ibid.*, pp. 48–50.

76. G. Vacca, 'Discorrendo di socialismo e di democrazia', *ibid.*, pp. 117–52.

77. P. Ingrao, 'Democrazia borghese o stalinismo? No: democrazia di massa', *ibid.*, pp. 153–62.

78. V. Gerratana, 'Quando la democrazia e sovversiva', *ibid.*, pp. 81–90.

well when supplemented by forms of participatory democracy which educated people in the virtues of citizenship and enabled them to have a more direct say in the running of government. Indeed Gerratana believed that:

> We owe to such forms of direct democracy – and I mean by that all the channels which succeed in putting pressure upon representative institutions and on the organs of executive power – the fact that democracy has managed to survive so far in Italy.[79]

Achille Occhetto went further: direct democracy enabled 'the effective passage from the private appropriation of the social product to the real socialisation of the economy and of politics'.[80] Bobbio's paradoxes would be sundered by the resulting 'comprehensive and spontaneous development of the many-sided capacities of man', although it required 'a full socialization of the forms of knowledge previously employed as instruments of domination, with the goal of putting technology, information, the education system and all the organization of society in the service of this objective'.[81]

Even Occhetto's Utopian vision could not satisfy some to the left of the PCI. Antonio Negri berated the PCI for its social-democratic stance.[82] A former professor of 'state doctrine', [*dottrina dello Staio*] at Padua university, a somewhat ironic post given his views and the fascist origins of this subject in Italian universities, Negri had achieved fame through his involvement with a group initially known as 'Workers' Power' [*Potere Operaio*], then as 'Workers' Autonomy' [*Autonomia Operaio*], in the late 1970s. For Negri, the crisis of the Italian economy and the creation of a large group of unemployed was no time to support the state but for 'storming heaven' so 'that cursed heaven will be no more'.[83] Negri simply ignored Bobbio's arguments and asserted that ensuring the right class governs *does* circumvent the problem of how government is exercised. He professed a millenarian form of communism, maintaining that the nature of production in mass society had provided the propitious conditions for the emergence of the 'new-social worker' of communist society, who identifies in a multifaceted way with all aspects of production.[84] Significantly he was arrested in 1979 and accused of involvement in the kidnapping and murder of the republic's President, Aldo Moro, who had done much to facilitate the receptivity to the 'historic compromise' within the Christian Democrats. Although these unfounded charges were dropped

---

79. *Ibid.*, p. 88.

80. A. Occhetto, 'Sul concetto di "democrazia mista" ', *ibid.*, pp. 96–7.

81. *Ibid.*, p. 98.

82. A. Negri, 'Esiste una dottrina marxista dello stato', *Aut Aut*, March–June 1976, pp. 35–50 (included in the English translation of *Which Socialism?* as ch. 6) and Bobbio's reply in *Quale socialismo?* pp. xii–xiii. (*NB:* This preface was omitted in the English edition.)

83. A. Negri, *Il dominio e il sabotaggio: sul metodo marxista della trasformazione sociale*, Milan: Feltrinelli, 1978, p. 78.

84. *Cf.* A. Negri, *Marx oltre Marx*, Milan: Feltrinelli, 1979.

in 1983, he was subsequently tried and condemned (*in absentia*) for armed insurrection. His election as a Radical deputy gave him temporary legal immunity while awaiting trial, which he used to escape to France, where he still lives.

Most of these criticisms were aimed at a straw target. For Bobbio had not denied the inadequacies of liberal democracy but had doubted whether Marxism had the resources to transcend these problems in a realistic manner; a charge his critics failed to answer. For these reasons Bobbio denied that a 'third' way exists between liberal democracy and Marxism, and believed that the PCI must therefore give up its pretensions to combine the two and concentrate on how to achieve a socialism compatible with liberal democracy.[85] His own proposal is outlined in detail in *The Future of Democracy*.[86] Very briefly, he argues that socialists need to establish a plausible basis for the more equitable division of resources on which a socialist democracy must rest. Moreover, these foundations must be consonant with the traditional liberal political rights protecting the individual. Marxists have usually disregarded this problem on the grounds that it will not arise in conditions of superabundance in a classless society. Given that the first condition is unlikely to be met, and that the clashes between different interests cannot be avoided without an undesirable, and probably unattainable, socialisation of the individual, then the problem cannot be ignored. Bobbio contends that a solution lies in reconciling the individualist premises of liberalism with socialist notions of distributive justice. This consideration leads him back to the tradition of natural jurisprudence and the theory of a social contract underlying relations between citizens in political society. Rawlsian-style arguments, in particular, provide him with a means of generating a set of socialist rights from a consideration of individual liberty. This conclusion derives from Rawls's notion of the worth of liberty.[87] The classical liberal defence of freedom as absence of intentional coercion only makes sense, on this view, if the individual is thereby empowered to do what she or he desires. Thus Isaiah Berlin's famous example of negative freedom, as a man or nation struggling against its chains, implies a power to do those things which a chained person or people cannot do.[88] If the power to do something enters into the defence of freedom, then upholding an equal right to liberty could as plausibly involve an equal right to those basic resources (or 'primary goods') necessary for individual agency as the traditional right to be free from constraints; indeed the two are connected.[89]

Bobbio argues that just as the political rights of freedom of expression and assembly and to a vote regardless of sex, creed or race established the basis for

85. N. Bobbio, 'La terza via non esiste', *La Stampa*, 1 Sept. 1978, pp. 62– 6.

86. Bobbio, *The Future of Democracy*. The following paragraphs draw on my introduction to that volume, reproduced here as ch. 14.

87. J. Rawls, *A Theory of Justice*, Oxford: Oxford University Press, 1971, pp. 201–5.

88. I. Berlin, 'Two concepts of liberty', in *Four Essays on Liberty*, Oxford: Oxford University Press, 1969, p. xliii, n. 1.

89. Rawls, *Theory of Justice*, pp. 90–5.

parliamentary democracy, so the social rights generated by a Rawlsian-style 'social contract' provide the precondition for democratic control of various aspects of society, such as hospitals, schools, bureaucracies and so on. Schemes for 'direct' democracy, such as workers' self-management, fall foul of Bobbio's paradoxes. The decisions made in industry, for example, are more specialised than in national politics. The latter is concerned with the aggregation of policy preferences and values, and only subordinately with technique and the interests of specialised functions of prime importance to the former. While the nation is a largely inclusive community, involving all the relevant parties, workplace democracy cannot include all those affected by its decisions, such as consumers, workers' dependents, other factories and so on.[90] The guild socialists and Gramsci avoided these difficulties by assuming that a natural organic harmony existed between different economic functions, and that a heightened perception of the mutually beneficial interrelations between society's diverse parts would reduce conflict. However without this, untenable, assumption, the proposal shades into the representative model by degrees so as to co-ordinate between groups. In fact, it is likely to exacerbate, rather than diminish, inter-group hostility by strengthening group identity. Bobbio, in contrast, argues that representative democracy on the competitive party model could be extended to these new areas. Parties have the advantage that in order to obtain a majority they need to produce broad platforms which accord due weight to different group interests and co-ordinate compromises and trade-offs on the voters' behalf. Representatives provide the specialist knowledge needed to make informed decisions and avoid the inflation of political participation to an unsupportable degree.

To an Italian observer, Bobbio's proposal might appear to legitimise the process of *sottogoverno* or 'subterranean government' afflicting Italian democracy.[91] Italy's public administration has been characterised by the proliferation of various agencies, currently numbering some 45,000 and ranging from the massive state industrial corporations such as ENI (which controls the exploitation of hydrocarbons) to banks, welfare centres, museums, and state radio and television. These organisations have been gradually infiltrated by the political parties, which divide up the key positions among each other on the basis of their relative electoral and parliamentary strengths, and their importance in the forming of government coalitions – the infamous 'Cencelli' formula. Both the socialists and the PCI have benefited from this feature of Italian politics to achieve a high degree of control within 'civil society' (in Gramsci's sense of the term). This source of power was the PCI's main gain during the era of 'historic compromise' and since 'Craxi' became Prime Minister the socialist share has increased greatly. This system has attracted widespread criticism for its unrepresentativeness, the disproportion between the PSI's percentage of the vote and their 'subterranean' political power causing a

90. R. Lane, 'From political to industrial democracy', *Polity* 17, 1985, pp. 623–48.

91. *See* F. Spotts and T. Wieser, *Italy: A difficult democracy*, Cambridge: Cambridge University Press, 1986, ch. 7, for a useful analysis of this form of government.

particular scandal. While, in contrast with most other parties, no PCI politician has been accused of abusing his or her position for financial gain, the party cadre have nevertheless monopolised bureaucratic posts in areas under their control in ways which have antagonised the left and, arguably, subverted democracy. Curiously for a student of Pareto and Mosca, Bobbio pays little attention to the possibilities of collusion among members of the political class which the elite model of democracy creates, and to the opportunities it offers for the domination of politics by particular party oligarchies. Yet this has been a significant feature of Italian politics ever since unification. Bobbio accepted the justice of these arguments, and indeed distanced himself from the socialist party over this very issue, but believed that a solution resided in a strong legal framework incorporating the above-mentioned social rights and through increasing participation within the parties themselves, rather than in direct popular involvement in decision-making or by returning these agencies to the private sector. In this manner he hoped to meet in a practicable way the requirements of a form of government which was both democratic and socialist in character.[92]

Socialists working within the Anglo-American tradition may be uncertain as to the relevance of Bobbio's arguments to them. The left has long been committed to the social-democratic road in these countries and has rejected the Marxist idea of overcoming the bourgeois state. The question of how to unite socialism and democracy seems less relevant than the problem of how to proceed to a socialist system within a democratic system. But for Bobbio these are two sides of the same coin, since it is only through democracy that citizens without any leverage in the market can channel demands for a more equitable division of resources, whilst only democratic accountability can ensure that the ensuing increase of state power can be kept in check.[93]

Many on the left contend that socialism cannot be attained in this way. For example, Adam Przeworski argues, in his sympathetic and sophisticated critique of social democracy, that we must not confuse the struggle to reform capitalism with the quest for socialism. He maintains that '[r]eforms would lead to socialism if and only if they were (1) irreversible, (2) cumulative in effect, (3) conducive to new reforms, and (4) directed towards socialism'.[94] Orthodox Marxists in the 1890s, and apparently the PCI until very recently, believed that reformism would satisfy all these conditions due to the inherent tendency of the process of industrialisation to form a coherent working-class majority. As we noted above, such hopes proved illusory and successful socialist parties, such as the PCI, owe their electoral success to having discarded revolutionary goals for a broader package of piecemeal reforms. For Przeworski, whatever merits this policy may have in alleviating the worst abuses of capitalism, it can never effect a transition to socialism.

---

92. *Cf.* Bobbio, *Future of Democracy*, pp. 94–6, 124–7.

93. *Cf. ibid.*, ch. 4, pp. 96–101.

94. A. Przeworski, *Capitalism and Social Democracy*, Cambridge: Cambridge University Press, 1985, pp. 248–241.

Does it follow then that Bobbio has similarly given up the socialist goal as a result of choosing the social-democratic path? I believe Bobbio could offer two responses to such a contention. First, he would agree that reformism does not necessarily entail socialism. As he stressed in criticism of the PSI's proposed package of reforms, one needs to provide clear criteria to guide policy-making in a specifically socialist direction if reformism is not to degenerate into simply managing the system.[95] For Bobbio, the chief characteristic of socialist reforms derives from their enlarging individual liberty in a manner compatible with equality:

> I consider socialist liberty par excellence, those liberties which in rendering someone free produce more equality by eliminating discrimination: it is a form of liberty which is not only compatible with equality but is the pre-condition for it.[96]

Taking up a number of examples of recent socialist legislation in Italy, such as the workers' statute and the reform of family law, he argues that the freedom of persons previously discriminated against, in these cases of workers and wives respectively, has been increased by putting them on an equitable standing with other citizens, such as employers and husbands, with respect to access to the relevant goods and opportunities. In contrast, one can have legislation which is either egalitarian and illiberal or liberalising and inegalitarian. If socialist measures have occasionally committed the error of falling into the first category, the present danger comes from current neo-liberal governments passing laws 'which give a free hand to entrepreneurs to liberate themselves from the obstacles arising from the existence of unions and factory councils, but at the same time are designed to increase the gap between rich and poor'.[97]

Bobbio would also accept the second objection raised by Przeworski concerning the provisional nature of such socialist reforms; that they can never be regarded as definitive or as necessarily culminating in a fully achieved socialism. However, he regards this limitation a price worth paying for abiding by the democratic 'rules of the game'. Bobbio remains relatively optimistic about the progressive nature of democracy. If democracy entails accepting a plurality of views, and hence the potential instability and impermanence of any eventual socialist settlement, the conflicts between groups and individuals also has its beneficial effects. For it is 'through [them] [...] that the number of social demands expands to which governments must respond with collectively binding decisions'.[98] According to Bobbio, a pluralist socialism must be democratic. But the results of aggregating

---

95. N. Bobbio, 'Parole nella nebbia', *La Stampa*, 8 February 1987; B. Craxi, 'Se Bobbio legesse il programma del PSI', *ibid.*, 11 February 1987; N. Bobbio, 'E lui che non mi legge', *ibid.*, 12 February 1987.

96. N. Bobbio, 'Riformismo, socialism, egualianza', *Mondoperaio*, no. 5, May 1985, p. 70.

97. *Ibid.*

98. *Ibid.*, p. 66.

individual preferences by democratic procedures differ from those obtained by the market processes favoured by neo-liberals. As citizens, individuals are accorded equal weight, whereas as market consumers the distortions of differentials in the distribution of wealth and income prevail. Hence the same individual preferences can yield a different pattern of resource allocation under the two systems.[99] The future of socialism is therefore tied to the future of democracy. The value of Bobbio's work inheres in his having sketched a plausible form of democratic government suitable for a complex socialist society.

Bobbio's suggestions may appear to conflict with socialist ideals of solidarity and community. But a socialist society premised on the removal of all conflict may be realisable only by a naive, and ultimately repugnant, dismissal of the nature of the differences between both individuals and groups. He does not belittle the role to be played by popular participation; on the contrary, he considers attendance at mass demonstrations and the like as 'a civic duty [...] in certain circumstances'.[100] However, he does question the adequacy of such forms as a means of exercising democratic control in an intricate modern society and regards them as only workable on the assumption of a total, and ultimately undesirable, transformation of human relations. As Bobbio concluded in his reply to his critics, the question does not solely revolve around a choice of the means to a particular end, but of which socialism is worth striving for in the first place.[101]

---

99. *Ibid.*, pp. 66–9. *see* too Przeworski, *Capitalism and Social Democracy*, ch. 6. Bobbio made analogous arguments to these throughout the 1970s, when the articles in this book were written. *see* his collection of pieces from *La Stampa*, N. Bobbio, *Le ideologie e il potere in crisi*, Firenze: Le Monnier, 1981.

100. Bobbio, *Which Socialism?*, p. 73.

101. I'm very grateful to Paul Ginsborg, Roger Griffin, Stephen Gundle, Chris Pierson, John Thompson, and especially Danilo Zolo for their help in preparing this introduction.

Chapter Fourteen

The Future of Democracy: Bobbio and the Broken Promises of Democratic Theory

Most regimes today regard themselves as either democratic or as moving towards the establishment of democracy. This universal acceptance of democracy has produced considerable confusion in the use of the concept, since large differences clearly exist between these self-styled democratic political systems. The divergences in the practices of putative democracies have led to theoretical debate about the term's conceptual coherence and created a gulf between descriptive and prescriptive characterisations of democratic practice in the work of political scientists and political theorists respectively. Whereas the former argue that we must adapt our aspirations to the conditions of modern politics and modify our theory of democracy accordingly, the latter deny that empirical evidence can ever force changes in theories which are largely normative.[1] It is a great merit of Bobbio's book to have bridged this divide successfully by combining an historically sensitive analysis of democracy's substantive meaning with a sociologically aware discussion of the political implications of adopting a particular definition. This fruitful combination of history with social and political theory enables him to follow his examination of the values attributed to democracy with a number of suggestions about how democratic practice might be extended in the future. He thereby performs an important service, not only to his fellow scholars but equally to his fellow citizens. For awareness of the shortcomings of existing democracies and of the deficiencies of and discrepancies between theorists of democracy has a tendency to provoke disillusionment with the democratic idea itself, and to lead to its dismissal as fundamentally incoherent and impractical. The survival of democracy as a political form depends upon studies such as Bobbio's, which unite an account of the ideals of democracy with the specification of the institutional framework best suited to their realisation, and which offer a justification of the preference for one model over others. By providing a plausible future for democracy, Bobbio has contributed to ensuring that it will have one.

---

1. *See* G. Duncan and S. Lukes, 'The new democracy', *Political Studies* XI, 1963, pp. 156–77 for an influential analysis of the competing claims of 'empirical' and 'normative' theories of democracy, written from a radical perspective largely critical of the former. For a powerful critique of both schools of thought, stressing how both sides have hijacked the positive connotations associated with any political system calling itself democratic, *see* Q. Skinner, 'The empirical theorists of democracy and their critics: a plague on both their houses', *Political Theory*, I, 1973, pp. 287–306.

Bobbio's *The Future of Democracy*[2] was initially addressed to an Italian audience. This Chapter provides some preliminary context-setting and places it within current debates among democratic theorists. Accordingly, the first section offers a few details concerning the intellectual and political orientation of his thought, while the second section briefly links it to the relevant Anglo-American literature and the third section discusses Bobbio's own proposals against this dual background.

I

Norberto Bobbio was born in Turin in 1909.[3] The cultural and social environment of his native city has a special importance in explaining Bobbio's intellectual and ideological allegiances. During the 1920s and 1930s, the university continued to be a stronghold of the Italian liberal-empiricist tradition and, as such, something of an anomaly during the heyday of Crocean idealism and its left-wing (Gramscian/ communist) and right-wing (Gentilian/fascist) variants.[4] Teachers such as the economist Luigi Einaudi, the political scientist Gaetano Mosca and Bobbio's professor, the legal philosopher Gioele Solari, bred an unfashionable distrust of metaphysical political systems amongst their students, combined with a critical regard for the liberal institutions of the market and parliamentary democracy. These ideological choices, unusual at a time when both fascists and, with the exception of Croce, their main liberal and left-wing opponents were united in their condemnation of the earlier Giolittian régime, were reinforced by the peculiar social and political situation in Turin. We have become accustomed to associating the relatively advanced industrial and class structure of this city with Gramsci's theory of proletarian revolution. However, it also spawned a very different and more approving appreciation of the benefits of capitalism. Gramscian communism had to compete with, and was challenged by, radical liberal and reformist socialist alternatives, which, whilst accepting the need for social change, were critical of the Marxist programme. This tradition gave rise to an influential non-communist

---

2.   N. Bobbio, *The Future of Democracy: A defence of the rules of the game*, trans. Roger Griffin, ed. Richard Bellamy, Cambridge: Polity Press, 1987. The Italian edition appeared in 1984. This chapter provided the Introduction to the English translation.

3.   For a fuller account of Bobbio's life and works, *see* my 'A life in defence of the rules of the game', the Introduction to R. Bellamy (ed.) 'The legacy of Norberto Bobbio: assessments and recollections', *Critical Review of International Social and Political Philosophy* 7(3), 2004, pp. 67–73.

4.   For a discussion of Turin university life at this time, *see* Gioele Solari 'Aldo Mautino nella tradizione culturale torinese da Gobetti alla resistenza', in A. Mautino, *La formazione della filosofia politica di Benedetto Croce*, Bari: Laterza, 1953, pp. 3–132. The influence of Crocean idealism on Italian cultural life is traced in R. Bellamy, 'Liberalism and historicism: Benedetto Croce and the political role of idealism in modern Italy *c*. 1890–1952', in A. Moulakis (ed.), *The Promise of History*, Berlin/New York: W. de Gruyter, 1986, pp. 69–119. The whole period is splendidly described by Bobbio in his *Profilo ideologico del novecento italiano*, Turin: Einaudi, 1986.

anti-fascist movement initially centred on the Turin periodical *La Rivoluzione Liberale* [*The Liberal Revolution*] and later identified with the movement Giustizia e Libertá [Justice and Liberty], inspired by the ideas of Carlo Rosselli.[5]

Rosselli contended that the Marxist attribution of a complete opposition between liberalism and socialism was mistaken. Many of his criticisms hit only the straw man of the vulgar scientific Marxism of the time and his arguments concerning the incompatibility of individual freedom and historical determinism appear too crude as a result. More lasting, however, is the conclusion he drew from his analysis: namely, that Marxists had insufficiently addressed the problem of individual autonomy, essential to liberalism. Whilst Marxism correctly regarded social and economic reform as necessary preconditions for the liberation of the proletariat, this in itself did not guarantee the civil liberties of individuals after the revolution.[6] Socialism, in Rosselli's view, was distinguished from communism by its insistence that 'the process of elevating the masses and the reform of social relations on the basis of a principle of justice is brought into harmony with the liberty of individuals and of groups'.[7] Socialism must achieve its goals by 'the liberal method', the institutional framework of liberal democracy.[8]

The fascist and Stalinist régimes of the time had persuaded Rosselli and his followers that it was the liberal rather than the capitalist or communist character of a régime which was decisive in preserving basic political liberties. Moreover, fascism convinced them of the inadequacy of mere mass participation in elections as an adequate defence against authoritarianism.[9] Political education had always been a central problem for Italian intellectuals and a party system on the élitist model was seen as a possible solution. As Bobbio has pointed out, the theory of elites never formed part of the official doctrine of fascism. Contrary to a popular misconception, democratic writers such as Gobetti and Guido Dorso were far more interested in developing it.[10] Bobbio himself played an important role in reviving this tradition of Italian thought and produced new editions of the works of Mosca and Pareto.[11] In advocating this doctrine of liberal socialism, which combined the three elements of constitutionalism, parliamentarism and a competitive multi-party system, Italian theorists were very much influenced by the ideas and experience

---

5. For a discussion of the two schools of thought in Turin at the time, albeit with a bias towards the Gramscian faction, *see* A. Asor Rosa, 'Torino operaia e capitalista', in *Storia d'Italia* IV ii, Turin: Einaudi, 1975, pp. 1439–64. Norberto Bobbio gives a sympathetic account of reformist socialism in his *Profilo*, pp. 62–73.

6. Carlo Rosselli, *Socialismo liberale*, [1929], Turin: Einaudi, 1973.

7. *Ibid.*, p. 454.

8. *Ibid.*, p. 445.

9. On Carlo Rosselli, *see* A. Garosci, *La vita di Carlo Rosselli*, 2 vols, Rome/Florence/Milan: Edizioni U, 1946, and N. Tranfaglia, *Carlo Rosselli dall' interventismo a 'Giustizia e Libertà'*, Bari: Laterza, 1968.

10. N. Bobbio, *Saggi sulla scienze politica in Italia*, Bari: Laterza, 1971, pp. 247–8 and ch. IX.

11. Most of these studies are collected in his *Saggi sulla scienza politica*.

of English 'new liberals' and socialists within the Labour Party.[12] As Rosselli and others pointed out, the survival of democracy and the fate of the working class there was in marked contrast to events in both Italy and Russia.[13]

Bobbio's work continues the project of this movement to reconcile the demands of social justice with individual civil and political liberty. The vast bulk of recent commentaries on Italian politics have been concerned with exploring the Italian Communist Party's claim to provide a 'third way' for the development of Western polities, distinct from either liberal capitalism or state socialism. This proposal hinges on a radical theory of democracy, stemming from Gramsci, and the role it would play in a communist society involving collective ownership of the means of production.[14] The Italian Socialist Party, to which Bobbio belongs, has long distanced itself from this programme. In an earlier work, *Which Socialism?* (1976), Bobbio offered a number of trenchant criticisms of Marxism and in particular of the belief that notions of justice and rights are products of the bourgeois capitalist system and would be redundant under communism.[15] Drawing on the arguments of Marx and Lenin,[16] Marxists have argued that once class divisions are abolished through the suppression of private property then the 'bourgeois liberties' protecting the integrity of the individual will be redundant. The interests of all members of society will ultimately be compatible with each other. In the interim, a revolutionary party, speaking for the as-yet-unarticulated interests of the

---

12. Guido De Ruggiero's *History of European Liberalism* (1924) trans. R. G. Collingwood, Oxford: Oxford University Press, 1927, is an eloquent example of this Italian literature. Further details of this movement are given in R. Bellamy 'An Italian "new liberal" theorist: Guido De Ruggiero's *History of European Liberalism*', which forms Chapter Seven of this collection. Hobhouse, Hobson and G. D. H. Cole were the most influential English thinkers.

13. *See 'Il Movimento Operaio'* (1924) and *'Battaglia Storica'* (1926) in C. Rosselli, *Socialismo Liberale*, pp. 65–77, 77–79.

14. Donald Sassoon's *The Strategy of the Communist Party from the Resistance to the Historic Compromise*, London: Frances Pinter, 1981, and Anne Showstack Sassoon, *Gramsci's Politics*, London: Croom Helm, 1980, are influential sophisticated accounts in the hagiographical tradition. For a useful corrective, *see* T. Judt, '"The spreading notion of the town": some recent writings on French and Italian communism', *Historical Journal* XXVIII, 1985, pp. 1011–21.

15. N. Bobbio, *Quale Socialismo?: Discussione di un 'alternativa'*, Turin: Einaudi, 1976. The terms of this debate can also be traced to an earlier discussion between the 'Giustizia e Libertà' group and the PCI. *See* G. Amendola's 'Con il proletariato o contro il proletariato?', *Lo Stato Operaio* V, June 1931, p. 6 and the 'Risposta a Giorgio Amendola', in *Quaderni di giustizia e libertá*, 1 January 1932, p. 40. The discussion was continued after the war in the famous exchange between Bobbio and Galvano della Volpe in the 1950s. Details of these disputes are given in R. Bellamy, *Modern Italian Social Theory*, Cambridge: Polity Press, 1987, ch. 7.

16. Marx's most trenchant criticisms of 'bourgeois *Recht*' occur in 'On the Jewish question', in *Early Writings*, trans. R. Livingstone and G. Benton, Harmondsworth: Penguin, 1975, pp. 211–41. His advocacy of workers' councils can be found in 'The Civil War in France' in D. Fernbach (ed.) *The First International and After*, Harmondsworth: Penguin, 1974, pp. 187–236. Lenin's ideas on the revolutionary party and his attack on social democracy occur in *What is to be Done?*, trans. S. V. and Patricia Utechin, Oxford: Oxford University Press, 1963. For a concise introduction to their views and failings, *see* M. Levin, 'Marxism and democratic theory', in G. Duncan (ed.), *Democratic Theory and Practice*, Cambridge: Cambridge University Press, 1983, pp. 79–95.

proletariat, can legitimately assume power. Yet, as the disastrous political record of actually existing socialist countries has demonstrated, this theory has in practice simply involved placing power in a far more coherent and self-serving governing elite than has ever existed in liberal régimes. A legal philosopher by training, Bobbio stressed the need for a political and legal framework capable of preserving the rights of individuals to choose their representatives freely. In *The Future of Democracy*, he developed these arguments and mounted a detailed attack on various models of direct democracy. However, he also sketched an alternative of his own, whereby he aimed to show that socialist goals can only be achieved acceptably within a liberal-democratic institutional framework.

II

The manifest shortcomings of liberal-democratic states have induced many critics on the left to insist on the need for a profound transformation of the economy as both a necessary and sufficient condition for 'true' democracy to emerge. However, the experience of actually existing socialist states casts serious doubt on this claim. By contrast, Bobbio shows that the left must take the criticisms and proposals of liberal thinkers seriously if it is to provide a workable alternative of its own. Without in any way diminishing the deficiencies of western democracies and their apologists, he argues that not only the formal liberal civil and political rights but also the whole constitutional and institutional framework of liberal democracies are essential for democracy. According to Bobbio, liberal democracy is not a contradiction in terms, as Marxists have maintained, but more nearly a tautology. For 'if liberalism provides those liberties necessary for the proper exercise of democratic power, democracy guarantees the existence and persistence of fundamental liberties'.[17] He adopts a minimal definition of democracy as 'a set of rules [...] which establish *who* is authorised to take collective decisions and which *procedures* are to be used to choose them'.[18] These rules consist of the majority principle – that is, decisions are made by a simple majority vote – and a number of civil and political rights, to freedom of speech and association and one vote per citizen, which guarantee rough political equality between voters and a choice between real alternatives at elections

Bobbio follows theorists such as Schumpeter,[19] Dahl[20] and Sartori[21] in arguing that these requirements are best satisfied by the competitive model of different parties vying for the people's vote, rather than by the classical model

---

17. Bobbio, *Future of Democracy*, p. 26.

18. *Ibid.*, p .24.

19. J. A. Schumpeter, *Capitalism, Socialism and Democracy*, London: George Allen and Unwin, 1943.

20. R. A. Dahl, *Preface to Democratic Theory*, Chicago, University of Chicago Press, 1956.

21. G. Sartori, *Democratic Theory*, Detroit: Wayne State University Press, 1962.

of participatory democracy.[22] Bobbio gives four main reasons for this. First, the modern ethos is individualistic, so that no amount of rational argument will bring about an all-embracing general will. Second, this cultural orientation is reinforced by the diversification of modern industrial society, which makes it harder to form common interests. Third, direct democracy could not mean that we vote on each and every issue after a prolonged discussion of all the elements involved – there simply would not be enough hours in the day. The only solution would be to mandate delegates to vote in specified ways. The difficulty here is that we belong to too many diverse groups – for example as workers, parents, city dwellers, etc. – for this not to either shade into the competitive model by degrees or result in the false attribution of certain 'real interests' to the people as a whole. Finally, the increased complexity of modern society makes people ill-informed judges of their own interests, so that representatives can serve us better than we can ourselves.

Bobbio believes the competitive model is better suited to the pluralist nature of modern society. Its chief advantages are instrumental. He contends that political experts are likely to produce more effective policies than a badly informed populace. Moreover, the competitive model is more efficient than the participatory alternatives in turning votes into policies. One of the inherent problems of majority decisions is that certain minorities with intense preferences for a particular good may be consistently outvoted. Classical theorists claimed that the educative effects of the decision-making process would modify the majority's view to take the intensity of minority feeling into account. But this effect is only likely to obtain in small communities, where each person can take part in the making of important decisions and hear and be influenced by the opinions of everyone else. By contrast, advocates of the competitive party system assert that the pluralistic nature of modern society makes it inevitable that any majority will have to be made up of a number of minorities. Parties will therefore have to produce platforms which accord due weight to minority opinion and co-ordinate compromises and trade-offs on the voters' behalf.[23]

This latter solution does not give complete satisfaction, however, and Bobbio carefully enumerates the inadequacies of the competitive-party model and frequently refers to the failings of contemporary Italy to illustrate his criticisms. For example, in a two-party system the competition between parties may well lead to a movement to the middle ground, where most votes are to be found, and the exclusion of radical alternatives. Parties will deliberately seek to project a moderate image and shed ideological extremists. The electoral advantages of this strategy, for instance, has been a constant problem for the British Labour Party, dividing the leadership from many of its most ardent supporters. The same pressures to dilute ideology do not occur in a multi-party system, such as the Italian. In this instance, the parties will have the opposite incentive and stress ideological differences. Here, the drawback is that no one party is likely to gain an

---

22. *See*, e.g. Schumpeter, *Capitalism, Socialism and, Democracy*, p. 269.

23. *See*, e.g. Dahl, *Preface to Democratic Theory*, pp. 133–4.

overall majority and hence be totally responsible for implementing its manifesto. This fact makes government policy less accountable to the electorate. The ruling parties can always claim that the other coalition partners forced them to back down on their declared programme and that rescuing parts of it was better than it not being implemented at all. Finally, leaders of parties may identify more with each other in certain crucial respects than with those they represent. This circumstance could result in their colluding with each other in order to keep certain issues off the political agenda. They form a 'political class', to use Mosca's term, with common interests as actual or potential rulers.[24] Ever since unification, Italy has been governed by an elite group which has sacrificed ideological differences for the shared spoils of power. Even though the widening of the franchise has changed matters in significant ways, the clientelistic nature of politics continues to hinder the democratic control of government.

Since the Second World War, Italian political parties have obtained a great deal of patronage through their control of numerous state monopolies and quangos. For none of this power is anyone directly accountable to the electorate. The major parliamentary parties divide these positions up according to considerations dictated by the exigencies of forming coalitions or the need to obtain tacit consent for their programmes, so that certain groups gain an influence far beyond their electoral support. Their control of essential services is so extensive that the system has come to be known as 'subterranean government' or *sottogoverno*. Yet it is unlikely to be reformed, since all parties have a common interest in this system, which gives them the resources to offer their members numerous incentives for continuing their support beyond success at the polls or the implementation of their declared programme.[25]

During the 1950s, pluralists such as Dahl tended to minimise these difficulties. Dahl argued that the 'polyarchical' nature of contemporary society rendered the liberal fear of the 'tyranny of the majority' a chimera, since only 'minorities' could rule, not a single majority. This system overcomes the problem of weighing the intensity of preferences by ensuring that 'all the active and legitimate groups in the population can make themselves heard at some crucial stage in the process of decision'.[26] Two assumptions underlay this thesis. First, he maintained that 'social training' through the family, schools, newspapers and so on, produced a basic consensus on norms and values amongst at least the political leaders.[27] Second, he believed that political activity is a function of relative intensity.[28] The more

---

24. For a discussion of Mosca and modern pluralism, *see* R. Bellamy, *Modern Italian Social Theory*, ch. 3.

25. For an analysis of the underside of Italian politics, *see* P. A. Alum, *Italy: Republic without Government?*, London, Weidenfeld and Nicholson, 1973, chs 3 and 4 and Martin Clark, *Italy 1871–1982*, London: Longman, 1984, pp. 334–8.

26. Dahl, *Preface to Democratic Theory*, p. 137.

27. *Ibid.*, pp. 75–7.

28. *Ibid.*, p. 134.

strongly a group feels about an issue, the greater will be its activism in promoting it. However, both of these presuppositions seem empirically dubious. Differences in organisational skills, education and finances will give certain groups, for example big business, greater advantages than others can muster. Underprivileged groups, such as racial minorities or the poor, lack the resources to sustain organisation. They can only offer the distant hope of eventual success to maintain their support, whereas wealthier concerns, or ones that are better positioned socially, can offer a host of immediate short-term benefits to their members. Thus a polluting chemical plant can use its monopoly of local employment opportunities to undermine the case of environmentalists complaining of long-term damage. Unions can give their members extensive immediate private benefits but an association of the unemployed cannot firm up support in this way, even if it would be in the long-term collective interest of the jobless to join.[29] In addition, organisations such as corporations and bureaucracies can wield a subtle and coercive power over the choices voters make. Not only do they have more lobbying influence than the individual citizen but they may actually control the circumstances in which votes are made, by limiting the available alternatives through their monopoly of employment opportunities, credit facilities, knowledge and expertise in particular areas and so on. These are 'invisible powers', to use Bobbio's suggestive term, undermining democratic practices.[30]

The existence of these social and economic inequalities erodes in turn the citizen's allegiance to shared social values, on which Dahl counts. Greater wealth not only gives certain individuals or groups greater influence in the choosing and influencing of candidates and issues but also means that they are not necessarily affected equally by the results of democratic decisions they dislike. Consumption taxes such as VAT, for example, fall disproportionately on the rich and the poor. This produces cynicism on the part of the relatively powerless and encourages the self-interested 'free-riding' of those with power. In Italy, as Bobbio notes, the position has degenerated even further with the presence of organised criminal elements in the south, which use violence to obtain electoral support or stifle opposition.[31]

The weaknesses of existing democracies are thus all too evident to Italian observers, and have contributed to what Bobbio calls the 'broken promises' of democracy.[32] Democracy has not lived up to the expectations of its early proponents and failed to eliminate the additional influence in decision-making afforded to certain individuals, due to inequalities of wealth, power and knowledge, or even

---

29. These arguments are elaborated by Jack Lively in *Democracy*, Oxford: Basil Blackwell, 1975, pp. 21–4.

30. For a critique of American pluralists' blindness to these factors, *see* Steven Lukes, *Power: A Radical View*, London: Macmillan, 1974.

31. Judith Chubb, *Patronage, Power and Poverty in Southern Italy*, Cambridge: Cambridge University Press, 1982, provides a chilling account of this side of Italian politics.

32. Bobbio, *Future of Democracy*, pp. 26–41.

to inculcate a heightened political awareness and/or increase of civic virtue among the newly enfranchised masses. As a result, Bobbio retains a healthy scepticism about regarding democracy pure and simple as a panacea for all political ills.

Radicals, however, often argue as if these difficulties could be solved simply by extending democracy to cover practically all decision-making. We have already noted some of the drawbacks of this idea, such as the almost limitless inflation of political activity and the problem of insufficient knowledge amongst the electorate. A variation of this scheme is to have more participatory democracy in areas which are sufficiently well defined for its virtues to be realised, such as in the workplace and local government. This proposal has always appealed to socialist pluralists, such as G. D. H. Cole[33] and H. J. Laski,[34] and their ideas were much admired by the Italian liberal socialists. More recently advocates of participatory democracy, such as Carole Pateman[35] and Peter Bachrach,[36] have turned to this tradition for inspiration. Gramsci's support for 'factory councils' has also been assimilated to this line of thought.[37]

Bobbio points out two defects of this approach. First, unless one believes absolutely in the educative nature of political participation, then the mere extension of democracy in this way will not necessarily produce any better results. After all, even on small committees, intense minorities can be consistently denied an effective voice by the majority. Second, advocates of this devolved form of participation assert that it strengthens the links between the individual and national politics, that participation at the local level prepares the citizen for informed involvement outside this sphere. However, this claim is in contradiction with a further assumption made by socialist pluralists, namely that equal weight can be given to different interest groups by virtue of allowing them to be as self-managing as possible. They argue that the best way of strengthening the liberal freedoms of speech and association, so that they reflect social and economic reality, is to return to workers and others authority over their own lives in the various spheres in which they move. The problem with this proposal is that it has a tendency to exacerbate, rather than diminish, the conflicts between groups, by strengthening group identity. The decisions made in industry are more specialised than in national politics. The latter is concerned with the aggregation of policy preferences and values and only subordinately with technique and the interests of specialised functions. In industry, however, these become of prime importance. Whilst the nation is a largely inclusive community, involving all the relevant

---

33. *See*, e.g. G. D. H. Cole, *Self-Government in Industry*, London: G. Bell and Sons, 1919.

34. *See*, e.g. H. J. Laski, *Studies in the Problem of Sovereignty*, London: George Allen and Unwin, 1917.

35. Carole Pateman, *Participation and Democratic Theory*, Cambridge: Cambridge University Press, 1970.

36. Peter Bachrach, *The Theory of Democratic Elitism: A critique*, Boston, MA: Little, Brown and Co., 1967.

37. *See*, e.g. Showstack Sassoon, *Gramsci's Politics*, p. 227. For an alternative reading, *see* R. Bellamy, *Modern Italian Social Theory*, ch. 7.

parties, workplace democracy cannot include all those affected by its decisions, such as consumers, workers' dependents, other factories, and so on.[38] The guild socialists and Gramsci circumvented these difficulties by assuming that a natural organic harmony existed between different economic functions, and that a heightened perception of the mutually beneficial interrelations between society's diverse parts would reduce conflict. As Bobbio remarks, this is the pluralism of a feudal rather than a democratic society. Moreover, it fails to go much beyond the thesis of liberal pluralists; indeed Dahl in his recent work has essentially espoused a very similar theory.[39] As a result, all the attendant difficulties of the polyarchal view, outlined above, remain.[40]

III

Bobbio's vision of a possible future for democracy attempts to avoid the pitfalls of these various models. He addresses the two main issues raised by modern theorists:

1. the need to extend democratic control to a number of areas within society in a practical manner, and

2. to ensure that political equality consists of more than the formal entitlement of one vote per citizen.

He traces the difficulties of democratic theorists in meeting these two needs to certain tensions within liberalism. Traditionally socialists have tried to circumvent these problems by simply rejecting the liberal heritage altogether; Bobbio, however, engages directly with it. Liberalism originated, in Bobbio's account, as a political reaction to authoritarian government in early-modern Europe. Its main concern was to grant individuals civil liberties against the incursion of the state. This origin produced an ambiguity in the liberal attitude towards democracy. As a procedure it provides a means of legitimising a government by formally requesting the consent of all citizens. However, a number of problems arise immediately. For example, have those who did not vote at all, because they dislike all the options, given their consent? Should all opinions be weighed equally in any case? Liberalism has tended to avoid such questions by keeping the state's functions to a minimum and stressing the autonomy of society. Social processes are seen as essentially unplanned and hence fair, reflecting the merit and effort of the individuals involved. However, this view begins to come into conflict

---

38. Robert E. Lane, 'From political to industrial democracy?', *Polity* XVII, 1985, pp. 623–48, provides empirical evidence to support this contention.

39. R. A. Dahl, *After the Revolution?*, New Haven, CT and London: Yale University Press, 1970, for all its criticisms of participatory democracy, praises workers' self-management on the Yugoslav model, pp. 130–40. He has recently developed this argument in *A Preface to Economic Democracy*, Cambridge: Polity Press, 1985.

40. *See* F. M. Barnard and R. A. Vernon, 'Pluralism, participation and politics: reflections on the intermediate group', *Political Theory* III, 1975, pp. 180–197 and 'Socialist pluralism and pluralist socialism', *Political Studies* XXV, 1977, pp. 474–90, for useful conclusions along these lines.

with democratic political ideals. For the latter seem to require a different sort of equality, based on need or our common humanity.[41]

In addressing this question, Bobbio examines the ideas of J. S. Mill and the new contractarians. Mill reveals the ambivalence of the liberal position in paradigmatic fashion. Whilst he undoubtedly believed all should have equal civil rights, he was deeply suspicious about extending the franchise to include the propertyless and uneducated. His advocacy of plural votes for the better educated was perfectly in keeping with the liberal belief that the rewards of politics, like those of the market, should go to those who deserved them. Thus, although he approved of equality of opportunity, and hence opposed the unearned privilege of inherited wealth, or discrimination on grounds of sex, creed or colour, this did not extend to a commitment to giving everyone an equal say in government – quite the reverse.[42]

Even in Mill's time this was not an entirely satisfactory stance to take. We have already rehearsed the problems social and economic inequalities raise for modern democrats. Yet, even within classical liberalism, a dissonance was noted between the need for economic independence when voting and the impossibility of achieving this as long as some members of the community were subservient to others for their livelihood.[43] Meeting the claims of democracy, however, has not proved universally acceptable to those of liberal sentiments. Some have argued that the cost is too high, that the demands of individuals upon the resources of their fellow citizens for more welfare, better schooling and hospitals and so on 'overloads' government beyond its capacity to pay for such schemes.[44] Others go further: they invoke the traditional liberal antipathy to government and insist on the inviolability of the individual against external interference. In recent theories, such as Nozick's, neo-liberal or libertarian thinkers have argued that defending individual liberty entails an entitlement right to the products of our labour or skill in the market, which makes taxation an infringement of the integrity of the individual similar to physical coercion.[45] Bobbio contests the comparison, pointing out that liberal rights against the state were asserted with a view to curbing the powers of hereditary monarchs, not elected governments. The theory also sets the limits to state interference impossibly high. Most libertarians accept that a minimal state will be needed to enforce recognition of the contractual rights and duties basic to the free-market economy. But if taxation is equivalent to coercion how is this to be funded? They would appear to be hoist with their own petard.[46]

---

41. These ambiguities have been traced by David Miller, 'Democracy and social justice', in P. Birnbaum, J. Lively and G. Parry (eds), *Democracy, Consensus and Social Contract*, London and Beverley Hills: Sage, 1978, pp. 75–100.

42. J. S. Mill, *Utilitarianism, Liberty, Representative Government*, London: Dent, 1964, p. 283.

43. J.-J. Rousseau, *The Social Contract and Discourses*, London: Dent, 1968, p. 42.

44. S. Brittan, *The Economic Consequences of Democracy*, London: Temple Smith, 1977.

45. R. Nozick, *Anarchy, State and Utopia*, New York, NY: Basic Books, 1975, p. 25.

46. J. Gray, *Liberalism*, Milton Keynes: Open University Press, 1986, pp. 76–7.

Bobbio argues that, in spite of these contradictions within liberalism, we cannot ignore liberalism or even reject it outright. Despite the disconcertingly reactionary character of many of its new forms, liberalism continues to thrive 'because', Bobbio writes, 'it is rooted in a philosophical outlook which, like it or not, gave birth to the modern world: the individualistic conception of society and history'.[47] He berates the left for never having come to terms with this conception. Apart from anarchism, the left has tended to advocate 'organic' views of community, which regard the individual as a mere part of a greater whole, and accordingly has produced schemes for functional rather than individual representation. Bobbio criticises this line of reasoning as regressive and unsuited to the conditions of modern society. Today, 'the starting point for every scheme for human emancipation is the individual with his *passions* (to be channelled or tamed), his *interests* (to be regulated and coordinated), and with his *needs* (to be satisfied or repressed)'.[48] He contends that the contractarian tradition provides the best foundation for establishing agreements in an individualist society and points to the proliferation of contractual obligations within modern societies, not only for the purposes of commercial exchanges but also between governments and citizens – as in union pay and strike agreements – and even between governments in foreign treaties. A contractual arrangement within the liberal tradition of Hobbes, Locke and Kant represents a procedure whereby all interested parties may consent freely to a given social set-up and make trade-offs of certain personal liberties for the greater advantages they feel will derive. As a result, contractualism is well suited to the pluralist and individualist nature of the modern world, since it offers an uncontentious basis for our social and political obligations without sacrificing individual liberty. The task for the democratic left, therefore,

> is to see whether, starting with the same incontestable individualist conception of society and using the same institutional structures, we are able to make a counter proposal to the theory of social contract which neo-liberals want to put into operation; one which would include in its conditions a principle of distributive justice and which would hence be compatible with the theoretical and practical tradition of socialism.[49]

Bobbio believes that John Rawls has designed such a new type of social contract, one capable of underpinning the equality of status required by members of the modern democratic polity.[50] Rawls maintains that 'the public culture of a democratic society' is committed to seeking forms of social co-operation which can

---

47. Bobbio, *Future of Democracy*, p.116.

48. *Ibid.*

49. Bobbio, *Future of Democracy*, p.117.

50. Bobbio refers to J. Rawls, *A Theory of Justice*, (Oxford: Clarendon Press, 1974), but in many respects his argument is closer to the argument Rawls was later to elaborate in *Political Liberalism*, New York, NY: Columbia University Press, 1993. The account of Rawls that follows consequently refers to an article in which Rawls elaborated some of the key ideas of that later work, which was not published at the time this chapter was originally written.

be pursued on a basis of mutual respect between free and equal persons.[51] This co-operation does not imply the co-ordination of social activity by an outside agency but simply involves the acceptance of certain common procedures to regulate political conduct. However, he adds, it must also contain fair terms specifying the basic rights and duties of citizens within society, so that the benefits produced by everyone's efforts are distributed fairly between generations over time.[52] Rawls argues that we can arrive at such a scheme via a process of 'reflective equilibrium', whereby we abstract from our present situation and arrive by philosophical reflection at the substantive basis of our political and moral convictions.[53]

He adopts the device of a hypothetical 'original position' to arrive at two principles of justice which he believes agents would choose freely if they were ignorant of their present abilities and social position as fair for society as a whole.[54] These are:

1. Each person has an equal right to a fully adequate scheme of equal basic rights and liberties, which scheme is compatible with a similar scheme for all.

2. Social and economic inequalities are to satisfy two conditions: first, they must be attached to offices and positions open to all under conditions of fair equality of opportunity; and second, they must be to the greatest benefit of the least advantaged members of society.[55]

The two principles are 'lexically ordered', so that the first takes priority over the second and 2(i) has precedence over 2(ii). Together they aim to meet and harmonise the respective claims of liberty and equality in modern democratic societies.[56]

In Rawls's view this goal entails that citizens be accorded equal respect in the pursuit of their idea of the good.[57] As various critics noted[58] and Rawls came to concede,[59] his theory assumes a particular type of agent possessing a sense of justice and a capacity to conceive a conception of the good. His ideal polity would also rule out those individuals who believed that their personal conception of the good involved enforcing others to abide by it too. Thus, for example, whilst he does not exclude religious groups who require strict conformity from their members, he could not countenance the formation of a theocratic state. The theory

51. J. Rawls, 'Justice as fairness: political not metaphysical', *Philosophy and Public Affairs* XIV, 1985, pp. 225–6.

52. *Ibid.*, p. 232.

53. *Ibid.*, p. 220.

54. *Ibid.*, pp. 234–6.

55. *Ibid.*, p. 237.

56. *Ibid.*, p. 231, n. 14.

57. *Ibid.*, p. 245.

58. *See*, e.g. V. Haskar, *Equality, Freedom and Perfectionism*, Oxford: Clarendon Press, 1979, ch. 10.

59. J. Rawls, 'Kantian constructivism in moral theory', *Journal of Philosophy* 77, 1980, pp. 526 f.

of justice forms, in his view, an 'overlapping consensus' between different groups and individuals, with divergent beliefs and life-styles, as to the fair procedures for making political demands in a democratic society where mutual toleration and fairness must be the norm.[60]

Numerous criticisms have been made of Rawls's theory concerning the viability of his derivation of the principles from the original position and the conception of social justice he espouses. These need not concern us here.[61] The appeal of the Rawlsian project to Bobbio is that his notion of 'pure procedural justice' appears to undercut the popular notion that the market mechanism of unplanned outcomes rewarding the abilities people prefer is intrinsically fairer than any other system. Whatever its defects, Rawls's theory purports to demonstrate that showing people equal concern and respect entails according them social and political as well as civil rights. In particular, Rawls's idea of a new type of social contract as the basis for a democratic society provides Bobbio with the framework for the consensual norms he requires for his proposed extension of democratic practices.[62]

According to Bobbio, the main issue for democrats today is not 'who can vote?' but 'where can you vote'.[63] The ideal of democracy involves the notion that we are free only when we have made the collective decisions which bind us by choosing from a range of valid alternatives and without restraint or coercion by or of others. Meeting this requirement means granting not only equal civil and political rights but social rights as well. However a further difficulty with modern democracy stems from the diversification and specialisation of contemporary life, which has produced the growth of numerous agencies outside our control – bureaucracies, technocracies, and international corporations. These 'invisible powers' have invaded our everyday life in ways which no amount of parliamentary legislation can check adequately. Bobbio contends that just as the civil rights of freedom of expression and assembly regardless of sex, creed or colour established the framework for parliamentary democracy, so social rights provide the precondition for democratic control of the various aspects of social life.

At first it might seem that Bobbio's proposal does not differ substantially from the calls of other theorists for more democracy, and must suffer from similar drawbacks to theirs. However, Bobbio does address the two main objections we

---

60. Rawls, 'Justice as fairness', pp. 248–51.

61. Those interested may consult N. Daniels *Reading Rawls*, Oxford: Blackwell, 1975, for an overview of some of the early criticisms.

62. In *A Theory of Justice*, pp. 544–5, Rawls explicitly rejected the idea that raising income might be necessary for self-respect. However, in a recent [at the time this chapter was first published] discussion of his ideas in Oxford, he seemed to accept that the 'difference principle' (2ii) entailed regarding democracy as not just a legitimising device but as linked to a definite system of income distribution in society. Bobbio certainly believes, rightly or wrongly, that Rawls's theory leads to a form of liberal socialism. *See* N. Bobbio, G. Pontara, S. Veca, *Crisi della democrazia e neocontrattualismo*, Rome: Riuniti, 1984, pp. 55–85. R. Plant, in *The Market, Equality and the State*, London: Fabian Society, 1984, similarly notes the bearing of Rawlsian arguments for social as well as political equality.

63. Bobbio, *Future of Democracy*, p. 32.

noted about these schemes. First, we disputed the claim that increased political participation led to greater social awareness. Bobbio tackles this difficulty by appealing to a Rawlsian-style social contract to create an agreed framework for how politics should be conducted. The 'rule of law' derived from the concept of justice, provides a shared political culture and the juridical foundation for political pluralism. The second, related, problem for direct democracy was its inefficiency in turning preferences into policies and the potential for relevant opinions or intensely held minority preferences to be ignored as a result. Bobbio seeks to rectify this difficulty by maintaining political parties as the medium for increasing the democratisation of society. He argues that they provide the best basis for providing voters with political choices and representing their diverse interests. Thus, although political debate occurs within a single system of beliefs about how democratic politics should be conducted and what our social rights and obligations are, these commitments facilitate rather than inhibit the expression of a plurality of political views. For it adds up to a shared conceptual and institutional framework for the effective competition between differing individuals about how society should be run.

IV

Bobbio seeks to adapt the foundations and institutions of liberal democracy to meet the demands and criticisms of socialists. He fully accepts the left's contention that the inequalities of wealth and influence, the growth of bureaucratic and corporate organisations and the increasing complexity, sophistication and specialisation of modem societies have undermined the democratic accountability of governments and empowered other agencies that have never been subject to public scrutiny. The Marxist solution of simply identifying the individual's interest with those of the community has long been discredited and Bobbio aligns himself with a prominent tradition of Italian socialist thought in rejecting it. Instead he suggests a reform of liberal justifications for civil and political equality to include social equality as the natural extension and partner of the other two. Following Rawls, he proposes a new social contract as the basis of a democratic society, which places our social and political rights and duties on an uncompromising individualist ethical foundation. He complements this socialist reformulation of liberal theory with a number of proposals for restructuring the institutional framework of liberalism. He argues that we need to render not only the state but society democratically accountable. However, in order to avoid the counter-productive inflation of political activity and the particularist tendencies of traditional radical calls for participatory democracy, he maintains that a multi-party system operating within a strong legal framework guaranteeing citizen's rights provides the most practicable avenue for reform.

Bobbio seeks to link liberal democratic means to socialist goals. This project involves not only the democratisation of society but the socialisation of democracy as well. Though many will dispute some or all of his arguments and proposals, his book is nevertheless to be valued as offering a spur to the reappraisal and the detailed working-out of what, in practical as well as theoretical terms, 'democratic socialism' means.

Chapter Fifteen

The Antinomies of Norberto Bobbio: The Rule of Law and the Rule of Democracy

A distinctive feature of Norberto Bobbio's work was the links he established between legal and political theory, particularly in his later writings. However, though he fully appreciated the interrelated character of law and politics, a tension between the two remains within his thinking and lies at the heart of his account of democracy as certain 'rules of the game'.[1] This tension arises out of what I shall call the Hobbes challenge and concerns the degree to which 'law' can rule in and of itself. If the rule of law can only be sustained through the rule of persons, then defining and seeking to constrain democracy in terms of a certain set of rules poses a paradox – for who is to decide what those rules are? Citizens acting through established democratic procedures, the courts, some other body? Whatever body or figure is chosen, the rule of law will have been displaced by the rule of the person or persons who deem what the rules or laws are.

Bobbio had a lifelong fascination with Hobbes[2] and rather relished antinomies and paradoxes – most notably in his famous account of the 'broken promises of democracy'.[3] Yet he never really grasped this particular nettle. However, it proves crucial for democrats to do so. If a primary reason for adopting democracy is because Platonic theories of what Dahl calls Guardianship fail to convince,[4] then the rules of the democratic game must surely be themselves subject to democratic protection and scrutiny? It is not clear, though, that Bobbio accepted this conclusion. Bobbio rightly noted that democracy has never existed without the defence of those liberal rights that largely animate it. But that is not the same as saying that all liberal democracies must be constitutional democracies – indeed, many are not. Nevertheless, he seems to have assumed that they must be.

Bobbio's basic mistake in this regard was to have seen democracy in Hobbesian terms as a (flawed) form of popular sovereignty. In truth, it is an anti-Hobbesian process that seeks to de-sovereigntise sovereignty, through placing all citizens on a par with each other as equally authors of the law – albeit through their elected representatives – and equally subject to it. In other words, democracy is a form of the rule of persons that encapsulates the central notion of the rule of law as treating all as equals. To show why this is so, we need to outline the Hobbesian challenge and then explore how democracy provides the most adequate response.

---

1. N. Bobbio, *The Future of Democracy: A defence of the rules of the game*, trans. R Griffen, ed. and introduced by Richard Bellamy, Cambridge: Polity Press, 1987.

2. *See* the essays collected in N. Bobbio, *Thomas Hobbes*, Turin: Einaudi, 1989.

3. Bobbio, *The Future of Democracy*, pp. 26–41.

4. R. A. Dahl, *Democracy and its Critics*, New Haven, CT: Yale University Press, 1989, ch. 4.

Hobbes's challenge to the rule of law

If we were ruled by philosopher-kings, who simply discovered the law through their devotion to truth and justice and could be counted on to apply it with an angelic rectitude and a divine omniscience, then the rule of law would be unproblematic. The law's agents, whether we called them monarchs, legislators or judges, would be free from the uncertainties as well as the biases that animate politics. They would act as the mere mouthpieces of a superior wisdom, offering infallibly just solutions that harmonised the individual's interest with that of the public. Clearly this is a fantasy, yet many versions of the concept of rule of law have a tendency to embrace it. The danger lies with potentially bad political rulers. Enshrine good laws in the constitution and entrust a special caste of legal guardians to oversee them and the rule of persons can be subordinated to the rule of law.

Unfortunately, this solution simply begs the very questions that lie at the heart of the problem. As Joseph Raz noted in a classic essay, some accounts of the rule of law use the term as a catch-all slogan for every desirable policy one might wish to see enacted. He cites as an instance of this approach the International Congress of Jurist's equation of the rule of law with the creation and maintenance of 'the conditions which will uphold the dignity of man as an individual' – a requirement that includes 'not only recognition of his civil and political rights but also the establishment of the social, economic, educational and cultural traditions which are essential to the full development of his personality'.[5] However, people reasonably disagree over the nature of the right and the good. Though most people will find the general aim of the ICJ's declaration unexceptionable, many will differ over what human dignity consists in and requires. Likewise, they will dispute the various ways such aims might be achieved by making all equal under the law – including what formal and substantive procedures and entitlements would need to be in place. Thus, if the rule of law depends on agreement on these contested issues, then it begs the question of who is to decide whose view is to prevail (or alternatively, of how agreement on them might be arrived at).

A more formal approach, which tempted Bobbio in his early writings on law,[6] attempts to overcome these difficulties.[7] This strategy focuses on the benefits, values and constraints inherent in the very existence of legal forms and procedures. After all, people often obey laws with which they disagree simply out of respect for the advantages of living in a law-governed environment. Law facilitates social interaction and helps curbs the abuse of power. It can even provide regular procedures for contesting and changing laws and decisions that they dislike. None of these considerations need involve substantive agreement with the goodness of the law. Yet, legality *per se* can only play a limited role in protecting against oppression and domination – even dictatorships, to the extent they are régimes,

---

5.   J. Raz, *The Authority of Law*, Oxford: Clarendon Press, 1979, pp. 210–11.

6.   N. Bobbio, *Teoria della norma giuridica*, Turin: Giappichelli, 1958.

7.   For the contrast between 'formal' and 'substantive' approaches, *see* P. Craig, 'Formal and sub-stantive conceptions of the Rule of Law: an analytical framework', *Public Law* 3 (Autumn), 1997, pp. 467–87.

are to some degree legal régimes. To avoid oppressive and dominating laws, we need not just laws but good laws. However, even good laws cannot rule in and of themselves – they need to be enacted and cannot be expected to cover all possible eventualities and infallibly guide those entrusted to uphold them towards the right answer.

Does this return us to the original dilemma of relying on good persons to give us good laws? This question brings us to the Hobbes challenge. Stated crudely, Hobbes argued that in circumstances of conflicting interests and deep disagreements about values and judgements, laws would only be equitably and coherently drafted and applied by all individuals being equally in awe of a sovereign who was outside the law and whose power was indivisible. For a start, the meaning of laws is rarely clear, so that 'all Laws, written and unwritten, have need of Interpretation' and these interpretations are usually controversial. Even when the meaning of laws is clear, their bearing on particular situations often is not – producing another source of controversy. Indeed, even if laws could be defined in an absolutely clear manner as to both their meaning and application, self-love, partiality and passion can lead people to employ them in self-serving ways and hence into conflict with each other. Hobbes believed these difficulties arise as much with the hypothetical imperatives of the Law of Nature as human laws. Therefore, laws or rules do not themselves provide the basis for social co-operation. Rather, a peaceful society results from having a political authority vested with the power to formulate, interpret and apply the laws and, crucially, to overrule rival views of their bearing in any given case. The claim that laws could be set above those sovereign person or persons empowered to enact and implement them was incoherent for Hobbes. It could only mean to set up another power able to judge and enforce these laws 'which is to make a new Sovereign' leading to an infinite regress with the need 'for the same reason a third, to punish the second; and so continually without end, to the Confusion, and Dissolution of the Common-wealth'.[8] On this view, law is not only subject to political contestation but intrinsically political, by virtue of being the creation of political authority.

Of course, as H. L. A. Hart observed, the sovereign's rule is recognised in part because it has legal foundations. In his terminology, we need 'secondary' rules of recognition to identify what counts as law as well as the 'primary' rules or laws that are created within a recognised legal system.[9] Among these secondary rules are those identifying the sovereign as authorised to decide what the law is. Such rules do place a legal constraint on personal rule, but not necessarily a very strong one. It is not just that tyrants have a habit of securing legal legitimacy for their rule after, rather than before, seizing power. Political rulers of all stripes habitually claim that the rule of law simply requires obedience to their commands as the legally recognised authorities. Yet if government is by definition the agency authorised by law to issue laws, then on this interpretation the rule of law barely constrains the rule of persons. To say all acts of government must have a

---

8.   T. Hobbes, *Leviathan*, ed. Richard Tuck, Cambridge: Cambridge University Press, 1991, p. 169.
9.   H. L. A. Hart, *The Concept of Law*, 2nd edn, Oxford: Clarendon Press, pp. 94–5.

foundation in law becomes almost a tautology. If law is merely (and only) what the lawful government decrees, then anything the lawful government decrees is authorised by law and what is not authorised or so decreed is illegal and so cannot be an action of the government.[10]

True, it would be wrong to dismiss this view completely. After all, British courts have frequently done a valuable job in restraining ministers and officials from acting beyond their remit. A government (or other body) that has to act within and according to its legally defined powers can be held to account in ways bodies or people that are not so constrained cannot. The rule of the socially influential and wealthy, of the mafia or of the mob, reveal in their different ways the disadvantages of lawless compared to lawful government. However, the Hobbes challenge emerges again, since some body of people, be they judges or other politicians, have to decide if the government has breached the rules. And although they too will be legally constituted, at some point some person or persons possesses the competence to decide questions regarding its own competence.[11] Meanwhile, an underlying set of problems remains: namely, why should the powerful have accepted to be rule-bound in the first place, unless it had somehow become in their interest to do so, and how can the legal forms of legislation and judging ensure that the law prevails rather than the will of those authorised to make decisions?

Therefore, the central dilemma posed by the rule of law is how to enjoy the benefits of legality while overcoming the Hobbes challenge. The law cannot rule without legislators and the judiciary. Can the rule of persons be modified by the rule of law if they are necessarily the instruments through which it governs? It is sometimes claimed that by ruling through law, those who make and enforce it are somehow led to be ruled by it in their turn. Fidelity to law is an intrinsic aspect of a coherent legal system and, for that to obtain, the laws and judging must possess certain desirable qualities.[12] Yet that view ends up perilously close to the fantasy of a system of good laws under the jurisdiction of beneficent philosophical kings.

Somehow the Hobbes challenge has to be tackled at its heart – the problem of the sovereign ruler. As I will attempt briefly to show, this is precisely what democracy attempts to do. However, Bobbio's characterisation of democracy in legalistic terms as 'the rules of the game' simply reintroduces the Hobbes challenge rather than dissolving it – for who decides what those rules are? Defining democracy in terms of the 'rules of the game' is at best tautologous, since any practice involves rules; at worst, to mistake its sources and purpose.

---

10. Raz, *The Authority of Law*, pp. 212–13.

11. It is sometimes argued that a democratic account of the rule of law requires a constitutional or other court to uphold the rights and procedures intrinsic to democracy (e.g. by J. H. Ely, *Democracy and Distrust: A theory of judicial review*, Cambridge, MA: Harvard University Press, 1980, and, in more qualified terms, by R. Dworkin, 'Political judges and the rule of law', in *A Matter of Principle*, Oxford: Clarendon Press, 1986, ch. 1. However, at least one reason why this proposal proves unsatisfactory is that these criteria are as disputable as any other law or right, so that placing their protection in the hands of a court suffers from parallel difficulties and is itself subject to the Hobbes challenge. I provide a detailed critique of this thesis in R. Bellamy, *Political Constitutionalism*, Cambridge: Cambridge University Press, 2007, ch. 3.

12. Lon L. Fuller, *The Morality of Law*, New Haven, CT: Yale University Press, 1964, ch. 2.

Democracy and the rule of law

Somewhat misleadingly, democracy is sometimes identified with popular sovereignty, suggesting rule by the will of a homogeneous people. It was this view above all that Bobbio was keen to criticise as impractical and incoherent. As modern analysts have shown,[13] democracy is better understood as a mechanism whereby the various peoples found in any community settle their disagreements and provisionally agree on a common definition of the rules. Without a degree of social pluralism, no democracy exists – for it is this social circumstance that obliges people to agree to be rulers and ruled in turn, sharing power with others on an equitable basis. They can only rule by co-operating with others, constructing a majority through diverse coalitions between different minorities. Without disagreement, though, democracy has no point – for its role is to offer a fair procedure for resolving our differences where a common rule is necessary. In this scenario, it is the democratic process, not the people *per se*, that is authoritative. Sovereignty exists not in the demos but in the procedures for voting.

Within this set-up, the rule of law simply is the democratic organisation of rule-making. For it is the obligation to vote on an equal basis to others, to accept the decision even if you voted the other way – notions that are at the heart of democracy, that encapsulates the core meaning of the rule of law, that laws should be equitable and apply equally to all. As Hobbes's great critic, the English republican James Harrington, observed, it is only when all are equal in the making of the laws that they will be 'framed by every private man unto no other end (or they may thank themselves) than to protect the liberty of every man'.[14] And that 'or they may thank themselves' indicates that what ensures democracy performs this function are not its rules – since they too need to be subject to democratic vigilance and revision – but the political involvement of citizens themselves.

Conclusion

To conclude: a central theme of Bobbio's thinking was the inter-connection between law and politics. He regarded law as a human, institutional artefact. I think his acknowledgement of the constructed character of law largely explains his lifelong fascination with Hobbes. However, he never faced up to the full consequences of the Hobbesian challenge. He always gave way to the temptations of a naturalist or Kantian tendency to prioritise an already existing law over politics. But if the Hobbes challenge is sound that cannot be the case. That challenge can only be met by seeing law as the outcome of a certain sort of democratic politics. In which case, the rules of the democratic game have to be seen as intrinsic to a democratic society and practices rather than as pre-existing legal or constitutional norms.

---

13. *See*, e.g. Dahl, *Democracy and its Critics*, ch. 16.
14. J. Harrington, *The Commonwealth of Oceana*, ed. J. G. A. Pocock, Cambridge: Cambridge University Press, 1992, p. 20 and *see also* Skinner, *Liberty*, pp. 74–77.

Index

www.ingramcontent.com/pod-product-compliance
Lightning Source LLC
Chambersburg PA
CBHW072050020426
42334CB00017B/1450